ANIMAL RIGHTS

ISSN 1546-6736

ANIMAL RIGHTS

Kim Masters Evans

INFORMATION PLUS® REFERENCE SERIES
Formerly Published by Information Plus, Wylie, Texas

GALE
CENGAGE Learning™

Detroit • New York • San Francisco • New Haven, Conn • Waterville, Maine • London

Animal Rights

Kim Masters Evans
Paula Kepos, Series Editor

Project Editors: Kathleen J. Edgar, Elizabeth
Manar

Rights Acquisition and Management: Barb
McNeil, Sara Teller, Robyn Young

Composition: Evi Abou-El-Seoud, Mary Beth
Trimper

Manufacturing: Cynde Lentz

For product information and technology assistance, contact us at
Gale Customer Support, 1-800-877-4253.
For permission to use material from this text or product,
submit all requests online at **www.cengage.com/permissions.**
Further permissions questions can be e-mailed to
permissionrequest@cengage.com

Cover photograph: Image copyright Ragne Kabanova, 2009. Used under license from Shutterstock.com.

Gale
27500 Drake Rd.
Farmington Hills, MI 48331-3535

ISBN-13: 978-0-7876-5103-9 (set)
ISBN-13: 978-1-4144-3369-1

ISBN-10: 0-7876-5103-6 (set)
ISBN-10: 1-4144-3369-7

ISSN 1546-6736

This title is also available as an e-book.
ISBN-13: 978-1-4144-5765-9 (set)
ISBN-10: 1-4144-5765-0 (set)
Contact your Gale sales representative for ordering information.

Printed in the United States of America
1 2 3 4 5 6 7 13 12 11 10 09

TABLE OF CONTENTS

PREFACE

Animal Rights is part of the *Information Plus Reference Series*. The purpose of each volume of the series is to present the latest facts on a topic of pressing concern in modern American life. These topics include the most controversial and studied social issues in the twenty-first century: abortion, capital punishment, care of senior citizens, the environment, health care, immigration, minorities, national security, social welfare, women, youth, and many more. Even though this series is written especially for high school and undergraduate students, it is an excellent resource for anyone in need of factual information on current affairs.

By presenting the facts, it is the intention of Gale, Cengage Learning, to provide its readers with everything they need to reach an informed opinion on current issues. To that end, there is a particular emphasis in this series on the presentation of scientific studies, surveys, and statistics. These data are generally presented in the form of tables, charts, and other graphics placed within the text of each book. Every graphic is directly referred to and carefully explained in the text. The source of each graphic is presented within the graphic itself. The data used in these graphics are drawn from the most reputable and reliable sources, such as from the various branches of the U.S. government and from major independent polling organizations. Every effort has been made to secure the most recent information available. Readers should bear in mind that many major studies take years to conduct and that additional years often pass before the data from these studies are made available to the public. Therefore, in many cases the most recent information available in 2009 is dated from 2006 or 2007. Older statistics are sometimes presented as well, if they are of particular interest and no more-recent information exists.

Even though statistics are a major focus of the *Information Plus Reference Series*, they are by no means its only content. Each book also presents the widely held positions and important ideas that shape how the book's subject is discussed in the United States. These positions are explained in detail and, where possible, in the words of their proponents. Some of the other material to be found in these books includes historical background, descriptions of major events related to the subject, relevant laws and court cases, and examples of how these issues play out in American life. Some books also feature primary documents or have pro and con debate sections that provide the words and opinions of prominent Americans on both sides of a controversial topic. All material is presented in an even-handed and unbiased manner; readers will never be encouraged to accept one view of an issue over another.

HOW TO USE THIS BOOK

Animals have been important to humans for around 2 million years as sources of food and other natural products, objects of worship and sport, and beasts of burden. Nevertheless, it was not until the seventeenth century that animal welfare began to concern Western society. What legal and moral rights do animals currently possess in the United States and how does society balance such rights with animals' enormous economic value? How do "abolitionists" and "welfarists" differ on these and other issues? In what ways should governments protect, regulate, and control wildlife? Under what conditions are farm animals raised and slaughtered? Should research animals be used in medical and veterinary investigations, product testing, and science classes? Do horse racing, greyhound racing, sled dog racing, and rodeos cause unwarranted harm to animal participants? How should entertainment animals, service animals, and pets be treated? These and other basic questions are discussed in this volume.

Animal Rights consists of nine chapters and three appendixes. Each chapter is devoted to a particular aspect of animal rights in the United States. For a summary of the information covered in each chapter, please see the synopses provided in the Table of Contents at the front of the book. Chapters generally begin with an overview of the basic facts and background information on the chapter's topic, then proceed to examine subtopics of particular interest. For example, Chapter 7, Entertainment Animals, begins with a brief overview of wild and domestic animals that have been used for entertainment. This is followed by an examination of the history of entertainment animals in the United States. Next, the chapter describes the major U.S. laws that govern the use of animals in entertainment and their welfare. Then the use of animals in different types of entertainment venues is examined in detail, including circuses, zoos, movies and television, and animal theme parks. The chapter also features sections on unwanted animals, the effects of captivity on carnivores, and the use of elephants in circuses and zoos. Readers can find their way through a chapter by looking for the section and subsection headings, which are clearly set off from the text. They can also refer to the book's extensive Index, if they already know what they are looking for.

Statistical Information

The tables and figures featured throughout *Animal Rights* will be of particular use to readers in learning about this topic. These tables and figures represent an extensive collection of the most recent and valuable statistics on animal rights, as well as related issues—for example, graphics cover what species are on the federal list of endangered and threatened animals, the number of people who participate in recreational/sport fishing (or angling), what percentage of people believe that buying and wearing clothing made of animal fur is morally acceptable, and what type of animals are pursued by the vast majority of hunters. Gale, Cengage Learning, believes that making this information available to readers is the most important way to fulfill the goal of this book: to help readers understand the issues and controversies surrounding animal rights in the United States and reach their own conclusions.

Each table or figure has a unique identifier appearing above it for ease of identification and reference. Titles for the tables and figures explain their purpose. At the end of each table or figure, the original source of the data is provided.

To help readers understand these often complicated statistics, all tables and figures are explained in the text. References in the text direct readers to the relevant statistics. Furthermore, the contents of all tables and figures are fully indexed. Please see the opening section of the Index at the back of this volume for a description of how to find tables and figures within it.

Appendixes

Besides the main body text and images, *Animal Rights* has three appendixes. The first is the Important Names and Addresses directory. Here, readers will find contact information for a number of government and private organizations that can provide further information on aspects of animal rights in the United States. The second appendix is the Resources section, which can also assist readers in conducting their own research. In this section, the author and editors of *Animal Rights* describe some of the sources that were most useful during the compilation of this book. The final appendix is the Index.

ADVISORY BOARD CONTRIBUTIONS

The staff of Information Plus would like to extend its heartfelt appreciation to the Information Plus Advisory Board. This dedicated group of media professionals provides feedback on the series on an ongoing basis. Their comments allow the editorial staff who work on the project to make the series better and more user-friendly. The staff's top priority is to produce the highest-quality and most useful books possible, and the Advisory Board's contributions to this process are invaluable.

The members of the Information Plus Advisory Board are:

- Kathleen R. Bonn, Librarian, Newbury Park High School, Newbury Park, California

- Madelyn Garner, Librarian, San Jacinto College, North Campus, Houston, Texas

- Anne Oxenrider, Media Specialist, Dundee High School, Dundee, Michigan

- Charles R. Rodgers, Director of Libraries, Pasco-Hernando Community College, Dade City, Florida

- James N. Zitzelsberger, Library Media Department Chairman, Oshkosh West High School, Oshkosh, Wisconsin

COMMENTS AND SUGGESTIONS

The editors of the *Information Plus Reference Series* welcome your feedback on *Animal Rights*. Please direct all correspondence to:

Editors
Information Plus Reference Series
27500 Drake Rd.
Farmington Hills, MI 48331-3535

CHAPTER 1
THE HISTORY OF HUMAN-ANIMAL INTERACTION

At the heart of the animal rights debate is the issue of how humans and animals should interact with each other. Are animals a natural resource for humans to use as they choose? Or are animals free beings with the right to live their lives without human interference? Is there an acceptable compromise somewhere in between? People answer these questions differently depending on their cultural practices, religious and ethical beliefs, and everyday experiences with animals. To understand how the debate has evolved over the centuries, it is necessary to examine history and see how the human-animal relationship developed and changed over time.

PREHISTORIC TIMES

Evolutionary science holds that humans are animals that have changed and adapted over hundreds of thousands of years to take on their current form. Biologists classify the human animal as a member of the order Primate, along with chimpanzees and gorillas. Scientists believe that humans and other primates shared a common ancestor millions of years ago and that at some point human animals split off to form their own evolutionary path. About 2 million years ago human primates began using stone tools and weapons. This was the beginning of the Stone Age. The use of stone-tipped spears allowed humans to hunt large game, such as wooly mammoths. Humans at that time survived by hunting and fishing and by foraging for edible vegetation, nuts, and seeds; hence, they are called hunter-gatherers. Most lived as nomads, traveling in small groups from place to place. Once they had exhausted all the animals and plants in an area, they would move to a new location.

The earliest known cave drawings date back approximately 30,000 years. Many cave drawings depict rhinoceroses, lions, buffalo, mammoths, and horses. Figure 1.1 shows a cave painting of a horse.

The vast majority of prehistoric cave drawings depict animals, not people. Some scientists believe that humans were in awe of the wild and fierce animals that they hunted. The hunters may have believed that they could exert some kind of magical power over animals by drawing pictures of them. Even though little is known for certain about the religious beliefs of the time, it is thought that prehistoric humans believed in a hidden world that was inhabited by the spirits of their dead ancestors, animals, and birds. People may have offered sacrifices of animals or other food to keep the spirits happy.

A belief system called animism has been traced back to the Paleolithic Age (the earliest period of the Stone Age). Animism is the belief that every object, living or not, contains a soul. Thus, animals, trees, and even rocks had spiritual meaning to prehistoric peoples. Some wild animals may have been worshipped as gods by early humans.

Changing Climate

Around 15,000 to 13,000 BC the massive glaciers that had covered much of the northern hemisphere during the Great Ice Age began to subside. The habitats and food supplies for both humans and animals began to change. The hunter-gatherers had increasing difficulty finding the big game they had hunted before. Scientists believe that mammoths and many other large animals were driven to extinction around 10,000 BC because of climate changes, overhunting by humans, or both. Humans turned to hunting smaller animals and began gathering and cultivating plants in centralized locations. This major shift from nomadic life to settled existence had a tremendous effect on the human-animal relationship.

HUMANS DOMESTICATE ANIMALS

Between 13,000 and 2,500 BC humans domesticated dogs, cats, cattle, goats, horses, and sheep from their wild counterparts. Even though the terms *taming* and *domestication* are often used interchangeably, they are not the same. Individual wild animals can be tamed to behave in

FIGURE 1.1

Cave painting of a horse, c. 13,000 BC, Lascaux, France. *AP Images.*

ing for leftovers. In either event, humans soon found dogs to be a welcome addition. The arrangement benefited both sides, as domesticated wolves helped humans with hunting and guarding duties and shared the food that was obtained.

The ancient Egyptians are usually credited with domesticating wild cats (*Felis silvestris libyca*, originating in Africa and southwestern Asia) around 4,000 BC. The Egyptians most likely raised cats to protect their grain stores from rats and mice. Cat domestication is strongly associated with the establishment of permanent settlements and the growing and storage of grains. Cats became important to agricultural societies, just as dogs had been important to hunting cultures.

Domestication of Livestock

The domestication of livestock—chiefly pigs, cows, sheep, horses, and goats—is thought to have occurred between 9,000 and 5,000 BC as agriculture became more of a factor in human societies scattered across Asia and Europe.

History shows that the most suitable animals for domestication (and use by humans) are those that naturally live in groups with a hierarchical social structure. This allows humans to assume a dominant role in the hierarchy and exert control over the animals' behavior. The ability to keep and control groups of meat-supplying animals allowed humans to give up their previously nomadic lives and produce excess food. This freed people to build cities and roads, invent new things, and cultivate the arts.

ANCIENT CULTURES AND RELIGIONS

The peoples of most ancient civilizations were polytheistic (believed in more than one god). Many ancient peoples worshipped animals as gods, used animals to represent their gods, or thought that their gods could assume animal form when they wished.

Some early civilizations also worshipped heavenly bodies, such as the sun and moon. These cultures believed that the stars and planets had magical influences over earthly events. They tracked the positions and aspects of the heavenly bodies closely and believed that such information could be used to foresee the future. Astrology and the zodiac evolved from these beliefs and were adopted by people in many different cultures, including the Babylonians, Egyptians, Hindus, and early Chinese, who used 12 different animals to represent different years in a 12-year cycle. (See Table 1.1.) Most ancient zodiacs used animals to represent some or all the constellations. In fact, the word *zodiac* comes from the Greek term *zodion kuklos*, meaning "circle of little animals."

Even though ancient Indians had varied spiritual beliefs, many of these beliefs were blended together into the practice

a docile manner around humans. By contrast, domestication is a process that takes place with an entire animal species over many generations.

Characteristics of Domesticated Animals

Domesticated animals are not just tamer than their wild ancestors; they are different genetically. Over the ages, desirable qualities, such as size and disposition, were engrained by breeding only those animals that displayed them. This explains some of the physical differences between wild and domesticated animals. For example, most domesticated species are smaller and fatter and have smaller teeth and brains than their wild ancestors.

Domestication of Dogs and Cats

The dog is thought to have been the first animal to be domesticated by humans, sometime around 13,000 to 10,000 BC, from its wolflike ancestor *Canis lupus*. Scientists believe that humans either adopted cubs and raised them or just began to accept into their groups some of the less fierce wolves that hung around their camps scroung-

TABLE 1.1

Chinese zodiac

Rat	Ox	Tiger	Rabbit	Dragon	Snake	Horse	Sheep	Monkey	Rooster	Dog	Boar
1912	1913	1914	1915	1916	1917	1918	1919	1920	1921	1922	1923
1924	1925	1926	1927	1928	1929	1930	1931	1932	1933	1934	1935
1936	1937	1938	1939	1940	1941	1942	1943	1944	1945	1946	1947
1948	1949	1950	1951	1952	1953	1954	1955	1956	1957	1958	1959
1960	1961	1962	1963	1964	1965	1966	1967	1968	1969	1970	1971
1972	1973	1974	1975	1976	1977	1978	1979	1980	1981	1982	1983
1984	1985	1986	1987	1988	1989	1990	1991	1992	1993	1994	1995
1996	1997	1998	1999	2000	2001	2002	2003	2004	2005	2006	2007
2008	2009	2010	2011	2012	2013	2014	2015	2016	2017	2018	2019

SOURCE: Created by Kim Masters Evans for Gale, 2009

of Hinduism around 3,000 BC. In general, Hindus believe that animals and people experience rebirths after they die. In other words, a human can be reincarnated as an animal, or vice versa. This means that all life forms are to be respected. Because Hindus consider virtually everything to be divine, they worship many animal gods and believe that their gods can take many forms, including human-animal forms.

Buddhism was founded during the sixth century by Siddhartha Gautama (c. 563–c. 483 BC), an Indian philosopher who came to be called Buddha. Buddha believed that animals were important spiritually and were evolving toward a higher consciousness, just as humans were. Therefore, Buddhists consider it wrong to cause any harm to an animal or any other living being.

Jainism also originated in India and is similar in many respects to Buddhism, although it is perhaps much older. The Jains are so adamantly opposed to killing any life form that they allow themselves to be bitten by gnats and mosquitoes rather than swatting them. They often carry brooms so they can brush insects out of their path to avoid stepping on them. The Jains strongly condemn the eating of any meat. They became well known in later centuries for their animal hospitals.

Archaeological evidence indicates that livestock raising was practiced in ancient China and that horse-drawn chariots were in use. A Chinese emperor of the first century BC established the Garden of Intelligence, one of the largest zoos in the world. Confucianism is based on the teachings of Confucius (551–479 BC), a Chinese philosopher who became famous for his sayings about how to live a happy and responsible life. In general, Confucius encouraged respect for animals, but not reverence. In other words, animals were not to be treated as deities.

Taoism is a spiritual philosophy that developed in China during the fifth and fourth centuries BC. Taoists believe that there is a power that envelops and flows through all living and nonliving things and that all life should be respected.

Hebrew Tribes and Judaism

The origins of Judaism lie with Hebrew tribes that populated the Mesopotamian region of the Middle East. Even though the Hebrews followed various worship practices, including animism, they eventually developed a central religion known as Judaism. The followers of Judaism came to be called Jews. Judaism was unique among the many religions of the time because it was monotheistic. The Jews worship only one god instead of many gods, and the Hebrew God is anthropomorphic, or humanlike.

According to the first book (Genesis) of the Hebrew Bible, God created the earth and populated it with all kinds of creatures. God granted humans "dominion over the fish of the sea, and over the birds of the air, and over all the wild animals of the earth, and over every creeping thing that creeps upon the earth." This idea of dominion can be interpreted in many ways and was to have a profound effect on Western civilization for centuries to come. However, the Old Testament states that "a righteous man regards the life of his animals."

Arabic Cultures and Islam

The first kingdom appeared in the Arabian desert around 1,000 BC. Before that time the region was inhabited by scattered families and clans, many of whom were nomads, called Bedouins, who raised camels. The Bedouins were animists who believed that spirits lived within all natural things. They also worshipped their ancestors and heavenly bodies.

Over the next few centuries society became more centralized, and the worship of many gods became common in temples and cults throughout the Arabian Peninsula. Islam was founded by the prophet Muhammad (c. AD 570–632), who believed in only one god. The Koran is the Islamic sacred text and includes many references to animals, particularly camels. Falcons, pigeons, cats, and horses were also considered important in early Islamic cultures. Legend has it that Muhammad was so fond of cats that he once cut a hole in his robe to keep from disturbing a cat that had fallen asleep on his sleeve. Muhammad also spoke highly of horses and considered their breeding to be an honorable task. The Arabs bred fast horses that were used in warfare, transportation, and sporting events.

Although the Koran does not specifically mention animal souls, it does teach respect for all living creatures.

Classical Greece

Even though Greece was associated with a variety of cultures, the classical Greek period from 500 to 323 BC was the most influential for future ideas about animals. The classical Greeks did not have one central philosophy but followed the teachings of various schools established by wise men and philosophers. Some of the most famous were Socrates (470?–399? BC), Plato (c. 428–c. 347 BC), and Aristotle (384–322 BC).

In general, animals were widely used for food, clothing, and work in Greek society. These uses were not questioned on moral or philosophical grounds because the people believed that everything in nature had a purpose. In other words, plants existed for animals and both plants and animals existed for the welfare and enjoyment of humans. However, the philosopher and mathematician Pythagoras (569?–475? BC) and his followers did not eat meat because they believed that animals had souls. Many other Greeks, including Plato, recommended a vegetarian diet for ethical or practical reasons.

Plato's student Aristotle is considered the father of zoology in Western history. He wrote extensively about animal anatomy, behavior, and reproduction in *History of Animals* and *On the Parts of Animals*. Aristotle believed that there was a natural hierarchy in which humans, animals, plants, and inanimate objects were arranged by their level of perfection. This arrangement came to be called the *scala naturae* or "ladder of nature." Later philosophers called it the "Great Chain of Being."

The top rungs of Aristotle's ladder were occupied by humans, because Aristotle believed that they alone had rational souls that were capable of belief, reason, and thought. Below the humans were animals; Aristotle believed that animals had limited souls that allowed them to feel, but not to reason. Plants had the lowest forms of souls and ranked the lowest on the ladder. Among humans, Aristotle believed that there was a natural hierarchy, with free men ranked above slaves, women, and children. Aristotle's ideas about the rank of humans and animals in society would influence thinking in Western cultures for centuries.

Christianity

Christianity began as a sect of Judaism during the first century AD. Its followers believe that God had come among them in the form of a human named Jesus Christ (4? BC–AD 29?). They set down their beliefs in scriptures that came to be known as the New Testament of the Bible.

Jesus' followers considered his death to be a human sacrifice, similar to the animal sacrifices that were common in Jewish religious practice. This symbolism played an important role in the new religion. The New Testament mentions many animals, but mostly in the context of everyday life and as food sources. Christians did maintain the belief from the Hebrew Bible that humans had dominion over animals. The importance of the human soul was central to Christian theology. Many Christian philosophers of later centuries, such as Saint Augustine of Hippo (354–430), argued that only humans (not animals) had rational minds and souls.

Roman Empire

The Roman Empire actually began as a single city, the city of Rome, which became a republic in 510 BC. The Romans had a warrior mentality and built their empire by conquering other peoples and cultures. The rulers of the Roman Empire delighted in brutal competitions and sports and invented many "games" to entertain their citizens. The Coliseum of Rome was a massive arena that featured events in which wild animals fought to the death with each other or with humans. Ancient texts describe the deaths of bulls, lions, tigers, elephants, and other animals. Often, the animals were chained together or tormented with burning irons and darts to make the fighting fiercer.

Historical evidence shows that the Romans were fond of horses. Their economy, troops, and postal service were dependent on the work done by horses. The Romans also raised livestock and kept cats and dogs as pets or working animals. Christianity became the official religion of the Roman Empire in AD 325. This put an end to the killing of humans in the Coliseum, because the human soul is sacred to Christianity. There is no evidence that animal games ceased, however, until the empire became too poor to acquire exotic and wild animals for them.

MEDIEVAL PERIOD

In general, Europe's medieval period, also called the Middle Ages, is considered the era from the fall of the Roman Empire in the late fifth century through the sixteenth century. The early centuries of the period are called the Dark Ages, because few known scientific and cultural achievements were made by Western societies during this time. Once the Roman emperors were gone, the authorities of the Christian church began to hold great power over the peoples of Europe.

Saint Francis of Assisi (1182–1226) is arguably the most famous animal lover of the medieval period in Europe. The Franciscan friar was said to preach to birds and animals and release captured animals from traps. There are many legends about the saint, the most famous being that he once convinced a wolf to stop terrorizing a town and eating the livestock. Saint Francis was said to have "the gift of sympathy" for animals and in modern Catholicism is the patron saint of animals and ecology.

One of the most influential philosophers of the Middle Ages was Saint Thomas Aquinas (1225?–1274). In 1264 he published *Of God and His Creatures*, in which he included a section titled "That the Souls of Dumb Animals Are Not Immortal." Aquinas argued that animals can neither understand nor reason and that their actions are driven entirely by natural instincts rather than by "art" or self-consciousness. Because animals can comprehend only the present and not the future, Aquinas believed that their souls are not immortal like human souls.

Crusades

During the medieval period the Christian church worked to stamp out paganism, cults, animal worship, and all other non-Christian beliefs. Many Crusades, or holy wars, were launched between 1095 and 1291 to try to conquer the Muslims, who had taken over Jerusalem. Thousands of people (and horses) on both sides were killed in these wars.

Domestic crusades were also launched against groups and individuals throughout Europe who were considered dangerous to the church or its teachings. Medieval people became obsessed with the devil and believed that he and his servants assumed human and animal forms. Even though different animals were suspected of being agents of the devil at different times and places, the cat was by far the most closely associated with evil. During the Middle Ages cats were burned at the stake, along with their owners, on suspicion of being witches. By the beginning of the fourteenth century, Europe's cat population had been severely depleted.

In 1347 the bubonic plague began to sweep across Europe. Called the Black Death, it killed 25 million people (nearly a third of Europe's population) in only three years. The disease was spread to humans by fleas on infected rodents. Centuries of cat slaughter had allowed the rodent population to surge out of control. The persecution of cats during the Middle Ages seems to have been unique to Europe. In Asia and the Middle East during the same period, cats retained their prestige as protectors of grains and other food supplies.

AGE OF ENLIGHTENMENT AND THE USE OF VIVISECTION

The centuries immediately following the Middle Ages are called the Age of Enlightenment because waves of intellectual and scientific advancement spread throughout Europe. Many superstitions and customs disappeared as societies became more urban and less rural. Church authorities began to lose much of their power over people's lives. Medical researchers gained permission to perform autopsies (mostly on executed prisoners) to learn about human anatomy. Autopsies had been forbidden by the church for cen-

turies, and little medical progress had been made in the field of anatomy. Animal experimentation was to become a major research tool of modern medicine.

In 1543 the Belgian doctor Andreas Vesalius (1514–1564) published "Some Observations on the Dissection of Living Animals" in *De humani corporis fabrica* (*On the Structure of the Human Body*). Vesalius hoped to convince other doctors that the study of anatomy was essential to improving medical care. He advocated cutting open living animals to teach students about blood circulation.

During the 1600s the French philosopher and mathematician René Descartes (1596–1650) published some influential essays in which he argued that animals could not think at all. Descartes said that only humans had eternal souls; thus, only humans could reason. He described the human gift of language as proof that humans were philosophically different from animals. Descartes was fascinated with the field of mechanics and extended its ideas to non-human animals. He wrote that animals were mechanical things like clocks and therefore could not feel pain. This helped make it socially acceptable to cut open animals while they were still alive for medical and scientific purposes. The process became known as vivisection and was widespread in Europe in the seventeenth and eighteenth centuries.

Literature from this time describes live dogs being nailed to tables in classrooms and dissected to learn about their anatomy. Writers dismissed the cries of the dogs as being similar to the screeching sounds that a piece of machinery makes when it is forcibly taken apart.

BLOOD SPORTS

As the Middle Ages drew to a close, sports in which animals were pitted against each other became popular in England. These "blood sports" included bull- and bear-baiting with dogs, cockfighting, and dogfighting.

Baiting began as more of a practical matter than a sport. Medieval people believed that an animal that was whipped immediately before slaughter would provide more tender meat. Whippings administered by butchers eventually evolved into events where teams of dogs were allowed to set upon bulls and bite and tear at their flesh. Such baitings soon became popular entertainment and were expanded to include other animals, such as bears. Baiting events were generally held in a ring or arena or in a field near a town's shops.

Most church authorities considered animal blood sports to be harmless pastimes, but this was not true of the Puritans. The Puritans were a Christian group that wanted to change the Church of England. In 1583 the Puritan social reformer Philip Stubbes (c. 1555–c. 1610) published *The Anatomie of Abuses* in which he asked, "What Christian heart can take pleasure to see one poor beast rend, tear, and kill another?" The Puritans took power over the British Parliament in the mid-1600s and outlawed baiting and other blood sports for a short time. When the Puritans were thrown out of power, blood sports returned and became even more popular.

MOVE TO NORTH AMERICA

During the seventeenth century many Puritans fled England for North America. The Puritans brought their unique perspective on animals with them. In 1641 the Massachusetts Bay Colony enacted a Body of Liberties that set out the fundamental rights of the colonists. Included in these rights was Article 92, which stated, "No man shall exercise any Tirranny or Crueltie towards any Bruite creature which are usuallie kept for man's use." This is generally considered the first modern law against animal cruelty; however, it did not have a major effect on American laws or customs regarding animals.

Livestock was vitally important to the new colonies because of its economic value. Thus, laws were passed making it a capital crime to kill a farm animal without the owner's permission.

EUROPEAN PHILOSOPHERS ARGUE AGAINST CRUELTY TO ANIMALS

Meanwhile, in Europe new social and philosophical movements were to have far-reaching effects on the welfare of animals. During the seventeenth and eighteenth centuries several notable philosophers and writers spoke out against the mistreatment of animals. The philosopher and political theorist John Locke (1632–1704) wrote that children should be taught from an early age that torturing and killing any living thing was despicable. In 1713 the poet Alexander Pope (1688–1744) wrote the article "Against Barbarity to Animals" for London's *Guardian* newspaper.

The Scottish philosopher David Hume (1711–1776) advocated "gentle usage" of animals for the sake of humanity. The German philosopher Immanuel Kant (1724–1804) argued that cruelty to animals easily escalated to cruelty to humans and should therefore be stopped. Stopping animal cruelty for the sake of humans became a popular idea and was embraced more easily than the idea of preventing cruelty just for animals' sake.

In 1751 the British artist William Hogarth (1697–1764) released a series of etchings and engravings called *The Four Stages of Cruelty*. The graphic images depicted the life of a fictional boy named Tom Nero who graduates from harming animals as a child to harming people as an adult. In the first scene the boy, in a white cap, tortures a dog with an arrow. Even though one boy tries to stop him, the boys are surrounded by other children also torturing animals. In the second scene Tom Nero is shown as a young man beating a horse on the street, while other acts of animal cruelty take place around him. The third scene shows fully grown Tom Nero immediately after he has murdered his girlfriend. In the fourth scene Tom Nero has been hanged for his crime, and his body is being dissected at a medical school.

Hogarth's intention was to illustrate some of the horrors of animal cruelty, but the connection between cruelty to animals and cruelty to humans was what captured people's attention. Even those who did not care about animal issues could see the dangers to civilized society of ignoring animal cruelty.

In 1764 the "mechanical animal" theory advocated by Descartes during the previous century was attacked by the French philosopher Voltaire (1694–1778) in *Dictionnaire philosophique portatif*. Voltaire argued that the scientists who dissected live animals found "organs of feeling" within them similar to those of humans, thus proving that animals could indeed feel pain.

In 1776 the Anglican clergyman Humphrey Primatt (1736–1779) published *A Dissertation on the Duty of Mercy and Sin of Cruelty to Brute Animals*. Primatt wrote, "Pain is pain, whether it be inflicted on man or on beast." He equated cruelty to animals with sin and even atheism and complained that legal authorities were doing little to stop it. Primatt argued that eliminating barbaric practices against animals might cut down on the number of "shocking murders" that were occurring.

One of the most poignant pleas for animals was made by the British philosopher and political scientist Jeremy Bentham (1748–1832). In 1789 he published *An Introduction to the Principles of Morals and Legislation*, in which he advocated making cruelty to animals punishable by law. Bentham wrote, "The question is not, Can they reason? Nor, Can they talk? but, Can they suffer?" Toward the end of the eighteenth century a few court cases were successfully tried against people who had abused animals, but only because the animals did not belong to the guilty parties.

BRITISH LAW TAKES HOLD

Modern legal protections for animals date back to nineteenth-century England. In 1822 Richard Martin (1754–1834), a member of the Parliament, sponsored a bill prohibiting cruelty to cattle, horses, and sheep. It became the first anticruelty law of its kind.

"Humanity Martin," as he came to be called, soon learned that having a law in effect and getting it enforced were two different things. The authorities were not interested in spending time gathering evidence and prosecuting animal abuse cases. Martin conducted his own investigations and was helped in his efforts by a group of people led by the Reverend Arthur Broome. In 1824 this group became the Society for the Prevention of Cruelty to Animals (SPCA).

In 1835 Martin's original act was expanded to protect dogs and bulls. In addition, cockfighting and the practice of baiting were outlawed. In 1840 the SPCA was recognized by Queen Victoria (1819–1901) and became the Royal Society for the Prevention of Cruelty to Animals (RSPCA). The RSPCA appointed inspectors to patrol the markets and slaughterhouses of London and other large cities looking for abuses. The group continued to push for new and tougher legislation against animal cruelty.

Many people involved in furthering animal welfare in England were also involved in other humanitarian movements of the time, including child welfare and antislavery causes. They believed that these issues were all related by common problems: abuse of power and the domination of the strong over the weak using cruel measures. There was also a growing moral belief that permitting cruelty to animals would lead to violence against humans and weaken society in general. It was also during the mid-1800s that the keeping of pets became popular among the middle classes.

U.S. LAW

Early U.S. law was patterned after British common law, which viewed animals as pieces of property. However, the reform movements that swept England during the nineteenth century also reached the United States. The Animal Legal and Historical Center (2009, http://www.animallaw.info/historical/statutes/sthusny1829.htm) notes that in 1829 New York State passed the first law against animal cruelty, which read: "Every person who shall maliciously kill, maim or wound any horse, ox or other cattle, or any sheep, belonging to another, or shall maliciously and cruelly beat or torture any such animal, whether belonging to himself or another, shall, upon conviction, be adjudged guilty of a misdemeanor."

Within the next decade similar laws were passed in states throughout the Northeast and Midwest. Some state laws covered only livestock, whereas others included all domestic animals. Some laws applied only if the animal belonged to someone other than the abuser.

In 1866 Henry Bergh (1811–1888) founded the American Society for the Prevention of Cruelty to Animals (ASPCA; 2009, http://www.aspca.org/about-us/history.html). Fashioned after the RSPCA, the ASPCA received permission from the New York Legislature to enforce anticruelty laws in the state. This meant that ASPCA officers could arrest and seek convictions of animal abusers. Bergh was elected the first ASPCA president and held that post for 22 years. Similar societies soon formed in other major cities, including Philadelphia, Pennsylvania, and Boston, Massachusetts.

Vivisection, which had been practiced at Europe's medical schools for some time, had also been incorporated into U.S. medical training. According to the New England Anti-

Vivisection Society, in "About NEAVS" (January 26, 2009, http://www.neavs.org/aboutneavs/history_1895_1920.htm), in 1871 Harvard University established one of the first vivisection laboratories in the country. Even though various antivivisection societies were started in the United States, their attempts to outlaw the practice failed.

The first federal law in the United States dealing with animal cruelty was the 28-Hour Law of 1873. This law required that livestock being transported across state lines be rested and watered at least once every 28 hours during the journey.

MODERN TIMES

By the early twentieth century American society was becoming increasingly urban and industrial. Working animals, such as horses, were gradually replaced with machinery on farms and city streets. The growing middle class had more time and money for leisure activities, many of which involved animals—hunting, fishing, keeping pets, and visiting wildlife refuges, circuses, zoos, and animal parks. Horse racing and greyhound racing both became popular sports in the 1930s as many states legalized this type of gambling.

In 1938 the Food, Drug, and Cosmetics Act was passed. This legislation required animal testing of certain chemicals and drugs to ensure their safety for human use. It was to have a profound effect on the human-animal relationship and later debates on the topic of animal rights. Following World War II (1939–1945) the use of animals in medical and scientific research exploded. The demand for dogs and cats in the laboratory led to animal procurement laws in many states, allowing scientists to obtain test subjects from dog pounds and animal shelters.

By this time, the country's animal protection organizations had largely turned their attention from farm animals to pets. Some people within these groups were deeply opposed to the use of animals in research, whereas others saw it as a regrettable necessity. Differences in opinion led to splintering and the formation of new organizations. The Animal Welfare Institute and the Humane Society of the United States (HSUS) were both founded in the early 1950s.

Animal protection groups began to develop separate identities and missions. Some retained a local focus, whereas others focused on national issues. They gained an ally in Senator Hubert Humphrey (1911–1978, D-MN), who championed animal causes as well as civil rights and other social movements. Humphrey was instrumental in the passage of the Humane Methods of Slaughter Act of 1958, which required the use of humane slaughter methods at slaughterhouses subject to federal inspection. It was the first piece of federal animal protection legislation in 85 years.

The next year Congress passed the Wild Horse Annie Act to outlaw the use of motorized vehicles and the poisoning of watering holes "for the purpose of trapping, killing, wounding, or maiming" wild horses on federal lands.

In the 1960s another animal issue, this time dog-related, achieved national prominence because of the efforts of a handful of people. Pepper was a family pet that disappeared from her backyard in Pennsylvania in 1965 and wound up dead in a New York City laboratory. Pepper's family diligently tracked down what had happened to her and helped expose a network of shady animal dealers and pet thieves selling animals by the pound to research laboratories. The public demanded action. In 1966 Congress passed the Laboratory Animal Welfare Act, which required the licensing of animal dealers and the regulation of laboratory animals. It is still the primary federal law that covers the welfare of animals used in research and public exhibitions and that regulates aspects of the handling, transport, care, and commerce related to covered animals. The major provisions of the act and its four amendments are shown in Table 1.2.

Several other federal laws were passed in the 1960s and 1970s designed to protect wild animals, including eagles, seals, and endangered species. Some animal protection issues were intertwined with causes devoted to conservation, ecology, and the environment. "Save the Whales" became a popular slogan.

Animal Rights Becomes an Issue

In 1975 a new twist developed in an old movement. The Australian philosopher Peter Singer (1946–) published the book *Animal Liberation: A New Ethics for Our Treatment of Animals*, which calls for a fundamental change in the human-animal relationship. Singer argues that animals are victimized by humans on a massive scale because of a social evil called speciesism, a term coined by British psychologist Richard D. Ryder (1940–) that Singer uses for the widespread belief that the human species is superior to all others. Singer equates humans' mistreatment of animals throughout history with racism and sexism and blames speciesism for the systematic abuse of animals in agriculture, research, and other human activities. The year after Singer's book was published, Animal Rights International was founded by the social reformer Henry Spira (1927–1998).

Some people working for animal causes embraced the idea that animals are not resources to be protected by benevolent humans but individual beings with their own interests and rights. This meant that humans could not use animals for any purpose (food, clothing, sport, entertainment, etc.) because it was morally and ethically wrong to do so. This opened a new agenda in the animal welfare movement that went beyond calls for kind treatment and humane methods of slaughter. Adherence to the most rad-

TABLE 1.2

The Animal Welfare Act and its amendments

Laboratory Animal Welfare Act Public Law 89-544 (August 24, 1966)

Authorizes the Secretary of Agriculture to regulate transport, sale, and handling of dogs, cats, nonhuman primates, guinea pigs, hamsters, and rabbits intended to be used in research or "for other purposes."
Requires licensing and inspection of dog and cat dealers and humane handling at auction sales.

Animal Welfare Act of 1970 Public Law 91-579 (December 24, 1970)

Expands the list of animals covered by the act.
Incorporates exhibitors into the act and defines research facilities.
Exempts retail pet stores, state and county fairs, rodeos, purebred dog and cat shows, and agricultural exhibition.
Directs development of regulations regarding recordkeeping and humane care and treatment of animals in or during commerce, exhibition, experimentation, and transport.
Establishes inspections, and appropriate anesthetics, analgesics, and tranquilizers. Includes regulations on dog and cat commerce.

Animal Welfare Act Amendments of 1976 Public Law 94-279 (April 22, 1976)

Primarily refines previous regulations on animal transport and commerce.
Licenses, method of payment, and penalties for violations are discussed.
Introduces and defines "animal fighting ventures."
Exempts animals used in hunting waterfowl, foxes, etc.
Makes it illegal to exhibit or transport via interstate or foreign commerce animals used in fighting ventures such as dogs or roosters.

Food Security Act of 1985, Subtitle F-Animal Welfare also called "The Improved Standards for Laboratory Animals Act" Public Law 99-198 (December 23, 1985)

Clarifies and specifies "humane care" specifics such as sanitation, housing, and ventilation.
Directs development of regulations to provide exercise for dogs and an adequate physical environment to promote the psychological well-being of nonhuman primates.
Specifies that pain and distress must be minimized in experimental procedures and that alternatives to such procedures be considered by the principal investigator.
Defines practices that are considered to be painful.
Stipulates that no animal can be used in more than one major operative experiment with recovery (exceptions are listed).
Establishes the Institutional Animal Care and Use Committee (IACUC).
Forms an information service at the National Agricultural Library to assist those regulated by the act.
Explains the penalties for release of trade secrets by regulators and the regulated community.

Food, Agriculture, Conservation, and Trade Act of 1990, Section 2503-Protection of Pets Public Law 101-624 (November 28, 1990)

Establishes a holding period for dogs and cats at shelters and other holding facilities before sale to dealers.
Requires dealers to provide written certification regarding each animal's background to the recipient.

SOURCE: Adapted from "Animal Welfare Act and Regulations," in *Animal Care: Animal Welfare Act and Regulations*, U.S. Department of Agriculture, Agricultural Research Service, National Agricultural Library, Animal Welfare Information Center, 2006, http://www.nal.usda.gov/awic/legislat/usdaleg1.htm (accessed January 8, 2007)

ical animal rights theory meant that eating meat and killing all types of animals were wrong. So were zoos and circuses, hunting and fishing, and experimenting on animals to find cures for human diseases—no matter how humanely any of these activities were carried out.

This philosophical leap was too much for many people, and the idea that animals had rights like humans was not generally embraced. The public supported anticruelty laws and animal protection measures (within reason) but did not go so far as to say that animals have a moral standing in society that makes it inherently wrong to eat or use them.

Opponents of animal rights argued that to do so would go against centuries of tradition and beliefs, disrupt many accepted systems for feeding and entertaining people, have crippling economic consequences, hurt millions of people who earned their living through animals, and impede scientific progress. Because of such arguments, most Americans of the 1970s rejected the idea of animal rights. So did most of the traditional animal protection organizations, though they continued their work to educate and reform.

However, this idea did not go away. More books examining this issue were published, and new organizations formed, including People for the Ethical Treatment of Animals (PETA) in 1980. Many others followed. These animal rights groups were much bolder than traditional animal welfare organizations. They held protest marches and publicly condemned companies and research institutions using animals for various purposes. The radical group Animal Liberation Front raided laboratories and farms to "free" animals and destroy property.

Some animal rights groups worked through the legal system to achieve change, filing lawsuits and working with prosecutors to strengthen animal protection laws. The more traditional animal protection groups supported these efforts. Legal reform was one area in which the entire animal movement found some common ground. The traditional groups increased their political power during the 1980s through swelling membership rolls, and animal issues gained momentum in society, particularly among pet owners.

LINK BETWEEN ANIMAL ABUSE AND VIOLENCE AGAINST PEOPLE

As illustrated in Hogarth's artwork, there has long been a belief that cruelty toward animals and cruelty toward humans are related. In more recent times this belief has been reinforced by scientific and anecdotal evidence. According to Joshua K. Marquis (2009, http://communities.justicetalking.org/blogs/day17/archive/2007/08/14/animal-abuse-its-association-with-other-violent-crimes.aspx), the district attorney of Clatsop County, Oregon, many notorious serial killers and mass murderers—including Jeffrey Dahmer (1959–1994); Ted Bundy (1946–1989); and Albert Henry DeSalvo (1931–1973, also known as the Boston Strangler)—are known to have tortured and killed animals. Marquis also notes that many of the children who have carried out school shootings since the 1990s (notably Eric Harris [1981–1999] and Dylan Klebold [1982–1999], who killed 12 fellow students, one teacher, and themselves at Columbine High School in Littleton, Colorado, in April 1999) had a history of cruelty to animals before they began committing violent acts against humans.

Many animal welfare activists, sociologists, psychologists, and law enforcement officials agree that a person who has abused animals will likely become involved in further antisocial and/or criminal behavior at some point. As a result, animal abuse is increasingly recognized as a serious crime in itself, with more states bringing felony charges against offenders. Additionally, successful programs have been created across the United States that join animal welfare organizations, local law enforcement, animal control officers, and child protective services so that all parties can be trained to look for signs of both animal abuse and domestic violence.

RECENT RECORD OF THE ANIMAL MOVEMENT

By the 1990s the major animal welfare organizations were starting to achieve sufficient financial support and political clout to successfully pursue their efforts for change in two main areas: the courts and the ballot box. In 2009 the HSUS Animal Protection Litigation Section (2009, http://www.hsus.org/in_the_courts/) employed 13 lawyers and was engaged in dozens of lawsuits pertaining to animal issues around the country. In many of the cases the HSUS was partnered with one or more other animal welfare or conservation organizations, such as the ASPCA or Defenders of Wildlife. Targets of the litigation included various corporate entities involved in animal-related businesses and government agencies in charge of implementing laws and regulations that pertain to animals.

Table 1.3 lists the major pieces of animal-related federal legislation that were passed or amended between 1958 and 2007. The table is adapted from the HSUS report *The State of the Animals III: 2005* (December 31, 2005, http://www.hsus.org/web-files/PDF/hsp/SOA_3-2005_Chap7.pdf). The report notes that the animal movement rose "from political oblivion in the first half of the twentieth century to a position where lawmakers would listen if the context and the proposal were timely and supported by the societal and political mood."

One of the major issues at the federal level is funding for the Animal Welfare Act (AWA). Figure 1.2 shows federal monies appropriated (assigned) to enforcement of the AWA between 1970 and 2005. Table 1.4 lists the annual AWA appropriations for fiscal years (FYs) 2002 through 2007. Nearly $17.5 million was appropriated to the AWA in FY 2007. Animal advocates believe this amount is far too small to adequately ensure that the AWA is properly enforced by the U.S. Department of Agriculture (USDA). USDA records shown in Table 1.5 list the number and types of AWA inspections conducted during FY 2007. During that year 13,316 compliance inspections were completed at the 9,249 facilities covered by the AWA. In addition, 1,683 noncompliance (prelicensing) inspections were also conducted. As shown in Table 1.6, 16,487 inspections were conducted in FY 2007, which was down almost 20% from FY 2006, when 20,311 inspections were performed, but up dramatically from FY 2002, when only 12,226 inspections were conducted. Table 1.7 shows there

TABLE 1.3

Federal animal protection legislation passed or amended, selected years 1958–2007

Year	Federal legislation passed/amended
1958	Humane Methods of Slaughter Act
1959	Wild Horses Act
1962	Bald and Golden Eagle Act
1966	Endangered Species Act
	Laboratory Animal Welfare Act
1970	Animal Welfare Act (amendments to Laboratory Animal Welfare Act)
1971	Wild Free-Roaming Horse and Burro Act
1972	Marine Mammal Protection Act
1973	Endangered Species Act amendments
	CITES
1976	Animal Welfare Act amendments
	Horse Protection Act
	Fur Seal Act
1978	Humane Methods of Slaughter Act amendments
1985	Animal Welfare Act amendments (focus on alternatives and pain and distress)
	PHS Policy on animals in research revised
1990	Animal Welfare Act amendments
1992	Wild Bird Conservation Act
1993	International Dolphin Conservation Act
	Driftnet Fishery Conservation Act
	NIH Revitalization [Reauthorization] Act mandates development of research methods using no animals
1995	USDA ends face branding
1999	Ban on the interstate shipment of "crush videos"
2000	Chimpanzee Health Improvement, Maintenance, and Protection Act
2002	Dog and Cat Protection Act
	Interagency Coordinating Committee on the Validation of Alternative Methods (ICCVAM) Authorization Act
	Safe Air Travel for Animals Act
	Ban on interstate transportation of birds and dogs for fighting purposes
2003	Captive Exotic Animal Protection Act
2007	Pets Evacuation and Transportation Standards Act

SOURCE: Adapted from Andrew N. Rowan and Beth Rosen, "Table 1. Federal Legislative Summary, 1958–2003," in *The State of the Animals III: 2005*, Humane Society of the United States, December 31, 2005, http://www.hsus.org/web-files/PDF/hsp/SOA_3-2005_Chap7.pdf (accessed April 17, 2009). Data from B. Unti and A. N. Rowan, "A Social History of Postwar Animal Protection," in *The State of the Animals: 2001*, Humane Society of the United States, 2001.

were 575 enforcement cases under the AWA during FY 2007, up from 482 cases in FY 2005. In total, $946,184 was collected in civil penalties related to AWA violations in FY 2007.

In 2004 the HSUS launched a new arm called the Humane Society Legislative Fund (HSLF). According to the HSLF (2009, http://www.fund.org/about_us/), the organization "works to pass animal protection laws at the state and federal level, to educate the public about animal protection issues, and to support humane candidates for office." One of the goals of the HSLF is to convince voters at election time to support candidates it considers animal-friendly on the issues. It does this through targeted media campaigns and mass mailings to potential voters. The HSLF also compiles a Humane Scorecard for each session of Congress that grades every legislator on his or her voting and bill-sponsorship record as it relates to animal issues. Humane Scorecards for the 103rd session (January 1993–January 1995) through the 110th session (January 2007–January 2009) are available on the organization's Web site.

Many animal protection groups have actively pursued stricter state laws dealing with animal cruelty and neglect. Table 1.8 is a listing compiled by the HSUS of state animal anticruelty laws as of July 2008. The HSUS (2009, http://www.hsus.org/legislation_laws/state_legislation/animal_cruelty_laws_where_does_your_state_stand.html) urges its members to push for felony state anticruelty laws that meet all the following criteria:

- Cover all species of animals

- Include first-time offenders

- Include large fines and long prison sentences as penalties

- Do not include exemptions

- Include counseling provisions for convicted abusers

- Prevent convicted abusers from owning or living with animals in the future

One of the ways in which animal organizations achieve change at the state level is through initiative petitions. These are petitions dealing with specific issues that receive enough signatures from the public to spur the inclusion of proposed measures on ballots during state elections. According to the HSUS, in *State of the Animals III*, initiative petition drives coordinated by animal protection groups were largely unsuccessful until 1990, when a new approach was undertaken. The HSUS and the Fund for Animals began selectively targeting specific animal issues in states where research indicated a good chance for collection of the signatures and of the money needed to put particular measures on the ballot and win support for them on election day.

In the summer of 2008 the HSUS and other animal groups successfully waged a petition drive in California that resulted in inclusion of a measure called Proposition 2 on the state's ballot in November of that year. Proposition 2 was passed by California voters. It will implement a ban in 2015 on the use of certain confinement techniques for farm animals. Its passage was heralded as a major victory for animal welfare proponents and criticized by opponents as an economic blow to the farming industry.

FIGURE 1.2

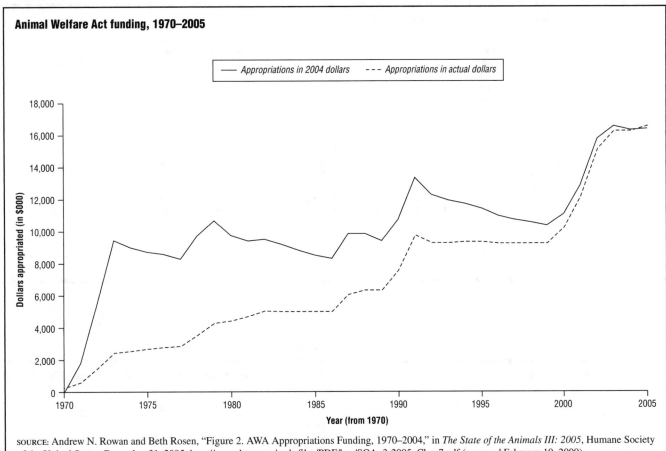

Animal Welfare Act funding, 1970–2005

Legend: —— Appropriations in 2004 dollars   - - - Appropriations in actual dollars

Y-axis: Dollars appropriated (in $000)

X-axis: Year (from 1970)

SOURCE: Andrew N. Rowan and Beth Rosen, "Figure 2. AWA Appropriations Funding, 1970–2004," in *The State of the Animals III: 2005*, Humane Society of the United States, December 31, 2005, http://www.hsus.org/web-files/PDF/hsp/SOA_3-2005_Chap7.pdf (accessed February 19, 2009)

TABLE 1.4

Animal Welfare Act funding, 2002–07

Fiscal year	Annual appropriation for enforcement of the Animal Welfare Act
2007	$17,473,000
2006	$17,303,000
2005	$16,485,000
2004	$16,303,000
2003	$16,301,000
2002	$15,167,000

SOURCE: "Table 2. Appropriations for Animal Welfare, FY 2002–2007," in *Animal Care Annual Report of Activities: Fiscal Year 2007*, U.S. Department of Agriculture, Animal and Plant Health Inspection Service, September 2008, http://www.aphis.usda.gov/publications/animal_welfare/content/printable_version/2007_AC_Report.pdf (accessed January 13, 2009)

TABLE 1.5

Animal Welfare Act inspections, by facility type and inspection category, fiscal year 2007

	Total number of regulated facilities[a]	Compliance inspections	Pre-licensing/pre-registration inspections	Attempted inspections
Dealers	5,239	6,909	1,160	956
Exhibitors	2,490	3,626	393	440
In-transit carriers[b]	186	787	0	23
In-transit handlers	246	222	0	26
Research facilities	1,088	1,657	1	39
Not yet licensed/registered	—	115	129	4
All facilities	9,249	13,316	1,683	1,488

Notes: Inspections for compliance are unannounced inspections and re-inspections. These do not include pre-licensing or pre-registration inspections, auction market observations, or attempted inspections. Pre-licensing/pre-registration inspections are announced. Observations of licensed and unlicensed auction markets are made to locate unlicensed dealers. Attempted inspections could not be performed for certain reasons—usually because there was no one available at the facility when the inspector arrived unannounced.
[a]A facility is the holder of the license or registration. Each facility may have only one license and/or registration number but may be physically divided into two or more sites.
[b]In-transit carriers is a category representing commercial airlines. Each airline may have two or more animal transportation sites at each airport it serves. Due to frequent changes in airline activities and other factors, the number of sites may vary.

SOURCE: "Table 3. FY 2007 AWA Inspections," in *Animal Care Annual Report of Activities: Fiscal Year 2007*, U.S. Department of Agriculture, Animal and Plant Health Inspection Service, September 2008, http://www.aphis.usda.gov/publications/animal_welfare/content/printable_version/2007_AC_Report.pdf (accessed January 13, 2009)

TABLE 1.6

Animal Welfare Act inspections, fiscal years 2002–07

Fiscal year	Number of inspections
2007	16,487
2006	20,311
2005	18,290
2004	13,886
2003	14,152
2002	12,226

SOURCE: Adapted from "Table 4. Total Number of Inspections Performed, FY 2005–2007," in *Animal Care Annual Report of Activities: Fiscal Year 2007*, U.S. Department of Agriculture, Animal and Plant Health Inspection Service, September 2008, http://www.aphis.usda.gov/publications/animal_welfare/content/printable_version/2007_AC_Report.pdf (accessed January 13, 2009); *FY 2004 AWA Inspections*, U.S. Department of Agriculture, Animal and Plant Health Inspection Service, 2004, http://www.aphis.usda.gov/animal_welfare/downloads/awreports/awreport2004.pdf (accessed February 2, 2009); *FY 2003 AWA Inspections*, U.S. Department of Agriculture, Animal and Plant Health Inspection Service, 2003, http://www.aphis.usda.gov/animal_welfare/downloads/awreports/awreport2003.pdf (accessed February 2, 2009); and *FY 2002 AWA Inspections*, U.S. Department of Agriculture, Animal and Plant Health Inspection Service, 2002, http://www.aphis.usda.gov/animal_welfare/downloads/awreports/awreport2002.pdf (accessed February 2, 2009)

TABLE 1.7

Animal Welfare Act enforcement cases, fiscal years 2005–07

Fiscal year	2005	2006	2007
Cases	482	480	575
IES review	302	249	391
Warnings	83	283	219
Stipulations	191	95	87
Submitted to OGC	73	80	76
ALJ decision	78	96	82
No violations	67	53	208
Submitted externally/penalty	82	24	11
Stipulations paid	$262,200	$263,596	$160,184
Civil penalty	$614,132	$644,220	$946,184

Chart key

Cases—Number of cases investigated.
IES review—Number of cases received by IES for review.
Warnings—Number of letters of warning issued.
Stipulations—Number of cases closed with a stipulation paid.
Complaints—Number of formal complaints sent by APHIS and USDA's OGC to USDA's Administrative Law Court.
ALJ decisions—Number of formal decisions from Administrative Law Judges.
No violations—Number of cases closed with no violations found.
Stipulations paid—Amount of money collected as a result of stipulation agreements.
Civil penalty—Total amount of money collected as a result of Administrative Law Judge decisions.

Notes: IES = Investigative and Enforcement Services.
OGC = USDA Office of the General Counsel.
ALJ = Administrative Law Judge

SOURCE: "Table 9. AC Enforcement for Cases Referred to IES," in *Animal Care Annual Report of Activities: Fiscal Year 2007*, U.S. Department of Agriculture, Animal and Plant Health Inspection Service, September 2008, http://www.aphis.usda.gov/publications/animal_welfare/content/printable_version/2007_AC_Report.pdf (accessed January 13, 2009)

TABLE 1.8

State animal anti-cruelty laws, July 2008

State	Statute number of cruelty law	Felony	Classification of crime/maximum level of penalty	Maximum fine	Maximum jail time	Psychological counseling	Cross reporting of animal cruelty	Year enacted into a felony	Other significant circumstances or penalties
Alabama	§13A-11-241	Yes	Class C felony on the first offense (cruelty in the first degree).	$5,000	10 years			2000	"Cruelty to a dog or a cat"—only felony
	§13A-11-14	No	Class B misdemeanor						All other animals
Alaska	11.61.140	Yes	Class C felony on the third offense.	$50,000	5 years			2008	All animals; may prohibit ownership of animals for up to 10 years.
Arizona	13-2910	Yes	Class 6 felony on the first offense.	$150,000	1 year			1999	All animals. Cruel neglect or abandonment resulting in serious physical injury or cruel mistreatment is a felony.
Arkansas	5-62-101	No	Class A misdemeanor.	$1,000	1 year	May order (2001)			**No felony.** Misd. includes all animals
California	597	Yes	Felony can apply on first conviction.	$20,000	1–3 years	Mandatory	May report	1988	All animals
Colorado	18-9-202 H.B. 1057 (2006)	Yes	Aggravated cruelty is a class 5 felony and any subsequent offense would be a class 4 felony.	Minimum $1,000 Maximum $500,000	Class 5: Min 1 year, Max 3 years. Class 4: Min 2 years, Max 6 years.	*May* order an evaluation or anger management treatment on the 1st offense. *Shall* order on the 2nd offense.		2002	Felony includes all animals; Details of the felony and punishment can be found at: §18-1-105 a person convicted of an **animal cruelty** or aggravated **animal cruelty** offense is prohibited from owning an animal after the conviction
Connecticut	53-247	Yes		$5,000	5 years	May order animal cruelty prevention or counseling and education program.		1996	Felony applies to all animals;
Delaware	11 Del. C. §1325	Yes	Class F felony	$5,000	3 years			1994	Felony applies to all animals Cruelty to animals; class A misd; class F felony; with felony conviction, may not own animals for 15 yrs.
District of Columbia	D.C. Code 22-1001	Yes	Felony	$25,000	5 years			2001	Felony applies to all animals, except: rats, bats or snakes
Florida	828.12	Yes	Felony of the third degree	$10,000	5 years	Psychological counseling/ anger management treatment is mandatory for acts of intentional torture/torment.	May report	1989	Felony applies to all animals; defendants found guilty of "intentional" cruelty must pay a minimum fine of $2,500.
Georgia	16-12-4 (b) and (c)	No	First offense—misdemeanor Second offense—misdemeanor for unjustifiable pain/suffering Second offense of causing death is a high aggravated misdemeanor	$1,000 (up to) $5,000 (up to) $10,000 (up to)	Up to 1 year Up to 1 year 3 months to 1 year	Sentencing judge may require psychological evaluation and shall consider the entire criminal record of the offender.		2000	Causing death or unjustifiable physical pain or suffering to any animal, by act omission or willful neglect.
		Yes	First offense Second offense	$15,000 $100,000	1–5 years				Felony applies to all animals; causing death or rendering part of the animal useless or disfiguring the animal.

The History of Human-Animal Interaction

TABLE 1.8

State animal anti-cruelty laws, July 2008 [CONTINUED]

State	Statute number of cruelty law	Felony	Classification of crime/maximum level of penalty	Maximum fine	Maximum jail time	Psychological counseling	Cross reporting of animal cruelty	Year enacted into a felony	Other significant circumstances or penalties
Hawaii	711-1109	Yes	Class C Felony	$10,000	5 years			2007	Felony only applies to dog, cat, rabbit, so long as not bred for consumption, guinea pig, domestic rat or mouse, or caged bird
Idaho	25-304 Penalties 25-3520A Definitions: 25-3502	No	3 stages of misdemeanor	$5,000–$9,000	6 months to 1 year				**No felony** Applies to all animals; exception for poisoning—jail: state max of 3 years, county max of 1 year. Max fine of $5,000.
Illinois	510 §3.02 and 510 70/4.01 and 70/16	Yes	Class 3 felony for torture on 1st offense. Class 4 felony for aggravated cruelty	$50,000	3–5 years 1–3 years	May order; Shall order for juveniles		1999	Felony applies to torture of any/all animals. Convicted or anyone residing in the same household may not adopt any forfeited animals.
Indiana	35-46-3-12	Yes	Class D felony on the first conviction or torture or mutilation.	$10,000	3 years	Mandatory evaluation and treatment		1998 In 2002 felony on the first.	Felony applies to all animals. A person who knowingly or intentionally beats a vertebrate animal commits cruelty to an animal, a Class A misdemeanor. 35-50-2-7 Fixed term 1½ years, with not more than 1½ years added for aggravating circumstances or not more than 1 yr subtracted for mitigating circumstances.
Iowa	717B.3A—Animal torture 717B.1 717B.2	Yes	Second offense committed is a Class D felony	$7,500	5 years	Shall order		2000	Felony applies to injury to animals other than livestock and does not apply to any game, fur-bearing animal, fish, reptile, or amphibian. Injury to an animal belonging to another person. Animal abuse is an aggravated misdemeanor.
Kansas	21-4310, Amended by S.B. 408 (2006)	Yes	First offense is a non-person felony	$500–$5,000	30 days to 1 year	Evaluation is mandated		2006	Intentionally and maliciously killing, injuring, maiming, torturing, burning or mutilating any animal
Kentucky	525.135 525.130 class A mis.	Yes	First offense of a Class D felony.	$1,000–$10,000 $500—for misdemeanor	1–5 years for felony 1 year—for misdemeanor			2003—2nd offense; 2008—1st offense	Felony applies to torture of a dog or a cat, only.
Louisiana	La. R.S. 14:102.1 (2004)	Yes		$25,000	10 years		Yes	1995	Felony applies to all animals accept chickens; community service shall be ordered for the misdemeanor offenses and a fine of up to $1,000.

TABLE 1.8

State animal anti-cruelty laws, July 2008 [CONTINUED]

State	Statute number of cruelty law	Felony	Classification of crime/maximum level of penalty	Maximum fine	Maximum jail time	Psychological counseling	Cross reporting of animal cruelty	Year enacted into a felony	Other significant circumstances or penalties.
Maine	§7-4011 Civil	No	If two or more convictions of civil or criminal animal cruelty charges a felony or max fine is charged.	$5,000	Not ordered in civil prosecution	Shall order if JV May order for all others		2001	Felony applies to all animals; If someone kills or tortures an animal to frighten or intimidate a person or forces a person to injure or kill an animal they are guilty of a Class D crime. If convicted the court shall prohibit the defendant from owning or having animals on their property permanently.
	§17-1031 Criminal	Yes	Felony penalty for the first violation of aggravated animal cruelty	$10,000	5 years				
Massachusetts	272 §77 and 266 §112	Yes	First conviction is a felony.	$2,500	5 years in the state prison or 2½ in the house of correction		May report	1804 increased penalties in 2004	Felony applies to all animals; felony if time is served in the state prison.
Maryland	Criminal Law, §10-606	Yes	First conviction of aggravated cruelty is a felony	$5,000	3 years	May order		2001	Felony covers all animals; 2002 court case—man was also ordered to not own any dogs in the future.
Michigan	750 §50b	Yes	Felony	$5,000	4 years	May order		1931	Felony applies to all animals; may also order up to 500 hours community service. And the defendant not to own or possess animals for a period of time not to exceed the period of probation... a second conviction the court may order the defendant to permanently relinquish animal ownership.
Minnesota	343.21	Yes	Felony	$10,000	2 years	May order		2001	Felony only on cruelty to a pet. Court may limit the possession of pets or probation w/no control of a pet.
Mississippi	97-41-16	No		$1,000	6 months				No felony 97-41-1 was found unconstitutionally vague; it lacked words of intent 2006 law to now include cats in misdemeanor code.
	97-41-1	No		$1,000	6 months				97-41-16—Kill, maim or wound a dog.
	97-41-15	No-for livestock only	Special-felony for livestock (does not include companion animals or wildlife) $500	$1,500-$10,000	12 months-5 years				97-41-15-Maliciously, mischievously kills, maim or wound, injure any livestock—felony—penalties to the left §97-41-23-Kill or injure a public service animal—felony—$5,000 and/or up to 5 years in jail.
Missouri	578.012	Yes	Class D felony (first offense of torture or mutilation)	$5,000	5 years			1994	Applies to all animals; animal abuse is a class A misdemeanor but the 2nd offense is a felony.
Montana	45-8-217	Yes	First offense of aggravated cruelty is a felony	Up to $2,500	2 years (Dept. of corrections)			1993	Felony applies to all animals; deliberate cruelty; court may prohibit ownership of animals for any period of time. Misdemeanor: MCA §45-8-211 $1,000 and 2 years in Dept. of Corrections.

TABLE 1.8

State animal anti-cruelty laws, July 2008 [CONTINUED]

State	Statute number of cruelty law	Felony	Classification of crime/maximum level of penalty	Maximum fine	Maximum jail time	Psychological counseling	Cross reporting of animal cruelty	Year enacted into a felony	Other significant circumstances or penalties
Nebraska	28-1009	Yes	The first conviction of torture, beating or mutilation is a IV degree felony	$10,000	5 years		Yes	2002—2nd offense, 2003—1st offense	Applies to all animals in captivity. Lesser offense: Class I misdemeanor for second offense of abandonment or cruel neglect.
Nevada	574.100	Yes	The third offense committed is a felony	$10,000	5 years	Mandatory for juveniles		1999	Applies to all animals, specific exemptions for rodeo and ranching.
New Hampshire	RSA 644:8	Yes	First offense of beating or torturing	$4,000	7 years			1994	Felony applies to all animals; 2nd offense of certain acts is a felony. Court may also prohibit future ownership of other animals for any period or impose other restrictions.
New Jersey	4:22-17	Yes	Crime of the fourth degree on the first offense (felony equivalent)	$15,000	3–5 years	Shall order juveniles for certain animal cruelty offenses		2001	Felony applies to all animals; a second offense is a crime of the third degree. The court may also sentence the convicted to community service and bonding requirements.
New Mexico	30-18-1	Yes	"Extreme cruelty to animals" is a felony in the first offense Fourth offense committed of "cruelty to animals" is a felony	$5,000	18 months	May order Shall order for JV's.		1999	Felony applies to all animals; court may order an animal cruelty prevention program.
New York	353-a 55.10 penal law	Yes	Aggravated cruelty to a companion animal is a Class E felony	$5,000 ($80)	4 years ($70)			1999	Felony only applies to dogs, cats, and companion animals.
North Carolina	14-360	Yes	First offense of cruelly beating, mutilating, torturing, poisoning or killing any animal is a Class I felony	$1,000	6 months			1998	Felony applies to all animals; basic animal cruelty is a class 1 misdemeanor. It is a class 1 misdemeanor to instigate or promote animal cruelty.
North Dakota	36-21.1-02	No	Class A misdemeanor	$2,000	1 year				**No felony** Misdemeanor law only
Ohio	959.13	Yes	Second offense committed is a 5th degree felony	$2,000	1 year	May order		2002	Felony only applies to companion animals and on the 2nd offense. First offense is a class 1 misdemeanor, with a maximum 6 months in jail and a $1000 fine. "Harassing a service dog or police dog" is a felony of the 3rd degree and the offender must pay vet, replacement, and training costs.
	959.02	No	1st degree misdemeanor	$1,000	180 days				1st degree is ordered for "injuring" an animal whose value is over $300. This applies to the property of another.

TABLE 1.8

State animal anti-cruelty laws, July 2008 [CONTINUED]

State	Statute number of cruelty law	Felony	Classification of crime/maximum level of penalty	Maximum fine	Maximum jail time	Psychological counseling	Cross reporting of animal cruelty	Year enacted into a felony	Other significant circumstances or penalties
Oklahoma	21-1685	Yes	Felony on first offense committed	$5,000	5 years in state jail, 1 year in a county jail			1887	Felony applies to all animals; aggravated animal abuse in the 1st degree.
Oregon	167.322	Yes	Class C felony on the first offense	$100,000	5 years	May order		1995	Felony applies to all animals
Pennsylvania	18-5511	Yes	The second offense committed on a dog or cat is a felony of the 3rd degree. First offense committed on a zoo animal is a felony of the 3rd degree	$15,000	7 years	May order (the court may order a presentence mental evaluation)		1995	Felony only applies to zoo animals (1st offense) and dogs and cats (on the 2nd offense) based on deliberate cruelty. First offense is a misdemeanor of the 1st degree. 18-1103—sentencing
Rhode Island	4-1-3	Yes	First offense committed is a felony	$1,000	2 years	§4-1-36—May order an evaluation		1896	Felony applies to all animals; Any penalty of over 1 year in jail or a fine of over $1000 is a felony. (law does not specify the word "felony")
	4-1-4	Yes		$1,000					Dismembering any animal maliciously or killing any animal or poisoning any animal. 10 hours of community restitution.
South Carolina	47-1-40	Yes	First offense is a felony	$5,000	5 years			2000	Felony applies to all animals;
South Dakota	40-1-21 and 40-1-27	No No	Class 1 misdemeanor	$1,000	1 year				**No felony** 40-1-21 killing the animal of another. 40-1-27 treating one's own animal inhumanely 406. 22-22-42 Bestiality Class 6 felony, 2nd offense is a Class 5 felony. Several other statutes w/no penalties mentioned: 40-1-2.2 unjustifiable or unreasonable physical pain or suffering is caused. 40-1-2.4 40-1-20. Poisoning animal of another.
Tennessee	39-14-202 39-14-212	Yes	First offense of aggravated cruelty is a felony		9 months minimum (mandatory) no suspended sentence or probation until 9 months are served.	Shall order	Yes	2001 2002 Felony on the 1st offense was passed in 2004	First offense of aggravated cruelty to a pet is a felony. Includes failure to provide food/water with a substantial risk of death or death. Court may order forfeiture of companion animals, and limit ownership in the future.
Texas	Sec. 42.09 Sec. 12.21 Sec. 12.35	Yes	Felony of the 3rd degree if the person has been convicted two times prior. The first offense is a lesser felony.	$10,000	2 years	Mandatory for juveniles		1997	All animals that are your own; state jail felony on the first offense of most egregious, 3rd degree felony on second. It is not illegal to kill one's own animal, no matter how cruelly or by what means. Separate section for livestock animals including horses.

TABLE 1.8

State animal anti-cruelty laws, July 2008 [CONTINUED]

State	Statute number of cruelty law	Felony	Classification of crime/maximum level of penalty	Maximum fine	Maximum jail time	Psychological counseling	Cross reporting of animal cruelty	Year enacted into a felony	Other significant circumstances or penalties
Utah	76-9-301	Yes	Third degree felony	$5,000	5 years	Mandatory for juveniles		2008	Felony for torture of a dog or cat; misdemeanor applies to all animals; The court may order the defendant to no longer possess or retain custody of any animal during the period of probation, parole or other.
Vermont	352	Yes	First act of cruelty committed is a felony	$7,500	5 years	May order		1998 improved 2004	Felony applies to acts of aggravated cruelty to all animals; any sentence less than 2 years is a misdemeanor. Defendant may have forfeited the right to ever own animals again.
Virginia	3.1-796.122	Yes	First offense committed is a felony	$2,500	5 years	May order		1999—felony Upgraded in 2002.	Dog or cat for felony on the first offense. All other animals if 2nd offense. The animal must die as a result of his/her injuries for the felony to apply. Any person convicted of violating this section may be prohibited from possession or ownership of companion animals.
Washington	16.52.205	Yes	First offense committed is a class C felony	$10,000	5 years	May order		1994	Felony applies to all animals
West Virginia	61-8-19	Yes	First offense committed is a felony	$1,000–$5,000	5 years	Shall order an evaluation	Yes	2003	All animals included in felony; §61-8-19—a court shall prohibit convicted from owning or residing with any animal for 5 yrs (if mis) and 15 yrs (for a felony). For a misdemeanor the max fine is $2000 and 1 year. Cross reporting required.
Wisconsin	For livestock §61-3-27 §951.18 (2004) §951.02—mistreating For service dogs (S.B. 181 2006)	Yes Yes	Felony only applies to animals with "value" over $100 Felony	$10,000	5 years			1986	Felony if the animal's value is over $100, but does not include dogs. Felony applies to all animals; aggravated cruelty, mutilating or animal fighting. A court may order that the violator may not own, possess or train any animal or species for up to five years. If someone intentionally injures a service dog or allows his/her dog to injure a service dog, he/she is guilty of a Class I felony. If someone intentionally causes the death of a service dog or takes possession of a service dog without consent of the owner, he/she is guilty of a Class H felony. (S.B. 181 (2006))

TABLE 1.8

State animal anti-cruelty laws, July 2008 [CONTINUED]

State	Statute number of cruelty law	Felony	Classification of crime/maximum level of penalty	Maximum fine	Maximum jail time	Psychological counseling	Cross reporting of animal cruelty	Year enacted into a felony	Other significant circumstances or penalties
Wyoming	§6-3-203	Yes	Felony	$5,000	2 years			2003	Felony applies to all animals; court may prohibit or limit the defendant's ownership, possession or custody of animals.
Puerto Rico	Law 439 Amends 67		Grave offense in the 4th degree					2004	Animal abuse is a felony offense.
Virgin Islands	§181	Yes	Felony	$2,000–$5,000	2 years			2005	Applies to any non-human mammal, except for "pests," can be banned from having custody of an animal for up to 20 years.

Note: Forty-five states, the District of Columbia, Puerto Rico and the Virgin Islands have laws making certain types of animal cruelty a felony offense.

SOURCE: "Fact Sheet: State Animal Anti-Cruelty Law Provisions," in *Animal Cruelty Laws: Where Does Your State Stand?* Humane Society of the United States, July 2008, http://www.hsus.org/web-files/PDF/state_cruelty_chart.pdf (accessed January 13, 2009)

CHAPTER 2
THE ANIMAL RIGHTS DEBATE

According to *Merriam-Webster's Collegiate Dictionary* (2003), a right is a "power or privilege to which one is justly entitled." In *The Animal Rights Crusade: The Growth of a Moral Protest* (1992), James M. Jasper and Dorothy Nelkin define a right as "a moral trump card that cannot be disputed." The term *human rights* came into usage during the late 1700s to refer to generally recognized privileges (or freedoms) that every person should enjoy.

RIGHTS AND SOCIETY

The United Nations has the Universal Declaration of Human Rights (1998, http://www.un.org/rights/50/decla .htm), which states, "Everyone has the right to life, liberty and security of person." The declaration specifies dozens of particular human rights, including the right to be free from slavery, torture, and cruel or degrading treatment.

The U.S. Declaration of Independence, written in 1776, states, "We hold these truths to be self-evident, that all men are created equal, that they are endowed by their Creator with certain unalienable Rights, that among these are Life, Liberty and the pursuit of Happiness." Even though the United States' founding fathers considered these rights to be inherent, they did note that people form governments to "secure these rights." Thus, even though rights have a moral basis, they are upheld through the law.

Since the 1970s a debate has arisen about whether animals have moral rights that should be recognized and protected by human society. This is largely a philosophical question, but the answer has many practical consequences. For example, if animals have a right to life, then it is wrong to kill them. If animals have a right to liberty, then it is wrong to hold them in captivity. If animals have a right to pursue happiness and enjoy security, then it is wrong to interfere in their natural lives.

Societies and governments make decisions about who should be granted rights and how those rights should be secured. In general, an individual's legal right to life and liberty ends if that person infringes on someone else's right to life and liberty. In some states a person who kills another person can be executed by the government. At the very least, the government can restrict the killer's liberty. People debate the moral issues involved in such affairs, but the legal issues are generally spelled out clearly in U.S. law.

Sometimes it is not considered morally or legally wrong for one person to kill another—for example, in the case of self-defense or in defense of others. The same holds true for a person killing an animal. There is general moral and legal agreement that killing an attacking tiger or rabid dog is reasonable and right behavior. In human society the moral and legal arguments that protect a person acting in self-defense begin to melt away as the threat level decreases. Killing an unarmed burglar or trespasser may or may not be perceived as justified under the law. Killing a loud, annoying neighbor crosses over the line.

This line is set much lower when it comes to killing animals. People can sometimes kill animals that burgle or trespass, make too much noise, or become a nuisance, without moral or legal condemnation. The same holds true for animals that taste good, have attractive skin or pelts, or are useful laboratory subjects. Why is it acceptable to kill an animal for these reasons, but not a human?

People answer this question in different ways, depending on their belief system and moral and social influences, including religion, philosophy, and education. The following are some of the most common reasons people give for denying animals rights:

- Animals do not have souls.

- God gave humans dominion over the animals.

- Humans are intellectually superior to animals.

- Animals do not reason, think, or feel pain like humans do.

- Animals are a natural resource to be used as humans see fit.

- Animals kill each other.

Animal Rights Activists and Welfarists

Some people believe it is not acceptable to use animals for any human purpose at all. They believe animals have moral rights to life, liberty, and other privileges that should be upheld by society and the rule of law. These are the hardcore believers in animal rights, the fundamentalists of the animal rights movement. When they speak out, write, march, or otherwise publicize their beliefs, they are called animal rights activists. An activist is someone who takes direct and vigorous action to further a cause (especially a controversial cause).

Other people believe some animals have (or should have) moral and/or legal rights under certain circumstances. They may rescue abandoned pets, lobby for legislation against animal abuse, feed pigeons in the park, or do any number of other things on behalf of animals. These people are broadly categorized as animal welfarists. Their adherence to the idea of animal rights generally depends on the circumstances. For example, a welfarist might defend the rights of pet dogs and cats but eat chicken, steak, or pork for dinner.

This is unacceptable to animal rights fundamentalists. They argue that all animals (not just the lovable or attractive ones) have rights that apply all the time (not just when it is convenient). Such fundamentalists face opposition from a variety of sources. Some of this opposition is driven by moral and philosophical differences of opinion. Some is also driven by economics.

Many animals (alive or dead) have financial value to humans. Livestock farmers, ranchers, pharmaceutical companies, zookeepers, circus trainers, jockeys, and breeders are among the many people who have a financial interest in the animal trade. If humans were to stop using animals, these people would be out of work. Many others would be deprived of their favorite sport and leisure activities. Given such economic arguments and the moral and philosophical arguments noted previously, those opposed to the idea of animal rights feel as strongly about the topic as those who support it.

THE HISTORY OF THE ANIMAL RIGHTS DEBATE

It was not until the 1970s that the question of animal rights became a major social issue. In 1970 the British psychologist Richard D. Ryder (1940–) coined the term *speciesism* to describe prejudice and discrimination practiced by humans against animals. Ryder's ideas received little publicity, but they were embraced by the Australian philosopher Peter Singer (1946–). In 1975 Singer published the influential book *Animal Liberation: A New Ethics for Our Treatment of Animals*, which describes in vivid detail the ways in which animals are subjected to pain and suffering on farms, in slaughterhouses, and in laboratory experiments. Singer publicizes the notion of speciesism and calls for an end to it. He argues that speciesism is similar to racism and sexism, in that they all deny moral and legal rights to one group in favor of another.

Henry Spira (1927–1998) formed Animal Rights International after attending one of Singer's lectures. Spira was a social reformer who had worked in the civil rights and women's liberation movements. Barnaby J. Feder notes in the obituary "Henry Spira, 71, Animal Rights Crusader" (*New York Times*, September 15, 1998) that Spira turned his attention to the animal rights movement after he "began to wonder why we cuddle some animals and put a fork in others." Spira was instrumental in bringing various animal groups together to work for common causes. Many people credit him with pressuring cosmetics companies to seek alternatives to animal testing for their products during the late 1980s.

By 1980 the animal rights movement had become prominent enough to attract the attention of critics. In *Interests and Rights: The Case against Animals* (1980), the philosopher Raymond G. Frey argues that animals do not have moral rights. He insists that animal lives do not have the same moral value as human lives because animals cannot and do not undergo the same emotional and intellectual experiences as humans.

In 1979 the organization Attorneys for Animal Rights was founded by the lawyer Joyce Tischler. The group held the first national conference on animal rights law in 1980. The next year it successfully sued the U.S. Navy and prevented the killing of 5,000 burros at a weapons-testing center in California. In 1984 the group adopted a new name: the Animal Legal Defense Fund (ALDF). One of ALDF's goals is to end the belief that animals are merely property. The group's anticruelty division also works with state prosecutors and law enforcement agencies to draft felony anticruelty laws and stiffen penalties for violations.

The British philosopher Mary Midgley joined the debate when she published *Beast and Man: The Roots of Human Nature* (1978) and *Animals and Why They Matter* (1983). Midgley argues that Charles Darwin's (1809–1882) *On the Origin of Species by Means of Natural Selection* (1859) was the catalyst for ending the moral separation that humans felt toward animals because it proved that humans were in fact animals. Midgley compares speciesism to other social problems, such as racism, sexism, and age discrimination.

It was during the 1970s and 1980s that some animal rights advocates began using high-profile tactics, such as sit-ins at buildings and protest marches on the streets, to attract public attention to their cause. These are examples of civil disobedience (refusing in a nonviolent way to obey government regulations or social standards). A radical element of the movement went even further by breaking into laboratories and fur farms to release animals and damaging buildings and equipment. Some people who used these methods referred to themselves as part of the Animal Liberation Front (ALF). ALF followers became known as the "domestic terrorists" of the animal movement.

People for the Ethical Treatment of Animals (PETA) was founded in 1980 and quickly came to prominence. One of the group's cofounders infiltrated a research laboratory and obtained photographs of the primates being held there. The incident attracted national media attention and greatly helped Spira's efforts to reduce animal use in cosmetic testing. Animal issues also became important to a larger number of Americans in the 1980s.

Many in the scientific community were disturbed by this new wave of moral and social opposition to the use of animals in research. The Foundation for Biomedical Research was founded in 1981 to defend such usage and promote greater understanding of its medical and scientific benefits among the general public. The foundation began tracking and reporting on the activities of criminal animal activists who broke into laboratories to release animals and/or destroy property.

In 1983 Tom Regan of North Carolina State University published *The Case for Animal Rights*. He argues that animal pain and suffering are consequences of a bigger problem: The idea that animals are a resource for people. Regan presents detailed philosophical arguments outlining why he believes animals have moral rights as "subjects-of-a-life." Regan states that acknowledging the rights of animals requires people to cease using them for any purpose, not just those associated with pain and suffering.

Frey responded to the growing pro-vegetarian movement in 1983 with *Rights, Killing, and Suffering: Moral Vegetarianism and Applied Ethics*. The idea of moral vegetarianism (adhering to a vegetarian diet for moral reasons, rather than for physical reasons) dates back centuries. The Italian artist Leonardo da Vinci (1452–1519) once wrote in his notebook, "The time will come when men such as I will look upon the murder of animals as they now look upon the murder of men." Moral vegetarianism was advocated by the Indian leader Mahatma Gandhi (1869–1948) in the early 1930s as a moral duty of humans toward animals and gained new life during the animal movement of the 1970s. Frey, however, argues that a widespread adherence to a vegetarian lifestyle would result in the collapse of animal agriculture and other animal-based industries and massive social disruption.

In 1984 Ernest Partridge of the University of California, Riverside, attacked Singer's speciesism philosophy and Regan's animal rights view in "Three Wrong Leads in a Search for an Environmental Ethic: Tom Regan on Animal Rights, Inherent Values, and 'Deep Ecology'" (*Ethics and Animals*, vol. 5, no. 3). Partridge maintains that both Singer and Regan miss a crucial point about the nature of rights: that rights have no biological basis, only a moral basis. In other words, it does not matter how humans and animals are alike or dissimilar in biology. What really matters is that no animals exhibit the capacities of "personhood," such as rationality and self-consciousness. Partridge contends that the lack of personhood effectively disqualifies animals from being rights holders.

Carl Cohen of the University of Michigan also attacked Singer's and Regan's views in "The Case for the Use of Animals in Biomedical Research" (*New England Journal of Medicine*, vol. 315, no. 14, October 2, 1986). Cohen acknowledges that speciesism exists, but denies that it is similar to racism or sexism. He argues that racism and sexism are unacceptable because there is no moral difference between races or between sexes. However, he writes that there is a moral difference between humans and animals that denies rights to animals and allows animals to be used by humans.

Animals as Property

In 1988 researchers at Harvard University obtained a patent for the OncoMouse—a mouse that had been genetically engineered to be susceptible to cancer. This was the first patent ever issued for an animal. Animal rights groups, led by the ALDF, challenged the issuance of the patent in court, but the case was dismissed because the court found that the ALDF had no legal standing in the matter. Since that time, several other animals have been patented, including pigs, sheep, goats, and cattle.

In 1995 Gary L. Francione published *Animals, Property, and the Law*, in which he argues that there is an enormous contradiction between public sentiment and legal treatment when it comes to animals. Francione notes that most of the public agrees that animals should be treated humanely and not subjected to unnecessary suffering, but he claims that the legal system does not uphold these moral principles because it regards animals as property.

Francione compares the situation to the one in the slave states before the Civil War (1861–1865). Even though there were laws that supposedly protected slaves from the abuse of slave owners, they were seldom enforced. Slaves, like animals, were considered property, and the law protects the right of people to own and use property as they see fit. Property rights date back to English common law. According to Francione, the law has always relied on the assumption that property owners will treat their property appropriately to protect its economic value. Under this reasoning, the courts of the nineteenth century refused to recognize that a badly beaten slave was "abused," as defined by the law.

Francione believes this same logic gives legal support to common practices in which animals are mistreated—for example, in the farming industry or in laboratory testing. He explains that humans are granted "respect-based" rights by the law and that animals are only considered in terms of their utility and economic value. Francione points out that animals are treated by the legal system as "means to ends and never as ends in themselves." In other words, existing animal laws protect animals because animals have value to people, not because animals have inherent value as living beings.

Bob Torres also believes that exploitation lies at the root of human-animal interactions. In *Making a Killing: The Political Economy of Animal Rights* (2007), he states, "Animals labor to produce commodities or to be commodities, and they do this as the mere property of humans. We generally talk of this relationship in magnanimous terms, describing our 'care' of animals as 'husbandry,' or as us being guardians of their 'welfare,' yet, underneath these comfortable and bucolic notions of animal-human relations, there is a system of exploitation that yields value for the producer while denying the animal her right to live fully."

PHILOSOPHICAL ARGUMENTS

At the base of the animal rights debate is philosophy. Philosophical discussions involve abstract ideas and theories about questions of ethics and morality. These can be difficult subjects to comprehend and apply to real-life situations, but philosophy is important because it explains people's motivations and why people feel the way they do about a particular issue. Philosophical arguments are commonly used to either justify or condemn certain actions toward animals.

Not all people involved in the animal movement believe in animal rights. Many are motivated to work for animal causes for other reasons. Historically, the most common motivator has been concern for animal welfare, or welfarism.

Welfarism

Welfarism is defined as the beliefs associated with the social system known as the welfare state. The term *welfare state* was first used during the 1940s to refer to a society in which the government has the primary responsibility for the individual and social welfare of its citizens. When applied to animals, welfarism assumes that humans have the primary responsibility for the welfare of animals. Welfarists acknowledge that society uses animals for various purposes. Their goal is to reduce the amount of pain and suffering that animals endure. Welfarism centers on compassionate and humane care and treatment.

The best-known welfarist organization in the United States is the American Society for the Prevention of Cruelty

to Animals (ASPCA; 2009, http://www.aspca.org/about-us/policy-positions/), which was founded in 1866. Its mission is "to provide effective means for the prevention of cruelty to animals throughout the United States." The ASPCA defines itself not as an animal rights organization but as an animal welfare or animal protection organization. Even though the ASPCA does advocate for stronger anticruelty laws, it does not actively promote issues such as vegetarianism or banning the use of animals in medical research.

The Humane Society of the United States (HSUS) was founded in 1954. It is an animal organization that fits into the welfarist category, but its agenda is more sweeping than that of the ASPCA, encompassing protection of wild and marine animals as well as companion animals. Even though it defines itself as an animal protection organization, critics charge that the HSUS quietly supports an animal rights agenda because it is openly against the use of animals in research, inhumane farming practices, and the fur industry.

Animal welfarists believe humans have a responsibility to ensure the well-being of animals and reduce their suffering. This responsibility is upheld by society in the form of anticruelty laws. However, these laws do not prevent farm animals from being slaughtered for food or laboratory animals from being experimented on, usually without anesthetic to numb their pain. In these situations, welfarists work for humane slaughtering methods and the prevention of "unnecessary" or excessive suffering during experimentation.

Utilitarianism

Utilitarianism is a philosophy popularized by the British philosopher and political scientist Jeremy Bentham (1748–1832) in *An Introduction to the Principles of Morals and Legislation* (1789). The basic premise of utilitarianism is that right actions are those that maximize utility. Bentham defines utility as either the presence of positive consequences—"benefit, advantage, pleasure, good, or happiness"—or the absence of negative consequences—"mischief, pain, evil, or unhappiness." In other words, right actions are those that maximize the best consequences or minimize the worst consequences. An important aspect of utilitarianism is that the interests of all parties involved in a particular situation must be considered. Likewise, the consequences to all parties involved must be taken into account. This is a difficult enough task when only humans are involved; it becomes much more complicated when animals are taken into consideration.

Singer uses a form of utilitarian logic in *Animal Liberation*. He argues that the suffering endured by animals on farms and during slaughtering far outweighs the pleasure and nutrition that the meat gives to humans. Likewise, he contends that laboratory animals suffer so much that this outweighs their usefulness to humans as test subjects. Singer concludes that the moral consequences of these practices (and other practices in which animals suffer) are so severe that they must be abolished. As a result, advocates of Singer's theory are often called liberationists or abolitionists. Even though his book is frequently called the bible of the animal rights movement, Singer does not specifically call for animal rights in the book. He has stated, however, that he believes the term is politically useful for drawing attention to animal suffering.

Many philosophers reject the notion that utilitarianism can be applied to human-animal situations because, historically, animals have not been considered to have interests at all, or their interests have not been considered equal to human interests. In 1992 the philosopher Peter Carruthers wrote *The Animals Issue: Moral Theory in Practice*, in which he argues that utilitarianism is not an acceptable moral theory for examining animal issues because it equates animal lives and suffering with human lives and suffering, an idea Carruthers calls "intuitively abhorrent" and a violation of "common-sense beliefs." In *Interests and Rights*, Frey also discounts the utilitarian theory as a model of morality for dealing with animals, saying that animals do not have interests because they do not experience wants, desires, expectations, or remembrances.

Contractarianism

Contractarianism is another philosophy that is used to examine morality. According to this theory, society establishes right actions (or moral norms) through an arrangement in which individuals (called agents) voluntarily agree to abide by certain rules of morality. Following these rules is beneficial to both individuals and society in general. Even though there are many different models of contractarianism, the most common are based on the writings of the German philosopher Immanuel Kant (1724–1804) and the American philosopher John Rawls (1921–2002). Kant believes the moral code arising out of contractarianism reflects what rational agents would choose under ideal circumstances. Rawls expands this view by saying that the right actions are those that rational agents would choose if they were unaware of their own personal ambitions or prejudices.

When contractarianism is used to discuss human society, the rational agents are assumed to have direct duties. In other words, the rational agents know they are bound by a moral contract and are responsible for acting accordingly. The rational agents also have direct rights under the contract and have duties to those who lack the rationality to enter into the contract, such as babies, small children, and the mentally challenged.

Some philosophers use the contractarian model to explain the moral relationship between humans and animals. In *Animals Issue*, Carruthers argues that contractarianism is the best moral model for describing the human-animal relationship, but he concludes that animals do not have moral standing under the contract because they do not qualify as rational agents. He notes that humans have only indirect duties toward animals, one of which is to treat them humanely out of respect for the feelings of the rational agents (other humans) who care about them. Carruthers does, however, extend direct rights to human beings who are not rational agents (such as babies), noting that this is necessary to maintain social stability.

In the contractarian model, humans are moral agents, meaning that they make decisions and take actions based on morality. Many philosophers believe animals are amoral—neither moral nor immoral. For example, a lion that kills a baby zebra to feed her cubs is acting out of instinct. The action is neither morally good nor morally bad. Some opponents of animal rights argue that because animals do not make decisions based on morality, they are not part of the moral contract and do not have moral rights. Tibor R. Machan is an outspoken critic of the notion of animal rights. In *Putting Humans First: Why We Are Nature's Favorite* (2004), he argues that animals cannot have rights because they are not capable of making moral decisions.

In practice, the moral code of contractarianism seems to provide some protections for selected species of animals. For example, in American society there is widespread moral repugnance to the idea of eating dogs and cats or killing animals with sentimental or patriotic significance (such as bald eagles). These views might be argued to be rooted in their moral and philosophical impact on humans and could therefore be extensions of the contractarian model.

Rights View

The rights view is defined and defended by Regan in *Case for Animal Rights* and in many subsequent books. He maintains that all beings who are "subjects-of-a-life with an experiential welfare" have inherent value that qualifies them to be treated with respect and gives them a right to that treatment. In other words, living beings with conscious awareness and self-identity deserve moral rights. Regan does not define exactly which animals fall into this category, but higher species, such as vertebrates (animals with a spinal cord) fit his criteria.

This philosophy is fundamentally different from welfarism and utilitarianism. The rights view holds that animals have moral rights to certain privileges and freedoms, just as humans do. It does not mean that animals have exactly the same rights as humans. Most animal rights advocates believe that animals at least have the right to life and the right to freedom from bodily interference.

The philosopher best known for criticizing the animal rights view is Carl Cohen. In 2001 Cohen and Regan coauthored *The Animal Rights Debate*, which presents a point-counterpoint examination of the issue. Cohen sums up his argument against animal rights: "Animals cannot be the bearers of rights, because the concept of rights is *essentially human*; it is rooted in the human moral world and has force and applicability only within that world." He admits that animals are sentient (conscious of sensory impressions), feel pain, and can experience suffering, but insists that sharing these traits with humans does not make animals morally equal to humans.

Cohen writes that some people confuse rights with obligations and assume that because humans have obligations to animals, it means that animals have rights. This assumption is called symmetrical reciprocity, and he believes it is based on false logic. The difference, Cohen explains, is that an obligation is what "we ought to do," whereas a right is "what others can justly demand that we do."

Cohen states that humans are moral agents who are restrained by moral principles from treating animals inhumanely. This means that humans should not inflict "gratuitous" pain and suffering on animals. However, it does not mean that humans must stop every activity that could or does harm animals in some way. Medical research on animals is an example. He believes that scientists have moral obligations to humanity to use animals in their experiments if that is the best way for them to achieve their goals. According to Cohen, "Our duties to human subjects are of a different moral order from our duties to the rodents we use."

Cohen's overall conclusion—that rights do not apply to animals because rights are essentially human—is a point commonly made by those who oppose the animal rights movement. Many of them find it ludicrous to even debate the issue. Adrian R. Morrison is a scientist engaged in animal research and a vocal critic of the animal rights movement. In "Understanding the Effect of Animal-Rights Activism on Biomedical Research" (*Actas de Fisiología*, vol. 8, 2002), he notes that few philosophers besides Cohen and almost no scientists bother to dispute in detail the philosophy behind the animal rights view. Morrison suggests that most scientists and philosophers "think the subject to be too far from reality to be worth the trouble."

PRACTICAL IMPLICATIONS

Assuming that animals have rights would have massive consequences to society. If animals have moral rights to life and freedom from bodily interference, then they cannot be purposely killed, harmed, or kept in captivity by humans. Billions of domesticated animals would be spared from slaughter and would have to be released from cages and pens.

PETA (2009, http://www.peta.org/) states its position quite bluntly:

- Animals are not ours to eat.

- Animals are not ours to wear.

- Animals are not ours to experiment on.

- Animals are not ours to use for entertainment.

- Animals are not ours to abuse in any way.

Implementation of these beliefs would mean the elimination of all commercial animal operations: livestock and fur farms, animal research facilities, circuses, zoos, animal parks and aquariums, game ranches, hunting lodges, animal breeding facilities, pet stores, dog and horse racetracks, and so on. All the people working in these businesses would be put out of work. The economic consequences would be enormous. Animal rights advocates point out that dismantling the slave trade after the Civil War was costly as well, but it was done anyway because it was the right thing to do.

Besides an economic cost, there would be a scientific cost. Medical and scientific research has relied on animal test subjects for centuries. Some research and development would have to stop until alternatives could be found. Students in schools and universities would have to learn anatomy and biology without dissecting animals. Doctors, surgeons, and veterinarians in training would have to practice on something besides animals. Cloning, twinning, and other genetic manipulation of animals would have to stop. Eliminating the use of animals would disrupt the entire scientific community. Animal rights activists believe the move is overdue because it would force scientists to think about their research in new ways. Many school districts have already implemented alternatives to animal dissection, including computer models that accurately mimic animal bodies.

There are also implications to private individuals in terms of dining, fashion, sport, recreation, and leisure. None of these activities could include the personal use of animals. Hunting, fishing, eating meat, wearing leather, and keeping pets would come to a stop. The activity that would affect the most Americans would be the elimination of meat and animal products (milk, eggs, cheese, and so on) from their diet. Most animal rights advocates and liberationists are vegetarians or vegans. They believe a vegetarian diet would not only help animals but also would be healthier for humans and better for the environment.

Opponents of animal rights are always eager to point out that keeping pets would be forbidden if animals had rights. Ingrid Newkirk, a PETA cofounder, has been quoted as saying that pets are a symbol of the human manipulation of animals, and the notion of pets should be phased out. This idea is controversial even within the animal rights community because it is so radical. Many people involved in both the animal rights and animal welfare movements refer to pets as "companion animals" and to owners as "animal guardians" or "animal caretakers." These terms are intended to downplay the ownership element between humans and animals.

Legally, most animals are considered property. In fact, the term *cattle* derives from a Latin word meaning "property." This raises difficulties for pet owners who wish to ensure that their pets will be properly cared for in the event the owners die or become incapacitated. In "What Is a Pet

Trust" (2007, http://www.pettrustlawyer.com/pages/What _is_a_Pet_Trust.php), Rachel Hirschfeld notes that pets cannot inherit money through wills, because pets are legally considered to be property. Pet owners can designate a caretaker in their wills and leave money to that person intended for pet care, but the arrangement is not legally enforceable by the courts. Hirschfeld recommends another option, called a trust, to pet owners. A trust is a legally enforceable arrangement that allows a person to leave money to another person (called a trustee) for management of certain assets, such as property. Pet trusts have become extremely popular as a means for pet owners to ensure that their pets will be cared for after the owners' death. In 2009, 39 states and the District of Columbia had laws in place specifically allowing for pet trusts.

Carolyn B. Matlack suggests in "Sentient Property: Unleashing Legal Respect for Our Companion Animals" (*Animal Law Section*, Summer 2003) that companion animals receive a new property classification under the law: sentient property (feeling property). She argues that courts could determine the best interests of sentient property based on the testimony of experts, as is done for young children and the mentally disabled.

Even wild animals are categorized by ownership. Private landowners assume power of ownership over wild animals on their land. As long as the animals are not protected by specific legislation, property owners may kill them as they please. Wild animals inhabiting government lands are considered public property and are treated as such. The mission of the U.S. Fish and Wildlife Service (December 29, 2006, http://www.fws.gov/help/mission.cfm) is "to conserve, protect and enhance fish, wildlife, and plants and their habitats for the continuing benefit of the American people."

Public and private landowners exhibit implied animal ownership when they grant hunters permission to hunt on lands under their control. If these animals are assumed to have moral rights, then they can no longer be considered property.

Many animal welfarists are uneasy with the animal rights movement. They worry that it draws attention away from goals that are more easily obtainable for animals in the near future. They also worry that the radical statements and actions of some animal rights activists will turn the public against the entire animal movement. Radical animal rights activists have been known to demonstrate in the nude, splash paint on people wearing fur coats, and destroy and vandalize property. Many have spent time in prison for their actions.

Even though welfarists and liberationists/abolitionists sometimes work together to achieve change, there is a philosophical gulf between them. This was made clear by the animal rights advocate Joan Dunayer in *Speciesism* (2004).

Dunayer supports the idea that humans and animals should have "absolute moral equality." She accuses animal rights groups of compromising their beliefs by campaigning for welfarist reforms in animal treatment, rather than for complete liberation. Dunayer compares the plight of animals to that of prisoners in Nazi concentration camps during World War II (1939–1945), arguing that the prisoners would have begged their supporters on the outside to work for liberation rather than for more humane living conditions or kinder slaughtering techniques.

In 2008 the philosophical fight between the two factions intensified over the passage of a ballot initiative in California. Proposition 2 (a ban on certain confinement techniques for some farm animals) was championed by the HSUS and other mainline animal welfare groups. Animal rights advocates were bitterly opposed to it. In "A Losing Proposition" (2008, http://animalrights.about.com/ od/proposition2ca2008/a/FrancioneProp2.htm), Francione criticizes the measure, noting that "animals raised for food in California will still be tortured. The only difference will be that the torture will have the stamp of approval of the Humane Society of the United States." He states that the money spent on so-called humane ballot measures would be better spent on promoting veganism. Other animal rights activists derisively say that welfarists endorse "happy meat," instead of working to free farm animals from slavery and exploitation.

Abolitionists ask welfarists to give up meat and leather; close down all circuses, zoos, animal parks, aquariums, and racetracks; and stop laboratories from using animals. Most welfarists are not willing to go so far, preferring to focus on finding practical solutions to problems such as pet overpopulation and cruelty to domestic animals.

At the other end of the spectrum is the radical element of the animal movement. This element does not debate philosophy but takes direct action—sometimes illegally—to free animals from farms and laboratories. The ALF is not really a group, as it has no leadership structure, but is instead a set of guidelines. The ALF (2009, http://www.animalliberation front.com/ALFront/alf_credo.htm) states that "the . . . short-term aim is to save as many animals as possible and directly disrupt the practice of animal abuse. [The] long-term aim is to end all animal suffering by forcing animal abuse companies out of business." The ALF also states that any vegans or vegetarians who carry out actions according to ALF guidelines can regard themselves as part of the ALF. These actions include liberating animals from "places of abuse" and inflicting "economic damage" on the people involved. ALF followers are urged to take precautions to prevent harming humans and animals. The ALF receives funding from the ALF Supporters Group, which consists of people who believe in the ALF guidelines but do not want to be involved in criminal activities.

FIGURE 2.1

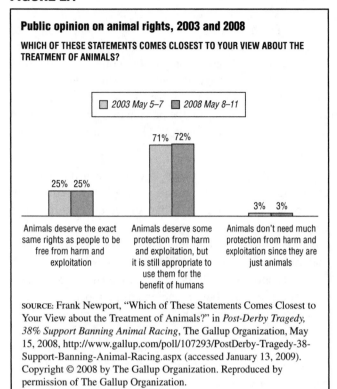

Public opinion on animal rights, 2003 and 2008

WHICH OF THESE STATEMENTS COMES CLOSEST TO YOUR VIEW ABOUT THE TREATMENT OF ANIMALS?

SOURCE: Frank Newport, "Which of These Statements Comes Closest to Your View about the Treatment of Animals?" in *Post-Derby Tragedy, 38% Support Banning Animal Racing*, The Gallup Organization, May 15, 2008, http://www.gallup.com/poll/107293/PostDerby-Tragedy-38-Support-Banning-Animal-Racing.aspx (accessed January 13, 2009). Copyright © 2008 by The Gallup Organization. Reproduced by permission of The Gallup Organization.

FIGURE 2.2

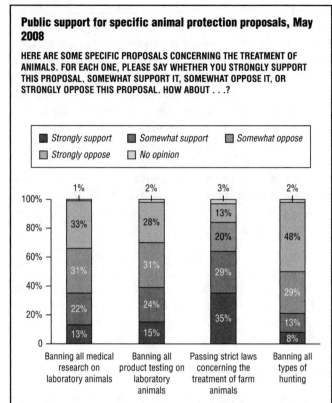

Public support for specific animal protection proposals, May 2008

HERE ARE SOME SPECIFIC PROPOSALS CONCERNING THE TREATMENT OF ANIMALS. FOR EACH ONE, PLEASE SAY WHETHER YOU STRONGLY SUPPORT THIS PROPOSAL, SOMEWHAT SUPPORT IT, SOMEWHAT OPPOSE IT, OR STRONGLY OPPOSE THIS PROPOSAL. HOW ABOUT . . .?

SOURCE: Frank Newport, "Here Are Some Specific Proposals Concerning the Treatment of Animals. For Each One, Please Say Whether You Strongly Support This Proposal, Somewhat Support It, Somewhat Oppose It, or Strongly Oppose This Proposal. How about...?" in *Post-Derby Tragedy, 38% Support Banning Animal Racing*, The Gallup Organization, May 15, 2008, http://www.gallup.com/poll/107293/PostDerby-Tragedy-38-Support-Banning-Animal-Racing.aspx (accessed January 13, 2009). Copyright © 2008 by The Gallup Organization. Reproduced by permission of The Gallup Organization.

PUBLIC OPINION

In May 2008 the Gallup Organization conducted a poll to determine Americans' opinions regarding animal rights issues. The results are based on telephone interviews with 1,017 adults aged 18 and older.

As shown in Figure 2.1, 25% of those asked believed animals deserve the same rights as people. A large majority (72%) said animals deserve some protection but can still be used to benefit people. Only a tiny percentage (3%) felt animals do not need much protection from harm and exploitation. These results are virtually identical to results obtained by Gallup in a May 2003 poll on the same subject.

The poll participants in 2008 were also asked whether they supported or opposed four specific proposals concerning the treatment of animals. (See Figure 2.2.) More than 60% favored passing strict laws regarding the treatment of farm animals. About 50% favored a ban on animal sports (such as dog racing and horse racing), and 40% supported a ban on all product testing performed on laboratory animals. Just over one-third favored a similar ban on medical research testing on animals. Support was far lower (20%) for a total ban on hunting.

Some of these same animal issues were addressed in another Gallup poll also conducted in May 2008. This poll dealt with questions of morality. Participants were asked to rate 16 specific issues or actions as generally "morally acceptable" or generally "morally wrong." Three of the moral issues/actions were animal related. (See Table 2.1.) Just over half (56%) of respondents rated medical testing on animals as morally acceptable. Slightly less (54%) said buying and wearing clothing made of animal fur was morally acceptable. Moral support for the cloning of animals was far lower. Only 33% of poll participants rated it as morally acceptable.

TABLE 2.1

Public opinion on the morality of various issues, May 2008

NEXT, I'M GOING TO READ YOU A LIST OF ISSUES. REGARDLESS OF WHETHER OR
NOT YOU THINK IT SHOULD BE LEGAL, FOR EACH ONE, PLEASE TELL ME WHETHER
YOU PERSONALLY BELIEVE THAT IN GENERAL IT IS MORALLY ACCEPTABLE OR
MORALLY WRONG.

	Morally acceptable	Morally wrong
	%	%
Divorce	70	22
Gambling	63	32
The death penalty	62	30
Medical research using stem cells obtained from human embryos	62	30
Sex between an unmarried man and woman	61	36
Medical testing on animals	56	38
Having a baby outside of marriage	55	41
Buying and wearing clothing made of animal fur	54	39
Doctor-assisted suicide	51	44
Homosexual relations	48	48
Abortion	40	48
Cloning animals	33	61
Suicide	15	78
Cloning humans	11	85
Polygamy, when one husband has more than one wife at the same time	8	90
Married men and women having an affair	7	91

SOURCE: Lydia Saad, "Next, I'm Going to Read You a List of Issues.
Regardless of Whether or Not You Think It Should Be Legal, for Each One,
Please Tell Me Whether You Personally Believe That in General It Is
Morally Acceptable or Morally Wrong," in *Cultural Tolerance for Divorce
Grows to 70%*, The Gallup Organization, May 19, 2008, http://www.gallup
.com/poll/107380/Cultural-Tolerance-Divorce-Grows-70.aspx (accessed
February 19, 2009). Copyright © 2008 by The Gallup Organization.
Reproduced by permission of The Gallup Organization.

CHAPTER 3
WILDLIFE

Wildlife are animals that have not been domesticated by humans. This does not mean that wild animals live without human interference. Humans control, manage, manipulate, use, and kill wildlife for various reasons. Humans tend to think of wild animals in terms of the threat they pose to people or the value they hold for them.

Some wildlife threaten human safety, health, property, and/or quality of life. This is true of large carnivores (such as lions, tigers, and alligators), poisonous snakes and spiders, disease-carrying animals (such as rats), and animals that endanger moving vehicles. In addition, there are carnivores (such as coyotes and bobcats) that prey on livestock and pets, herbivores that eat crops and lawns, beavers that dam up streams, and wild animals that invade or damage human spaces. Many rodents, skunks, rabbits, deer, and birds are considered nuisance animals.

However, many wild animals, even dangerous ones, have value to humans. This value might be economic, educational, or emotional in nature. Valuable wildlife fall into the following categories:

- Wild animals that produce products people want to eat, wear, or use. This category includes deer, buffalo, elk, wildfowl, fur-bearing creatures, many fish and marine mammals, and animals such as tigers and bears with bones and organs that are used in traditional medicines.

- Wild animals that humans kill for sport through hunting or fishing. In the United States people primarily hunt native game, such as deer, bears, rabbits, squirrels, and waterfowl. Exotic (foreign) animals are imported and killed at some hunting ranches. African lions, giraffes, antelopes, gazelles, Cape buffaloes, Corsican sheep, and Angora goats are some of the most popular. Sport fish include a variety of fresh- and saltwater species.

- Wild animals that can be manipulated to do labor or entertain people. For example, elephants are used as beasts of burden in many Asian countries. They also perform in circuses and shows, along with bears, primates, birds, lions, tigers, dolphins, seals, whales, and other trainable animals. Some wild animals even have military uses, particularly dolphins, whales, and sea lions.

- Wild animals that humans enjoy watching, hearing, feeding, or photographing. This category is very diverse and ranges from songbirds in the backyard to whales in the open sea. (See Figure 3.1.) It includes a variety of animals that humans can encounter in the wild and at refuges, sanctuaries, zoos, parks, and entertainment venues.

- Wild animals that are useful in scientific and medical research. These include primates and some strains of rats, mice, and rabbits.

- Wild animals kept as pets. This includes a wide variety of species, some of which are dangerous to humans. Keeping wild animals as pets is highly controversial and, in many states, illegal.

Animal rights advocates believe wild animals should not be used at all—not for food, clothing, entertainment, companionship, or any other purpose. They consider wild animals not as commodities but as free beings with the right to live undisturbed in their natural habitat. Animal welfarists are concerned that wild animals are exploited and mistreated because of human greed and ignorance. They work to publicize the fate of animals in captivity and to save them from mistreatment.

Most people consider wildlife a valuable natural resource, such as water or coal. They may disagree about how wild animals should be used, but they generally agree that humans have the right to use them, especially if the supply is plentiful. Wild species threatened by extinction are a different matter, however, as many people rally to conserve them. Successful conservation ensures that the species will continue to thrive in the future.

FIGURE 3.1

A humpback whale. *Image copyright Richard Fitzer, 2009. Used under license from Shutterstock.com.*

Every aspect of wildlife-human interaction raises questions in the animal rights debate. For example:

• The American bison was nearly extinct in the nineteenth century. Thanks to conservationists, the species was saved and is even thriving. By 2000 bison burgers were being sold at trendy restaurants. Is it acceptable to save an endangered species and then eat it?

• The government allows people to kill deer to keep the population under control. Otherwise, a lack of food could lead to starvation among the deer population. Is hunting deer more humane than letting them starve?

• Many people enjoy experiencing wildlife up close for its entertainment and educational value. Should wild animals be kept in captivity to satisfy this desire?

These are just some of the major questions in the animal rights debate.

HISTORY

Problems with wildlife management plagued the first European colonists in North America. Historical records show that the colonists fought off animal predators, includ-

ing wolves, coyotes, cougars, bears, and mountain lions. They also lost domesticated animals to wild predators. Livestock, particularly hogs, sometimes wandered away and lived in the wild. Their offspring were feral animals (animals born and living in the wild that are descendants of domesticated animals). The colonists killed wild and feral animals whenever they could because they were a threat to livestock and crops. The colonists found wolves to be particularly bothersome. Early governing bodies established wolf bounty acts that paid people for killing wolves.

By the early 1700s official hunting seasons for certain species were established in some colonies. Over the next century state governments set up fish and game departments and enacted hunting restrictions, requiring licenses and setting limits on the number of some species that could be killed during each hunting season.

Colonization severely depleted the ranks of some native wild species through a combination of overhunting and disease. The introduction of livestock brought new animal diseases that were devastating to some native species. Passenger pigeons and heath hens died out altogether. Bison, elk, and beaver stocks were severely diminished, though they did not become extinct.

Development of the Conservation Movement

Late in the nineteenth century people began to become aware of the value of natural resources, such as land, water, and wildlife, and worked to conserve wilderness spaces and protect them from development. Early conservationists initiated programs that helped wild animals by preserving natural habitats, but they were not always motivated by the same concerns that drove people involved in the animal welfare movement. Many prominent conservationists were avid hunters. Many welfarists were (and are) opposed to hunting for sport. The ethical battle over hunting that began between conservationists and welfarists in the nineteenth century continues into the twenty-first century.

GOVERNMENT ENACTS REGULATION LAWS. In the twentieth century dozens of federal laws were enacted that regulated wildlife. Table 3.1 lists the most notable ones. The first federal wildlife law was the Lacey Act of 1900, which banned the transportation of illegally taken wildlife across state lines. It also established regulations regarding the importation of wildlife into the country. Many laws were designed to fund conservation efforts through hunting fees. For example, the Migratory Bird Hunting and Conservation Stamp Act of 1934 required people to purchase a stamp before they could hunt waterfowl. The Federal Aid in Wildlife Restoration Act of 1937 added a special tax on guns and ammunition.

By the early twenty-first century wildlife in the United States was extensively regulated. In "Digest of Federal Resource Laws" (January 14, 2009, http://www.fws.gov/laws/lawsdigest/Resourcelaws.html), the U.S. Fish and Wildlife Service (USFWS) lists more than 160 federal laws that have been passed dealing with the control, preservation, eradication, and management of wildlife. Some laws pertain directly to particular species, whereas others address the preservation of habitat and the use of federal lands.

GOVERNMENT AGENCIES THAT CONTROL WILDLIFE

Wildlife issues in the United States are overseen by various federal and state agencies. At the federal level, the USFWS is the primary agency. Originally called the U.S. Commission on Fish and Fisheries, the USFWS was formed in 1871 to examine problems with declining food-fish stocks and recommend remedies. In 1903 the agency was given oversight of the first national wildlife refuge, Pelican Island, a 3-acre (1.2-ha) bird sanctuary in Sebastian, Florida.

The USFWS (April 9, 2009, http://www.fws.gov/refuges/) states that in 2009 it managed over 150 million acres (60.7 million ha) in more than 550 refuges in the National Wildlife Refuge System. It also manages migratory bird conservation, oversees thousands of wetlands and other management areas, and operates dozens of national fish hatcheries, fishery resources offices, and ecological services field stations. The USFWS administers and enforces

TABLE 3.1

Major federal laws impacting wildlife, 1900–97

Major federal laws impacting wildlife	Year enacted
Lacey Act	1900
Game and Bird Preserves Act	1905
Weeks-McLean Act	1912
National Park Service Act	1916
Migratory Bird Treaty Act	1918
Migratory Bird Conservation Act	1920s
Tariff Act (Enhanced Lacey Act)	1930
Animal Damage Control Act	1931
Fish and Wildlife Coordination Act	1934
Migratory Bird Hunting and Conservation Stamp Act (Duck Stamp Act)	1934
Taylor Grazing Act	1934
Federal Aid in Wildlife Restoration Act (Pittman-Robertson Act)	1937
Bald Eagle Protection Act	1940
Federal Aid in Sport Fish Restoration Act (Dingell-Johnson Act)	1950
Whaling Convention Act	1950
Tuna Conventions Act	1950
Fisherman's Protective Act	1954
Fish and Wildlife Act	1956
Great Lakes Fishery Act	1956
Multiple Use Act	1960
Surplus Grain for Wildlife Act	1961
Refuge Recreation Act	1962
Wilderness Act	1964
Refuge Revenue Sharing Act	1964
Land and Water Conservation Fund Act	1965
Anadromous Fish Conservation Act	1965
National Wildlife Refuge System Administration Act	1966
Endangered Species Preservation Act	1966
Fur Seal Act	1966
National Environmental Policy Act	1969
Endangered Species Conservation Act	1969
Federal Wild and Free Roaming Horses and Burros Act	1971
Marine Mammal Protection Act	1972
Endangered Species Act	1973
Alaska National Interest Lands Conservation Act	1980
Fish and Wildlife Conservation Act	1980
National Aquaculture Act	1980
Salmon and Steelhead Conservation and Enhancement Act	1980
Atlantic Salmon Convention Act	1982
Northern Pacific Halibut Act	1982
Atlantic Striped Bass Conservation Act	1984
Pacific Salmon Treaty Act	1985
The North American Wetlands Conservation Act	1986
South Pacific Tuna Act	1988
The African Elephant Conservation Act	1988
Dolphin Protection Consumer Information Act	1990
Non-Indigenous Aquatic Nuisance Prevention and Control Act	1990
Wild Bird Conservation Act	1992
Alien Species Prevention and Enforcement Act	1992
Rhinoceros and Tiger Conservation Act	1994
National Wildlife Refuge System Improvement Act	1997

SOURCE: Created by Kim Masters Evans for Gale, 2009

many federal wildlife laws and issues import and export permits under those laws.

The USFWS works with the U.S. Customs and Border Protection and the U.S. Department of Agriculture (USDA) to monitor wildlife trade and stop illegal shipments of protected plants and animals. The USFWS also enforces the country's participation in the Convention on International Trade in Endangered Species of Wild Fauna and Flora (CITES). This international agreement regulates the importing and exporting of thousands of species. Other federal agencies involved in controlling wild populations include the Wildlife Services (WS) of the USDA, the Bureau of Reclamation, and the National Park Service.

FIGURE 3.2

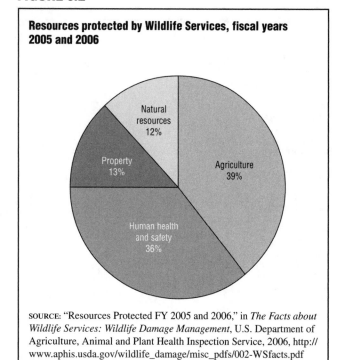

Resources protected by Wildlife Services, fiscal years 2005 and 2006

SOURCE: "Resources Protected FY 2005 and 2006," in *The Facts about Wildlife Services: Wildlife Damage Management*, U.S. Department of Agriculture, Animal and Plant Health Inspection Service, 2006, http://www.aphis.usda.gov/wildlife_damage/misc_pdfs/002-WSfacts.pdf (accessed January 15, 2009)

The WS is the primary federal agency in charge of controlling wildlife that can damage agriculture, property, and natural resources or threaten public health and safety. It operates the National Wildlife Research Center in Fort Collins, Colorado.

GOALS OF GOVERNMENT WILDLIFE REGULATION

Historically, wildlife control efforts in the United States have focused on protecting human interests and preserving endangered species. Human interests include health, safety, property, and resources (e.g., livestock, crops, trees, lawns, structures, water, food supplies, vehicles, and pets). Figure 3.2 shows the breakdown of the resources protected by the WS in fiscal years (FYs) 2005 and 2006. Protection of agricultural resources received the most funding (39%), followed by human health and safety (36%), property (13%), and natural resources (12%). Wild animals that threaten human interests are subject to removal or elimination.

Protecting Health and Safety

Violent confrontations between wild animals and people are relatively rare in contemporary times. Of greater concern is the danger from zoonotic diseases (diseases that can be passed from animals to people). Zoonotic diseases associated with wild animals include rabies, West Nile virus, Lyme disease, bovine tuberculosis (a respiratory disease associated with buffalo, bison, and deer), chlamydiosis (a respiratory disease most commonly found in tropical birds, such as parrots), histoplasmosis (a lung disease transmitted through bird and bat droppings), salmonellosis (an intestinal illness transmitted through contaminated feces, particularly from infected reptiles), and granulocytic ehrlichiosis (a tickborne disease similar to Lyme disease).

One of the most feared zoonotic diseases is rabies. In the early twentieth century rabies killed an average of a hundred people annually, but a combination of control methods greatly reduced its threat. By the end of the century only one or two people died each year from the disease. The Centers for Disease Control and Prevention (CDC) conducts rabies epidemiology (the study of the distribution and causes of disease in populations). In *Rabies Surveillance in the United States during 2007* (September 15, 2008, http://www.cdc.gov/rabies/docs/rabies_surveillance_us_2007.pdf), Jesse D. Blanton et al. of the CDC report that there were 7,258 reported cases of animal rabies in the United States in 2007. Wild animals, primarily raccoons, bats, and skunks, accounted for 93% of those cases.

Blanton et al. note that vaccination campaigns for domestic animals (e.g., dogs and cats) have been waged since the 1940s in an effort to stem the transmission of rabies to humans. In the 1990s state and federal wildlife officials began distributing baits laden with oral rabies vaccine to some at-risk populations of wild animals, such as raccoons, foxes, and coyotes.

Besides diseases, humans face dangers posed by collisions between moving vehicles and wild animals and birds. According to the USDA's Animal and Plant Health Inspection Service (APHIS), in *Protecting People from Predators, Wildlife Conflict and Collisions, and Wildlife-Borne Disease* (2007, http://www.aphis.usda.gov/wildlife_damage/misc_pdfs/Fy%202007%20Notebook%20Sections/Protecting%20People/Protecting%20People.pdf), between 1 million and 1.5 million collisions between deer and automobiles occur each year, costing $1.1 billion in repairs to vehicles. The Insurance Institute for Highway Safety notes in "Fatal Crashes with Deer Jump in November" (*Status Report*, vol. 43, no. 10, November 25, 2008) that between 2000 and 2007, 1,538 people had been killed in these collisions, with 233 in 2007 alone. The USDA and the Federal Aviation Administration (FAA) state in the joint report *Wildlife Strikes to Civil Aircraft in the United States 1990–2007* (June 2008, http://wildlife.pr.erau.edu/BASH90-07.pdf) that 82,057 animal strikes by civilian aircraft were reported to the FAA between 1990 and 2007. Birds were responsible for 97.5% of the strikes, followed by terrestrial mammals (2.1%), bats (0.3%), and reptiles (0.1%). In January 2009 an airliner leaving New York City's LaGuardia Airport was forced to land in the Hudson River after losing power in both engines due to a reported bird strike. All 155 passengers and crew survived.

Protecting Property and Pleasure

APHIS states in *Wildlife Damage Management* (2007, http://www.aphis.usda.gov/wildlife_damage/misc_pdfs/002-

WSfacts.pdf) that wildlife causes an estimated $944 million worth of damage annually to agriculture. Another $71 million in livestock is lost to wild predators. The U.S. General Accounting Office (GAO; now the U.S. Government Accountability Office) estimates in *Wildlife Services Program: Information on Activities to Manage Wildlife Damage* (November 2001, http://www.gao.gov/new.items/d02138 .pdf) that 273,000 sheep and lambs, 147,000 cattle and calves, and 61,000 goats and kids were lost to wild predators in 1999. Coyotes are blamed for most of the losses. Wild predators are primarily a problem in western states, where ranchers graze their livestock on open rangelands.

The GAO report involved an extensive investigation into wildlife damage across the country and was the most recent comprehensive study available as of mid-2009. Table 3.2 lists wildlife problems reported by each state in 2001. Birds, especially Canada geese, are a problem in 39 states. Coyotes are mentioned as an issue in 20 states. Beavers are considered a problem in 18 states. Figure 3.3 shows the occurrence of damage and threat to resources by wildlife reported by the WS in FY 2007. The greatest damage and threat was to agriculture (44%), followed by property (43%), health and safety (11%), and natural resources (2%).

Federal and state wildlife agencies use a variety of direct control methods to deal with so-called nuisance wildlife, including relocation, poisons, sharpshooters, contraceptives, and repellents. The WS issues an annual report on its wildlife dispersal and control methods. As of April 2009, the most recent report available was for FY 2007. The WS (http://www.aphis.usda.gov/wildlife_damage/annual% 20tables/2007%20PDRs/FY%202007%20Individual%20 PDRs/National%20Tables/PDR_G_FY2007_National.pdf) dispersed 15.3 million animals during FY 2007, killed or euthanized approximately 2.4 million, and freed 36,823 animals. As shown in Figure 3.4, dispersal accounted for 86.2% of the total, followed by killing (13.6%), and freeing of animals (0.2%). Table 3.3 lists the 20 most-killed species in FY 2007. European starlings were, by far, the most-killed species. Nearly 1.2 million of these birds were killed. European starlings are not native to the United States. According to the USDA, the birds were first brought to this country in 1890 as part of a scheme to introduce all the bird species mentioned in the writings of William Shakespeare (1564–1616). European starlings have thrived in the United States. They are considered a problem because they compete with native bird species and destroy agricultural crops. Overall, birds make up 13 of the 20 species most killed by the WS in 2007. Nonbird species on the list include coyotes, northern pikeminnows, beavers, feral hogs, brown tree snakes, raccoons, and striped skunks.

PROBLEM HORSES. Wild horse and burro populations on public lands are managed by the Bureau of Land Management (BLM). The GAO assesses the BLM's wild horse program in *Bureau of Land Management: Effective Long-*

Term Options Needed to Manage Unadoptable Wild Horses (October 2008, http://www.gao.gov/new.items/d0977.pdf). According to Table 3.4, as of February 2008 there were 33,105 of these animals scattered across the western states. The table also provides information on designated Herd Management Areas and the appropriate management level (AML) per state. AMLs have been established by the federal government as the maximum number of wild horses or burros appropriate for a particular area. As of February 2008, populations in all but Wyoming and Oregon exceeded their AMLs.

The BLM states in "Factsheet on Challenges Facing the BLM in its Management of Wild Horses and Burros" (April 14, 2009, http://www.blm.gov/wo/st/en/prog/wild _horse_and_burro/new_factsheet.html) that its policy "is to manage healthy herds of wild horses and burros on healthy Western rangelands." The animals are gathered and held in holding pens. Some are adopted out to private citizens or organizations.

In December 2004 Congress passed the FY 2005 Omnibus Appropriations Bill, which included an amendment allowing some "excess" wild horses and burros to be sold at auction "without limitation." The bill applied to animals greater than 10 years old and those that have unsuccessfully been offered for adoption at least three times. The amendment was added by Senator Conrad Burns (1935–; R-MT), who argued that the animals damage valuable grazing land and that maintaining them in holding pens is too expensive for the federal government. Critics complained that the phrase "without limitation" means that the animals can be slaughtered for horse meat.

In May 2005 Maryann Mott reported in "Wild Horses Sold by U.S. Agency Sent to Slaughter" (*National Geographic*) that 41 wild horses sold by the BLM had been slaughtered for meat at a slaughterhouse in Illinois. According to Mott, a BLM spokesman stated the agency was "very upset" to learn the horses had been slaughtered. Animal groups were furious about the news. An additional 52 wild horses that had also been sold to the slaughterhouse were bought back by the Ford Motor Company. Ford (2009, http://www.ford.com/en/goodWorks/environment/nature AndWildlife/saveTheMustangs/default.htm) also established a Save the Mustangs fund to build public awareness and raise contributions to save wild horses. Ford reports that in 2009 about $215,000 had been raised for the fund. The money is used to find "good homes" for wild horses available for sale from the BLM.

According to the GAO, approximately 235,700 of the government's wild horses and burros were adopted between 1971 and 2007. Figure 3.5 shows the number of animals removed from the wild and adopted per year from 1989 to 2007. The GAO notes that 8,400 animals have become eligible for sale since the 2005 amendment, but

TABLE 3.2

Examples of and concerns connected with resources damaged by wildlife, by state and type of injurious wildlife, 2001

State	Injurious wildlife	Resource damaged (annual damage estimate, if available)	Emerging concerns
Alabama	Fish-eating birds (e.g., cormorants, pelicans, herons, egrets)	Catfish ($4 million)	Wildlife diseases pose greater threats to humans, livestock, and pets; populations of fish-eating birds continue to increase; and diminished sport trapping is adding to the increase in beaver populations.
	Beavers	Timber ($19 million), transportation infrastructure	
Alaska	Arctic foxes	Aleutian Canada goose (threatened), nesting seabirds	Increased air travel throughout the state, coupled with immense populations of migratory birds and other wildlife, has created an urgent need for state and federal management of wildlife threats. Also, farmers and ranchers need assistance with damage from birds and predators.
Arizona	Coyotes, black bears, mountain lions	Livestock	Increased human populations and increased recreational use of public lands emphasize the need to deal with risks of wildlife disease transmission.
	Blackbirds	Dairy cattle, feedlot cattle (disease risk from contaminated feed and water)	
Arkansas	Blackbirds	Rice crops ($3.5 million)	The growing rice and aqua cultures industries require additional protection from the increasing populations of fish-eating birds.
	Fish-eating birds	Catfish ($2.3 million)	
California	Coyotes, black bears, mountain lions	Livestock (nearly $2 million)	Increased airline traffic and population growth of many bird species has created a greater need for wildlife control at airports; the recent surge in the number of direct attacks on humans creates an increased need to protect humans from large predators such as coyotes, black bears, and mountain lions.
	Birds, rodents	Row crops, fruit and nut crops, vineyards	
	Feral cats, red foxes, raccoons, coyotes, striped skunks, raptors	Threatened or endangered species (e.g., California red-legged frog, salt marsh harvest mouse, Sierra Nevada big horn sheep, Monterey Bay western snowy plover)	
Colorado	Coyotes	Sheep and lambs ($1.5 million), black-footed ferrets (endangered)	Human population growth, especially in rural and semi-rural areas, creates an increased potential for human-wildlife conflicts.
Connecticut	Starlings, blackbirds	Dairy cattle (salmonella risk from contaminated feed and water)	Preventing wildlife-borne diseases from affecting humans and livestock has become a growing concern with the recent out breaks of rabies, West Nile virus, salmonella, and E. coli; increased air travel and growing bird populations also call for increased wildlife control at airports.
	Canada geese, blackbirds, mute swans	Vegetable crops, cranberries	
	Birds, bats, squirrels, monk parakeets, ospreys	Buildings, landscaping, utilities	
Delaware	Snow geese	Coastal salt marsh habitat	West Nile virus is a major health concern. In fiscal year 2000, Delaware reported that four horses tested positive for the virus. Growth in air travel, coupled with growth in deer and bird populations, has created a greater need for wildlife control at airports.
	Canada geese	Grain crops, golf courses ($75,000)	
Florida	Raccoons, red foxes, coyotes, feral hogs, ghost crabs, armadillos	Threatened or endangered sea turtles (e.g., leatherback, hawksbill, loggerhead turtles)	Wildlife continue to threaten the safety of air travelers at many airports, but resource constraints have prevented Wildlife Services from resolving the hazards; livestock producers suffer losses from coyote and vulture predation, and direct assistance from Wildlife Services, rather than advice, would help reduce these losses.
	Foxes, coyotes, black rats, skunks, raccoons, snakes, armadillos, dogs	Endangered beach mice (e.g., Perdido Key, Anastasia Island, Choctawhatchee beach mice)	
	Red foxes, rats, coyotes, raccoons, feral cats	Threatened or endangered birds (e.g., roseate tern, least tern, Puerto Rican parrot)	
	Beavers	Flooded timber lands, croplands, roadways ($620,000)	
Georgia	Armadillos, raccoons, coyotes	Ground-nesting birds (e.g., bobwhite quail)	Increased habitat loss, human population growth, and the adaptability of many wildlife species to human environments increase the need for professional resolution of wildlife problems. Of concern are deer, geese, beavers, vultures, cormorants, pigeons, feral hogs, and raccoons.
	Beavers	Landscapes, pastures, timber, sanitation lines, culverts, highways, wells ($152,000)	
	Resident Canada geese, while-tailed deer	Crops, property, neighborhood landscapes and gardens	
Hawaii	Feral goats, sheep, pigs, deer	Endangered waterbirds, plants	The state is concerned about the time and expense involved in complying with the National Environmental Policy Act (conducting environmental analyses of Wildlife Services' actions performed for nonfederal cooperators), and the associated administrative requirements.
	Tree frogs	Horticulture, parrots, Axis deer	
	Rats	Agricultural products, native plants, seabirds, turtles	

TABLE 3.2

Examples of and concerns connected with resources damaged by wildlife, by state and type of injurious wildlife, 2001 [CONTINUED]

State	Injurious wildlife	Resource damaged (annual damage estimate, if available)	Emerging concerns
Idaho	Coyotes, black bears, mountain lions, wolves, red foxes	Sheep, lambs ($1.5 million)	Efforts to control crop damage by the sandhill crane have been limited by the lack of resources. Populations of ravens and red foxes have increased, to the detriment of the sage grouse.
	Ravens, coyotes, badgers, red foxes	Sage grouse, endangered northern Idaho ground squirrels	
Illinois	Canada geese, white-tailed deer	Private and municipal property	Bird predation at fish production facilities—an emerging agricultural industry in Illinois—is a concern, as is the transmission of wildlife-borne diseases such as West Nile virus.
	European starlings	Private and industrial property, risk of disease (histoplasmosis)	
Indiana	Canada geese	Private and industrial property ($169,000 in property damage reported in fiscal year 2000)	Over 12,000 people used Indiana's toll-free wildlife conflicts hotline during its first 2 years of service, preventing an estimated $100,000 in wildlife damage; now an additional person is needed to respond to calls.
	Starlings	Property damage (e.g., buildings and equipment), risk of disease (histoplasmosis)	
Iowa	Coyotes	Sheep, cattle, hogs ($20,000 in confirmed losses to coyotes)	Requests for assistance continue to increase, especially in regard to livestock predators (especially coyotes) and beavers.
	Beavers	Roads, crops, bridges	
Kansas	Blackbirds (grackles, starlings, cowbirds)	Livestock feed (more than $660,000 in damage at three feedlots during a recent winter)	Wildlife Services' success in addressing blackbird problems at feedlots has fueled demand for similar services statewide.
Kentucky	Starlings, Canada geese	Agriculture, residential and industrial property, aquaculture, golf courses, parks, utility structures	Increased urbanization and expansion into formerly rural areas, coupled with escalating wildlife populations, have led to a rise in wildlife-human conflicts.
Louisiana	Blackbirds, cowbirds, egrets, cormorants, white pelicans, herons	Sprouting rice ($5 million to $10 million a year in damage), strawberries, pecans, crawfish, catfish	Increased damage by birds is becoming more difficult to control, despite the more than $17 million spent annually by aquaculture facilities throughout the state. Beavers are another source of increasing wildlife damage in the state.
	Beavers	Threatened Louisiana pearlshell (a mussel), timber, roadways, bridges, public utilities. Nearly $5 million in beaver-caused losses was reported between 1998 and 2000.	
Maine	Birds, deer, moose, raccoons, skunks, black bears	Blueberries, strawberries, vegetable crops, beehives, campsites, summer homes, fences	Increasing predation from a rising cormorant population is harming the commercial, pen-raised Atlantic salmon industry and is thought to be the primary cause of the dwindling wild Atlantic salmon population.
	Beavers	Commercial timberlands, municipal roads, highways	
Maryland	Canada geese, vultures	Crops, waterfront properties	The state has an increased need to protect humans, their pets, and livestock from wildlife-borne diseases. Rabies and West Nile virus are two major health concerns on the East Coast.
Massachusetts	Canada geese, blackbirds	Cranberries, vegetables, dairy feed	Preventing the spread of wildlife-borne diseases to humans and livestock is a growing concern, given the recent outbreaks of rabies, West Nile virus, salmonella, giardia, and E. coli.
	Eider ducks, swans, cormorants, gulls	Trout hatcheries, shellfish	
Michigan	Starlings	Dairies, feedlots	Wolf populations will likely increase and expand from the Upper to the Lower Peninsula, causing increased demand for prompt and professional response in wolf management services. Also, demand for help in reducing damage by congregating starlings has grown significantly.
	Gray wolves (endangered)	Livestock	
	Deer	Bovine tuberculosis in cattle (projected impact to the state's producers is $121 million over 10 years)	
Minnesota	Gray wolves	Cattle, horses, sheep, poultry, dogs	As the wolf population continues to expand, the need for Wildlife Services' professional assistance is expected to increase. Nuisance bear complaints are also increasing.
	Beavers	Private property, roads, timber, fish habitat	
Mississippi	Double-crested cormorants, American white pelicans	Aquaculture (about $5 million)	Feral hogs are causing more crop damage and posing a disease threat (pseudorabies) for the domestic hog industry. Canada geese and black bears are becoming a growing concern for property owners.
	Beavers	Roads, bridges, drainage structures, agricultural fields, private property, timber (several million dollars a year in damage)	
	Black bears	Beehives, crops, private property	
Missouri	Beavers, muskrats	Crops, roads, levees	The state's resident Canada goose population has quadrupled since 1993, causing increased damage; the feral hog population is also increasing, and the state needs Wildlife Services' help with this problem.
	Blackbirds, herons	Rice crops, aquaculture	
	Canada geese	Crops, lawns, golf courses (more than $122,000 in turf and crop damage in fiscal year 2000)	
Montana	Grizzly bears, Rocky Mountain gray wolves (threatened or endangered)	Livestock (predators caused a $1.1 million loss to state's sheep industry in 2000)	With the successful reintroduction and recovery of Rocky Mountain gray wolves in nearby states, Montana Wildlife Services expects a growing demand for its expertise in handling wolf-related livestock predation issues.

TABLE 3.2

Examples of and concerns connected with resources damaged by wildlife, by state and type of injurious wildlife, 2001 [CONTINUED]

State	Injurious wildlife	Resource damaged (annual damage estimate, if available)	Emerging concerns
Nebraska	Coyotes, foxes, mountain lions, bobcats	Livestock	Areas requiring increased attention include wildlife management at airports, livestock predation, and public protection from wildlife-borne diseases. Increased public awareness of Wildlife Services' professional role in these issues has increased the demand for its services.
	Prairie dogs	Rangeland	
	Blackbirds	Feedlots	
Nevada	Rodents	Public health risk of sylvatic plague (wild form of bubonic plague)	Aviation safety is a growing concern. Population growth and city development around Nevada's major airports has created an ideal habitat for migratory birds such as Canada geese, mallard ducks, and American coots.
	Coyotes, mountain lions	Livestock; humans and pets in urban areas	
New Hampshire	Black bears	Apiaries, row crops, livestock	Controlling the spread of West Nile virus is an emerging concern, along with rabies, Lyme disease, salmonella, and chronic wasting disease. Also, the 10-year trend of increasing conflicts associated with bears and bird feeding activities needs to be addressed.
	Deer	Apples, fruit crops, ornamental shrubbery	
	Woodchucks	Earthen dams and levees, wild lupine (essential to the endangered Karner blue butterfly)	
	Gulls	Roseate and common tern recolonization efforts	
New Jersey	Canada geese	Human health effects of goose feces, human safety threats from aggressive geese, crops, turf	The state's large population of resident Canada geese will pose increasing challenges for the protection of human health and safety, as well as property, at schools, hospitals, airports, and urban and suburban areas. The spread of West Nile virus is another concern.
	Deer, blackbirds	Crops, fruit trees, vegetables	
	Red foxes, raccoons, opossums	Threatened and endangered shorebirds (e.g., piping plovers, least terns, black skimmers)	
New Mexico	Coyotes, cougars, bobcats, black bears	Livestock (losses in excess of $1.6 million in 1999)	Coyotes are becoming an increasing problem in urban and suburban areas, killing pets and other domestic animals and posing safety risks to humans. Wildlife Services' assistance will be needed to resolve conflicts between humans and the black-tailed prairie dog, a candidate threatened species.
	Prairie dogs, pocket gophers, ground squirrels	Agricultural crops, pasture land, turf, human health and safety (nearly $500,000 in rodent damage in fiscal year 2000)	
	Sandhill cranes, snow geese	Crops (e.g., alfalfa, chile, wheat)	
New York	Cormorants, gulls	Catfish, bait fish, crawfish, sport fish	Bat and raccoon rabies remain a health concern, and urban winter crow roosts are emerging as a unique problem to city residents, resulting in conflicts over droppings, noise, odor, and fear associated with zoonotic disease.
	Canada geese	Property, crops	
North Carolina	Beavers	Timber, crops, roads, drainage systems, landscapes. In fiscal year 2000, Wildlife Services prevented about $8.5 million in damage to such resources: nearly $9 saved for every $1 spent.	Threats to public safety, not only by wildlife at airports, but also by the rapidly growing beaver population, must be addressed. A rabid beaver's recent attack on a human has increased public awareness of this issue.
North Dakota/ South Dakota	Coyotes, foxes	Cattle, sheep, poultry	More work at airports is needed, and the threat of rabies transferring from skunks to humans or domestic animals continues to be a concern.
	Blackbirds	Sunflowers and other grain crops (over $5 million in losses annually in the upper Great Plains), feedlots	
	Canada geese and other waterfowl	Grain crops (damage increased by 80 percent in 2000, resulting in $162,000 in losses)	
Ohio	Coyotes, vultures	Cattle, sheep, poultry	Increasing populations of gulls, vultures, and starlings are causing significant human health and safety issues and crop and property damage.
	Raccoons	Human health and safety	
	Rooftop nesting gulls	Property	
	Blackbirds, Canada geese	Crops, property	
Oklahoma	Beavers	Dams, timber, crops, roads, private property	Feral hogs cause many problems (livestock predation, crop destruction); Canada geese are growing in number and are damaging crops.
	Coyotes	Cattle, sheep, goats, poultry	
	Canada geese	Crops (especially winter wheat)	
Oregon	Canada geese	Turf grass seed, other crops	Successful wolf reintroduction in Idaho means future wolf coflicts with livestock in Oregon. Wolves will hamper present predator control efforts because control tools and methods will be restricted around wolves.
	Cougars	Human safety (Wildlife Services addressed 386 cougar complaints in 2000; 118 involved threats to humans)	
	Black bears, beavers	Timber	

TABLE 3.2

Examples of and concerns connected with resources damaged by wildlife, by state and type of injurious wildlife, 2001 [CONTINUED]

State	Injurious wildlife	Resource damaged (annual damage estimate, if available)	Emerging concerns
Pennsylvania	Deer	Human safety (automobile collisions)	The state's large population of resident Canada geese will pose increasing challenges over time, as will increasing populations of deer, vultures, and gulls. Emerging public health issues (e.g., West Nile virus) will also be a challenge.
	Canada geese	Landscape, crops (program annually assists over 300 residents with goose-related problems)	
	Starlings	Livestock facilities	
Rhode Island	Canada geese, gulls, crows, turkey vultures	Property, turf, vegetable crops	The needs of some citizens are currently unmet. Increasingly, the program is able to respond to requests for assistance only from entities that can fully fund it. Preventing wildlife-borne diseases is a growing concern.
	Mute swans	Pond water quality	
	Monk parakeets, ospreys	Landscaping, utilities	
South Carolina	Beavers	Timber, crops, roads, levees, dams	The demand for beaver management has overwhelmed the program, yet some counties cannot afford to share the costs. At the same time, the vulture population and related complaints have increased.
	White-tailed deer	Landscaping, human safety (automobile collisions), human health (tick-borne diseases)	
Tennessee	Canada geese	Turf (at golf courses, parks, etc.)	The growing number and variety of wildlife-human conflicts pose a challenge to the program, especially in terms of wildlife control at airports and urban damage by large birds.
	Beavers	Roads, bridges, timber, wildlife management areas	
	Vultures	Municipal utility structures, residential property	
Texas	Coyotes, foxes	Human health (rabies)	The feral hog population in the state exceeds 1 million. Hogs damage many crops (e.g., corn, rice, peanuts, hay), and they prey on lambs, kids, fawns, and ground nesting birds. Also, damage by migratory birds (e.g., cattle egrets, vultures, cormorants) has increased, taxing the program's response abilities.
	Coyotes	Sheep and goats	
	Beavers	Dams, dikes, railroad track beds, timber, roads, pastures, crops	
	Blackbirds	Citrus crops, rice, feedlot operations	
	Feral hogs	Agricultural crops, livestock	
Utah	Coyotes, mountain lions, black bears	Sheep and lambs (nearly $2 million in losses in 1999, even with controls in place), endangered black-footed ferrets, sage grouse, mule deer fawns	Demands for wildlife damage management are increasing, yet the program already has more requests than it can address. Protection of native wildlife continues to be of importance.
	Skunks, raccoons, feral and urban waterfowl, pigeons	Human health and safety (threat of rabies, raccoon roundworm, salmonella, plague)	
Vermont	Raccoons	Human health (rabies), threatened Eastern spiney softshell turtle	Wildlife diseases like West Nile virus, Lyme disease, salmonella, and chronic wasting syndrome continue to emerge and need to be addressed.
	Starlings	Cattle feed at dairies	
Virginia	Coyotes, black vultures	Livestock	Challenges include finding a way to provide damage management services to low- and middle-income people and protecting Virginia's rare natural resources (e.g., the threatened piping plover and Wilson's plover).
	Beavers	Roads, railroads	
	Canada geese, crows, vultures, starlings, muskrats	Urban and suburban property, water quality, human health and safety. (Canada geese are involved in 26 percent of all requests for program assistance in Virginia.)	
Washington	Northern pikeminnows, gulls	Threatened and endangered salmon and steelhead	Increasing problems are caused by urban Canada geese and by predators (damage to livestock, agriculture, and forestry resources), but program resources are already strained.
	Starlings, feral pigeons, Canada geese, gulls	Bridges, buildings (bird feces are corrosive to paint and metal), fruit crops, public and private property, human health (over $6 million a year in damage to the fruit industry)	
	Coyotes	Livestock, endangered Columbian white-tailed deer, pygmy rabbits	
West Virginia	Coyotes, vultures	Sheep, cattle, goats	With its limited resources, the program concentrates on the highest priorities (human health and safety). As a result, though, program staff cannot make much-needed on-site evaluations of wildlife damage to property; rather, they make recommendations based on telephone interviews. Also, problems caused by starlings and roosting birds need attention.
	Raccoons	Human health (rabies)	
	Muskrats, beavers	Levees and dams	

only about 2,700 of them had been sold as of October 2008. Regardless, the BLM has managed to reduce the estimated population of the animals in the wild to just above the AML. (See Figure 3.6.) According to the GAO, BLM spending for off-the-range holding of wild horses and burros was approximately $21 million in 2007.

TABLE 3.2

Examples of and concerns connected with resources damaged by wildlife, by state and type of injurious wildlife, 2001 [CONTINUED]

State	Injurious wildlife	Resource damaged (annual damage estimate, if available)	Emerging concerns
Wisconsin	Deer	Crops (over $1 million a year in damage)	The endangered gray wolf population has grown from 34 wolves in 1990 to about 250 in 2000, and the wolf's recovery is considered a success. But problems, such as depredation on livestock and pets, have come with the wolf's recovery. Also problematic is the damage done by the burgeoning population of resident Canada geese, which now numbers over 70,000.
	Black bears	Crops, property, human safety	
	Beavers	Trout streams	
	Gray wolves	Livestock, pets	
	Canada geese	Municipal and private property	
Wyoming	Coyotes, black bears, red foxes, mountain lions, grizzly bears, wolves	Livestock (losses of over $5.6 million to predators in 2000)	As wolf and grizzly bear populations expand, new or different control methods will be needed to prevent unnecessary conflicts with them. Also, skunk rabies seems to be spreading westward across the state, and a program is needed to contain it.
	Skunks	Human health (rabies risk)	
	Coyotes	Black-footed ferrets	
Guam	Brown tree snakes	Power transmission lines, poultry and small animals, endangered species (e.g., Vanikoro swiftlets, Mariana crows, Guam fruit bats, Guam rails, Micronesian kingfishers), human health and safety	The magnitude and complexity of the work to control the brown tree snake pose significant challenges, and the administrative burden is increasing.
U.S. Virgin Islands	Black rats	Endangered sea turtles, migratory birds, native vegetation	Invasive species' impacts on native plants and animals is a major and growing problem.
	Roosting birds	Human health concerns	

SOURCE: "Table 6. Examples of Resources Damaged by Injurious Wildlife, and Related Emerging Concerns, by State," in *Wildlife Services Program: Information on Activities to Manage Wildlife Damage*, U.S. General Accounting Office, November 2001, http://www.gao.gov/new.items/d02138.pdf (accessed April 28, 2009)

FIGURE 3.3

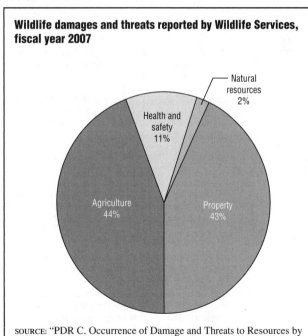

Wildlife damages and threats reported by Wildlife Services, fiscal year 2007

Natural resources 2%
Health and safety 11%
Agriculture 44%
Property 43%

SOURCE: "PDR C. Occurrence of Damage and Threats to Resources by Wildlife Reported by Wildlife Services—FY 2007," in *Program Data Reports: Wildlife Services' 2007 Annual Tables*, U.S. Department of Agriculture, Animal and Plant Health Inspection Service, August 4, 2008, http://www.aphis.usda.gov/wildlife_damage/annual%20tables/2007%20PDRs/Content/wp_c_ws_PDR_C_Piechart.shtml (accessed January 15, 2009)

FIGURE 3.4

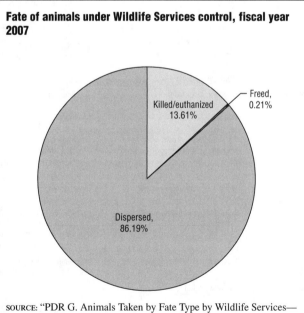

Fate of animals under Wildlife Services control, fiscal year 2007

Killed/euthanized 13.61%
Freed, 0.21%
Dispersed, 86.19%

SOURCE: "PDR G. Animals Taken by Fate Type by Wildlife Services—FY 2007," in *Program Data Reports: Wildlife Services' 2007 Annual Tables*, U.S. Department of Agriculture, Animal and Plant Health Inspection Service, August 19, 2008, http://www.aphis.usda.gov/wildlife_damage/annual%20tables/2007%20PDRs/Content/wp_c_ws_PDR_G_Piechart.shtml (accessed January 15, 2009)

Protecting Endangered and Threatened Species

The Endangered Species Act was passed in 1973. It built on protection measures first laid out in the 1966 Endangered Species Preservation Act. The purpose of the Endangered Species Act is to conserve the ecosystems on which endangered and threatened species depend and to conserve and recover listed species. An endangered species is in danger of extinction throughout all or a significant portion of its range. A threatened species is considered likely to become endangered in the future. Some species are listed as endangered in some areas of the country and only threatened in other areas.

According to the USFWS, in *Threatened and Endangered Species System* (http://ecos.fws.gov/tess_public/TESSBoxscore), as of January 19, 2009, there were 572 native species on the federal list of endangered and threatened animals—409 endangered species and 163 threatened species. (See Table 3.5.) Another 571 foreign animal species were listed as endangered or threatened. Animals are placed on the list based on their biological status and the threats to their existence. Some species are put on the list because they closely resemble endangered or threatened species.

The USFWS and the National Marine Fisheries Service (NMFS) share responsibility for administering the Endangered Species Act. They work in partnership with state agencies to enforce the act and develop and maintain conservation programs.

The Endangered Species Act prohibits any person from taking a listed species. Taking includes actions that "harass, harm, pursue, hunt, shoot, wound, kill, trap, capture, or collect" listed species or attempt to do so. Harm is defined as an action that kills or injures the animal and includes actions that significantly modify or degrade habitats or significantly impair essential behavior patterns such as breeding, feeding, and sheltering. These measures are designed to allow endangered and threatened species to repopulate. However, once a species does repopulate, it can be delisted (removed from the list of endangered species), and the taking prohibition no longer applies.

In addition, endangered species that pose a threat to humans and livestock can be killed under certain circumstances. In 1967 gray and red wolves were listed as endan-

TABLE 3.3

Top twenty animals killed by Wildlife Services, fiscal year 2007

Animal	Number killed	Type of animal
European starlings	1,176,647	Bird
Brown-headed cowbirds	335,289	Bird
Red-winged blackbirds	289,090	Bird
Coyotes	90,326	Terrestrial mammal
Feral (rock) pigeons	86,786	Bird
Northern pikeminnows	54,972	Fish
Chestnut mannikins	48,609	Bird
Beavers	25,039	Terrestrial mammal
Common grackles	24,843	Bird
Feral hogs	19,586	Terrestrial mammal
Double-crested cormorants	15,740	Bird
Canada geese	14,614	Bird
Blackbirds (mixed species)	13,835	Bird
Brown tree snakes	13,594	Reptile
Mourning doves	12,875	Bird
Raccoons	12,643	Terrestrial mammal
Zebra doves	12,439	Bird
Java sparrows	9,340	Bird
Striped skunks	7,782	Terrestrial mammal
Spotted doves	6,751	Bird

SOURCE: Adapted from "Table G. Animals Taken by Component/Method Type and Fate by the Wildlife Services Program—FY 2007," in *Program Data Reports: Wildlife Services' 2007 Annual Tables*, U.S. Department of Agriculture, Animal and Plant Health Inspection Service, August 19, 2008, http://www.aphis.usda.gov/wildlife_damage/annual%20tables/2007%20PDRs/FY%202007%20Individual%20PDRs/National%20Tables/PDR_G_FY2007_National%20by_Species_Alphabetically_All%20States.pdf (accessed January 16, 2009)

TABLE 3.4

Wild horse and burro program statistics, February 2008

State	Number of HMAs	Total AML*	Population estimate	HMA acreage BLM acreage	HMA acreage Other acreage	HMA acreage Total acreage
Nevada	102	13,098	16,143	15,772,485	1,695,925	17,468,410
Wyoming	16	3,725	3,439	3,638,330	1,137,121	4,775,451
Arizona	7	1,676	2,173	1,756,086	1,327,777	3,083,863
Oregon	18	2,715	2,473	2,703,409	259,726	2,963,135
Utah	21	2,151	3,096	2,379,850	362,817	2,742,667
California	22	2,237	3,878	1,946,590	471,855	2,418,445
Idaho	6	617	703	377,907	40,287	418,194
Colorado	4	812	933	366,098	38,656	404,754
Montana	1	105	170	28,282	8,865	37,147
New Mexico	2	83	97	24,505	4,107	28,612
Total	**199**	**27,219**	**33,105**	**28,993,542**	**5,347,136**	**34,340,678**

*This column represents the upper limit of AML according to BLM data.
Note: HMA = Herd Management Area, AML = Appropriate Management Level, BLM = Bureau of Land Management.

SOURCE: "Table 2. Summary Statistics on BLM's Wild Horse and Burro Program, by State, February 2008," in *Effective Long-Term Options Needed to Manage Unadoptable Wild Horses*, U.S. Government Accountability Office, October 2008, http://www.gao.gov/new.items/d0977.pdf (accessed January 14, 2009)

FIGURE 3.5

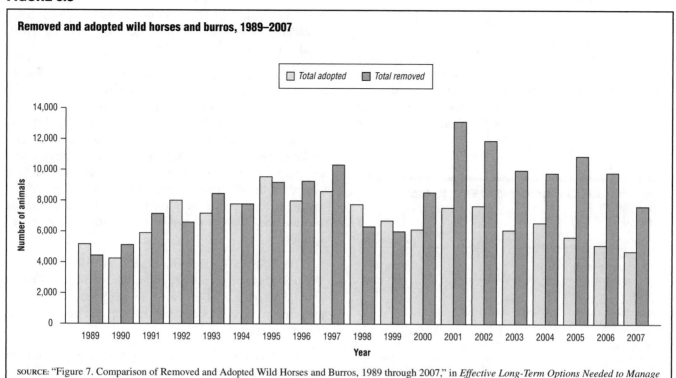

Removed and adopted wild horses and burros, 1989–2007

SOURCE: "Figure 7. Comparison of Removed and Adopted Wild Horses and Burros, 1989 through 2007," in *Effective Long-Term Options Needed to Manage Unadoptable Wild Horses*, U.S. Government Accountability Office, October 2008, http://www.gao.gov/new.items/d0977.pdf (accessed January 14, 2009)

FIGURE 3.6

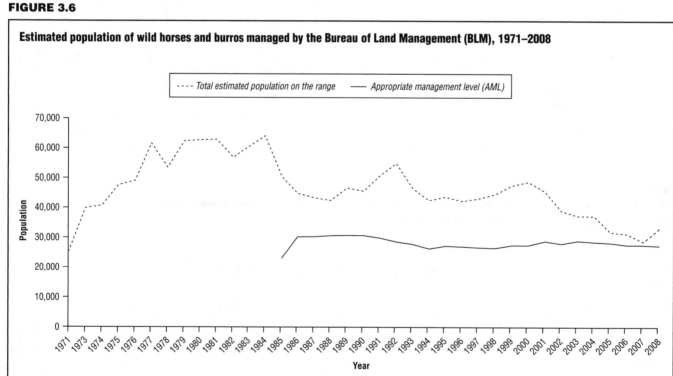

Estimated population of wild horses and burros managed by the Bureau of Land Management (BLM), 1971–2008

Note: All population levels are estimated based on aerial surveys that likely undercount the number of animals on the range. In 2000, BLM changed the time frame for its population counts from October 1 through September 30 of every year to March 1 through February 28 or 29 of every year. For AML levels prior to 1984, BLM was unable to provide estimated figures. For AML levels from 1984 through 1999, the figures are estimated and they do not necessarily reflect the upper limit of AML; from 2000 onward, the AML figures represent the upper limit of AML.

AML = Appropriate Management Level, BLM = Bureau of Land Management.

SOURCE: "Figure 5. Estimated Population of Wild Horses and Burros on the Range," in *Effective Long-Term Options Needed to Manage Unadoptable Wild Horses*, U.S. Government Accountability Office, October 2008, http://www.gao.gov/new.items/d0977.pdf (accessed January 14, 2009)

TABLE 3.5

List of U.S. endangered and threatened animal species as of January 19, 2009

Group	United States*		
	Endangered	Threatened	Total listings
Mammals	70	14	84
Corals	0	2	2
Reptiles	13	24	37
Amphibians	13	11	24
Fishes	74	65	139
Clams	62	8	70
Snails	24	11	35
Insects	47	10	57
Arachnids	12	0	12
Crustaceans	19	3	22
Birds	75	15	90
Animal totals	**409**	**163**	**572**

Note: 11 animal species are counted more than once in the above table, primarily because these animals have distinct population segments (each with its own individual listing status).
*United States listings include those populations in which the United States shares jurisdiction with another nation.

SOURCE: Adapted from "Summary of Listed Species Listed Populations and Recovery Plans as of Mon., 19 Jan 2009," in *Threatened and Endangered Species System*, U.S. Department of the Interior, U.S. Fish and Wildlife Service, January 19, 2009, http://ecos.fws.gov/tess_public/TESSBoxscore (accessed January 19, 2009)

FIGURE 3.7

A timber wolf. *Image copyright Geoffrey Kuchera, 2009. Used under license from Shutterstock.com.*

gered, because centuries of extermination had severely depleted their numbers. (See Figure 3.7.) In the 1990s the federal government began moving wolves from Canada and reintroducing them to certain areas of the western United States. This was highly controversial and drew strong condemnation from ranchers and other livestock owners. Some of the wolf populations were designated "nonessential experimental populations." This designation allowed government agencies and private citizens flexibility in controlling the wolves. For example, they could be killed, moved, or harassed to protect domestic livestock. By the twenty-first century wolf populations in some states had reached the government's recovery goals. However, attempts to delist these populations have been met with court challenges by some animal conservation groups. Before the species can be delisted, the USFWS requires that state and tribal governments have approved wolf management plans in place that will protect both the wolves and human interests.

INTERESTS OF HUMANS VERSUS THOSE OF ENDANGERED SPECIES. Protecting endangered and threatened species becomes extremely controversial when it threatens human economic interests. One example is the northern spotted owl. Its primary habitat is among old-growth trees (greater than 100 years old) in the coniferous forests of the Pacific Northwest, which were heavily logged in the 1960s. John Weier reports in "Spotting the Spotted Owl" (June 15, 1999, http://earthobservatory.nasa.gov/Study/SpottedOwls/) that in 1972 researchers at Oregon State University estimated that 85% to 90% of the owl's suitable habitat had already been eliminated. The researchers assessed the future harvest

plans of major logging companies and learned that most of the remaining old-growth trees in these forests were also to be cut down. The resulting publicity caused a major showdown between environmental conservation groups and the logging industry.

Environmental activists chained themselves to trees and damaged logging equipment to protest removal of the old-growth forests. Protest marches captured national headlines. There was tremendous political pressure to protect the owl's remaining habitat, particularly because approximately half of it was on federal lands. Since the mid-1980s the U.S. Forest Service (USFS) has tried to develop plans for managing federal forests in the Pacific Northwest that balance timber harvesting with habitat protection. Neither side has been happy with the proposals. The timber industry complains that protecting owls puts loggers out of work. Environmentalists believe all old-growth forests can be saved. In 1990 the USFWS added the northern spotted owl to the federal list of threatened species. The decision followed years of study and lawsuits filed by environmental groups and representatives of the timber industry.

The legal battles continued throughout the 1990s and into the first decade of the twenty-first century. In 1994 the administration of President Bill Clinton (1946–) formulated the Northwest Forest Plan in a futile attempt to satisfy both sides. The plan requires completion of biological surveys on dozens of plants and animals before logging is allowed on federal timberlands in the Northwest. It also includes other measures designed to protect owl habitat. Critics contend that this protection has caused people to lose jobs in the forest products industry.

In May 2008 the USFWS published *Final Recovery Plan for the Northern Spotted Owl (Strix Occidentalis Caurina)* (http://www.fws.gov/pacific/ecoservices/endangered/recovery/pdf/NSO%20Final%20Rec%20Plan%20051408.pdf). The plan includes data indicating that populations in a number of study areas have declined. (See Table 3.6.) Rates of fecundity (reproductive success) and survival have mostly declined or remained stable. The plan includes a complicated recovery strategy that sets aside designated areas of federal land as conservation areas for the owls. It was promptly challenged in court by a coalition of conservation groups who complained the plan provides less overall protection for owl habitat and opens up too much of the area for logging.

Similar conflicts between conservation and economic interests have raged in the United States over the protection of other animal species. These include the snail darter (a fish inhabiting the Tennessee River valley), Florida's gopher tortoises, jaguars in southern Arizona and New Mexico, and Coho salmon and sucker fish in Oregon's Klamath River basin.

TABLE 3.6

Spotted owl recovery plan study areas

Area	Fecundity	Survival	Population change
Wenatchee	Declining	Declining	Declining
Cle Elum	Declining	Declining?	Declining
Rainier	Stable	Declining	Declining
Olympic	Stable	Declining	Declining
Coast Ranges	Declining?	Stable	Declining
HJ Andrews	Stable?	Stable	Declining
Warm Springs	Stable	Stable	Declining
Tyee	Increasing	Stable	Stationary
Klamath	Stable	Stable	Stationary
S. Cascades	Declining	Stable	Stationary
NW California	Declining	Declining	Declining?
Hoopa	Increasing	Stable	Stationary
Simpson	Declining	Stable	Declining
Marin	Stable	Stable	NA

SOURCE: Adapted from "Table A1. Spotted Owl Demographic Study Areas," in *Final Recovery Plan for the Northern Spotted Owl (Strix Occidentalis Caurina)*, U.S. Fish and Wildlife Service, May 2008, http://www.fws.gov/pacific/ecoservices/endangered/recovery/pdf/NSO%20Final%20Rec%20Plan%20051408.pdf (accessed February 9, 2009)

INTERNATIONAL EFFORTS. On the international front, endangered wild animals are protected by CITES. Under the Endangered Species Act, the United States participates in CITES to prohibit trade in listed species.

CITES includes three lists:

- Appendix I—species for which no commercial trade is allowed. Noncommercial trade is permitted if it does not jeopardize species survival in the wild. Importers and exporters of Appendix I species must obtain permits.

- Appendix II—species for which commercial trade is tightly regulated and managed with permits.

- Appendix III—species that may be negatively affected by commercial trade. Permits are used to monitor trade in these species.

Listing of any species in Appendix I or II requires approval by a two-thirds majority of CITES member nations. The CITES appendices list thousands of animals from all over the world. Animals of major concern internationally include Asian and African elephants and primates.

WILDLIFE-RELATED RECREATION

The USFWS conducts a national survey on hunting, fishing, and other wildlife-related activities every five years. The latest survey as of mid-2009 was conducted in 2006 and published in 2007. The survey finds that 87.5 million U.S. residents aged 16 and older participated in wildlife-related recreation in 2006 and spent $122.3 billion on these activities. (See Table 3.7.) The largest number (71.1 million) were wildlife watchers, meaning that they observed, fed, or photographed wildlife around their home or away from home. Wildlife watchers spent $45.7 billion on these activities in 2006. Thirty million Americans reported angling (fishing) in 2006 and had total expenditures of $42 billion. Far fewer people, 12.5 million, participated in recreational hunting in 2006. Their expenditures totaled $22.9 billion.

Participation rates in hunting and fishing are of particular importance to the USFWS and to state fish and wildlife agencies, because the agencies collect taxes and fees associated with these activities. These monies include fees for hunting and fishing licenses, tags, and permits and a federal excise tax on certain hunting and fishing supplies. The excise tax supports the government's Wildlife and Sport Fish Restoration Program. (See Figure 3.8.) Collected funds are allocated to state fish and wildlife agencies for them to spend on wildlife-related programs. For example, Table 3.8 lists how the $215 million collected in 2007 from the hunting excise tax could be spent by state agencies on wildlife restoration programs.

Hunting

The number of people participating in hunting declined from 14 million in 1996 to 13 million in 2001 to 12.5 million in 2006. (See Figure 3.9.) The number of days and the

TABLE 3.7

Spending on wildlife-related recreation, 2006

Participants	87.5 million
Expenditures	$122.3 billion
Sportspersons	
Total participants[a]	**33.9 million**
Anglers	30.0 million
Hunters	12.5 million
Total days	**737 million**
Fishing	517 million
Hunting	220 million
Total expenditures	**$76.7 billion**
Fishing	42.0 billion
Hunting	22.9 billion
Unspecified	11.7 billion
Wildlife watchers	
Total participants[b]	**71.1 million**
Around the home	67.8 million
Away from home	23.0 million
Total expenditures	**$45.7 billion**

[a]8.5 million both fished and hunted.
[b]19.7 million both wildlife watched around the home and away from home.

SOURCE: "Total Wildlife-Related Recreation," in *2006 National Survey of Fishing, Hunting, and Wildlife-Associated Recreation*, U.S. Department of the Interior, U.S. Fish and Wildlife Service, and U.S. Department of Commerce, U.S. Census Bureau, November 2007, http://library.fws.gov/nat_survey2006_final.pdf (accessed January 14, 2009)

FIGURE 3.8

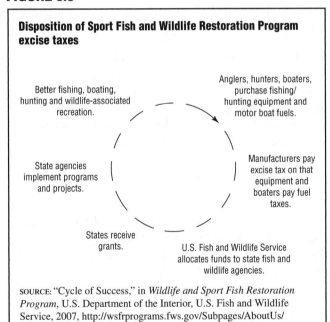

Disposition of Sport Fish and Wildlife Restoration Program excise taxes

Better fishing, boating, hunting and wildlife-associated recreation.

Anglers, hunters, boaters, purchase fishing/hunting equipment and motor boat fuels.

State agencies implement programs and projects.

Manufacturers pay excise tax on that equipment and boaters pay fuel taxes.

States receive grants.

U.S. Fish and Wildlife Service allocates funds to state fish and wildlife agencies.

SOURCE: "Cycle of Success," in *Wildlife and Sport Fish Restoration Program*, U.S. Department of the Interior, U.S. Fish and Wildlife Service, 2007, http://wsfrprograms.fws.gov/Subpages/AboutUs/WSFRPrograms2007.d7.ppt#1 (accessed January 19, 2009)

amount of money spent by hunters have also declined. (See Figure 3.10 and Figure 3.11.) The vast majority of hunters surveyed in 2006 (nearly 11 million) pursued big game, such as deer, elk, and bear. (See Figure 3.12.) About 5 million hunters reported hunting small game, such as squirrels and

TABLE 3.8

Wildlife Restoration Program excise tax, 2007

$215M—2007

Can be used for:
• Reintroduction of declining wildlife species
• Wildlife population surveys
• Species research
• Hunter education
• Acquisition of wildlife habitat
• Shooting ranges

SOURCE: "Wildlife Restoration," in *Wildlife and Sport Fish Restoration Program*, U.S. Department of the Interior, U.S. Fish and Wildlife Service, 2007, http://wsfrprograms.fws.gov/Subpages/AboutUs/WSFRPrograms2007.d7.ppt#1 (accessed January 19, 2009)

FIGURE 3.9

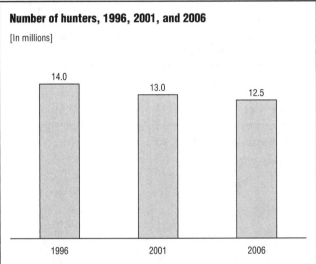

Number of hunters, 1996, 2001, and 2006

[In millions]

1996	2001	2006
14.0	13.0	12.5

SOURCE: "Number of Hunters," in *2006 National Survey of Fishing, Hunting, and Wildlife-Associated Recreation*, U.S. Department of the Interior, U.S. Fish and Wildlife Service, and U.S. Department of Commerce, U.S. Census Bureau, November 2007, http://library.fws.gov/nat_survey2006_final.pdf (accessed January 14, 2009)

rabbits. Just over 2 million hunters targeted migratory birds. Approximately 1 million hunters hunted other types of wild animals. Note that these numbers total more than 12.5 million, because some hunters hunt multiple types of animals.

OPPOSITION TO HUNTING. Hunting is bitterly opposed by some animal protection groups. In January 2004 the Fund for Animals (FFA, now a part of the Humane Society of the United States) released the report *A Dying Sport: The State of Hunting in America*. The report provides statistics on hunter demographics and expenditures and the number of animals killed by hunting each year. The FFA estimates that 115 million animals were killed by hunters during the 2002–03 hunting season. The animal protection group In Defense of Animals (IDA) claims that hunters injure millions of other animals, damage habitats, and disrupt the eating, migration, hibernation, and mating habits of protected animals. For

FIGURE 3.10

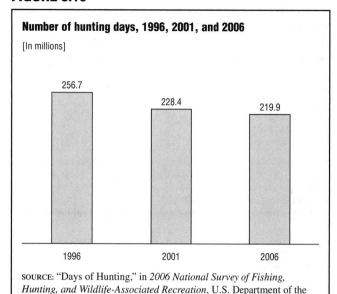

Number of hunting days, 1996, 2001, and 2006

[In millions]

SOURCE: "Days of Hunting," in *2006 National Survey of Fishing, Hunting, and Wildlife-Associated Recreation*, U.S. Department of the Interior, U.S. Fish and Wildlife Service, and U.S. Department of Commerce, U.S. Census Bureau, November 2007, http://library.fws .gov/nat_survey2006_final.pdf (accessed January 14, 2009)

FIGURE 3.12

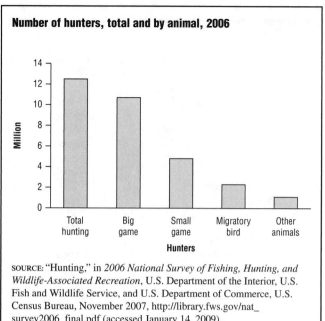

Number of hunters, total and by animal, 2006

SOURCE: "Hunting," in *2006 National Survey of Fishing, Hunting, and Wildlife-Associated Recreation*, U.S. Department of the Interior, U.S. Fish and Wildlife Service, and U.S. Department of Commerce, U.S. Census Bureau, November 2007, http://library.fws.gov/nat_ survey2006_final.pdf (accessed January 14, 2009)

FIGURE 3.11

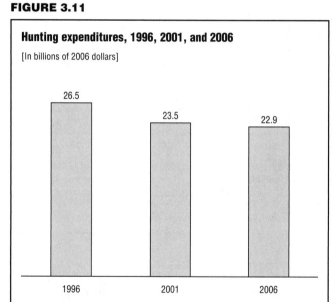

Hunting expenditures, 1996, 2001, and 2006

[In billions of 2006 dollars]

SOURCE: "Hunting Expenditures," in *2006 National Survey of Fishing, Hunting, and Wildlife-Associated Recreation*, U.S. Department of the Interior, U.S. Fish and Wildlife Service, and U.S. Department of Commerce, U.S. Census Bureau, November 2007, http://library.fws .gov/nat_survey2006_final.pdf (accessed January 14, 2009)

example, the IDA estimates in "Hunting Facts" (2009, http://www.idausa.org/facts/hunting.html) that for every animal killed instantly by hunters, at least two wounded animals die slow painful deaths from hunting injuries. Furthermore, it states that careless hunters also kill and wound domestic animals and people each year. IDA complains that "hunters and hunting organizations also promote the idea that hunting is necessary for 'wildlife management' and 'conservation.' 'Wildlife management' and 'conservation' are euphemisms used to describe programs that ensure that there are always enough animals for hunters to hunt. Because they make their money primarily from the sale of hunting licenses, the major function of wildlife agencies is not to protect individual animals or biological diversity, but to propagate 'game' species for hunters to shoot."

HUNTING AND TRAPPING ON NATIONAL WILDLIFE REFUGES. Most people assume that national wildlife refuges are truly refuges, where animals are protected from hunting and trapping. However, federal law allows the government to permit secondary uses, such as hunting, on wildlife refuges if a review of the potential effects indicates that protected wildlife will not be adversely affected. Other allowed secondary uses include fishing, wildlife watching, and environmental education programs.

The USFWS notes in "Where Can I Go Hunting?" (April 2009, http://www.fws.gov/hunting/wherego.html) that hunting was permitted on 317 of the nation's 550 national wildlife refuges.

A killing method that receives much criticism from animal protection groups is the trapping of fur-bearing animals. Welfarists consider traps to be especially cruel because the panicked animals are often trapped for a long period before being discovered and killed; sometimes they chew off their own limbs to escape. Trapping is used as a control method on federal lands, including refuges. It is done by refuge staff, by trappers under contract to the refuges, and by members of the public who obtain special permits.

The Animal Protection Institute (API) examined USFWS data collected in 1997 as part of an investigative study of trapping at wildlife refuges around the country. The API (2008, http://www.bancrueltraps.com/b1_problem.php) claims that many nontarget species are captured in body-gripping traps at refuges, including river otters, feral and domestic cats and dogs, rabbits, geese, alligators, ducks, hawks, owls, eagles, and bears. Some of these animals are killed immediately by the trapping devices or die from injuries sustained during trapping. Others are released unharmed following their discovery by the trappers.

HUNTING AS A WILDLIFE CONTROL AND CONSERVATION METHOD. Government wildlife agencies maintain that hunting is necessary to manage wildlife populations. Some animal protection groups are openly skeptical that hunting is an effective solution to overpopulation. The IDA points out in "Hunting Facts" that hunters seek out not starving animals but large and healthy ones. It argues that hunting is not about conserving species but about human power, status, and collecting wild animal heads and antlers as trophies.

Deer are the animals most often associated with hunts designed to prevent overpopulation. The deer population exploded in the latter part of the twentieth century for a variety of reasons, including lack of natural predators. The USFWS and state wildlife agencies commonly justify hunting as a humane method of killing deer that would otherwise starve because of overpopulation. By contrast, animal welfare groups believe hunting actually aggravates population problems, claiming it upsets the natural ratio between bucks (male deer) and does (female deer) and results in higher reproduction rates. The IDA states that deer make up only a small percentage of the animals killed by hunters and claims that the vast majority of hunted wild species are not considered overpopulated. It believes that sport hunting should be banned and that natural predators, such as wolves and mountain lions, should be reintroduced wherever possible to control deer populations.

Hunters defend their sport and their role in conserving wildlife just as vigorously. The U.S. Sportsmen's Alliance (USSA) and the Safari Club International (SCI) are major groups representing the interests of hunters. The USSA operates the Sportsmen's Legal Defense Fund (SLDF). The SLDF and the SCI intervene in lawsuits filed by anti-hunting groups against government wildlife management and natural resources agencies. The SCI also operates Sportsmen against Hunger, a program that donates wild game meat to hunger-relief agencies.

Hunting proponents note that hunting fees support government conservation programs. In "The Federal Duck Stamp Program" (March 23, 2004, http://www.fws.gov/duckstamps/Info/Stamps/stampinfo.htm), the USFWS states that the duck stamp has raised over $700 million since its

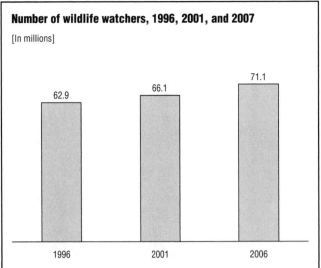

FIGURE 3.13

Number of wildlife watchers, 1996, 2001, and 2007

[In millions]

62.9	66.1	71.1
1996	2001	2006

SOURCE: "Number of Wildlife Watchers," in *2006 National Survey of Fishing, Hunting, and Wildlife-Associated Recreation*, U.S. Department of the Interior, U.S. Fish and Wildlife Service, and U.S. Department of Commerce, U.S. Census Bureau, November 2007, http://library.fws.gov/nat_survey2006_final.pdf (accessed January 14, 2009)

inception in 1934 and this money has purchased 5.2 million acres (2.1 million ha) of land for the wildlife refuge system.

Critics claim the government uses money obtained from hunting fees to set aside more areas for hunting. They want greater focus on activities such as wildlife watching and environmental education at wildlife refuges. The USFWS indicates in *2006 National Survey of Fishing, Hunting, and Wildlife-Associated Recreation* (November 2007, http://library.fws.gov/nat_survey2006_final.pdf) that the number of wildlife watchers increased from 62.9 million in 1996 to 66.1 million in 2001 to 71.1 million in 2006. (See Figure 3.13.) The number of days spent wildlife watching increased from 314 million in 1996 to 372 million in 2001 and then declined to 352 million in 2006. (See Figure 3.14.) The expenditures of wildlife watchers increased from $37.7 billion in 1996 to $43.8 billion in 2001 to $45.7 billion in 2006. (See Figure 3.15.)

TROPHY HUNTING AND CANNED HUNTS. Trophy hunting is the hunting of animals, particularly exotic species, for collection of the carcasses or parts thereof (such as the head or horns) as trophies, or symbols, of the hunter's conquest over the animal. One type of trophy hunting conducted by commercial enterprises is called canned hunting. This is a type of hunting in which animals are fenced in or otherwise enclosed in a space for the enjoyment of trophy hunters.

The Humane Society of the United States (HSUS) estimates that there are hundreds of canned hunt operators in the United States, mostly in Texas. Many offer a "no kill, no pay" policy. The most common animals involved in canned hunting are exotic species of antelope, deer, goats, sheep,

FIGURE 3.14

Number of away-from-home wildlife watching days, 1996, 2001, and 2006

[In millions]

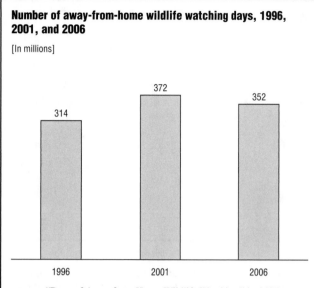

SOURCE: "Days of Away-from-Home Wildlife Watching," in *2006 National Survey of Fishing, Hunting, and Wildlife-Associated Recreation*, U.S. Department of the Interior, U.S. Fish and Wildlife Service, and U.S. Department of Commerce, U.S. Census Bureau, November 2007, http://library.fws.gov/nat_survey2006_final.pdf (accessed January 14, 2009)

FIGURE 3.15

Wildlife-watching expenditures, 1996, 2001, and 2006

[Billions of 2006 dollars]

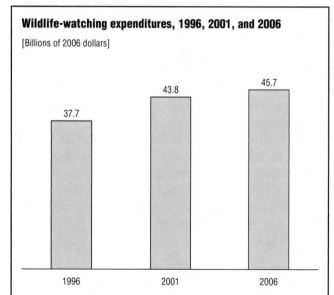

SOURCE: "Wildlife-Watching Expenditures," in *2006 National Survey of Fishing, Hunting, and Wildlife-Associated Recreation*, U.S. Department of the Interior, U.S. Fish and Wildlife Service, and U.S. Department of Commerce, U.S. Census Bureau, November 2007, http://library.fws.gov/nat_survey2006_final.pdf (accessed January 14, 2009)

cattle, swine, bears, zebra, and big cats. Hunters generally pay a set price for each exotic animal killed.

One of the oddest types of trophy hunting is so-called Internet hunting, in which participants pay to use their computer to control a hunting rifle at a game ranch and kill

captive animals. In "Internet Hunting: Killing for Couch Potatoes" (2009, http://www.hsus.org/wildlife_abuse/cam paigns/internet/) the HSUS calls it "hunting for couch potatoes" and "pay-per-view slaughter." The HSUS reports that as of August 2008 Internet hunting had been outlawed by 38 states. (See Figure 3.16.)

The HSUS and other animal welfare groups are opposed to all types of canned hunting. They consider it unsportsmanlike and cruel. Animal welfare groups believe that many relatively tame animals dumped by zoos, circuses, and exhibitors wind up victims of canned hunts. These animals are not afraid of humans and make easy targets for trophy hunters. There are many surplus exotic animals in the United States because of overbreeding. The HSUS believes canned hunts provide a financial incentive that aggravates the problem. Unwanted and purposely over-bred exotic animals are passed on by breeders and dealers to game and hunting preserves specializing in canned hunts.

RECREATIONAL FISHING. In *2006 National Survey of Fishing, Hunting, and Wildlife-Associated Recreation*, the USFWS reports that the number of U.S. residents aged 16 and older participating in recreational/sport fishing (or angling) decreased from 35.2 million in 1996 to 34.1 million in 2001 to 30 million in 2006. (See Figure 3.17.) The number of days spent fishing by the anglers in each of these years also declined. (See Figure 3.18.) Fishing expenditures decreased from $48.6 billion in 1996 to $40.6 billion in 2001, but then increased to $42 billion in 2006. (See Figure 3.19.)

The federal government's Sport Fish Restoration Program funnels excise tax receipts from the sale of certain fishing and boating equipment to various state and federal programs and agencies devoted to furthering sports fishing. Table 3.9 shows the ways in which the $349 million raised in 2007 could be spent by these agencies.

WILD ANIMAL COMMODITIES

Many wild animals are killed purely for their fur or parts. The most common wildlife commodities are:

- Fur from minks, beavers, foxes, rabbits, bears, and seals

- Hides from tigers, leopards, and other big cats

- Rhinoceros horns, reindeer antlers, snake blood, shark fins, various organs, and the penises from seals, tigers, and rhinoceroses (these items are believed by some people to act as aphrodisiacs—supplements that enhance sexual performance)

- Bones, claws, paws, fangs, brains, eyeballs, tails, and internal organs from tigers (all are used in traditional Asian medicines)

- Bile from wild boars, bears, and snakes (used in aphrodisiacs and traditional Asian medicines)

FIGURE 3.16

States with Internet hunting bans as of August 19, 2008

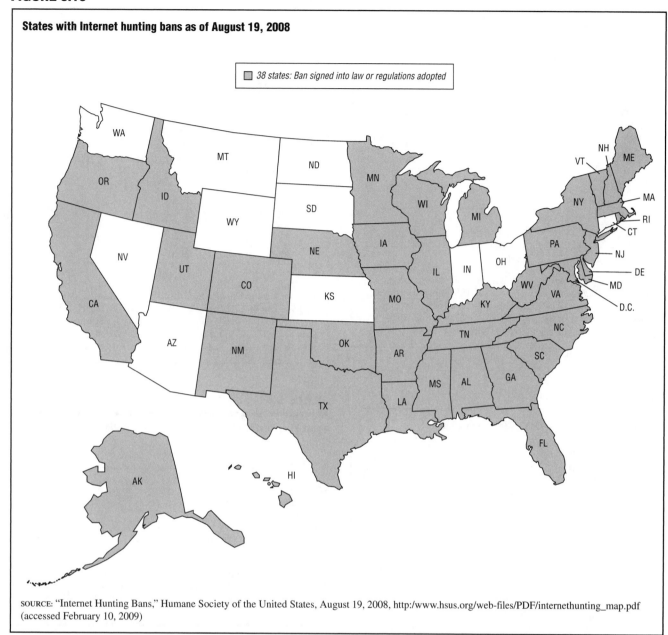

☐ *38 states: Ban signed into law or regulations adopted*

SOURCE: "Internet Hunting Bans," Humane Society of the United States, August 19, 2008, http://www.hsus.org/web-files/PDF/internethunting_map.pdf (accessed February 10, 2009)

- Elephant tusks (for ivory)
- Bear paws (considered a delicacy in some Asian countries)

Seals

Many animals used in the fur trade are bred and raised in cages on farms. Some animals, however, are still trapped or killed in the wild, particularly seals. The killing of seals for fur was a high-profile issue of the animal rights movement during the 1970s. Greenpeace activists traveled to hunting areas to splash dye on seals and draw media attention to their slaughter.

The killing of seals caught public attention because seals—usually babies only a few weeks old—on ice floes were clubbed in the head, then dragged with hooks across the ice. Animal welfarists who witnessed seal hunts claimed to have seen seals skinned while still alive and conscious. Seal hunters argued that clubbing was humane and killed the seals quickly. Seals swimming in the water were shot instead of clubbed. Critics claimed that many of these seals were injured and drowned after they sank below the surface.

In 1972 the United States banned all imports of seal products. A decade later the European Union put strict importation limits on seal pelts. As a result, Canada's seal fur industry was virtually eliminated. However, Clifford Krauss reports in "New Demand Drives Canada's Baby Seal Hunt" (*New York Times*, April 5, 2004) that Canada's seal fur industry became larger than ever because of high demand from eastern Europe and China. Krauss notes that

FIGURE 3.17

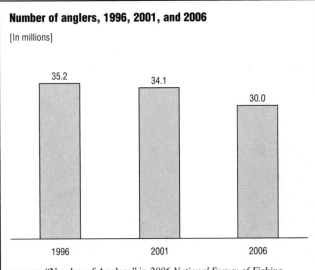

Number of anglers, 1996, 2001, and 2006

[In millions]

SOURCE: "Number of Anglers," in *2006 National Survey of Fishing, Hunting, and Wildlife-Associated Recreation*, U.S. Department of the Interior, U.S. Fish and Wildlife Service, and U.S. Department of Commerce, U.S. Census Bureau, November 2007, http://library.fws .gov/nat_survey2006_final.pdf (accessed January 14, 2009)

FIGURE 3.19

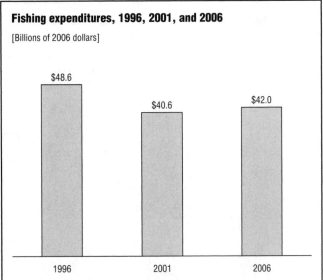

Fishing expenditures, 1996, 2001, and 2006

[Billions of 2006 dollars]

SOURCE: "Fishing Expenditures," in *2006 National Survey of Fishing, Hunting, and Wildlife-Associated Recreation*, U.S. Department of the Interior, U.S. Fish and Wildlife Service, and U.S. Department of Commerce, U.S. Census Bureau, November 2007, http://library.fws .gov/nat_survey2006_final.pdf (accessed January 14, 2009)

FIGURE 3.18

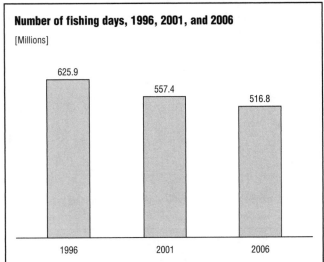

Number of fishing days, 1996, 2001, and 2006

[Millions]

SOURCE: "Days of Fishing," in *2006 National Survey of Fishing, Hunting, and Wildlife-Associated Recreation*, U.S. Department of the Interior, U.S. Fish and Wildlife Service, and U.S. Department of Commerce, U.S. Census Bureau, November 2007, http://library.fws .gov/nat_survey2006_final.pdf (accessed January 14, 2009)

TABLE 3.9

Sport Fish Restoration Program excise tax, 2007

$349M—2007

Can be used for:
• Fish research
• Reintroducing declining sport fish species
• Restoring aquatic habitat
• Aquatic education
• Constructing boat ramps and fishing piers
• Boating access

SOURCE: "Sport Fish Restoration," in *Wildlife and Sport Fish Restoration Program*, U.S. Department of the Interior, U.S. Fish and Wildlife Service, 2007, http://wsfrprograms.fws.gov/Subpages/AboutUs/WSFRPrograms2007 .d7.ppt#1 (accessed January 19, 2009)

baby seals are still clubbed to death on the ice, but new regulations mean that only seals older than two weeks are subject to the hunt. At this age the seals have lost their pure white fur and developed a gray spotted coat. According to Krauss, the renewed hunt has not aroused widespread public protest because "tougher hunting rules, including stiffer regulations to avert skinning the seals alive, have muted the effort to stop the hunt and eased the consciences of Canadians."

In 2004 many animal welfare and rights groups launched new campaigns against Canadian seal hunting. Dozens of groups, including the American Society for the Prevention of Cruelty to Animals, the HSUS, the FFA, and Greenpeace, joined together to form the Protect Seals Network. (See Table 3.10.) The network calls for a boycott of Canadian seafood to protest the seal hunt.

According to the article "Seal Hunt 2009 Makes Its First 19,000 kills" (CBC News, March 26, 2009), the annual catch quota for the Canadian seal hunt was 280,000 for the 2009 hunting season. The size of the seal population was estimated at 5.6 million. Another article, "Newfoundland's Northeast Coast Sealers Staying Home" (CBC News, April 15, 2009), notes that the selling price for a seal pelt in 2009 was expected to be only around $15, a very low value compared to previous years.

Animal organizations worldwide that support the Protect Seals Network, 2009

American Society for the Prevention of Cruelty to Animals (ASPCA)
Anima (Denmark)
Animal (Portugal)
Animalia (Finland)
Animal Alliance of Canada
Animal Right Collective of Halifax (ARCH, Canada)
Atlantic Canadian Anti-Sealing Coaltion (Canada)
Animal Friends Croatia
Animal Protection Institute (API) (USA)
Animal Rights Sweden
Asociacion Nacional Para la Defensa de los Animales (ANDA, Spain)
Bont Voor Dieren (Fur For Animals, The Netherlands)
Born Free Foundation (United Kingdom)
CETA (Life, Ukraine)
Compassion in World Farming (CIWF, Ireland)
Dyrevernalliansen (Norwegian Animal Welfare Alliance)
Earth Island Institute (USA)
Environment Voters (Canada)
Eurogroup for Animal Welfare
The Franz Weber Foundation (Switzerland)
Fundación Altarriba (Spain)
Fondation 30 Millions d'Amis (France)
GAIA (Belgium)
Global Action Network (Canada)
Greenpeace
The Humane Society of the United States (HSUS)
International Wildlife Coalition (IWC)
Asian, Australian, Canada, and United Kingdom branches of Humane Society
  International (HSI)
LAV (Lega Anti Vivisezione, Italy)
The Marine Mammal Center (USA)
Massachusetts Society for the Prevention of Cruelty to Animals (USA)
Marchig Animal Welfare Trust (United Kingdom)
Nova Scotia Humane Society (Canada)
Ocean Futures Society (USA)
One Voice (France)
Organization International pour la Protection des Animaux (France)
Respect for Animals (United Kingdom)
Royal Society for the Prevention of Cruelty to Animals (RSPCA, United Kingdom)
Sea Shepherd Conservation Society (USA)
Scandinavian Anti-Sealing Coalition (Norway, Sweden)
STS/PSA (Schweizer Tierschutz/Protection Suisse des Animaux/Swiss Animal Protection)
Svoboda Zvirat (Freedom for Animals, Czech Republic)
Vancouver Humane Society (Canada)
The Responsible Animal Care Society (TRACS, Canada)
Vier Pfoten e.V. (Germany)
VITA (Russia)
World Society for the Protection of Animals (WSPA)

SOURCE: "The Protect Seals Network," in *Protect Seals*, Humane Society of the United States, 2009, http://www.hsus.org/marine_mammals/protect_seals/the_protect_seals_network.html (accessed January 19, 2009)

Big Cats

There is a huge market for wild animal parts throughout Asia, particularly in China. Many parts are used in traditional remedies for various illnesses and diseases. In addition, animal penises are sold as aphrodisiacs. The animal most sought after is the tiger. Tiger hides are popular, and tiger bones are ground up and used in medicines for rheumatism and arthritis. Tiger penises are used in aphrodisiacs, soups, and various medicines.

Tigers are listed as endangered under the Endangered Species Act. Leopards are classified as either endangered or threatened, depending on the location of the wild population. According to the USFWS, many tigers are worth more

dead than alive. The animals breed easily in captivity and have been extremely overbred in the United States. Baby tigers are popular at zoos and animal parks, but they grow up quickly and are expensive to care for as adults. Unwanted and overbred tigers from zoos, refuges, and game parks can wind up in the hands of unscrupulous dealers who kill the animals for their valuable parts. Federal law allows the possession of captive-bred tigers, but only if their use enhances the propagation or survival of the species. It is illegal to kill the animals for profit or sell their parts, meat, or hide in interstate commerce. It is not illegal to donate the animals.

Elephants

Ivory is a hard creamy white substance found in the tusks of African elephants and some male Asian elephants. Demand for ivory was so high during the twentieth century that hundreds of thousands of elephants were poached (illegally killed) for it. Conservation groups estimate that more than half the population of African elephants was wiped out during the 1980s alone. In 1990 an international ban on ivory trade was established under CITES. Even though the ban helped to severely reduce elephant poaching, it did not eliminate the problem. It is believed that hundreds of elephants are still killed illegally each year for their ivory.

The article "Huge Population of Endangered Asian Elephants Living in Malaysian Park" (ScienceDaily.com, January 17, 2009) states that the Wildlife Conservation Society estimated the Asian elephant population at 30,000 to 50,000. The elephants are endangered due to habitat loss and poaching. According to the article "Ivory Poaching at Critical Levels: Elephants on Path to Extinction by 2020?" (ScienceDaily.com, August 1, 2008), in 2008 University of Washington researchers reported that the total African elephant population was less than 470,000, down from more than 1 million in the late 1980s. It is believed that ivory poaching claims approximately 8% of the population each year. The researchers fear that the elephants will be largely extinct in the wild by 2020 unless this trend is reversed.

WHALING AND COMMERCIAL FISHING

Whaling

Whaling has been an industry in northern seas for hundreds of years. The oil and blubber from whales were popular commodities in many markets. By the beginning of the twentieth century whaling had taken a significant toll on whale populations. The United States banned commercial whaling in 1928. In 1946 the International Whaling Commission (IWC) was founded by 24 member countries (including the United States) as a means of self-regulating the industry and limiting the number and type of whales that could be killed. In 1986 all IWC member countries agreed to ban commercial whaling after most whale populations were placed under Appendix I of the CITES agreement. However, whaling was still allowed for "scientific purposes."

Conservation and animal rights groups have complained for years that some IWC member countries, particularly Japan, kill many whales under this loophole. Whalers and some scientists say that some whale species are not endangered and should be subjected to controlled hunts.

In 2002 Iceland rejoined the IWC after dropping out in 1991, but with the reservation that it would not support a ban on commercial whaling. This started an internal battle within the IWC about what the commission's role should be. Some countries believe the IWC's focus should be entirely on conservation. Others would like to see the IWC become more industry-friendly. The IWC (http://www.iwcoffice.org/commission/iwcmain.htm) notes that in January 2009 it had 84 member countries.

Commercial Fishing

Commercial fishing of many species is blamed for a host of environmental and conservation problems in the world's oceans. Overfishing and poor management have caused severe declines in some populations. In 2009 the Food and Agriculture Organization (FAO) of the United Nations released *The State of World Fisheries and Aquaculture, 2008* (ftp://ftp.fao.org/docrep/fao/011/i0250e/i0250e.pdf). According to the FAO, commercial fisheries and aquaculture provided approximately 121 U.S. tons (110 million t) of food fish (fish for human consumption) in 2006. Commercial fisheries accounted for just over half of the total. The FAO estimates that 8% of the world's marine fishery resources were depleted in 2007. Another 19% were overexploited and 1% were recovering from depletion. More than half (52%) of stocks were described as "fully exploited," meaning that they were producing catches at or near their maximum sustainable limits. Only approximately 20% of marine stocks were "moderately exploited" or "under exploited." The FAO reports that most of the world's top 10 marine fishery species were either fully exploited or overexploited.

In "Rapid Worldwide Depletion of Predatory Fish Communities" (*Nature*, vol. 423, no. 6937, May 15, 2003), Ransom A. Myers and Boris Worm report that commercial fishing has decreased the world's population of large predatory ocean fishes by 90%. These fish include blue marlin, cod, tuna, and swordfish. Scientists find that the most sought-after species were quickly diminished by overfishing and then replaced by less desirable species. These replacement species were also depleted quickly. Technological advances such as global positioning systems and sonar have allowed commercial fishing companies to better find and follow great schools of fish in previously uncharted waters.

Another criticism of commercial fishing is that it endangers marine mammals and other fish besides those the fisherman want to catch. Experts estimate that thousands of nontarget specimens are killed each year after becoming entangled in fishing nets and devices. According to Earthtrust (October 8, 2008, http://www.earthtrust.org/fsa.html), a nonprofit wildlife conservation organization, approximately 7 million dolphins were killed between 1959 and 1991 because of purse seining in the eastern tropical Pacific. Purse seining is a fishing technique in which giant nets are encircled around schools of fish. It is a popular way to capture tuna. Schools of tuna are frequently accompanied by pods of dolphins. In fact, some fishermen chase and set their nets around dolphins to capture the nearby tuna. Because dolphins are mammals, they require air to breathe. The dolphins get caught and drown in the nets. Negative publicity about the problem during the 1980s led consumers to demand changes in tuna fishing and labeling.

In 1990 the Dolphin Protection Consumer Information Act was passed, establishing an official definition of "dolphin-safe" tuna. Canners must meet certain criteria before they can label their tuna dolphin-safe, and U.S. fishermen modified their fishing techniques to meet the criteria. Purse-seine fishing is still widely practiced by foreign fishing industries, particularly in Mexico and South America.

In 2002 the NMFS announced in the press release "Commerce Department Determines No Significant Adverse Impact of Fishing on Dolphin Populations" (December 31, 2002, http://www.publicaffairs.noaa.gov/releases2002/dec02/noaa02168.html) its finding that the tuna purse-seine industry has "no significant adverse impact" on dolphin populations in the eastern tropical Pacific. This finding allows foreign fishermen using the technique to import their fish into the United States as dolphin-safe if an onboard observer certifies that no dolphins were killed or seriously injured during the catch.

Critics claim that purse-seine fishing is inhumane to dolphins even if they are released from the nets alive because it can separate baby dolphins from their mothers. In January 2003 the Earth Island Institute and eight other environmental, conservation, and animal welfare groups (including the HSUS) filed suit against the NMFS in federal court to halt implementation of the ruling. In August 2004 a federal judge ruled that the "dolphin-safe" label cannot be used on any tuna products caught by netting dolphins.

The Scripps Institution of Oceanography at the University of California, San Diego, notes in the press release "Dolphin Population Stunted by Fishing Activities, Scripps/NOAA Study Finds" (November 24, 2008, http://scrippsnews.ucsd.edu/Releases/?releaseID=939) that in 2008 commercial fishing continued to threaten dolphin populations in the eastern Pacific Ocean. The populations had not rebounded as expected since purse-seining restrictions went into effect in the 1990s. The institute indicates that commercial fishing activities have reduced calf survival rates and birth rates. It is believed that temporary separation of mothers from nursing calves during netting may be to blame for these lower rates.

CHAPTER 4
FARM ANIMALS

Farm animals are animals that are kept for agricultural purposes. This includes domesticated animals such as cows and chickens, and wild animals that are raised in confinement, including mink and fish. Animals are farmed for a variety of reasons. Most are raised to be killed. Meat from cattle, hogs, and chickens provides the bulk of protein in the American diet, whereas animals with beautiful fur are killed for their pelts. However, some farm animals are more useful and profitable alive. These animals produce something of value to humans, such as milk, eggs, wool, or honey, or are farmed for their skills, such as horses, mules, and burros. Whatever the reason, the cultivation of farm animals is an enormous business.

Each year the U.S. Department of Agriculture (USDA) publishes a comprehensive report on the demographics, economic value, and health of the nation's livestock. The report *2007 United States Animal Health Report* (http://www.aphis.usda.gov/publications/animal_health/content/printable_version/ahr2007.pdf) was published in September 2008 and includes data through 2007. Table 4.1 shows the production value for the top money-making livestock commodities in 2007. Farm animals and their output accounted for $118.2 billion in value. Figure 4.1 shows a breakdown of value by percentage. Cattle, milk from milk cows, broilers (chickens raised for meat), and swine (hogs and pigs) made up the vast majority of the total in 2007.

The number of animals involved in the agricultural industry is staggering. In 2007 U.S. farms included 8.9 billion broilers and nearly 514 million cattle, swine, and egg-laying hens. (See Table 4.2.) Table 4.3 shows slaughter statistics for 2007 for a variety of farmed animals. Over 9.5 billion farm animals were slaughtered in 2007.

In 2007 more farm animals were living in the United States than there were humans on Earth. The use and well-being of these animals is of major importance to people concerned with animal rights and welfare. Animal rights activists abhor the idea that animals are commodities at all. They believe that animals should not be used for any purpose, especially to feed humans. Welfarists focus their attention on the treatment of farmed animals—how they are housed, fed, transported, and slaughtered. The Gallup Organization conducted a poll in May 2008 in which 64% of respondents indicated that they "strongly" (35%) or "somewhat" (29%) support the passage of strict laws concerning the treatment of farm animals (See Figure 4.2.)

People in the U.S. livestock business argue that farm animals are well treated. They point to the high productivity of the industry as proof. In other words, farm animals must be thriving because there are so many of them. The American Meat Institute (AMI; April 2009, http://www.animalhandling.org/), a trade organization that represents the meat and poultry industry, sums up this viewpoint by stating: "Optimal handling is ethically appropriate, creates positive workplaces and ensures higher quality meat products." The link between humane animal treatment and high production of good-quality products is commonly cited by the livestock industry.

Critics argue that high productivity is an indicator of the efficiency of the overall system, not the welfare of individual animals. They have a long list of complaints about how farm animals are raised and slaughtered in the United States.

Farming animals is an old and respected business. It feeds people and supplies products they want. Forcing farmers to radically change the way they treat animals might jeopardize the relatively cheap and plentiful supply of animal products that Americans enjoy. Would society tolerate this just for the sake of the animals? This is the ultimate question at the center of the farm animal debate.

TABLE 4.1

Value of production of selected farm animal commodities, 2007

Cattle	$36,066,735,000
Milk from milk cows	$35,652,656,000
Broilers	$21,460,211,000
Swine	$13,467,996,000
Eggs	$6,678,147,000
Turkeys	$3,710,846,000
Catfish and trout	$532,381,000
Sheep	$383,576,000
Honey	$153,233,000
Miscellaneous poultry	$50,783,000
Wool	$30,258,000
Total	**$118,186,822,000**

SOURCE: Adapted from "Table A1.2. Value of Production for Selected Agricultural Commodities for 2006 and 2007," in *2007 United States Animal Health Report*, U.S. Department of Agriculture, Animal and Plant Health Inspection Service, September 2008, http://www.aphis.usda.gov/publications/animal_health/content/printable_version/ahr2007.pdf (accessed January 13, 2009)

TABLE 4.2

Selected farm animals, inventories and numbers sold, 2007

All farms	2007
Livestock and poultry	
Cattle and calves inventory	96,347,858
Beef cows	32,834,801
Milk cows	9,266,574
Cattle and calves sold	74,071,936
Hogs and pigs inventory	67,786,318
Hogs and pigs sold	206,807,181
Layers inventory	349,772,508
Broilers and other meat-type chickens sold	8,914,828,122

SOURCE: Adapted from "Table 1. Historical Highlights: 2007 and Earlier Census Years," in *2007 Census of Agriculture, United States Summary and State Data, Volume 1*, U.S. Department of Agriculture, National Agricultural Statistics Service, February 2009, http://www.agcensus.usda.gov/Publications/2007/Full_Report/usv1.pdf (accessed February 6, 2009)

FIGURE 4.1

Percentage breakdown of value of production of selected farm animal commodities, 2007

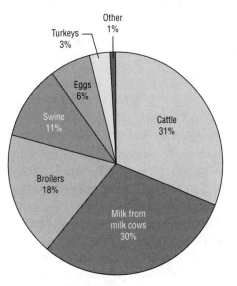

SOURCE: Adapted from "Table A1.2. Value of Production for Selected Agricultural Commodities for 2006 and 2007" and "Table A1.10. Poultry Production in the United States, 2006 and 2007," in *2007 United States Animal Health Report*, U.S. Department of Agriculture, Animal and Plant Health Inspection Service, September 2008, http://www.aphis.usda.gov/publications/animal_health/content/printable_version/ahr2007.pdf (accessed January 13, 2009)

TABLE 4.3

Slaughter statistics, selected farm animals, 2007

	Total commercial and farm slaughter
Chickens	9,031,035,000
Turkeys	264,969,000
Hogs and pigs	109,277,000
Cattle	34,451,000
Ducks	27,311,000
Other cows	3,178,000
Sheep and lambs	2,769,000
Dairy cows	2,497,000
Goats	827,300
Calves	758,000
Bison	67,000

Note: Rounded to nearest thousand.

SOURCE: Adapted from "Table A1.15. Slaughter Statistics, 2007," "Table A1.10. Poultry Production in the United Sates, 2006 and 2007," "Table A1.7. Hog and Pig Production, 2006 and 2007," "Table A1.3. Cattle and Calves Production, 2006 and 2007," "Table A1.4: Milk Cow Production, 2006 and 2007," and "Table A1.8. Sheep Production in the United States, 2006 and 2007," in *2007 United States Animal Health Report*, U.S. Department of Agriculture, Animal and Plant Health Inspection Service, September 2008, http://www.aphis.usda.gov/publications/animal_health/content/printable_version/ahr2007.pdf (accessed January 13, 2009)

LIVESTOCK PROTECTION LAWS

In the 1800s a number of laws were enacted in England and the United States to protect animals from abuse, neglect, and mistreatment by their owners. Some of these laws specifically included livestock, whereas others did not. Many state anticruelty laws excluded what they called "customary agricultural practices." These laws were often interpreted not to apply to animals raised for food.

The 28-Hour Law of 1873 was the first federal law dealing with livestock welfare. It required that livestock being transported across state lines be rested and watered at least once every 28 hours during the journey. At the time, livestock transport was done by rail, and for more than 130 years the law was only enforced on railroad transport of livestock. In 2005 the animal group Compassion over Killing conducted an undercover investigation of a pig transport operation and produced videos documenting the suffering allegedly inflicted on pigs forced to

FIGURE 4.2

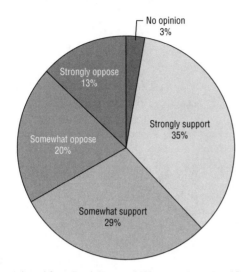

Public support for strict laws concerning the treatment of farm animals, May 2008

HERE ARE SOME SPECIFIC PROPOSALS CONCERNING THE TREATMENT OF ANIMALS. FOR EACH ONE, PLEASE SAY WHETHER YOU STRONGLY SUPPORT THIS PROPOSAL, SOMEWHAT SUPPORT IT, SOMEWHAT OPPOSE IT, OR STRONGLY OPPOSE THIS PROPOSAL. HOW ABOUT PASSING STRICT LAWS CONCERNING THE TREATMENT OF FARM ANIMALS?

No opinion 3%
Strongly oppose 13%
Somewhat oppose 20%
Strongly support 35%
Somewhat support 29%

SOURCE: Adapted from Frank Newport, "Here Are Some Specific Proposals Concerning the Treatment of Animals. For Each One, Please Say Whether You Strongly Support This Proposal, Somewhat Support It, Somewhat Oppose It, or Strongly Oppose This Proposal. How about Passing Strict Laws Concerning the Treatment of Farm Animals?" in *Post-Derby Tragedy, 38% Support Banning Animal Racing*, The Gallup Organization, May 15, 2008, http://www.gallup.com/poll/107293/Post Derby-Tragedy-38-Support-Banning-Animal-Racing.aspx (accessed January 13, 2009). Copyright © 2008 by The Gallup Organization. Reproduced by permission of The Gallup Organization.

travel by truck for long time periods. The USDA launched its own investigation after learning that more than 150 pigs transported by truck for more than 28 hours in the summer heat arrived dead at a livestock facility in Texas. Compassion over Killing and other animal welfare organizations petitioned the USDA to include truck transport under the provisions of the 28-Hour Law. In September 2006 the USDA announced in the press release "USDA Reverses Decades-Old Policy on Farm Animal Transport" (http://www.hsus.org/farm/news/ournews/usda_reverses_28 _hour_policy.html) that it officially agreed and concluded that "'trucks' which operate as express carriers or common carriers" for livestock would be covered under the law.

The Animal Welfare Act was enacted in 1966 to provide protection for animals used for certain purposes, but the regulations enforcing the law specifically excluded livestock.

The major legislation of the twentieth century to affect livestock was the Humane Methods of Slaughter Act of 1958. The law required slaughter by humane methods at slaughterhouses subject to federal inspection.

This meant that livestock had to be rendered insensitive to pain before being slaughtered. The act excluded chickens and all animals slaughtered using techniques associated with religious rituals. For decades, animal welfare organizations have been contesting the USDA policy that excludes some animals, particularly chickens and turkeys, from coverage under this law. In 2005 the Humane Society of the United States (HSUS) and other plaintiffs filed a lawsuit against the USDA challenging the policy that excludes birds from the act. The case was finally heard in November 2007. In March 2008 a federal judge dismissed the case, ruling that the original definition of *livestock* in the act did not include poultry.

Concern Grows

Following the Humane Methods of Slaughter Act, farm animals did not receive much attention until a 1964 book by Ruth Harrison (1920–2000) was published. *Animal Machines: The New Factory Farming Industry* described the brutality inflicted on livestock in Britain by the modern farming industry. In 1975 Peter Singer (1946–) published *Animal Liberation: A New Ethics for Our Treatment of Animals*, which detailed similar problems on U.S. factory farms. It was also during the 1960s and 1970s that the vegetarian movement gained momentum.

The plight of farm animals became a major issue with animal rights activists and welfarists. In the 1980s and early 1990s several groups dedicated to livestock concerns formed, among them the Farm Animal Reform Movement, the Humane Farming Association, Farm Sanctuary, and United Poultry Concerns. Since 2000 these and other groups began publicizing abuses that occur in the agricultural industry and have achieved new legislation to protect farm animals.

Specific goals include:

- Banning the slaughter of horses for food
- Drafting legislation for poultry that enables them to be covered under the Humane Methods of Slaughter Act
- Protecting animals at the slaughterhouse that have been injured during transport and are unable to walk (so-called downed animals)
- Outlawing the keeping of veal calves and pregnant and nursing hogs in small iron crates so that they cannot move
- Outlawing the keeping of chickens in so-called battery cages
- Publicizing the abuse and mishandling of animals at slaughterhouses

ANIMAL PRODUCTS

Animal products are used in many ways by modern society. People consume and wear them and buy items every day that contain animal-derived components. According to

FIGURE 4.3

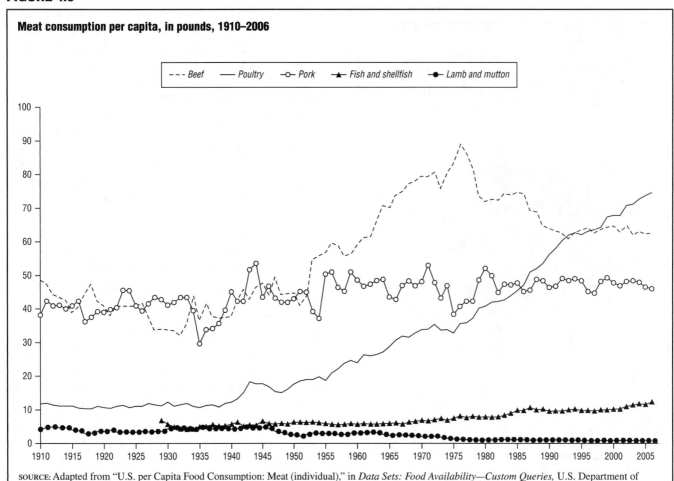

Meat consumption per capita, in pounds, 1910–2006

- - - Beef   —— Poultry   —○— Pork   —▲— Fish and shellfish   —●— Lamb and mutton

SOURCE: Adapted from "U.S. per Capita Food Consumption: Meat (individual)," in *Data Sets: Food Availability—Custom Queries,* U.S. Department of Agriculture, Economic Research Service, February 15, 2007, http://www.ers.usda.gov/Data/FoodConsumption/FoodAvailQueriable.aspx (accessed January 26, 2009)

the Economic Research Service (ERS), in *Data Sets: Food Availability—Custom Queries* (March 6, 2009, http://www.ers.usda.gov/Data/FoodConsumption/FoodAvaiQurriable.aspx), Americans consumed 200.6 pounds (90.9 kg) of meat per capita (per person) during 2007. From 1909 until 1939 the annual meat consumption averaged 111.6 pounds (50.6 kg) per person. After World War II (1939–1945) Americans began consuming more meat. The annual per capita consumption climbed steadily throughout the remainder of the century.

For much of the twentieth century, beef and pork accounted for most of the meat consumed in the United States. (See Figure 4.3.) Concerns about the fat and cholesterol content of red meat led to greater demand for chicken and turkey. Figure 4.3 shows that these "white" meats began to make up a larger share of meat consumption. By 2006 beef (32%) and pork (23%) accounted for 55% of the pounds of meat consumed per year, whereas poultry made up 39%. (See Figure 4.4.) Consumption of fish, shellfish, lamb, and mutton was much lower.

Animals killed for meat must be processed immediately. This means that meat animals must arrive alive at the slaughterhouse. They cannot be humanely euthanized with drugs as pets are when put to sleep because humans will be consuming them. Those parts that are not readily edible by humans are rendered into other marketable products. Bones, hooves, beaks, feet, feathers, fat, and inedible organs and tissues are recycled at one of several hundred rendering plants in the United States. The fat is processed for industrial use, and the other byproducts are ground into a powder or boiled to make gelatin. Tallow (rendered fat) is used to make soap, candles, and lubricants.

According to the National Renderers Association, in "US Production, Consumption, and Export of Rendered Products for 2002–2007" (April 15, 2008, http://national renderers.org/assets/US_Production_Consumption_and _Export_of_Rendered_Products_for_2002_2007.pdf), nearly 8.6 million tons (7.8 million t) of animal byproducts were produced by the rendering industry in 2007. Of this, 2.9 million tons (2.6 million t) was inedible tallow and greases. The remainder included bone meal, edible tallow, lard, poultry fat, inedible feather meal, and miscellaneous products.

FIGURE 4.4

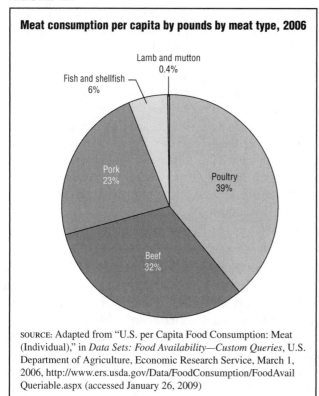

Meat consumption per capita by pounds by meat type, 2006

Lamb and mutton 0.4%

Fish and shellfish 6%

Poultry 39%

Beef 32%

Pork 23%

SOURCE: Adapted from "U.S. per Capita Food Consumption: Meat (Individual)," in *Data Sets: Food Availability—Custom Queries*, U.S. Department of Agriculture, Economic Research Service, March 1, 2006, http://www.ers.usda.gov/Data/FoodConsumption/FoodAvail Queriable.aspx (accessed January 26, 2009)

Rendered byproducts are sold to a variety of industries and become ingredients in lubricants, paints, varnishes, waxes, soaps, candles, cement, pharmaceuticals, pet food, toothpaste, and cosmetics (such as lipstick and shampoo). Gelatin is an ingredient in many food products, including some types of ice cream, yogurt, candy, and marshmallows. Before the 1990s a primary use of rendered byproducts was as a protein supplement (or food source) for livestock. In 1997 the U.S. Food and Drug Administration (FDA) outlawed the use of most mammal-based protein in feed intended for cattle. This is to prevent the spread of disease, particularly mad cow disease, should it appear in the United States. Rendering plants also process whole carcasses of farm animals that die of illness or injury and other dead animals, including euthanized pets.

ROUTINE FARMING PRACTICES

Historically, farm animals have not been covered by animal welfare legislation. As a result, some practices relating to the treatment of farm animals are considered standard by farmers but may be thought of as cruel or inhumane by animal activists and other people. Such practices include culling, castration, dehorning, branding, and various forms of physical alteration. Culling means the rejection of inferior or undesirable animals. Because it costs money to feed and care for livestock, unwanted farm animals are usually killed. This is particularly true in the hen-breeding business. Male chicks of laying breeds will never lay eggs and are not suitable meat chickens. Millions of them are routinely killed each year when they are only one day old.

Another ancient farming practice is animal castration (removal of the male sex organs). Humans have used castration to control the reproduction of farm animals for centuries. This is particularly true in cattle and hog farming. Only the males with the most desirable characteristics are allowed to remain intact for breeding purposes. This is believed to be beneficial for herd management, because castration reduces aggressive behavior and physical confrontations between males that might damage their meat. In addition, sexually mature males release hormones that can affect the taste of meat.

The vast majority of cattle are dehorned to make them easier to handle and to prevent them from accidentally or intentionally injuring each other. In grown cattle the fully developed horns are cut off, but a more common practice is to treat the emerging horn buds of baby calves with a caustic salve to prevent horns from developing. According to Todd Duffield, in "Cattle Preconditioning: How to Dehorn Calves to Minimize Pain" (February 12, 2009, http://www.cattlenetwork.com/Cattle_Preconditioning _Content.asp?ContentID=290743), this procedure causes "minimal" pain and the use of a local anesthetic block is unnecessary.

Branding and other forms of identification, such as ear notching, are used to distinguish ownership. Cattle and swine have their tails clipped to prevent them from chewing on each other's tails and to improve cleanliness and reduce disease. Chicken beaks are trimmed to reduce injuries that might result from the animals pecking at each other.

All these procedures are regarded as practical and necessary by farm animal producers and considered inhumane by many animal welfarists. Castration, dehorning, branding, beak trimming, tail clipping, and ear notching are widely conducted in the United States without the use of anesthetics or pain medication. Use of a local anesthetic is recommended (but not required) in Canada and is required by law in most cases in the United Kingdom.

FACTORY FARMING

What Is a Farm?

The farming of livestock has changed dramatically over the past century. Many people think of a farm as a rural collection of barns and fields run by one farming family. In reality, some farms are massive industrial-type facilities owned and operated by large corporations. These are called factory farms. Even though they make up a small percentage of U.S. farms, they handle a large percentage of the animals killed for food in the United States.

TABLE 4.4

Farms by animal type, 2007

All farms	2007
Livestock and poultry	
Cattle and calves inventory	963,669
Beef cows	764,984
Milk cows	69,890
Cattle and calves sold	798,290
Hogs and pigs inventory	75,442
Hogs and pigs sold	74,789
Layers inventory	145,615
Broilers and other meat-type chickens sold	27,091

SOURCE: Adapted from "Table 1. Historical Highlights: 2007 and Earlier Census Years," in *2007 Census of Agriculture, United States Summary and State Data, Volume 1*, U.S. Department of Agriculture, National Agricultural Statistics Service, February 2009, http://www.agcensus.usda.gov/Publications/2007/Full_Report/usv1.pdf (accessed February 6, 2009).

In *2007 Census of Agriculture* (February 2009, http://www.agcensus.usda.gov/Publications/2007/Full_Report/usv1.pdf), the USDA defines a farm as an establishment that produces or sells $1,000 or more of agricultural products during a year. According to the 2007 census, there were just over 2.2 million farms in the United States, just over half of which produced livestock. The breakdown by animal type is shown in Table 4.4. Cattle and calf farms accounted for the largest number (963,669) of the total.

Consolidation of Agricultural Businesses

The USDA reports in *2007 Census of Agriculture* that in 2007, 1.9 million farms were owned and operated by individuals and families. About 96,000 farms were owned by corporations, but many small farms operate under contract to corporations. The farmers may sign away ownership of their animals and be paid to raise them to a contracted age or weight. Then the animals are turned over to the companies for finishing or slaughtering.

How Factory Farms Work

The most visible symbol of factory farming is the animal feeding operation (AFO) or concentrated animal feeding operation (CAFO). The U.S. Environmental Protection Agency notes in "Animal Feeding Operations" (March 10, 2009, http://www.epa.gov/oecaagct/anafoidx.html#About%20Animal%20Feeding%20Operations) that an AFO is a facility that "congregate[s] animals, feed, manure and urine, dead animals, and production operations on a small land area." The difference between an AFO and a CAFO is based in part on how many animals are involved. Both feature highly concentrated confinement areas with no pasture or grazing land.

In this way, the animals can be housed, fed, medicated, and processed with the utmost efficiency. Every aspect of animal life and behavior is controlled to ensure that productivity and profits are maximized. The animals are kept in the smallest space possible and fed the cheapest food that will quickly and effectively fatten them up. Breeding facilities ensure a constant supply of replacements.

Modern technology is employed whenever it is economically feasible. Females are artificially inseminated rather than mated. Pregnancies are spaced close together to increase production. Mothers and offspring are separated quickly to keep the process moving. Antibiotics, hormones, and growth-enhancing drugs are administered to ensure rapid growth and to prevent deadly diseases. Slaughterhouses are run like assembly lines with an emphasis on speed and meat quantity.

Pros and Cons

The overwhelming advantage of the factory farming system to society is economic: satisfaction of the demand for meat at acceptable prices. Factory farming provides the United States with a continuous and relatively inexpensive meat supply. However, animal rights activists blame the factory farming system for many animal abuses. They believe the industry's emphasis on profits, efficiency, and productivity has contributed greatly to inhumane treatment and sloppy slaughtering of farm animals.

There is no doubt that industrial methods have changed the way in which farmers and animals interact. Traditionally, farmers had a lot of personal interaction with their animals during feeding and handling. Even though this did not change the ultimate usage of the animals, many people believe that it built a bond that led farmers to care more about the welfare of individual animals. Certainly sick or injured animals were more likely to be noticed and cared for in this system. Many small farms, particularly in communities that use traditional methods (such as Amish farms) still achieve this level of human-animal contact.

By contrast, factory farms are almost entirely automated. For example, on most chicken farms the food is dispensed by machines, and the eggs are collected on conveyor belts. The chickens rarely see people until they are gathered by human handlers into crates for their journey to the slaughterhouse. Such automation in modern animal husbandry saves money by reducing labor costs and increasing efficiency.

CATTLE

Cattle are bovines that descend from ancient animals called aurochs. They have complex four-compartment stomachs called rumens and eat vegetation. In nature, cattle swallow their food whole. Later, the partially digested food, or cud, is regurgitated into their mouths for them to chew. "Chewing the cud" is a well-known cattle trait. The natural lifespan for cattle is 20 to 25 years.

FIGURE 4.5

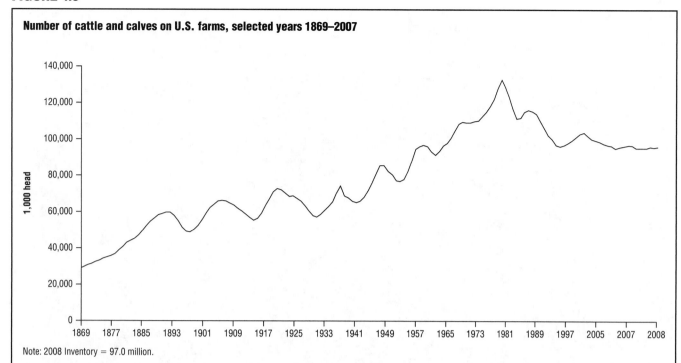

Number of cattle and calves on U.S. farms, selected years 1869–2007

Note: 2008 Inventory = 97.0 million.

SOURCE: "Figure 6.1C. Cattle and Calves: U.S. Inventory on January 1 for Selected Years, 1869–2007," in *2007 United States Animal Health Report*, U.S. Department of Agriculture, Animal and Plant Health Inspection Service, September 2008, http://www.aphis.usda.gov/publications/animal_health/content/printable_version/ahr2007.pdf (accessed January 13, 2009)

There are many different breeds of cattle. Some are specially bred for meat (such as Angus and Hereford), whereas others are bred to produce milk (such as Jerseys). Adult female cattle are called cows. They produce milk for their newborn calves for months. People learned long ago to take calves away from their mothers and collect the milk for human consumption. Young female cows that have not yet given birth are called heifers. Uncastrated adult male cattle are called bulls. They are used only for breeding purposes. Male cattle castrated before they reach sexual maturity are called steers. They are a major source of beef in this country.

There were 96.3 million cattle on U.S. farms in 2007. (See Table 4.2.) Figure 4.5 shows that the cattle inventory increased dramatically through the early 1970s and then declined, before leveling off in the mid-1990s.

Beef Cattle

HISTORY. At the beginning of the twentieth century, the U.S. cattle industry was concentrated in the western states. Cattle were herded by cowboys to markets in large cities with railroad hubs. Cattle were shipped by rail to massive stockyards and slaughtering/processing centers in places such as Chicago, Illinois, and Kansas City, Missouri. As refrigeration and electricity spread throughout the country, slaughterhouses were able to move away from the big cities and into rural areas.

During the 1950s large meat companies began setting up feedlots for cattle, first in the Great Plains and later further west. (See Figure 4.6.) Before that time cattle mostly ate grass, with some corn and other grains added to fatten them. They were slaughtered when they reached marketable size, around three to four years of age. U.S. farmers began producing a surplus of corn in the mid-1950s, and it became a primary feed for beef cattle. Cattle fed a diet rich in corn got fatter much faster and could be slaughtered much earlier than grass-fed cattle. Corn-fed beef had a rich fatty taste with a marbled texture and was more tender than grass-fed beef. It was also much cheaper. Heavy marketing by grocery stores led to huge demand for corn-fed beef.

PRESENT CONDITIONS. Figure 4.7 provides a percentage breakdown of cattle operations as of 2007 and their inventories as of January 1, 2008. More than 60% of the operations had 49 or less cattle per operation. These establishments accounted for approximately 10% of the total cattle inventory. Operations with herds of 50 to 99 cattle accounted for just over 10% of total cattle inventory. Operations with 100 to 499 cattle accounted for less than 20% of all operations but held roughly one-third of all cattle. Approximately 1% of cattle operations had herds of 500 to 999 cattle, accounting for 13% of total inventory. Around 2% of cattle operations had more than 1,000 cattle, accounting for 32% of the total inventory.

FIGURE 4.6

Cattle at a feedlot. *Image copyright Thoma, 2009. Used under license from Shutterstock.com.*

Most beef cattle are slaughtered around the age of 14 to 16 months. Calves spend the first six to eight months of their life with their mother, drinking milk and grazing on grass at farms and ranches around the country. This is called the cow-calf stage of the business. Following weaning, most calves are moved to large crowded feedlots (outdoor grassless enclosures) to be "finished" for slaughter. During finishing the cattle receive virtually no exercise to prevent muscle buildup and fat loss. The animals are given various drugs to help them digest the rich corn diet and fend off disease from the crowded and often dirty conditions.

In March 2002 the reporter Michael Pollan purchased an eight-month-old calf from a South Dakota ranch and chronicled the calf's life in "Power Steer" (*New York Times*, March 31, 2002). Following weaning, Pollan's calf spent several months in a backgrounding pen becoming accustomed to a corn diet before being shipped to a feedlot. At the feedlot, which was crowded with 37,000 cattle, the calf was fed a diet of corn, fat, protein supplements, and some alfalfa hay and corn silage for roughage. The calf was given antibiotics to help it digest this new diet.

Pollan notes that feedlot cattle must be fed antibiotics and antacids to overcome digestive problems from eating corn rather than grass. Corn-fed cattle are prone to severe bloat, indigestion, and other conditions that can weaken their immune system and make them susceptible to serious diseases. Thus, many are fed continuous low-level doses of antibiotics to keep them reasonably healthy. The corn diet damages their liver, but this is a trade-off acceptable to the beef industry because cow liver is not in high demand. Pollan's steer also received a hormone injection of synthetic estrogen to help him gain weight, a common and legal practice.

According to Pollan, the cattle on the feedlot lived amid a thick layer of manure during their entire stay, another reason that antibiotics are required for feedlot cattle. Generally, manure is not a concern until slaughtering time, when it is washed off the carcasses during processing. Pollan argues that this practice is not healthy for the people who will eat the beef or for the cattle living in this environment.

Ranchers use the feedlot system because it is much cheaper for them than finishing the cattle at the ranch.

FIGURE 4.7

FIGURE 4.8

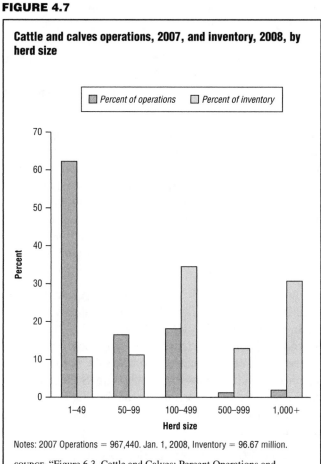

Cattle and calves operations, 2007, and inventory, 2008, by herd size

Notes: 2007 Operations = 967,440. Jan. 1, 2008, Inventory = 96.67 million.

SOURCE: "Figure 6.3. Cattle and Calves: Percent Operations and Inventory, by Herd Size," in *2007 United States Animal Health Report*, U.S. Department of Agriculture, Animal and Plant Health Inspection Service, September 2008, http://www.aphis.usda.gov/publications/animal_health/content/printable_version/ahr2007.pdf (accessed January 13, 2009)

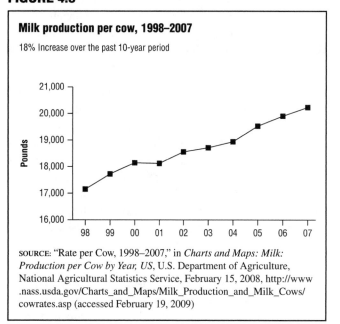

Milk production per cow, 1998–2007

18% Increase over the past 10-year period

SOURCE: "Rate per Cow, 1998–2007," in *Charts and Maps: Milk: Production per Cow by Year, US*, U.S. Department of Agriculture, National Agricultural Statistics Service, February 15, 2008, http://www.nass.usda.gov/Charts_and_Maps/Milk_Production_and_Milk_Cows/cowrates.asp (accessed February 19, 2009)

The price of beef is so low that profit margins on cattle are slim. Ranchers and farmers must cut costs wherever they can. Many ranchers sell their calves to corporations and companies running feedlots. Others retain ownership and pay rent to the feedlot during the finishing process.

Dairy Cattle

Dairy cattle are a valuable commodity because they produce milk that can be consumed as a drink or used to make other dairy products. The ERS states in *Data Sets: Food Availability* that the average per capita consumption in the United States during 2007 was 20.7 gallons (78.4 L) of milk, 27.4 pounds (12.4 kg) of cheese, and 25.2 pounds (11.4 kg) of frozen dairy products (mostly ice cream).

The USDA's National Agricultural Statistics Service reports in *Charts and Maps: Milk Production and Milk Cows* (February 15, 2008, http://www.nass.usda.gov/Charts _and_Maps/Milk_Production_and_Milk_Cows/milkprod .asp) that dairy cows produced more than 185 billion pounds (83.9 billion kg) of milk during 2007. The combination of factory farming, high-tech breeding, and modern

medicine has resulted in a higher production of milk per cow over time. Milk production per cow increased by 18% between 1998 and 2007 alone. (See Figure 4.8.)

Even though the public may assume that dairy cattle spend leisurely days in rolling fields of grass and are only occasionally milked, the reality is that dairy cows have become milk-producing machines. Most dairy cows live in small indoor stalls or are confined to large dirt pens called dry lots. To produce milk, the cows must have calves. Modern farmers keep dairy cows pregnant almost continuously, often through artificial insemination. They take the calves away from their mothers as soon as possible after birth to prevent the calves from drinking the valuable milk. Male calves and any cows that cease to produce milk are slaughtered for beef. Common health problems in dairy cows include mastitis (an udder infection) and lameness due to back and leg problems.

Many dairy cattle are given antibiotics and other drugs regularly. One of the most controversial drugs is called bovine growth hormone (BGH). Born Free USA indicates in "Get the Facts: The Destructive Dairy Industry" (2009, http://www.bornfreeusa.org/facts.php?more=1&p=373) that BGH can increase the amount of milk that a cow can produce by 25%. Animal welfarists note that BGH enlarges cows' udders to such a degree that the cows suffer from spine and back problems and have difficulty keeping their udders from dragging in dirt and manure. In "Bovine Somatotropin (bST or bGH)" (March 2008, http://www.id fa.org/reg/biotech/rbst_idfa_position.cfm), the International Dairy Foods Association states that BGH has been used in U.S. dairy herds since 1993. The association reports that the milk has been deemed safe for human consumption "by the Food and Drug Administration,...the World Health

Organization, the American Medical Association, the National Institutes of Health, the American Diabetic Association and regulatory agencies in 50 countries." The use of BGH, which is also called bovine somatotropin, is banned in Europe and Canada because of its effects on cow health.

Another criticism of the factory farming of dairy cattle is that the cows spend long periods standing on hard surfaces. This includes concrete floors, metal gratings, and dirt-packed dry lots. Welfarists contend this contributes to lameness problems in dairy cattle. Lameness is a major reason for cows to be culled (killed) during the raising process. Experts studying downed animals (those that cannot stand and walk because of injury or illness) arriving at slaughterhouses report that a large percentage of downers are dairy cows.

Veal

Veal is meat from young calves that are raised in a way that produces tender, light-colored flesh. This meat is highly prized for its pale color and delicate flavor. According to the American Veal Association, in "Industry Information: Facts" (2008, http://www.vealfarm.com/industry-info/facts.asp), veal farmers purchase unwanted calves from the dairy industry (mostly male Holstein calves) and raise them to the desired weight.

The Cattlemen's Beef Board and National Cattlemen's Beef Association (2008, http://www.veal.org/Content/Veal101Veal.aspx) explains that there are three main types of veal:

- Special-fed veal calves are fed a nutritionally complete milk supplement until they reach 18 to 20 weeks of age and typically weigh from 400 to 450 pounds [181 to 204 kg]. The meat is ivory or creamy pink, with a firm, fine and velvety texture. Approximately 85% of the veal consumed in the U.S. is special-fed veal. This is the veal industry's premium product.

- Bob veal calves are fed milk. They usually weigh less than 150 pounds [68 kg] and are approximately three weeks old when marketed. The meat has a light-pink color and a soft texture.

- Grain-fed veal calves are initially fed milk, and then receive a diet of grain, hay and nutrition formulas. The meat tends to be darker in color and has additional marbling and often visible fat. Grain-fed veal calves are usually marketed at 5 to 6 months of age and weigh from 450 to 600 pounds [204 to 272 kg].

THE CONTROVERSY. Veal production is harshly criticized by both animal rights supporters and welfarists. They view the early separation of calves from their mothers and the extremely confined conditions under which the calves live as inhumane. Calves are usually kept in narrow stalls or boxes that prevent them from turning around and are allowed no exercise that would help them build muscle. Also, critics accuse producers of feeding the calves diets that are extremely low in iron to prevent the flesh from darkening. This results in anemic calves that suffer from health problems and stress brought on by their living conditions. The British government has banned the use of veal crates that do not allow a calf to turn around and requires that calves be fed a diet containing sufficient iron and fiber.

American veal producers defend the use of individual stalls to raise their calves. They point out that this method reduces the spread of disease by preventing interaction among the calves. Each calf receives its own feed and does not have to compete with others for food. Also, each calf can receive individual attention to its nutrition and health needs. The American Veal Association claims in "Industry Information" that the stalls are designed so that calves "can comfortably lay in a natural position, stand up, groom themselves and interact with their neighbors."

In November 2006 Arizona voters passed a measure banning the use of confining crates for veal calves. It was the first state ban of its kind. In November 2008 an HSUS-backed legislative initiative called Proposition 2 was passed by California voters that outlaws the caging of farm animals in such a manner that the animals cannot stand, turn around, lie down, or fully extend their limbs. This law goes into effect in 2015 and will prohibit the use of very restrictive veal crates.

CONSUMPTION OF VEAL. Figure 4.9 shows annual consumption data for veal on a per capita basis. In *Data Sets: Food Availability*, the ERS notes that Americans consumed only 0.3 pounds (0.1 kg) of veal per person during 2007, down from a high of 8.4 pounds (3.8 kg) per person in 1944.

Cattle Slaughter

Cattle killed at federally inspected slaughterhouses are required by law to be killed humanely. In most plants the preferred method is use of a stun gun. Cattle are directed single-file through chutes that lead to the stunner. As each animal passes by, the stunner shoots a stun bolt into the animal's forehead to render it unconscious.

The animal is then hoisted up by one rear leg to hang from a bleed rail. At that time, its throat is cut so that the blood can drain out. Federal law requires that no animal fall into the blood of other slaughtered animals. This is why bloodletting is performed while the animal is suspended in the air. Following bloodletting, the animal moves down the line to a number of processing stations where the tail and hocks are cut off, the belly is cut open, and the hide is removed.

SPECIALLY DESIGNED METHODS. Temple Grandin (1947–) of Colorado State University is a renowned expert on cattle handling and slaughter. She maintains a comprehensive Web site (http://www.grandin.com) that provides information on this subject. Grandin designed the systems

FIGURE 4.9

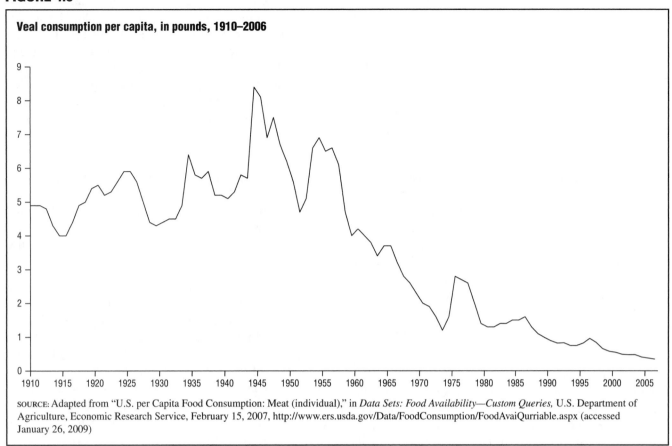

Veal consumption per capita, in pounds, 1910–2006

SOURCE: Adapted from "U.S. per Capita Food Consumption: Meat (individual)," in *Data Sets: Food Availability—Custom Queries,* U.S. Department of Agriculture, Economic Research Service, February 15, 2007, http://www.ers.usda.gov/Data/FoodConsumption/FoodAvaiQurriable.aspx (accessed January 26, 2009)

in use at most U.S. slaughterhouses and has written many guidance documents for the AMI.

Grandin suffers from autism and says it allows her to see the world "in pictures," as animals see it. She has published many books and articles on the proper design of livestock chute systems. For example, chutes must be curved to trick the animals into thinking they are going back to where they came. The chutes must have high walls to keep the animals from seeing what is going on around them. Each animal should only see the rear end of the animal in front of it as it walks toward the stunner.

Grandin's recommendations are designed to keep cattle moving efficiently and peacefully. This has both economic and welfare benefits. Cattle that balk (refuse to move ahead or try to go back down a chute) hold up production. Also, animals that panic are believed to release stress chemicals that taint their meat. Therefore, it is in the best interest of producers that their cattle remain calm in the slaughterhouse. Maintaining quiet and calm also leads to less stress for the animals, which is of importance to animal welfarists.

Grandin says that she is often asked if animals entering the slaughterhouse know they are about to die. She believes the animals do not suspect their fate, because if they did, they would all balk and panic. She reports that cattle will calmly walk into restraining devices covered with the blood of other cattle, as long as the previous cattle were also calm. However, cattle will refuse to approach a location in which a stressed animal has been killed. Grandin believes that animals that become agitated for several minutes release fear pheromones that other animals can smell.

In "Animal Welfare Audits for Cattle, Pigs, and Chickens That Use the HACCP Principles of Critical Control Points" (October 2007, http://www.grandin.com/welfare.audit .using.haccp.html), Grandin discusses an audit procedure with which slaughterhouses can be graded on how well they meet AMI guidelines. The audit procedure centers on five main performance categories that can be graded numerically:

- Stunning proficiency (the number of cattle stunned correctly on the first try)

- Insensibility on the bleed rail (the number of cattle that are still breathing, moving their eyes or blinking, making sounds, or trying to lift themselves up)

- Electric prod usage (the number of cattle that are prodded to keep them moving and the manner in which the prodding is performed)

- Slipping and falling cattle (the number of cattle that slip and fall while they are being moved through the plant)

- Vocalizing cattle (the number of cattle that moo, bellow, or make some other noise during handling and stunning)

In addition, the auditor assesses how the plant handles nonambulatory animals (downers), the condition of flooring and pens, truck unloading and handling procedures, the presence of drinking water in the pens, problems with overcrowding, and the general health condition of the cattle at the plant.

Grandin reports in "Survey of Stunning and Handling in Federally Inspected Beef, Veal, Pork, and Sheep Slaughter Plants" (January 7, 1997, http://www.grandin.com/survey/usdarpt.html), an audit she did for the USDA in 1996 of 10 federally inspected slaughterhouses in various states, that only three of the plants were able to stun at least 95% of the cattle with a single shot. She also describes problems with poor equipment maintenance, lack of management supervision, excessive use of electric prods, transport of downed animals with forklifts, and other such practices.

Grandin notes in "Corporations Can Be Agents of Great Improvements in Animal Welfare and Food Safety and the Need for Minimum Decent Standards" (April 4, 2001, http://www.grandin.com/welfare/corporation.agents.html) that in 1999 she was hired by McDonald's Corporation to audit the company's beef and pork suppliers for their compliance with the standards. She states that compliance greatly improved after McDonald's fired a supplier that failed the audit. For example, 90% of the plants audited after that firing were able to stun at least 95% of the cattle with a single shot. In addition, the use of electric prods was reduced or eliminated, and most abusive behavior by employees stopped.

Between 2001 and 2008 Grandin oversaw audits conducted for restaurants at dozens of beef and pork plants. The most recent audit findings as of mid-2009 were "2007 Restaurant Animal Welfare and Humane Slaughter Audits in Federally Inspected Beef and Pork Slaughter Plants in the U.S. and Canada" (2007, http://www.grandin.com/survey/2007.restaurant.audits.html) and "2008 Restaurant Animal Welfare and Humane Slaughter Audits in Federally Inspected Beef and Pork Slaughter Plants in the U.S. and Canada" (2008, http://www.grandin.com/survey/2008.restaurant.audits.html).

In 2007, 44 beef plants in the United States were audited. Grandin reports that 91% of the plants received excellent or acceptable scores on all audit criteria. One plant failed the audit for using electric prods on cattle inappropriately. Another plant failed for cutting the leg off of a cow that was still conscious. The latter incident was blamed on poor employee training by plant management. Overall, 28 of the plants stunned 99% to 100% of their cattle with the first captive bolt shot.

In 2008, 32 U.S. and Canadian beef plants were audited. Eight of the plants (25%) failed the audit. The failures were due to excessive use of electric prods, high vocalization scores, high rates of cattle falling and slipping, and mishandling of cattle by slaughterhouse employees. One plant failed because an animal on the bleed rail appeared to be partially sensible. Overall, 24 of the plants were able to stun 99% to 100% of their cattle with only one captive bolt shot.

Grandin notes that better stunning technology and equipment maintenance have led to continuous improvements in the audits she has conducted over the years. She warns plants that they must have zero tolerance for hoisting, skinning, or cutting any animal showing any obvious signs of sensibility or even partial return to sensibility after stunning.

PROBLEMS WITH THE PROCESS? Stories in the media since the late 1990s have exposed some problems with slaughterhouse procedures. In "'They Die Piece by Piece': In Overtaxed Plants, Humane Treatment of Cattle Is Often a Battle Lost" (*Washington Post*, April 10, 2001), Joby Warrick analyzed USDA records and conducted interviews with current and former slaughterhouse workers and federal inspectors. The workers, who made about $9 an hour, claimed to have seen many conscious cattle moving down the bleed rail.

A worker responsible for cutting off the cattle's hocks reported that dozens of conscious animals reached his station each day. He said the animals were blinking, moving, looking around, and making noises. Other workers also reported having to cut into living cattle. Workers in charge of stunning complained that the line moved so fast that they did not have time to do their job properly.

Warrick notes that the USDA had relaxed its oversight of slaughtering plants since 1998 and did not track the number of humane slaughter violations that occur each year. A records review, however, showed that inspectors found 527 violations between 1996 and 1997, including incidents in which "live animals were cut, skinned, or scalded."

Warrick reports that footage from hidden cameras at slaughterhouses show blinking cattle hanging from bleed rails. Other cattle twist, turn, and arch their backs as if trying to pull themselves upright. Footage also shows squealing hogs being lowered into the scalding water baths that are designed to soften the hides of dead animals. Industry officials claim that the videotaped incidents were staged by disgruntled employees and that unconscious animals kick and twitch by reflex.

Live animals on the bleed rail are a danger to line workers. According to Warrick, many workers are kicked by the animals and suffer broken bones and teeth. Even though the line is supposed to be stopped when a conscious animal is detected, workers said this does not happen.

Animal welfare activists say the allegations made by Warrick are not unusual. They blame many of the problems on the extremely fast line speed at slaughterhouses and the use of low-paid workers. According to Warrick, most plants process around 400 animals per hour. This figure has increased eightfold since the early 1900s.

Another major concern of welfarists relates to the problem of downed animals. Downed animals are primarily dairy cattle that collapse from illness, injury, or other causes. They may be tossed alive onto trash heaps, or dragged by chains or pushed by forklifts around stockyards and slaughterhouses. Animal welfare organizations consider the processing of these animals inhumane and have tried unsuccessfully since the 1990s to achieve legislation called the Downed Animal Protection Act, which would require that critically ill or injured farm animals be humanely euthanized at the stockyards. In December 2003 a downer cow in Washington State tested positive for bovine spongiform encephalopathy (BSE), commonly known as mad cow disease. This is an extremely serious disease in cattle. It has been linked to a similar fatal disease in humans believed to have eaten beef contaminated with BSE. The USDA promptly announced a ban on the processing of downer cattle for human consumption unless the downers are deemed fit for slaughter by an on-site federal veterinarian.

In 2008 a downer scandal at the Westland/Hallmark Meat Company in Chino, California, made national headlines. Andrew Martin reports in "Largest Recall of Ground Beef Is Ordered" (*New York Times*, February 18, 2008) that undercover video taken at the plant by the HSUS showed plant employees using forklifts to move cows that were too sick to walk to the slaughter line. The incident prompted the USDA to force the company to recall 143 million pounds (64.9 million kg) of beef that had been processed at the plant since 2006—the largest beef recall in history at that time. USDA officials admitted that most of the meat being recalled had probably already been eaten. The company reportedly supplied beef to the national school lunch program and two fast-food restaurants: Jack-in-the-Box and In-N-Out. The USDA noted that the plant failed to notify federal veterinarians about the downed cattle.

In May 2008 the USDA proposed a regulation that would ban all downers from the food supply, thereby eliminating the loophole that had previously allowed a federal veterinarian to determine the fitness of downers for slaughter. According to Andrew Martin, in "U.S. Moves to Prohibit Beef from Sick or Injured Cows" (*New York Times*, May 21, 2008), the U.S. secretary of agriculture Edward T. Schafer (1946–) noted that "cattle producers, transporters and slaughter establishments alike will be encouraged to enhance humane handling practices, as there will no longer be any market for cattle that are too weak to rise or walk on their own." In March 2009 President Barack Obama (1961–) announced that the ban had been adopted.

In September 2008 two former workers at the plant had been sentenced to jail terms for their roles in the scandal. One of the workers pleaded "no contest" to felony charges of animal abuse and misdemeanor charges of abuse to a downed animal. He received a nine-month sentence. The second worker pleaded guilty to misdemeanor charges of illegal movement of a nonambulatory animal and was given a six-month sentence.

RITUAL SLAUGHTER. The Humane Methods of Slaughter Act has exceptions for ritual slaughter—that is, slaughter conducted according to religious dictates. Ritual slaughter is practiced by some orthodox Jews and Muslims. Their teachings require that animals killed for food be moving and healthy when they are killed by having their throats slit. This was originally intended to ensure that sick animals were not eaten by humans. Meat from animals killed in this manner is said to be kosher in Jewish tradition and halal in Muslim tradition. Regarding ritual slaughter, the Humane Methods of Slaughter Act does require "simultaneous and instantaneous" cutting of the throat arteries "with a sharp instrument" to render the animal insensible (unconscious).

Animal welfarists complain that strict interpretation of the directives for ritual slaughter means that cattle are not stunned before being bled out. They may be jerked up to the bleed rail by a hind leg while still fully conscious. The jerking action can break the leg and tear apart joints, causing them severe pain. Their thrashing makes it more difficult for the cutter to cleanly cut their throats, which prolongs the entire process.

There are upright restraining devices that hold animals more humanely while their throats are being cut. The AMI strongly recommends the use of these devices, both for the welfare of the animals and the safety of the plant workers. Grandin and Gary C. Smith report in "Animal Welfare and Humane Slaughter" (November 2004, http://www.grandin.com/references/humane.slaughter.html) that throat cutting must be done precisely with a long razor-sharp knife to induce "near-immediate collapse." Otherwise, the animal can remain conscious for more than a minute. Animals that struggle against their restraints or become agitated stay conscious the longest.

Singer states in *Animal Liberation* that critics of ritual slaughter are often accused of being racist or anti-Semitic. He points out that parts of ritually killed animals wind up on supermarket shelves and are purchased by people who may not be aware of how the animal was killed. This is because Jewish law requires the removal of the lymph nodes and sciatic nerve from cattle. Singer says that this is difficult to do efficiently on the hindquarters of cattle, so often only the front portion is sold as kosher. The hindquarters are processed and sold in usual commercial markets.

In "Inquiry Finds Lax Federal Inspections at Kosher Meat Plant" (*New York Times*, March 10, 2006), Donald G. McNeil Jr. reports on an animal welfare controversy involving AgriProcessors Inc., a kosher slaughterhouse in Postville, Iowa. In 2004 an undercover investigator for People for the Ethical Treatment of Animals (PETA) captured video of cattle not being rendered unconscious by throat slitting. However, workers immediately used hooks to pull out the trachea and esophagus of each animal. This practice vastly speeds up the bleeding process. The video shows steers thrashing about for up to three minutes before passing out. According to McNeil, the video's release spurred outrage among Jewish organizations around the world—outrage at PETA for allegedly being "anti-Semitic" and at the processing plant for causing animal suffering. The plant has reportedly altered its slaughtering procedures since the issue became public.

A resulting six-month investigation by the USDA found that its inspectors at the plant knew that the practice was going on but ignored it because they assumed the USDA had no say over ritual slaughter techniques. In addition, the inspectors had accepted free gifts of meat from employees at the slaughter plant. In response, the agency suspended one of the inspectors for two weeks and issued warning letters to two other inspectors. McNeil reports that PETA learned about the USDA investigation only after PETA obtained a copy of the USDA inspector general's report under the Freedom of Information Act.

POULTRY

Poultry are domesticated birds cultivated for their eggs or meat. This includes chickens, turkeys, geese, and ducks. Chickens are by far the most common type of poultry raised in the United States. In 2007, 8.9 billion broilers and 349.8 million laying hens were produced in the United States. (See Table 4.2.) The sale of poultry and poultry products was valued at more than $30 billion in 2007, with broilers providing the bulk of the value. (See Figure 4.10.)

Chickens

Chickens were originally domesticated from wild Asian jungle fowl. In natural conditions chickens tend to live in small groups composed of one male chicken (called a rooster or cock) and a dozen or more female chickens (called hens). Chickens are known for their hierarchy, or "pecking order." Each member of the group has a particular rank that determines its place in society. The average natural lifespan of a chicken is 6 to 10 years, although they can live as long as 25 years.

Chickens are omnivores, meaning that they will feed on both vegetable and animal substances. They spend a good part of their day foraging and pecking at the ground for food. They also like to perch, flap their wings, and take dust baths. Hens prefer to lay eggs in a private nest. Young

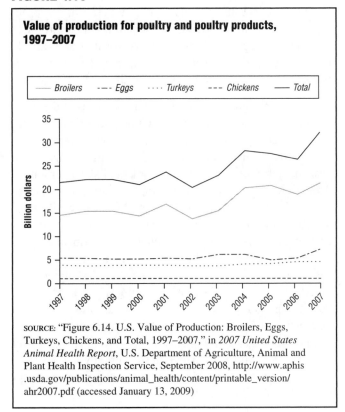

FIGURE 4.10

Value of production for poultry and poultry products, 1997–2007

SOURCE: "Figure 6.14. U.S. Value of Production: Broilers, Eggs, Turkeys, Chickens, and Total, 1997–2007," in *2007 United States Animal Health Report*, U.S. Department of Agriculture, Animal and Plant Health Inspection Service, September 2008, http://www.aphis.usda.gov/publications/animal_health/content/printable_version/ahr2007.pdf (accessed January 13, 2009)

hens above the age of five months produce 200 to 300 eggs per year. Unless the hen has recently mated with a rooster, however, the egg is infertile and does not develop into a chick. In the wild the hen would leave infertile eggs to rot or be eaten by predators.

CHICKEN BECOMES BIG BUSINESS. Before the 1920s chicken meat was not common in the American diet. Female chickens were valued on the farm for egg production. Besides being sometimes used for cockfighting, male chickens were not considered valuable. They were relatively scrawny and aggressive. This began to change in the 1920s, when enterprising farmers started cultivating chickens for meat. Scientific advances led to chicken breeds that were much meatier and grew faster. The use of vitamins, antibiotics, and growth hormones allowed mass production of chickens to become a thriving business. In the 1950s producers began using large CAFOs. This became the preferred method for raising chickens.

CHICKEN WELFARE CONCERNS. Chickens raised in crowded conditions are prone to aggression. They peck and claw at each other, which can cause feather loss and injury. Injured chickens may be pecked to death and even eaten by other chickens. As such, it is a common practice in the factory farming of chickens to debeak a certain percentage of chickens by removing part of the upper and/or lower beak. Toe clipping involves cutting off parts of the chicken claw. Producers explain these practices are for the good of the chickens because it spares them from becoming injured.

They claim the chickens do not experience any pain because beaks are similar to human fingernails.

United Poultry Concerns (UPC) is a nonprofit group that advocates for the humane treatment of domestic poultry. The UPC claims in "Debeaking Birds Has Got to Stop" (*Poultry Press*, vol. 17, no. 3, Winter 2007) that scientific studies show that chicken beaks contain nerves and pain receptors. Thus, debeaked chickens suffer pain, as noted by one experiment, which found that newborn chicks "were said to 'vocalize' in response to an increase in 'energy density' indicating they were feeling 'discomfort.'" The UPC notes that some types of debeaking techniques do not work properly the first time, so newborn chicks must go through the process a second time.

Animal welfarists say debeaking and toe clipping would not be necessary if chickens were raised in more natural environments. They believe it is the stress of living in cramped cages in buildings housing tens of thousands of other chickens that drives chickens to demonstrate aggressive behavior. Welfarists suggest that producers accommodate these brutal systems by mutilating the chickens instead of changing the way in which chickens are raised.

Chicken producers defend these practices as necessary. The National Chicken Council (NCC) is an industry organization for companies that produce, process, and market chickens. The NCC's voluntary *Animal Welfare Guidelines and Audit Checklist* (April 5, 2005, http://www.nationalchickencouncil.com/files/AnimalWelfare2005.pdf) states: "Today's chicken has been purposefully selected to thrive under modern management. We believe current good management practices that avoid destructive behavior, prevent disease, and promote good health and production are consistent with the generally accepted criteria of humane treatment."

BROILERS. Chicken meat is extremely popular in the United States. In *Data Sets: Food Availability*, the ERS indicates that the annual per capita consumption increased from 10.4 pounds (4.7 kg) per person in 1910 to 59.9 pounds (27.2 kg) per person in 2007. Billions of broilers are raised and slaughtered each year to keep up with the demand for chicken meat. Broiler production has increased dramatically over the last 46 years, from approximately 2 billion head in 1960 to 9 billion head in 2006. (See Figure 4.11.)

Broiler-type chicks are bred to gain weight fast. They start their lives at hatcheries. Day-old chicks are moved into chicken houses that may be hundreds of feet long and contain tens of thousands of chickens. These buildings are windowless and usually have dim lighting, because this is considered more calming. In modern chicken houses food and water are dispensed by machine. Chicks are vaccinated against common poultry diseases. Broilers are routinely given antibiotics and other drugs to overcome disease and speed up growth.

FIGURE 4.11

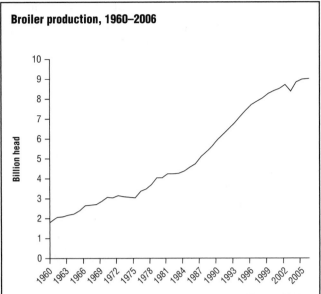

Broiler production, 1960–2006

SOURCE: "Figure 6.15A. U.S. Broiler Production, 1960–2006," in *2007 United States Animal Health Report*, U.S. Department of Agriculture, Animal and Plant Health Inspection Service, September 2008, http://www.aphis.usda.gov/publications/animal_health/content/printable_version/ahr2007.pdf (accessed January 13, 2009)

The NCC specifies in *Animal Welfare Guidelines and Audit Checklist* that bird density should not exceed 8.5 pounds per square foot (3.9 kg per 929 square cm) of living space. Because a typical broiler weighs 4 to 5 pounds (1.2 to 2.3 kg) at slaughter weight, two birds of this size would have approximately 1 square foot (929 square cm) of space under this system. The NCC also recommends that broilers not be debeaked unless they are used for breeding purposes.

LAYING HENS. Laying hens, or layers, are chickens specifically bred for their egg-laying abilities, rather than for meat production. There were 349.8 million layers on U.S. farms during 2007. (See Table 4.2.) These chickens produced 91 billion eggs that year. (See Figure 4.12.) This value is up dramatically from the early 1960s, when 63 billion eggs were produced by layers annually. However, egg consumption per capita in the United States has declined sharply since the 1940s, from a peak of 421.4 eggs per person in 1945 to 256.8 eggs per person in 2006. (See Figure 4.13.) Processed eggs (pasteurized and packaged nonshell eggs) have been steadily increasing since the 1960s because of demand from food manufacturers and restaurants.

In "The HSUS's Campaign to Ban Battery Cages" (April 2, 2009, http://www.hsus.org/farm/camp/nbe/), the HSUS calls laying hens "the most abused animals in all agribusiness." Animal protection groups are highly critical of three common practices in the factory farming of laying hens: killing male chicks, forced molting, and use of battery cages.

Laying-hen chicks are sorted by gender when they are one day old. Only the females are kept. The males are killed because they have not been bred for meat production and will not grow up to be meaty enough for human consumption. According to animal rights groups, millions of culled male chicks are thrown into garbage bags, where they suffocate. The poultry industry does not generally discuss its methods of culling male chicks, but it is widely believed that methods including suffocation and maceration (instantaneous death in a high-speed grinder) are commonly used.

Under natural conditions hens can lay eggs for more than a decade, but egg-laying production of hens in factory farms ceases dramatically after the first year. One method used by producers to rejuvenate laying is forced molting, in which all food is withheld from the hens for either a set number of days (usually 5 to 14), or until the hens lose a particular amount of weight. This forced fast mimics the conditions that wild chickens experience in the fall or winter, when food is not as plentiful. Lower food intake causes a hen to molt (lose her feathers). Also, her reproductive system temporarily ceases producing eggs. When food is fully restored, the hen is much more productive at making eggs than she was before.

Animal welfarists are extremely critical of forced molting, saying that because all food is withheld from the hens, it is much more brutal than natural molting. They equate the practice to forced starvation and note that food deprivation for the purpose of forced molting is banned in Europe.

FIGURE 4.12

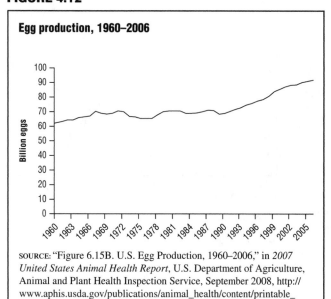

Egg production, 1960–2006

SOURCE: "Figure 6.15B. U.S. Egg Production, 1960–2006," in *2007 United States Animal Health Report*, U.S. Department of Agriculture, Animal and Plant Health Inspection Service, September 2008, http://www.aphis.usda.gov/publications/animal_health/content/printable_version/ahr2007.pdf (accessed January 13, 2009)

FIGURE 4.13

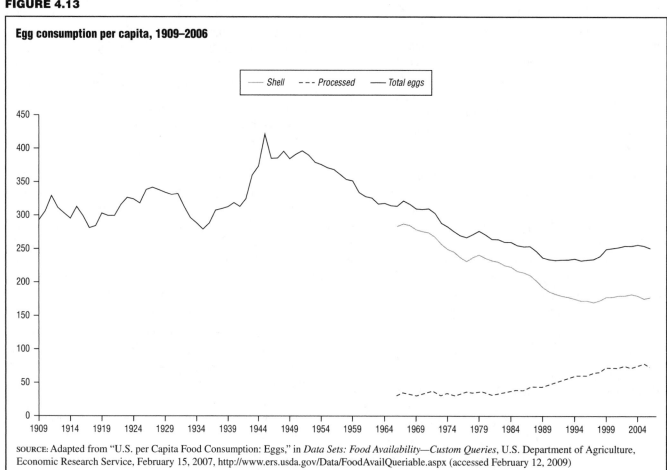

Egg consumption per capita, 1909–2006

SOURCE: Adapted from "U.S. per Capita Food Consumption: Eggs," in *Data Sets: Food Availability—Custom Queries*, U.S. Department of Agriculture, Economic Research Service, February 15, 2007, http://www.ers.usda.gov/Data/FoodAvailQueriable.aspx (accessed February 12, 2009)

The United Egg Producers states in *United Egg Producers Animal Husbandry Guidelines for U.S. Egg Laying Flocks* (2008, http://www.uepcertified.com/media/pdf/UEP-Animal-Welfare-Guidelines.pdf) that approximately 95% of all commercial laying hens in the United States are confined to plain-wire cages called battery cages. Animal welfarists complain the cages are so small that the birds cannot spread their wings or engage in nesting, perching, and other natural behaviors. In "HSUS's Campaign to Ban Battery Cages," the HSUS states that battery cages have been banned in Austria, Germany, Sweden, and Switzerland, and will be phased out throughout the European Union by 2012. Many animal welfare organizations urge consumers to buy eggs only from cage-free chickens. However, the HSUS notes that even cage-free chickens may suffer from welfare problems, including overcrowding within buildings, lack of access to the outdoors, debeaking, and/or forced molting.

Proposition 2, which was passed by California voters in November 2008, will profoundly affect the way in which chickens are caged in that state beginning in 2015. The new law will outlaw the caging of farm animals in such a manner that the animals cannot stand, turn around, lie down, or fully extend their limbs. Carla Hill reports in "Prop. 2 Probably Won't Hike Egg Prices" (*Los Angeles Times*, November 6, 2008) that Proposition 2 will affect 20 million layers that produce approximately 5 billion eggs yearly. It is estimated that the requirement will increase the production costs for California egg farmers by 20%. It is not anticipated to raise the price of eggs in the state, because out-of-state producers are expected to increase their supply to California. However, an analysis by the Agricultural Issues Center of the University of California, Davis, does not bode well for the state's egg farmers. Daniel Sumner notes that "the most likely outcome" of Proposition 2 will be "the elimination of almost all of the California egg industry over a few years."

CHICKEN SLAUGHTER. When they are ready to go to the slaughterhouse, chickens are gathered by their feet by handlers, who carry them upside down to put into crates. At the slaughterhouse the chickens are shackled upside down by their feet to a conveyor belt. The Humane Methods of Slaughter Act does not apply to poultry, which means that chickens do not have to be stunned unconscious before having their throats slit. Some plants do, however, use a stunning method based on the availability of electricity.

Each live chicken strapped to the conveyor belt has its head dunked into a water bath containing salt. An electric current is passed through the shackles to knock the chicken unconscious. Then the birds pass by an automated cutting blade that slits their throat. After the blood is drained (which takes about 90 seconds), the birds are dipped into scalding water baths to loosen their feathers before moving on to cutting stations.

In "Employee Describes Deliberate Torture of Chickens at Tyson Slaughter Plant" (*Poultry Press*, vol. 13, no. 1, Spring 2003), the UPC reports that in January 2003 PETA obtained a signed affidavit from Virgil Butler, who used to work at a chicken slaughterhouse in Arkansas from 1997 to 2002. Butler claimed to have witnessed many acts of brutality toward the birds, saying that other workers regularly ran over chickens with forklifts, stomped them to death, and even "rip[ped] the heads, legs, and wings off of live chickens." He also claimed that chickens were often not stunned or killed before entering the scalding baths. Butler described working one night when equipment breakdowns delayed the conveyor belt and allowed stunned chickens to wake up before their throats were slit. The workers did not have time to do the slitting, so they sent the chickens straight to the scalding baths.

As noted earlier, Grandin conducts audits of slaughter facilities. As of April 2009, her most recent audit results for chicken slaughter facilities were from 2005. During that year Grandin oversaw an audit based on NCC standards of 19 poultry plants. Her findings are reported in "2005 Poultry Welfare Audits: National Chicken Council Animal Welfare Audit for Poultry Has a Scoring System That Is Too Lax and Allows Slaughter Plants with Abusive Practices to Pass" (April 2, 2006, http://www.grandin.com/survey/2005.poultry.audits.html). Grandin is highly critical of the NCC standards and reports that five of the plants passed the audit even though they had committed "serious abuses." These incidents included four birds that had been scalded while still alive, operators throwing birds during handling, and a live bird found in the trash. Grandin points out that she oversaw a poultry audit at 26 plants during 2005 for a client with much higher animal welfare standards and found that none of the plants audited engaged in serious abuses. She concludes, "When plants are required to uphold a higher standard, they are capable of doing it. Unfortunately, there are some people in the producer community who want to make standards so low that even the worst places can pass."

Turkeys

Turkeys are one of the few domesticated animals native to North America. However, present-day turkeys have little resemblance to their wild ancestors. Modern turkeys are bred to gain weight quickly, particularly in the breast. Turkeys are raised much the same way that broiler chickens are raised. At around six weeks of age, the baby birds are moved into growing houses in which they spend the remainder of their lives. Conditions there are crowded, as they are for chickens, and can lead to feather-pecking and cannibalism. Turkeys are slaughtered similarly to chickens at around three to six months of age. Figure 4.14 shows that U.S. turkey production grew steadily from 1960 to the 1990s, peaking at around 300 million turkeys per year in the late 1990s. Production

FIGURE 4.14

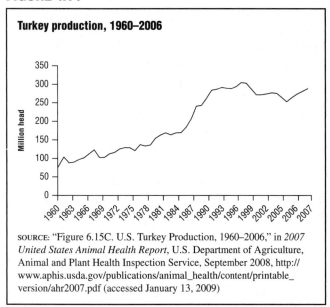

Turkey production, 1960–2006

SOURCE: "Figure 6.15C. U.S. Turkey Production, 1960–2006," in *2007 United States Animal Health Report*, U.S. Department of Agriculture, Animal and Plant Health Inspection Service, September 2008, http://www.aphis.usda.gov/publications/animal_health/content/printable_version/ahr2007.pdf (accessed January 13, 2009)

fell to around 250 million turkeys by 2005 and then began to rebound, reaching nearly 300 million turkeys in 2007.

Ducks and Geese

Domestic ducks and geese are raised for their meat, eggs, and feathers. Most ducks are raised indoors, similarly to chickens, and are fed fortified corn and soybeans. Geese are raised in covered enclosures for the first six weeks of their lives and then allowed to forage for grass in fields. Most ducks are raised in Wisconsin and Indiana, whereas most geese are raised in California and South Dakota. Federal law prohibits the use of hormones in duck and goose production. Ducks and geese are slaughtered with electrocution baths followed by throat slitting.

Duck and geese products are mostly sold in specialty markets. The tongues and feet of the animals are considered a delicacy in parts of Asia (particularly Hong Kong) and are also sold in Asian-American markets. High-value products from ducks and geese include down feathers, smoked meat products, liver pâté (paste), and foie gras (pronounced *fwah grah*, meaning "fat liver" in French).

FOIE GRAS CONTROVERSY. Foie gras is obtained by force-feeding male ducks and geese a rich mixture containing corn, fat, salt, and water over a short amount of time. This regimen causes the birds' livers to become fatty and hugely swollen, six to 10 times their normal size.

The feeding process, called gavage, is usually started two to four weeks before slaughter. It is accomplished using an electronic pump that forces food through a 12- to 16-inch tube that is placed down the bird's throat. The birds are force-fed several times a day and held in cramped cages or pens so that they cannot move. This prevents them from losing weight during the fattening process.

Animal welfarists are highly critical of gavage. The HSUS states that the birds suffer pain from swollen abdomens and lesions in their throats. It also says that autopsies conducted on birds subjected to gavage show severe liver, heart, and esophagus disorders.

Foie gras is a gourmet delicacy that is expensive, selling for up to $50 per pound. It is available at upscale restaurants and specialty stores. Most foie gras comes from France. As of April 2009, there were only two commercial producers of foie gras in the United States—Hudson Valley Foie Gras of Ferndale, New York, and Sonoma Foie Gras of Sonoma, California—and both process duck livers. The producers defend the use of the gavage process, saying that it does not gag the birds because they do not chew their food anyway.

In 2004 the California governor Arnold Schwarzenegger (1947–) signed a bill into law that will ban by 2012 the force feeding of ducks and geese to produce foie gras and ban the sale of the product in California. In 2006 the Chicago City Council passed an ordinance banning the sale of foie gras within the city limits. According to the HSUS, in "Force-Fed Abuse" (2009, http://www.hsus.org/farm/camp/ffa/), the production of foie gras has been banned in over a dozen countries, including Denmark, Finland, Germany, Israel, Norway, Poland, Sweden, Switzerland, and the United Kingdom.

HOGS AND PIGS

Hogs and pigs are domesticated swine. A pig is a young swine that is not yet sexually mature. A young female hog is called a gilt. A female adult hog is called a sow. The generic term *hog* is generally used to refer to all hogs. Hogs are curious and intelligent animals, supposedly smarter than dogs. They have sensitive noses, which they use to root around the ground for their food and explore their surroundings. Pregnant sows like to build nests of grass. Under natural conditions sows give birth to (or farrow) a litter of piglets twice per year. Each litter averages eight piglets that suckle for about three months. The normal life expectancy of a hog is 12 to 15 years.

Modern Hog Industry

Hogs have been popular farm animals for centuries. In *Part III: Changes in the U.S. Pork Industry, 1990–1995* (October 1997, http://www.aphis.usda.gov/vs/ceah/ncahs/nahms/swine/swine95/sw95Pt3.pdf), the Animal and Plant Health Inspection Service (APHIS) reports that the 1850 agricultural census showed an inventory of 30.4 million hogs. This number increased to 62.9 million hogs by 1900. Furthermore, in "The USDA's Role in Equine Health Monitoring" (June 1996, http://www.aphis.usda.gov/vs/ceah/ncahs/nahms/equine/equine98/eqrole.pdf), APHIS notes that 76% of U.S. farms produced hogs in 1900. Hogs were favored because hog meat and fat were so versatile.

FIGURE 4.15

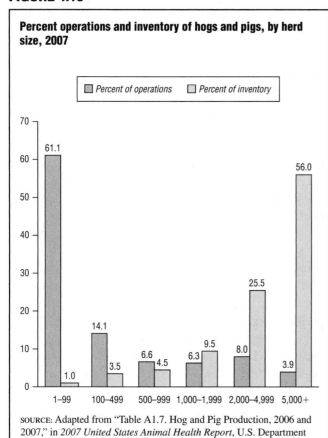

Percent operations and inventory of hogs and pigs, by herd size, 2007

SOURCE: Adapted from "Table A1.7. Hog and Pig Production, 2006 and 2007," in *2007 United States Animal Health Report*, U.S. Department of Agriculture, Animal and Plant Health Inspection Service, September 2008, http://www.aphis.usda.gov/publications/animal_health/content/printable_version/ahr2007.pdf (accessed January 13, 2009)

Pork could be canned, smoked, or cured to provide food for long periods of time. Lard (the fat produced from hogs) was widely used as cooking oil and in making candles.

The total U.S. hog inventory in 2007 was 67.8 million. (See Table 4.2.) Just over 61% of all hog farms had less than 100 hogs in 2007. (See Figure 4.15.) Only 3.9% of all hog farms raised 5,000 hogs or more. However, 56% of all hogs in the United States lived on farms that raised 5,000 hogs or more. The vast majority of hogs raised in the United States are concentrated on a few massive CAFOs. These facilities not only finish the hogs, as is done in the cattle industry, but also raise them. Major pork producers operate farrowing complexes, nurseries, and growing-feeding units.

The annual per capita consumption of pork products in the United States has changed less than the consumption of beef and chicken over the past century but still rose by about 20%. (See Figure 4.3.) In *Data Sets: Food Availability*, the ERS indicates that in 1910 the annual consumption was 38.2 pounds (17.3 kg) per person; by 2007 it was 47.3 pounds (21.5 kg) per person.

Hog-Raising Practices

Confinement buildings for hogs can be hundreds of feet long and contain up to 12,000 hogs. They typically feature concrete or slatted floors—concrete floors can be easily cleaned and slatted floors allow manure and urine to fall into pits below. Hogs are kept on short tethers or confined in cages and pens to prevent them from getting exercise, which might build muscle instead of fat and toughen the meat. Crowded conditions can lead to aggressive behavior among the hogs, including tail chewing, biting, and fighting. Tail docking and teeth clipping are commonly practiced to help prevent injuries from these behaviors. Antibiotics, hormones, and other drugs are routinely administered to speed growth and prevent deadly diseases.

GESTATION CRATES. Breeding sows are often kept in individual stalls or confined with tethers until they are ready to farrow. Gestation crates, as they are called, are typically around 7 feet (2.1 m) long and 2 feet (0.6 m) wide—just wide enough for the sow to lie down but not to turn around. The sow eats, urinates, and defecates where she stands. When she is ready to give birth, the sow may be moved to a farrowing pen in which she and her piglets will be kept tightly confined.

The USDA's National Animal Health Monitoring System conducts a national swine survey every five to six years. The report *Swine 2006* (http://www.aphis.usda.gov/vs/ceah/ncahs/nahms/swine/index.htm#swine2006) was published in October 2007. In "Info Sheet: Sow and Gilt Management in Swine 2000 and Swine 2006" (January 2009, http://www.aphis.usda.gov/vs/ceah/ncahs/nahms/swine/swine2006/Swine2006_sowgilt_infosheet.pdf), an excerpt report based on *Swine 2006*, the USDA notes that 2006, 67.7% of sows on U.S. farms were farrowed in total confinement facilities.

Industry officials defend the use of gestation crates, saying that the crates are necessary to keep aggressive sows from fighting with each other over food. Fighting can cause injuries that lead to miscarried fetuses. Pork producers believe caged sows receive beneficial individual attention to their health and nutrition needs. The National Pork Producers Council (2008, http://www.nppc.org/issues/sowhousing.htm) states that it supports gestation crates as a means to minimize aggression between sows and protect them from environmental extremes and exposure to hazards.

The use of gestation crates has been banned in the United Kingdom and Sweden. The European Union plans to phase out use of the crates by 2013. In 2002 Florida voters passed an amendment to the state constitution that outlaws the use of gestation crates. In 2006 and 2007 Arizona and Oregon voters, respectively, passed a similar measure banning the use of gestation crates for pigs. According to the National Pork Producers Council, Colorado pig farmers began a voluntary phase-out of gestation stalls in 2008. California pig farmers are bound by Proposition 2 to eliminate gestation stalls when that legislation goes into effect in 2015.

OTHER PRACTICES. Generally, week-old pigs are subjected to teeth clipping, tail docking, and ear notching. The males are castrated at this time. These procedures are done without anesthesia. Once the piglets reach around 55 pounds (25 kg), they are moved to indoor finishing pens. Piglets are raised to slaughter weight, typically 250 pounds (113 kg), at around four to six months of age. Spent breeding sows are usually slaughtered at around two to three years of age.

Animal welfarists are critical of hog-raising practices in the United States. They consider the intense confinement too stressful for intelligent and social animals such as hogs. They also condemn early weaning as cruel to sows and piglets. Factory-farmed hogs not only suffer from excessive crowding, stress, and boredom but also experience serious breathing disorders because of high concentrations of ammonia from their waste materials. Critics also note that hogs experience feet and leg deformities from standing on floors made of improper materials.

Hog Slaughter

Hogs are generally killed via electrocution or by stunning followed by bleeding out. Electrocution is accomplished by stunning the hog with a wand with sufficient shock to stop its heart. This is called cardiac arrest stunning and is the technique most large hog slaughter plants use. Hogs can also be given an electrical shock to the head to render them unconscious. Next, the animals are hoisted up by their back feet and bled via a small incision in the chest. Fully electrocuted hogs are also bled out in this manner. The dead hogs are then lowered into vats of scalding water to remove hair. The meat can then be processed.

According to Grandin's instructions for electrical stunning, a hog stunned with sufficient amperage in the correct location will feel no pain. Insufficient amperage and an improper current path will cause the animal pain. Grandin recommends that head-stunned hogs be bled out within 30 seconds of being stunned to prevent them from regaining consciousness.

As noted earlier, between 2001 and 2008 Grandin oversaw audits conducted for restaurants at dozens of beef and pork plants. The most recent audit findings as of mid-2009 were "2007 Restaurant Animal Welfare and Humane Slaughter Audits in Federally Inspected Beef and Pork Slaughter Plants in the U.S. and Canada" and "2008 Restaurant Animal Welfare and Humane Slaughter Audits in Federally Inspected Beef and Pork Slaughter Plants in the U.S. and Canada." In 2007, 27 Canadian pork plants were audited. Grandin reports that 92% of the pork plants received excellent or acceptable scores on all audit criteria. One pork plant failed the audit for hanging a conscious pig on the bleed line. The pig was restunned before being bled out. In 2008 23 U.S. pork plants were audited. One of the plants failed the audit due to excessive vocalization from the pigs in the restraining area. However, all the plants rendered all their pigs unconscious before the animals were shackled and hoisted to the bleed rail.

HORSES

APHIS reports in "USDA's Role in Equine Health Monitoring" that approximately 20 million horses lived on U.S. farms in 1900. This number declined significantly over the next century. In *2007 Census of Agriculture*, the USDA notes that there were just over 4 million horses living on 576,000 farms in the United States in 2007. The country's total horse inventory could be much higher, because exact inventories are not known for horses kept for racing, breeding, showing, and pleasure purposes.

Horsemeat Controversy

Banning the slaughter of horses for food is the goal of many animal welfare groups. Even though horses are not specifically cultivated in the United States for human consumption, there is a growing overseas market for this meat, primarily in Europe and Asia. Horsemeat is increasingly popular in these regions because of the scare concerning mad cow disease.

According to APHIS, in "Horse Transport" (October 2005, http://www.aphis.usda.gov/animal_health/animal _dis_spec/horses/horse_transport.shtml), over 2 million horses have been slaughtered between 1989 and 2005. APHIS indicates that some of the horses were blind, lame, or old. The horses were sold at auction terminals and transported in trailers to horse slaughter plants in the United States or Canada. At the time there were only three horse slaughter plants in the United States: two in Texas and one in Illinois. Horses slaughtered in the United States were covered by the Humane Methods of Slaughter Act. They had to be rendered unconscious before being hoisted onto the bleed rail and cut open. Like cattle, horses were stunned by a shot in the head with a bolt gun.

In November 2005 federal legislation was passed that prohibited for one year the use of federal funds for USDA-conducted ante mortem (predeath) inspections of horses at the three U.S. slaughter plants. Animal welfare groups believed this would effectively end horse slaughtering in the United States, because the Federal Meat Inspection Act of 1906 requires such inspections if the meat to be sold is for human consumption. The ban went into effect in March 2006. However, just before its effective date, the horse slaughter industry petitioned the USDA and received permission to conduct privately funded ante mortem inspections at the slaughter plants. Thus, horse slaughtering for human consumption was allowed to continue. The HSUS notes in "HSUS and Others Seek Injunction to Halt USDA in Its Attempt to Buck Congress on Horse Slaughter" (February 22, 2006, http://www.hsus.org/pets/pets_related

_news_and_events/usda_threatens_horse_slaughter.html) that it and several animal organizations and legislators were furious by what they saw as USDA circumvention of the intent of the law that was passed.

The Animal Welfare Institute (AWI; 2009, http://www .awionline.org/legislation/horse_slaughter) notes that in 2007 Texas and Illinois passed laws that closed down all horse slaughter plants in the United States. Regardless, the AWI complains that "tens of thousands" of American horses are shipped to Canada or Mexico for slaughter each year. In January 2009 the Conyers-Burton Prevention of Equine Cruelty Act of 2009 was introduced in the U.S. House of Representatives by Representatives John Conyers Jr. (1929–; D-MI) and Dan Burton (1938–; R-IN). The federal law would outlaw not only horse slaughter in the United States but also transport across international borders of live horses intended for slaughter for human consumption. As of April 2009, the bill remained in committee, meaning that it had not yet reached the House floor for a vote. Animal welfare groups advocate humane euthanasia for horses that are severely ill or injured and promote horse rescue and adoption programs.

FISH

Fish farming, or aquaculture, has been around for at least a millennium. Historians believe the Chinese practiced aquaculture in 900 to raise fish for their emperor's dinner table. China is still a leading producer of farmed fish. Commercial aquaculture is also a big business in the United States. According to the USDA, in *2007 Census of Agriculture*, there were 6,409 fish farms operating in the United States in 2007 that sold products worth more than $1.4 billion. Nearly all the rainbow trout and catfish consumed in the United States come from farm operations. Besides freshwater fish, saltwater fish are also raised in farm environments.

Fish farming is accomplished in one of two ways. Producers use netted enclosures in near-offshore ocean waters or they build separate enclosures inland. The second method is considered more environmentally friendly because the farmed fish and their waste are separated from fish living in natural waters. In-ocean farms occasionally lose fish to the surrounding waters, and environmentalists fear that these fish may spread diseases to their wild counterparts. In-ocean farms can also only be used for saltwater species, not freshwater. Fish farms typically keep as many fish as possible in the smallest amount of space possible. These confined operations can cause health problems, particularly sea lice infestation, in the farmed fish.

Several animal welfare groups oppose aquaculture, claiming that farmed fish are subjected to severe overcrowding in water pens contaminated with large amounts of fecal matter.

OTHER FARM ANIMALS

Inventory data for various other farm animals are shown in Table 4.5. The largest inventories of these animals in 2007 were sheep and lambs (5.8 million), goats (3.1 million), and bee colonies (2.9 million).

One farm animal of particular interest on this list is the bison (or American buffalo). The bison was driven to the brink of extinction in the 1800s due to overhunting of

TABLE 4.5

Production data on miscellaneous livestock, 2007

Item	Inventory 2007
Colonies of bees	
farms	27,908
number	2,902,732
Bison	
farms	4,499
number	198,234
Deer	
farms	5,654
number	269,537
Elk	
farms	1,917
number	68,251
Goats, all	
farms	144,466
number	3,140,529
Angora goats	
farms	7,215
number	204,106
Milk goats	
farms	27,481
number	334,754
Meat and other goats	
farms	123,278
number	2,601,669
Horses and ponies	
farms	575,942
number	4,028,827
Horses and ponies owned	
farms	501,528
number	3,224,964
Mules, burros, and donkeys	
farms	99,746
number	283,806
Alpacas	
farms	8,708
number	121,904
Llamas	
farms	26,060
number	122,680
Mink and their pelts	
farms	290
number	1,507,719
Rabbits and their pelts	
farms	27,137
number	616,129
Sheep and lambs	
farms	83,134
number	5,819,162
Other livestock	
farms	12,781

SOURCE: Adapted from "Table 31. Other Animals and Animal Products— Inventory and Number Sold: 2007 and 2002" and "Table 29. Sheep and Lambs—Inventory, Wool Production, and Number Sold by Size of Flock: 2007," in *2007 Census of Agriculture, United States Summary and State Data, Volume 1*, U.S. Department of Agriculture, National Agricultural Statistics Service, February 2009, http://www.agcensus.usda.gov/ Publications/2007/Full_Report/usv1.pdf (accessed February 6, 2009)

wild herds. Only a few hundred wild and farmed bison survived. In *2007 Census of Agriculture*, the USDA estimates that 4,499 farms had an inventory of 198,234 bison in 2007. Bison meat is being heavily marketed by the American business executive Ted Turner (1938–). In 2001 Turner opened a chain of restaurants called Ted's Montana Grills (http://www.tedsmontanagrill.com/) that feature bison meat. He also formed the company U.S. Bison to market the meat to upscale restaurants and consumers. According to Turner Enterprises (2009, http://www.tedturner.com/enterprises/ranches_Template.asp?page=ranches_faq.html), Turner's bison herd numbered approximately 50,000 in 2009, making it the largest privately owned herd in the world.

WELFARE-FRIENDLY FARMING?

The most strict animal rights activists are opposed to the farming of animals to produce products for human consumption and use. They often embrace a vegan lifestyle, in which no animal products are consumed or used. Others are vegetarians. Vegetarians do not eat meat, but may consume secondary products, such as milk or eggs. For example, lacto-vegetarians eat dairy products, whereas ovo-vegetarians eat eggs. Lacto-ovo vegetarians eat both.

Vegans and vegetarians make up a small but increasing minority of the U.S. population. In "How Many Adults Are Vegetarian?" (*Vegetarian Journal*, no. 4, 2006), Charles Stahler reports that 2.3% of U.S. adults consider themselves strict vegetarians. Many more people are part-time vegetarians or occasionally eat vegetarian meals. Not all vegetarians embrace their chosen diet for animal rights reasons— many have health, environmental, and/or religious reasons instead of or besides ethical ones.

There is also growing demand in the United States for meat and other products from animals that are raised or slaughtered using more humane methods. Food suppliers are beginning to make changes that represent significant reforms in animal welfare and slaughter. Some of these changes have no doubt been driven by pressure from vocal animal rights groups. For example, PETA has been conducting aggressive publicity and picketing campaigns against major fast-food chains in the United States, and many fast-food chains are implementing more welfare-friendly policies.

Some farmers have initiated reforms on their own. For example, some smaller hog farms are allowing their sows to farrow in straw-filled huts or barns instead of in gestation crates. Welfare-friendly farming is considered part of a larger movement called organic farming. Organic farming of crops involves no use of pesticides or herbicides. This produces a more natural product that many consumers consider healthier and more environmentally friendly. According to the ERS, in "Organic Agriculture" (October 30, 2008, http://www.ers.usda.gov/Briefing/Organic/), organic farming is one of the fastest-growing segments of U.S. agriculture.

TABLE 4.6

Number of organic certified livestock, 1997, 2003, and 2005

Item	1997	2003	2005	Change 1997–2005
U.S. certified animals		Number		Percent
Total livestock[a]	**18,513**	**124,346**	**196,506**	**961**
Beef cows	4,429	27,285	36,113	715
Milk cows	12,897	74,435	87,082	575
Hogs and pigs	482	6,564	10,108	1,997
Sheep and lambs	705	4,561	4,471	534
Total poultry[b]	**798,250**	**8,780,152**	**13,757,270**	**1,623**
Layer hens	537,826	1,591,181	2,415,056	349
Broilers	38,285	6,301,014	10,405,879	27,080
Turkeys	750	217,353	144,086	19,111

[a]Total livestock includes other and unclassified animals.
[b]Total poultry includes other and unclassified animals.
Note: Numbers may not add due to rounding.

SOURCE: Adapted from "U.S. Certified Organic Farmland Acreage, Livestock Numbers, and Farm Operations, 1997, 2003, and 2005," in *Briefing Rooms: Organic Agriculture: U.S. Organic Farm Sector Is Diverse*, U.S. Department of Agriculture, Economic Research Service, August 22, 2007, http://www.ers.usda.gov/Briefing/Organic/Farmsector.htm (accessed February 19, 2009)

Some livestock farmers offer meat and other products from animals cultivated using organic methods. The animals are not given antibiotics or other drugs (except some necessary vaccines) and are housed in more natural conditions than those used in factory farms. The farmers accommodate the animals' natural nutritional and behavior requirements. For example, ruminating animals are given access to pasture. According to the USDA, there were 196,506 organic cows, swine, sheep, and lambs and nearly 13.8 million organic chickens and other poultry on U.S. farms in 2005. (See Table 4.6.) These numbers have increased dramatically since 1997, when only 18,513 organic livestock and 798,250 organic poultry were recorded.

Farmers are not allowed to label their products as organic unless they meet specific requirements established by the U.S. government in the National Organic Program. The organic standards govern living conditions, access to the outdoors, feed rations, and health care practices. No growth hormones or genetic engineering are allowed, and the animals are not fed animal byproducts. There are also restrictions on manure management and slaughter procedures. The farmers must provide documentation to the USDA demonstrating that they are following these standards to use the organic label.

Some animal protection groups have implemented their own programs to define and certify welfare-friendly farming operations. In 2000 the American Humane Association (AHA) established the Free Farmed Program (now called the American Humane Certified Program). Producers that want to be certified by the AHA must meet specific standards for food and water management, living conditions, and transport, handling, and slaughter techniques. Humane Farm Animal Care (HFAC) is an independent nonprofit organization that administers the Certified Humane Raised and Handled Program. The HFAC program is funded by various animal welfare organizations, including the HSUS and the American Society for the Prevention of Cruelty to Animals. Products are labeled "Certified Humane" if the producers meet specific criteria for animal care that are enforced through an inspection and verification process.

It has also become common for livestock farmers to market products labeled "all natural," "cage free," "grass fed," "pasture raised," "free range," or "free roaming." Critics say that these labels are marketing ploys and are not clearly defined or verified by regulatory agencies or animal welfare groups. For example, the label "cage free" has no legally enforceable meaning.

In the fact sheet "Meat and Poultry Labeling Terms" =(August 24, 2006, http://www.fsis.usda.gov/FactSheets/Meat_&_Poultry_Labeling_Terms/index.asp), the USDA states that "a product containing no artificial ingredient or added color and is only minimally processed (a process which does not fundamentally alter the raw product) may be labeled natural. The label must explain the use of the term natural (such as—no added colorings or artificial ingredients; minimally processed)." However, the label can be applied to meat from animals that received antibiotics and other drugs to promote growth. Producers that market free-range or free-roaming chickens are required by the USDA to provide their chickens access to the outside. However, there is no verification process in place to prove this claim. Critics point out that the requirement is satisfied at some chicken houses by including a small door that leads out into a small caged area open to the environment.

The USDA definitions of *free range*, *pasture fed*, and *free roaming* for nonpoultry animals say that the animals must have been allowed to eat grass and live outdoors during at least part of their lives. Animal welfare groups claim the USDA rarely performs inspections to verify such claims but relies on the statements of livestock producers.

HUMAN HEALTH ISSUES

Because humans consume so many animal products, there is a correlation between the health of farm animals and human health. Even people who do not have moral or philosophical problems with the treatment or consumption of livestock are concerned about some factory farming methods.

Use of Antibiotics

One of the biggest concerns is the routine administration of low doses of antibiotics to farm animals to prevent them from developing diseases and to cure any that might already have diseases. This is called nontherapeutic, subtherapeutic, or preventive antibiotic use. Many people fear that it could lead to development of antibiotic-resistant diseases in animals and humans. Scientists already know

that some bacteria are able to adjust to and tolerate low dosages of weaker antibiotics. Once they achieve this resistance, stronger types of antibiotics are needed to kill them.

Animal-to-Human Disease Transmission

Another concern related to animal welfare is the fear that U.S. farm animals could transmit diseases to humans, either through live contact or from the consumption of tainted meat products.

Diseases that can be transmitted from animals to humans are called zoonoses. Zoonoses associated with farm animals include anthrax (an infectious disease caused by spore-forming bacterium), brucellosis (a flulike illness transmitted by bacteria), leptospirosis (a bacterial disease that can cause a variety of symptoms in humans), bovine tuberculosis (a respiratory disease), streptococcus suis (a meningitis-like disease mostly associated with pigs), orf (a viral skin disease), avian influenza, and ringworm (a fungal skin disease). Of major concern is a group of diseases called transmissible spongiform encephalopathies (TSEs). One TSE is called bovine spongiform encephalopathy (BSE), commonly known as mad cow disease. BSE devastated farm animal populations in England during the 1980s and 1990s. Millions of animals were killed because they either had the disease or as a precaution against the disease. Since 1990 the USDA has conducted a BSE surveillance program on U.S. cattle.

FUR FARMING

Fur farming is a unique agricultural enterprise for two reasons. First, most of the animals involved are wild instead of domesticated. Second, the animals are raised and killed for their pelts only. The most popular fur animal is the mink. According to FurKills.org, in "The Truth about Fur Farming" (2009, http://furkills.org/furfarming.shtml), it takes about 60 female mink or 35 male mink pelts to produce one fur coat.

Mink are wild animals that are kept in cages on fur farms. They typically breed in the early spring and give birth to litters in late spring. An average litter contains four or five kits (babies) that are weaned after six to eight weeks. The kits are vaccinated against common diseases. During the late summer and early fall the mink naturally molt (lose their summer fur) and regrow a thick winter coat. The mink are killed in late autumn or early winter. Some are retained for breeding purposes.

In *2007 Census of Agriculture*, the USDA reports that in 2007 there were 290 mink farms in the United States that contained more than 1.5 million mink. (See Table 4.7.) The U.S. Fur Commission (2009, http://www.furcommission.com/farming/Graphics/MapofStates.jpg) notes that the top five mink-pelt producing states in 2007 were Wisconsin, Utah, Oregon, Idaho, and Minnesota.

TABLE 4.7

Mink farms, 2002 and 2007, and by state, 2007

Geographic area		Farms
United States total		
United States	2007	290
	2002	310
States, 2007		
Alaska		1
Colorado		1
Hawaii		1
Idaho		25
Illinois		7
Indiana		1
Iowa		17
Maryland		1
Massachusetts		1
Michigan		12
Minnesota		26
Missouri		2
Montana		7
New Hampshire		1
New York		5
North Carolina		2
Ohio		8
Oregon		19
Pennsylvania		14
South Dakota		3
Utah		55
Washington		8
Wisconsin		73

SOURCE: Adapted from "Table 22. Mink and Their Pelts—Inventory and Number Sold: 2007 and 2002," in *2007 Census of Agriculture, United States Summary and State Data, Volume 1*, U.S. Department of Agriculture, National Agricultural Statistics Service, February 2009, http://www.agcensus.usda.gov/Publications/2007/Full_Report/usv1.pdf (accessed February 6, 2009)

TABLE 4.8

Public opinion on the morality of buying and wearing animal fur, 2001–08

NEXT, I'M GOING TO READ YOU A LIST OF ISSUES. REGARDLESS OF WHETHER OR NOT YOU THINK IT SHOULD BE LEGAL, FOR EACH ONE, PLEASE TELL ME WHETHER YOU PERSONALLY BELIEVE THAT IN GENERAL IT IS MORALLY ACCEPTABLE OR MORALLY WRONG. HOW ABOUT . . . [RANDOM ORDER]?

BUYING AND WEARING CLOTHING MADE OF ANIMAL FUR

	Morally acceptable %	Morally wrong %	Depends on situation (vol.) %	Not a moral issue (vol.) %	No opinion %
2008 May 8–11	54	39	3	1	2
2007 May 10–13	58	38	2	1	2
2006 May 8–11	62	32	2	2	2
2005 May 2–5	64	32	2	1	1
2004 May 2–4	63	31	2	2	2
2003 May 5–7	60	36	2	1	1
2002 May 6–9	59	35	2	2	2
2001 May 10–14	60	32	2	3	3

*Less than 0.5%.
(vol.) = Volunteered response.

SOURCE: "Next, I'm Going to Read You a List of Issues. Regardless of Whether or Not You Think It Should Be Legal, for Each One, Please Tell Me Whether You Personally Believe That in General It Is Morally Acceptable or Morally Wrong. How about Buying and Wearing Clothing Made of Animal Fur?" in *Moral Issues*, The Gallup Organization, 2008, http://www.gallup.com/poll/1681/Moral-Issues.aspx (accessed January 13, 2009). Copyright © 2008 by The Gallup Organization. Reproduced by permission of The Gallup Organization.

The fur industry is harshly criticized by animal rights activists and welfarists, who say the animals are kept in miserable conditions and in small cages. The HSUS explains that overbreeding by farmers to produce desirable coat colors leads to serious and painful deformities in the animals. The farming and slaughter of fur animals are not regulated by the USDA. The most common killing techniques are gassing, electrocution, and breaking of the animals' necks. Fur farming has been banned in many west European countries.

Animal welfarists and rights activists have conducted antifur campaigns since the 1960s. PETA's "I'd rather go naked than wear fur" campaign was begun in the 1990s and has featured celebrities such as Pamela Anderson (1967–) and Kim Basinger (1953–) posing nude. PETA activists also regularly disrupt fashion shows featuring fur-clad models and protest outside stores selling fur. In spite of these campaigns, fur sales have continued to rise. According to the Fur Commission, in the press release "Nine Years of Sustained Momentum for Global Fur Sales" (March 4, 2008, http://www.furcommission.com/news/newsF10p.htm), global fur sales increased by 11.3% between 2006 and 2007, exceeding $15 billion. Industry analysts indicate that fur demand is driven by weather and economy rather than by animal issues. A Gallup poll conducted in May 2008 found that 54% of those asked believed the buying and wearing of clothing made of animal fur was morally acceptable. (See Table 4.8.) This number was down slightly in 2008, compared to previous years.

Mink farmers defend their animal husbandry and slaughtering procedures as humane. They argue that mink in the wild rarely live longer than one year and insist that the mink are handled carefully, both for their welfare and to protect their valuable coats from damage. Producers also insist that the mink are killed quickly and humanely using veterinary-approved methods. The Fur Commission (2009, http://www.furcommission.com/farming/index.html) claims that "today's farm-raised furbearers are among the world's best cared-for livestock."

CHAPTER 5
RESEARCH ANIMALS

Research animals are animals that humans use solely for scientific research; medical and veterinary investigations and training; in the testing of drugs, cosmetics, and other consumer products; and in educational programs. It is not known how many animals are used in research, testing, and medical and veterinary training programs in the United States, but the number is certainly in the millions. Sharon Oosthoek notes in "How the 'Mouse Man' Changed Medical Research" (*New Scientist*), no. 2692, January 28, 2009) that approximately 25 million mice are used in the world's research laboratories annually. Some estimates put this figure much higher. The *Scientific American* (August 4, 2004) estimates that as many as 100 million animals per year (mostly mice and rats) may be used in the United States. People for the Ethical Treatment of Animals (2009, http://www.stopanimaltests .com/vivisectionactionpack.asp) puts this number at around 115 million. Millions more research animals may be kept as classroom pets or teaching aids to educate children in schools.

Living animals used as specimens to test drugs and products, practice medical and surgical procedures, and investigate diseases and bodily systems are called laboratory animals. Laboratory animals often die from these procedures or are euthanized by researchers after they are no longer needed. The plight of laboratory animals has been a major issue for animal rights advocates since the 1970s.

Increasingly, the use of dead animals to teach dissection skills to children is coming under fire. Dissection is a procedure in which an organism is cut apart for scientific examination. If the organism is alive at the time, the procedure is called vivisection. However, the term *vivisection* has come to be used to refer to all invasive research and testing performed on live animals for scientific purposes.

Live animals are used in modern medical research because some of their bodily systems mimic those of humans. This makes them useful test subjects for drugs, vaccines, and other products intended for humans. They are also useful training tools for doctors, surgeons, and veterinarians, who need to practice medical procedures, such as inserting a catheter, administering anesthesia, or performing operations.

People who support the use of animals in research are passionate in their belief that the benefits to people far outweigh the consequences to animals. They point out the important medical and veterinary advances that have resulted. On the contrary, animal rights activists uniformly condemn this use. The most extreme activists have broken into laboratories, released animals, and physically harassed the researchers involved. Animal welfarists work to minimize the pain these animals experience during testing and to improve their living conditions.

The Gallup Organization includes a question about laboratory animals in the morality poll it conducts each year. (See Table 5.1.) The latest poll conducted in May 2008 showed that 56% of respondents found "medical testing on animals" to be morally acceptable, whereas 38% found it morally wrong. Another 3% said the morality depends on the situation. These numbers show significant change from those obtained in 2001, when 65% stated testing on animals was morally acceptable and only 26% stated it was morally wrong. Nearly two-thirds (64%) of respondents opposed banning all medical research on laboratory animals, whereas 35% of respondents supported a ban. (See Figure 5.1.) Gallup pollsters also found that 59% of respondents opposed banning all product testing on laboratory animals. (See Figure 5.2.) Thirty-nine percent supported such a ban.

Science and Engineering Indicators is a report published by the National Science Foundation (NSF) every two years. Each report includes polls and questionnaires conducted on public understanding and attitudes about various topics related to science and engineering. The 2002 report (http://www.nsf.gov/statistics/seind02/pdfstart.htm) is the most recent of the reports to include public opinion polls on the use of animals in scientific research. NSF pollsters assessed public opinion on the use of mice versus the use of dogs and chimpanzees in medical research that

TABLE 5.1

Public opinion on the morality of medical testing on animals, 2001–08

NEXT, I'M GOING TO READ YOU A LIST OF ISSUES. REGARDLESS OF WHETHER OR NOT YOU THINK IT SHOULD BE LEGAL, FOR EACH ONE, PLEASE TELL ME WHETHER YOU PERSONALLY BELIEVE THAT IN GENERAL IT IS MORALLY ACCEPTABLE OR MORALLY WRONG. HOW ABOUT . . . [RANDOM ORDER]?

MEDICAL TESTING ON ANIMALS

	Morally acceptable %	Morally wrong %	Depends on situation (vol.) %	Not a moral issue (vol.) %	No opinion %
2008 May 8–11	56	38	3	*	3
2007 May 10–13	59	37	3	*	1
2006 May 8–11	61	32	5	*	2
2005 May 2–5	66	30	2	*	2
2004 May 2–4	62	32	4	*	2
2003 May 5–7	63	33	3	*	1
2002 May 6–9	63	30	3	1	3
2001 May 10–14	65	26	5	1	3

*Less than 0.5%.
(vol.) = Volunteered response.

SOURCE: "Next, I'm Going to Read You a List of Issues. Regardless of Whether or Not You Think It Should Be Legal, for Each One, Please Tell Me Whether You Personally Believe That in General It Is Morally Acceptable or Morally Wrong. How about Medical Testing on Animals?" in *Moral Issues*, The Gallup Organization, 2008, http://www.gallup.com/poll/1681/Moral-Issues.aspx (accessed January 13, 2009). Copyright © 2008 by The Gallup Organization. Reproduced by permission of The Gallup Organization.

FIGURE 5.1

Public support for banning all medical research on laboratory animals, May 2008

HERE ARE SOME SPECIFIC PROPOSALS CONCERNING THE TREATMENT OF ANIMALS. FOR EACH ONE, PLEASE SAY WHETHER YOU STRONGLY SUPPORT THIS PROPOSAL, SOMEWHAT SUPPORT IT, SOMEWHAT OPPOSE IT, OR STRONGLY OPPOSE THIS PROPOSAL. HOW ABOUT . . .?

BANNING ALL MEDICAL RESEARCH ON LABORATORY ANIMALS

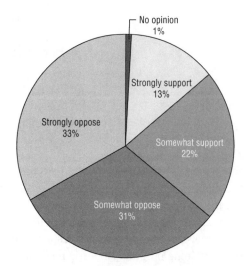

SOURCE: Adapted from Frank Newport, "Here Are Some Specific Proposals Concerning the Treatment of Animals. For Each One, Please Say Whether You Strongly Support This Proposal, Somewhat Support It, Somewhat Oppose It, or Strongly Oppose This Proposal. How about Banning All Medical Research on Laboratory Animals?" in *Post-Derby Tragedy, 38% Support Banning Animal Racing*, The Gallup Organization, May 15, 2008, http://www.gallup.com/poll/107293/PostDerby-Tragedy-38-Support-Banning-Animal-Racing.aspx (accessed January 13, 2009). Copyright © 2008 by The Gallup Organization. Reproduced by permission of The Gallup Organization.

causes pain and injury to the animals but produces new information on human health problems. The results indicate that in 2001, 68% of respondents approved of the use of mice in such a manner, whereas only 44% approved of the use of dogs and chimpanzees. This finding is not surprising, as people typically have more charitable feelings toward dogs and chimpanzees than they do toward mice.

Many people react emotionally to the thought of animals in distress. Scientists and researchers—those who work with the animals directly—use clinical terms to describe their work. They refer to laboratory animals as animal models and speak of them as specimens. Antivivisection groups gain support for their views by publicizing the gruesome details of experiments. Photographs of restrained animals with bolts through their brains or sores on their bodies can disturb the public, regardless of how scientifically justified the experiments may be.

HISTORY

Vivisection on animals and humans dates back to at least the ancient Greeks and Romans. By the Middle Ages moral and religious concerns prohibited most vivisection on humans. There was little debate about the morality of using animals for these purposes. The seventeenth-century French philosopher René Descartes (1596–1650) and his followers believed that animals were unthinking and unfeeling machines. In the next century the British philosopher and political scientist Jeremy Bentham (1748–1832)

summarized his very different thoughts on the subject in *An Introduction to the Principles of Morals and Legislation* (1789): "The question is not, Can they reason? Nor, Can they talk? but, Can they suffer?" (See Figure 5.3.)

Throughout the eighteenth and nineteenth centuries philosophers debated the moral issues involved in animal vivisection. According to historians, the poor and working-class people of the time opposed animal vivisection because they associated it with the dissection of human corpses. The unclaimed bodies of poor people and criminals were often turned over to medical colleges for dissection. There were also well-publicized cases of grave robbing and body snatching to supply researchers with human corpses. These events horrified the common people and made them suspicious of scientists and doctors engaged in medical research.

The modern antivivisection movement began in the nineteenth century. In *Animals' Rights, Considered in Relation to Social Progress* (1894), the humanitarian Henry S. Salt (1851–1939) writes that "the practice of vivisection is revolting to the human conscience, even among the ordinary members of a not over-sensitive society." This was

FIGURE 5.2

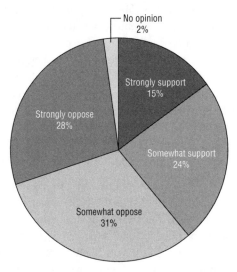

Public support for banning all product testing on laboratory animals, May 2008

HERE ARE SOME SPECIFIC PROPOSALS CONCERNING THE TREATMENT OF ANIMALS. FOR EACH ONE, PLEASE SAY WHETHER YOU STRONGLY SUPPORT THIS PROPOSAL, SOMEWHAT SUPPORT IT, SOMEWHAT OPPOSE IT, OR STRONGLY OPPOSE THIS PROPOSAL. HOW ABOUT . . . ?

BANNING ALL PRODUCT TESTING ON LABORATORY ANIMALS

No opinion 2%
Strongly support 15%
Somewhat support 24%
Somewhat oppose 31%
Strongly oppose 28%

SOURCE: Adapted from Frank Newport, "Here Are Some Specific Proposals Concerning the Treatment of Animals. For Each One, Please Say Whether You Strongly Support This Proposal, Somewhat Support It, Somewhat Oppose It, or Strongly Oppose This Proposal. How about Banning All Product Testing on Laboratory Animals?" in *Post-Derby Tragedy, 38% Support Banning Animal Racing*, The Gallup Organization, May 15, 2008, http://www.gallup.com/poll/107293/PostDerby-Tragedy-38-Support-Banning-Animal-Racing.aspx (accessed January 13, 2009). Copyright © 2008 by The Gallup Organization. Reproduced by permission of The Gallup Organization.

FIGURE 5.3

Jeremy Bentham. *The Library of Congress.*

only 76 years after the publication of *Frankenstein; or, The Modern Prometheus* (1818), a story by Mary Shelley (1797–1851) about a scientist who creates a mutant human from spare parts. The anthropologist Susan Sperling states in *Animal Liberators: Research and Morality* (1988) her belief that the antivivisectionists of the nineteenth century and the twenty-first century share a common fear: scientific manipulation of living beings.

The nineteenth century also witnessed organized efforts from animal welfare organizations to achieve legislation against animal cruelty in the United Kingdom and the United States. The Cruelty to Animals Act was passed in Britain in 1849 and amended in 1876 to restrict the use of animals in research. In 1875 the Society for the Protection of Animals Liable to Vivisection was founded by Frances Power Cobbe (1822–1904). It was later called the Victorian Street Society. In 1898 Cobbe founded the British Union for the Abolition of Vivisection, an organization that is still active.

Vivisection was also fought by welfarists in the United States. In 1871 Harvard University founded one of the first vivisection laboratories in the country, despite opposition from the Massachusetts Society for the Prevention of Cruelty to Animals. Various antivivisection groups were founded, including the American Anti-Vivisection Society in 1883 and the New England Anti-Vivisection Society (NEAVS) in 1895. The new antivivisection groups tried, unsuccessfully, to outlaw the practice of vivisection. Legislation was passed during the 1890s that outlawed repetition of painful animal experiments for the purpose of teaching or demonstrating well-known and accepted facts.

First Half of the Twentieth Century

In December 1903 the American writer Mark Twain (1835–1910) published the short story "A Dog's Tale" in *Harper's Magazine*. The story was written to protest cruelty to animals and their use in research. It is told from the viewpoint of a dog that lives with the family of a scientist. The dog saves the family's baby from a nursery fire but later sees her own puppy blinded and killed during an experiment performed by the scientist to impress his friends. Even though some critics condemned the work as overly sentimental, animal welfarists of the time were pleased that it brought public attention to the issue of animal experimentation.

In 1906 Congress passed the Pure Food and Drug Act (PFDA). The original act did not require any type of testing to ensure that a product was safe or effective. This would change after some tragic events occurred. According to Susan E. Wilson-Sanders of the University of Arizona, in "Mrs. Brown's Sad Story: A History of the Food, Drug, and Cosmetic Act" (October 1, 2008, http://www.uac.arizona.edu/VSC443/Alternmethod/Fdapap03.htm), many Americans were injured, sickened, or even killed by unsafe potions, "snake oils," and patent medicines sold by entrepreneurs during the early decades of the twentieth century. Some of these products contained incredibly toxic substances, such as dinitrophenol, a compound used to make explosives.

During the 1920s and 1930s hair dyes containing an aniline compound called paraphenylenediamine became popular. Even though it was well known that aniline compounds were harmful to the eyes, a cosmetics company still chose to introduce a brand of mascara called Lash-Lure that contained these chemicals. Doctors reported thousands of eye injuries caused by the product, and even a few deaths after patients suffered serious infections. Many states banned the use of aniline dyes in personal-care products. Wilson-Sanders reports that Lash-Lure contained 25 to 30 times more aniline than the amount commonly used in hair dyes.

Wilson-Sanders mentions several other popular cosmetic products of the time that caused injury, such as Anti-Mole, Berry's Freckle Ointment, Bleachodent (a teeth whitener), Dr. Dennis's Compound, Koremlu cream, and Dewsberry Hair Tonic. These products contained high concentrations of acids or other toxic chemicals. Whisker dyes marketed to men contained dangerous levels of silver or lead acetate. A popular depilatory (hair removal cream) contained rat poison.

According to Wilson-Sanders, doctors lobbied Congress throughout the 1930s to crack down on dangerous drugs and personal products sold to Americans, but they were opposed by powerful marketing groups. In 1937 nearly 100 people (mostly children) died after drinking a product called Elixir of Sulfanilamide that contained sulfa drugs dissolved in diethylene glycol (antifreeze). The public was outraged and pressured Congress to strengthen the original PFDA and include cosmetics. The Food, Drug, and Cosmetics Act (FDCA) was passed in 1938. It contained a requirement for animal testing.

Wilson-Sanders notes that the first tests were conducted on rats and could last less than one month. The testing requirements were gradually amended to include different species and to last for longer time periods. By 1957 drug testing had to be performed on rats or dogs for up to six months. By the 1980s testing was required to last 12 to 18 months. Testing on pregnant animals was instituted in the 1960s following the thalidomide tragedy. Thalidomide is a drug that was widely prescribed in Canada and Europe during the late 1950s to treat nausea in pregnant women. More than 10,000 babies with birth defects resulted. The drug had been extensively tested on animals, but it had not been tested on pregnant animals. New guidelines for testing the effects of drugs on animal reproduction and fetus development were incorporated into the FDCA.

Second Half of the Twentieth Century

Historians note that the antivivisection movement subsided with the advent of World War I (1914–1918) and did not resurge until the 1960s. One of the driving forces behind the movement's rebirth was the story of Pepper, a Dalmatian who disappeared from her family's backyard in Pennsylvania in July 1965. The family tracked the dog to an animal dealer in New York, but he refused to return the dog. The family enlisted the help of the Animal Welfare Institute, the Pennsylvania State Police, and Representative Joseph Resnick (1924–1969; D-NY), but they were too late. Pepper had been sold to a hospital in New York City that conducted an experiment on her and euthanized her.

The story was widely publicized and led to public outrage. Bills were introduced in the U.S. House of Representatives and the U.S. Senate calling for animal dealers and laboratories to be licensed and inspected by the U.S. Department of Agriculture (USDA) and be required to meet certain humane standards of care. The bills were opposed by strong lobbying groups and were in danger of failing, until a story ran in the February 4, 1966, issue of *Life* magazine.

"Concentration Camps for Dogs" was the story of a police raid on a dog dealer's facility in Maryland. The story included horrific photographs of abused dogs kept in filthy cages until they could be sold to research laboratories. According to the article, the dogs were to be sold at auction for $0.30 per pound. Letters flooded politicians' offices and editorials appeared in major newspapers around the country calling for federal legislation.

A few months later Congress passed the Laboratory Animal Welfare Act of 1966. It called for the licensing of animal dealers and the regulation of laboratory animals. The original act applied to dogs, cats, primates, guinea pigs, hamsters, and rabbits. In 1970 the act was renamed the Animal Welfare Act (AWA) and amended to cover several other warm-blooded animals. A year later the USDA decided to exclude rats, mice, and birds from coverage under the act, arguing that the department did not have the staff needed to regulate the huge numbers of such animals involved. It also noted that most of these small animals were used at research institutions that had other oversight protections in place to regulate their use.

The publication of *Animal Liberation: A New Ethics for Our Treatment of Animals* (1975) by the Australian philosopher Peter Singer (1946–) brought more coverage to the use of animals in scientific research. The book includes disturbing photographs and descriptions of animals being subjected to all sorts of painful procedures for questionable purposes. Singer argues that the pain and suffering inflicted on the animals is too high a moral price to pay for scientific research.

In 1976 the animal activist Henry Spira (1927–1998) led a campaign protesting the American Museum of Natural History's research on the effects of castration and mutilation on cats' sexual behavior. The campaign was hailed as a success by activists after the museum halted the research a year later. Spira then turned his attention to the testing of cosmetics on animals, particularly the Draize eye test, in which chemicals are put into the eyes of restrained animals.

Spira formed a coalition of animal welfare and antivivisection groups to educate the public about animal testing of cosmetics. In full-page advertisements in major newspapers, Spira accused major cosmetics companies of being cruel to animals. Public response was immediate. Several companies, including Revlon and Avon, announced their intention to cease animal testing and find new alternatives. In 1981 the Cosmetics, Toiletries, and Fragrance Association funded the founding of the Center for Alternatives to Animal Testing (CAAT) at Johns Hopkins University. By the end of the 1980s Revlon and Avon had ceased animal testing.

In 1985 Congress amended the AWA to require that researchers minimize animal pain and distress whenever possible through the use of anesthesia, analgesics (painkillers), and humane euthanasia. New requirements were added regarding the physical and psychological well-being of dogs and primates used in research work. Throughout the 1980s and 1990s animal welfare groups petitioned and sued the USDA to add mice, rats, and birds to the animals covered under the AWA but were unsuccessful. In 1990 AWA coverage was extended to horses and other farm animals.

Scientists engaged in animal research watched with concern as animal welfare and antivivisection groups launched aggressive publicity campaigns against them. In 1979 the National Association for Biomedical Research (2009, http://www.nabr.org/AboutNABR/tabid/373/Default .aspx) was founded with the mission of "advocating for sound public policy that recognizes the vital role that animals play in biomedical research." In 1981 the Foundation for Biomedical Research and the Michigan Society for Medical Research (MISMR) were founded with similar goals. These organizations work to counter claims by animal rights activists that animal research and testing are cruel practices with little to no scientific value.

PEOPLE FOR THE ETHICAL TREATMENT OF ANIMALS AND THE SILVER SPRING MONKEY CASE. In 1981 a little-known organization called People for the Ethical Treatment of Animals (PETA) gained national prominence through an exposé on paralysis experiments that were being conducted on monkeys at the Institute of Behavioral Research in Silver Spring, Maryland. The research

was funded by the National Institutes of Health (NIH) and led by the psychologist Edward Taub (1931–). It involved depriving monkeys of sensory input into their spinal cords to give them denervated arms, or arms in which the nerves were not active. The monkeys gnawed and licked their arms, producing wounds. Taub hired Alex Pacheco (1958–) to work as a laboratory assistant. He was not aware that Pacheco had cofounded PETA the year before. Pacheco secretly photographed the monkeys, then reported the lab to authorities. A subsequent raid led to the filing of animal cruelty charges against Taub.

The incident came to be known as the Silver Spring Monkey Case. Even though the charges against Taub were eventually dropped, the publicity made PETA famous. The monkeys were confiscated, and Congress forced the NIH to cease the research. This was viewed as a major triumph by people involved in antivivisection and the growing animal rights movement.

ANIMAL ENTERPRISE PROTECTION ACT. During the late 1970s and 1980s animal research institutions and animal industries experienced an increasing number of violent acts committed by animal rights extremists. As described in Chapter 2, activists broke into laboratories and fur farms to "liberate" animals and damage buildings and equipment. Some of these activists claimed to be part of the Animal Liberation Front (ALF), an emerging movement that embraced radical and illegal actions on behalf of animals. The rise of the ALF is described in the 1993 report *Report to Congress on the Extent and Effects of Domestic and International Terrorism on Animal Enterprises* (http://www.furcommission.com/resource/ perspect2.htm) by the U.S. Department of Justice. The report notes that even though PETA disavowed taking part in violent activities, the group publicized them on its Web site and praised the activists for their actions on behalf of animals.

Rising concern among research scientists and animal industries about animal activist violence led to passage in 1992 of the Animal Enterprise Protection Act. The law prohibits "causing physical disruption to the functioning of an animal enterprise." Three types of animal enterprises are defined:

- Commercial or academic enterprises using animals to produce food or fiber or for agriculture, research, or testing

- Zoos, aquariums, circuses, rodeos, and other legal sporting events

- Fairs and similar events designed to advance agricultural arts and sciences

Offenses that can be charged under the act include using the mail to cause physical disruption at animal enterprises and stealing, damaging, or causing the loss of property used by animal enterprises. Property includes animals and records.

HUNTINGDON LIFE SCIENCES BECOMES A TARGET.
PETA continued to use infiltration to secretly obtain photographs and videotapes, which were then publicized to make the public aware of the realities of animal research. In 1996 and 1997 the group conducted an eight-month undercover investigation at a Huntingdon Life Sciences (HLS) facility in New Jersey. The HLS is a major target of antivivisection groups because it is one of the largest contract companies conducting animal research. A PETA member began working at the HLS and secretly collected documents, photographs, and videotapes that PETA used to file a formal complaint against the HLS with the USDA. PETA also released some of the material to the media.

The HLS countersued PETA, claiming that the materials were obtained by illegal means and that PETA had violated the Economic Espionage Act and the Animal Enterprise Protection Act. In December 1997 a mutual settlement was reached in which PETA agreed to turn over all records taken from the HLS and cease trying to infiltrate HLS property for five years, and the HLS agreed to drop its lawsuit against PETA.

In 1999 Stop Huntingdon Animal Cruelty (SHAC), a new animal rights group, began using radical and violent means against HLS headquarters in the United Kingdom. Cars were firebombed and company executives were assaulted outside their homes. Several activists were arrested and jailed for violent crimes.

SHAC began targeting companies providing the HLS with services, funding, and equipment. Banks, brokerage houses, and investment companies with ties to the HLS were picketed and flooded with threatening letters, faxes, and e-mails. Employees were harassed and sometimes assaulted. Their homes were vandalized. The intimidation tactics were effective, as many companies decided to sever their business ties with the HLS. By 2002 no commercial bank in the United Kingdom would loan money to the company. According to Alan Cowell, in "Scene Shifts in Fight against British Testing Lab" (*New York Times*, January 22, 2002), the company's stock dropped in value from $3 per share in 1993 to $0.06 a share in 2002, even though the company was making a modest profit.

In 2002 the company moved its stock market listing to the United States. Cowell reports that the HLS was taken over "on paper" by Life Sciences Research, a company set up by the HLS and incorporated in Maryland. This arrangement allows the HLS to take advantage of U.S. privacy laws that protect the identity of certain investors. An American arm of SHAC known as SHAC USA was formed to lead an intimidation campaign against the HLS and companies that do business with it. In May 2004 SHAC USA and seven individuals associated with it were indicted in New Jersey under federal charges for violating the Animal Enterprise Protection Act, stalking, and conspiracy to commit terrorism. The case went to trial in

February 2006, and the organization and six of the individuals were found guilty. They were sentenced to various prison terms ranging up to six years. SHAC USA officially ceased to exist; however, animal activists developed a new Web site (http://www.shac7.com) that publicizes the case and seeks to raise money and moral support for the imprisoned individuals. The Web site summarizes the details of the case and continues to accuse the HLS of abusing animals. As of April 2009, two of the activists had been released from prison.

In "Animal Welfare" (2009, http://www.huntingdon.com/index.php?currentNumber=3&currentIsExpanded=0), the HLS defends its practices, stating that it is "committed to providing the highest levels of animal husbandry and welfare." It also notes that in 2003 it was accredited by the Association for Assessment and Accreditation of Laboratory Animal Care (AAALAC) and is one of only a few contract research organizations in the world to be accredited. The AAALAC is an independent nonprofit organization founded in 1965 by scientists and veterinarians engaged in animal research. The AAALAC (2009, http://www.aaalac.org/accreditation/benefits.cfm) notes that accreditation "demonstrates a willingness to go above and beyond the minimums required by law. It tells the public that the institution is committed to the responsible care and use of animals in science."

Mainstream antivivisection and welfarist groups condemn the violent tactics used by radical activists and instead wage public relations and political campaigns against the use of research animals.

FEDERAL LEGISLATION AND OVERSIGHT

Facilities that use certain species of live laboratory animals for research purposes must abide by laws and policies governing their use. Even though there are a few state laws that also apply, most of the applicable legislation and oversight is provided by federal agencies. Table 5.2 lists acronyms, laws, and regulations related to federal oversight of laboratory animal usage.

Animal Welfare Act

Animal Welfare Act (AWA) regulations are enforced by the Animal Care unit of the USDA's Animal and Plant Health Inspection Service (APHIS). The regulations govern the housing and care of the animals and include licensing, registration, veterinary, and record-keeping requirements. Covered facilities must register with the USDA.

The AWA does not apply to cold-blooded animals, rats, mice, or birds. According to the law, these animals do not fall under the definition of *animal*. This condition was made permanent in May 2002 as part of new federal legislation. The AWA does cover dogs, cats, rabbits, primates, guinea pigs, hamsters, marine mammals, and "other warm-blooded animals."

TABLE 5.2

Acronyms and common terms associated with laboratory animal oversight

AAALAC	Association for Assessment and Accreditation of Laboratory Animal Care International. Independent organization that accredits animal care and use programs.
AALAS	American Association for Laboratory Animal Science. Organization of laboratory animal technicians, veterinarians, and other professionals that serves society through education and the advancement of responsible laboratory animal care and use.
ACLAM	American College of Laboratory Animal Medicine. Organization that establishes standards for board certification in the veterinary medical specialty of laboratory animal medicine. Board certified veterinarians are known as ACLAM diplomats.
AHRQ	Agency for Healthcare Research and Quality. Agency of the Public Health Service.
APHIS	Animal and Plant Health Inspection Service. Component of the USDA that administers the Animal Welfare Act. Within APHIS, Animal Care (AC) is the agency that is responsible for ensuring compliance with the Animal Welfare Regulations.
AVMA	American Veterinary Medical Association. Professional organization of veterinarians.
AWA	Animal Welfare Act. Federal law regulating the use, sale, and handling of animals.
AWIC	Animal Welfare Information Center. Part of the United States Department of Agriculture's National Agricultural Library, AWIC provides information and publications on many aspects of animal welfare and alternatives to the use of animals.
Animal Welfare Regulations	USDA regulations that implement the Animal Welfare Act.
CDC	Centers for Disease Control and Prevention. Agency of the Public Health Service.
FDA	Food and Drug Administration. Agency of the Public Health Service.
FOIA	Freedom of Information Act. Statute allowing the public access to certain information on file in federal agencies.
Guide	Guide for the Care and Use of Laboratory Animals. Manual of standards for animal care and use developed under the auspices of the Institute for Laboratory Animal Research.
Health Research Extension Act of 1985	Federal law that mandates the PHS Policy.
HRSA	Health Resources and Services Administration. Agency of the Public Health Service.
IACUC	Institutional Animal Care and Use Committee. Committee charged with oversight of institutional animal care and use program.
IHS	Indian Health Service. Agency of the Public Health Service.
ILAR	Institute for Laboratory Animal Research. Component of the National Research Council, National Academy of Sciences, responsible for developing and disseminating information on humane care and appropriate use of animals.
IRAC	Interagency Research Animal Committee. Author of U.S. Principles and the focal point for coordinating federal policies involving all animal species needed for biomedical research and testing, especially their care, use, and conservation.
NIH	National Institutes of Health. Agency of the Public Health Service.
OLAW	Office of Laboratory Animal Welfare. NIH office with responsibility for implementation of the PHS Policy.
OPRR	Office for Protection from Research Risks. The OPRR Division of Animal Welfare was renamed the Office of Laboratory Animal Welfare in March, 2000.
PHS	Public Health Service. Component of the Department of Health and Human Services that includes eight different agencies.
PHS Policy	PHS Policy on Humane Care and Use of Laboratory Animals. Document that implements the Health Research Extension Act of 1985, and governs activities involving animals conducted or supported by PHS agencies.
Principles	United States Government Principles for the Utilization and Care of Vertebrate Animals Used in Testing, Research, and Training. Nine principles that provide a foundation for humane care and use of animals in the United States.
SAMHSA	Substance Abuse and Mental Health Services Administration. Agency of the Public Health Service.
USDA	United States Department of Agriculture. Federal agency responsible for implementation and enforcement of the Animal Welfare Act.

SOURCE: *Acronym Glossary and Additional Resources*, National Institutes of Health, Office of Laboratory Animal Welfare, January 22, 2001, http://grants1.nih.gov/grants/olaw/tutorial/glossary.htm (accessed February 20, 2009)

Under the AWA each research facility must have an attending veterinarian who is required to provide adequate veterinary care to the facility's animals. The law defines adequate veterinary care as "what is currently the accepted professional practice or treatment for that particular circumstance or condition." Each research facility must have an institutional officer who is responsible for legally committing the facility to meet AWA requirements. This officer or the chief executive officer of the facility must appoint an institutional animal care and use committee (IACUC) to assess the research facility's animal program, buildings, and procedures. The IACUC must include at least three members (a chairperson, a veterinarian, and a person not affiliated with the institute) to represent "general community interests." IACUC members have to be qualified based on their experience and expertise.

The IACUC is responsible for reviewing a research facility's animal use program and inspecting the facilities in which animals are housed and studied. These evaluations must be done at least once every six months. Written reports are required and must be made available to APHIS and to any federal agencies that provide funding to the

facility. The IACUC is also responsible for investigating any complaints lodged against the facility regarding the care and use of the animals. This includes complaints from the general public. The IACUC has the power to approve or disapprove proposed animal care and use activities and to ask for modifications in these activities. It can also suspend particular animal activities if it believes they are not being conducted in accordance with its wishes.

Under the AWA proposed animal activities must meet certain criteria. Some of the major requirements include:

- Procedures must "avoid or minimize discomfort, distress, and pain to the animals."

- Researchers must consider alternative procedures that will not cause more than momentary or slight pain and provide reasons in cases where alternatives cannot be used.

- Researchers must provide written assurance that the activities "do not unnecessarily duplicate previous experiments."

Any procedures that may cause more than momentary or slight pain or distress require that pain-relieving drugs be administered, "unless withholding such drugs is scientifically justified." Animals cannot be administered paralyzing drugs unless they are also given anesthesia. Those that experience severe or chronic pain or distress that cannot be relieved are required to be painlessly euthanized as soon as possible, unless researchers seek and receive an exemption from the IACUC.

APHIS publishes an annual report on its animal welfare activities. The most recent report as of mid-2009, *Animal Care Annual Report of Activities: Fiscal Year 2007* (http://www.aphis.usda.gov/publications/animal_welfare/content/printable_version/2007_AC_Report.pdf), was published in September 2008 and includes data through fiscal year (FY) 2007. According to APHIS, in FY 2007 there were 1,088 registered research facilities in the United States. (See Table 5.3.) This number has varied little since FY 2002, when 1,087 research facilities were registered with the USDA. In "Electronic Freedom of Information Act Reports" (January 9, 2009, http://www.aphis.usda.gov/animal_welfare/efoia/index.shtml), APHIS maintains lists of federal and nonfederal research institutions and Veteran's Administration hospitals required to comply with AWA regulations and standards. The lists include the names and addresses of the facilities, which are mostly colleges and universities, pharmaceutical companies, hospitals, and biotechnology laboratories.

All research facilities are required to comply with AWA regulations and standards. Federal facilities are not required to register with the USDA and are not subject to USDA inspections, though they are required to comply with USDA standards for animal care established under the AWA and must submit annual reports to the USDA

regarding their use of regulated laboratory animals. The AWA requires that nonfederal research facilities receive at least one inspection per year to determine compliance with the law.

All registered research facilities must submit annual reports to the USDA listing the number and species of animals used in research, testing, and experimentation and indicating whether pain-relieving drugs were administered. If the drugs were not administered for procedures that caused pain or distress, the report must explain why their use would have interfered with the research or experiment.

Health Research Extension Act

In 1985 the Health Research Extension Act (HREA) was passed. This act requires that facilities conducting animal research, training, and testing activities that receive funding from the Public Health Service (PHS) follow an animal welfare policy called the Public Health Service Policy on the Humane Care and Use of Laboratory Animals (PHSP). The PHS includes government agencies such as the Centers for Disease Control and Prevention, the U.S. Food and Drug Administration (FDA), and the NIH. The NIH is the main public source of funding for biomedical research in the United States.

The animal research facilities that fall under the HREA must follow the recommendations given in the PHS's *Guide for the Care and Use of Laboratory Animals* (1996) regarding housing, cleanliness, husbandry, veterinary care, and use of measures to alleviate pain and distress. The standards are similar to those found in the AWA, but the HREA applies to all vertebrates, including mice, rats, and birds.

The HREA requires facilities to file annual reports that describe their animal care and use programs and how they comply with the AWA and the PHSP. The PHSP is administered by the NIH Office for Protection from Research Risks. Research facilities that receive funding from the NIH must have at least five people on their IACUC. The NIH also reviews planned animal studies to ensure that animal models are appropriate and that no more animals than necessary are used.

In 2008 the NIH's Institute for Laboratory Animal Research (ILAR; November 17, 2008, http://www8.nationalacademies.org/cp/projectview.aspx?key=48959) began an update of *Guide for the Care and Use of Laboratory Animals* to reflect new technologies and scientific literature on laboratory animal care. The updated edition will be published in January 2010.

Food, Drug, and Cosmetic Act

Another major piece of federal legislation that affects laboratory animals is the Food, Drug, and Cosmetic Act of 1938 (FDCA), which has been amended several times. The FDCA defines drugs as:

TABLE 5.3

Research facilities registered under the Animal Welfare Act, fiscal years 2002–07

Fiscal year	Total facilities
2007	1,088
2006	1,072
2005	1,024
2004	1,079
2003	1,088
2002	1,087

SOURCE: Adapted from "Table 8: Registered Research Facilities, FY 2005–2007," in *Animal Care Annual Report of Activities: Fiscal Year 2007*, U.S. Department of Agriculture, Animal and Plant Health Inspection Service, September 2008, http://www.aphis.usda.gov/publications/animal_welfare/content/printable_version/2007_AC_Report.pdf (accessed January 13, 2009); *FY 2004 AWA Inspections*, U.S. Department of Agriculture, Animal and Plant Health Inspection Service, 2004, http://www.aphis.usda.gov/animal_welfare/downloads/awreports/awreport2004.pdf (accessed February 2, 2009); *FY 2003 AWA Inspections*, U.S. Department of Agriculture, Animal and Plant Health Inspection Service, 2003, http://www.aphis.usda.gov/animal_welfare/downloads/awreports/awreport2003.pdf (accessed February 2, 2009); and *FY 2002 AWA Inspections*, U.S. Department of Agriculture, Animal and Plant Health Inspection Service, 2002, http://www.aphis.usda.gov/animal_welfare/downloads/awreports/awreport2002.pdf (accessed February 2, 2009)

- Articles intended for use in the diagnosis, cure, mitigation, treatment, or prevention of disease in man or other animals; and

- Articles (other than food) intended to affect the structure or any function of the body of man or other animals

Drugs must receive FDA approval before they can be sold in the United States. Even though the FDA does not specify the tests that must be done, the agency does not allow human testing to occur if animal safety testing is considered inadequate or incomplete.

Cosmetics are defined as articles other than soap that are applied to the human body for "cleansing, beautifying, promoting attractiveness, or altering the appearance." Soaps are specifically excluded from the regulatory definition of cosmetics and so do not fall under the FDCA.

Cosmetic products and their ingredients (except for color additives) are not subject to premarket FDA approval. However, it is illegal to distribute cosmetics that contain substances that could harm consumers under normal use. Even though animal testing is not required by the law, it is recommended by the FDA to ensure product safety. Cosmetic products that are not adequately tested for safety must have a warning statement on their front label reading "WARNING—The safety of this product has not been determined."

Some consumer products are considered both a drug and a cosmetic under the law, such as dandruff shampoos, fluoride-containing toothpastes, combination antiperspirants/deodorants, and makeup products or moisturizers that contain sunscreens. These products are subject to provisions of the laws that apply to both drugs and cosmetics.

Other Federal Legislation

The Federal Hazardous Substances Labeling Act was passed in 1960. The Consumer Product Safety Commission administers the law as it applies to household products. This law affects animals because household products (such as cleaners) that contain hazardous chemicals must warn consumers about their potential hazards. A hazardous substance is defined as one that is toxic, corrosive, flammable, or combustible; that is extremely irritating or sensitizing; or that generates pressure through heat, decomposition, or other means. Toxicity tests are required to determine these conditions.

Other laws governing chemicals that must be tested for toxicity include the Federal Insecticide, Fungicide, and Rodenticide Act of 1947 and the Toxic Substances Control Act of 1976. Both of these laws are administered by the U.S. Environmental Protection Agency. Animals are commonly used to test the products regulated by all of this legislation.

In 2000 the Chimpanzee Health Improvement, Maintenance, and Protection (CHIMP) Act was passed, calling for the creation of a national sanctuary system for chimpanzees no longer needed in research programs conducted or supported by federal agencies. In 2002 the NIH awarded a contract to Chimp Haven Inc. to establish and operate a sanctuary under the CHIMP Act in Shreveport, Louisiana. Construction began in 2003, and the facility was dedicated in 2004. Most chimpanzees involved in federal research programs were bred or captured from the wild to be used in hepatitis and acquired immune deficiency syndrome (AIDS) research. The HSUS estimates in "Chimps Deserve Better" (February 9, 2009, http://www.hsus.org/animals_in_research/chimps _deserve_better/) that approximately 1,000 chimpanzees were being held at 10 research facilities around the country in 2009. Table 5.4 lists the research facilities and the self-described chimp sanctuaries known to the HSUS.

The CHIMP Act is extremely controversial because it allows the animals to be recalled for research purposes if there is a "public health need." Because the act does not call for permanent retirement of chimpanzees, many animal activist groups have called for its repeal.

LABORATORY ANIMALS AND THEIR USES

Determining the number of animals used for research in the United States is extremely difficult, because rats, mice, birds, and cold-blooded animals are not regulated by the AWA and do not have to be counted. It is widely agreed that rats and mice make up a huge majority of research animals.

There were just over 1 million AWA-registered animals used in live research during FY 2007. (See Table 5.5.) California laboratories used the most regulated animals (124,155), followed by New York (92,107), Pennsylvania (72,713), Massachusetts (68,136), Iowa (62,792), and Texas (55,623). Together, these six states accounted for 46% of all regulated research animals.

In *Animal Care Annual Report of Activities*, APHIS provides a breakdown of regulated research animals by species in FY 2007. Rabbits made up the largest number (23%, or 236,511), followed by guinea pigs (20%, or 207,257), hamsters (17%, or 172,498), farm animals (11%, or 109,961), dogs (7%, or 72,037), primates (7%, or 69,990), and cats (2%, or 22,687). (See Figure 5.4.) In addition, 13% (136,509) were miscellaneous animals. Overall, rabbits, guinea pigs, and hamsters accounted for 60% of the total, whereas dogs, cats, and nonhuman primates constituted 16% of all regulated animals. These latter species are the ones that arouse the most public concern in the research animal debate.

The total number of regulated research animals used annually between FYs 1973 and 2007 is shown in Table 5.6 and Figure 5.5. The number ranged between approximately 1.5 million and 2.2 million per year from

TABLE 5.4

North American chimp laboratories and self-described sanctuaries, 2009

Facility	Location	Type
Alamogordo Primate Facility	Alamogordo, NM	Laboratory
Bioqual	Rockville, MD	Laboratory
Center for Disease Control (CDC)	Atlanta, GA	Laboratory
Center for Great Apes	Wauchula, FL	Sanctuary
Chimp Haven	Shreveport, LA	Sanctuary
Chimpanzee and Human Communication Institute (CHCI), Central Washington University	Ellensburg, WA	Sanctuary
Chimpanzee Sanctuary Northwest	Cle Elum, WA	Sanctuary
Cleveland Amory Black Beauty Ranch	Murchison, TX	Sanctuary
Fauna Foundation	Quebec, Canada	Sanctuary
Food & Drug Administration (FDA)	Rockville, MD	Laboratory
Language Research Center, Georgia State University	Decatur, GA	Laboratory
MD Anderson Cancer Center	Bastrop, TX	Laboratory
New Iberia Research Center (NIRC)	New Iberia, LA	Laboratory
Primarily Primates, Inc	San Antonio, TX	Sanctuary
Primate Foundation of Arizona (PFA)*	Mesa, AZ	Laboratory
Primate Rescue Center	Nicholasville, KY	Sanctuary
Primate Sactuary of America (Chimp Aid)	San Antonio, TX	Sanctuary
Save the Chimps	Alamogordo, NM	Sanctuary
Save the Chimps	Ft. Pierce, FL	Sanctuary
Southwest National Primate Research Center (SWNPRC)	San Antonio, TX	Laboratory
Wildlife Waystation	Angeles National Forest, CA	Sanctuary
Yerkes National Primate Research Center	Atlanta, GA	Laboratory

*Note: PFA is scheduled to close in 2010. Its chimps are expected to be transferred to the MD Anderson Cancer Center

SOURCE: Adapted from "Chimpanzee Labs and Sanctuaries," in *Chimps Deserve Better*, Humane Society of the United States, 2009, http://www.hsus.org/animals_in_research/chimps_deserve_better/chimpanzee_labs_and_sanctuaries/?facility_type=&state= (accessed February 20, 2009)

FY 1973 to FY 1994 and then began to decline. It reached a low of 1,012,713 animals in FY 2006.

Biomedical Research

The vast majority of research animals are used in biomedical research. Biomedicine is a medical discipline based on principles of the natural sciences, particularly biology and biochemistry.

The NIH maintains the Computer Retrieval of Information on Scientific Projects (CRISP; http://www.crisp.cit.nih.gov/), which is a database of biomedical research projects that have received funding from federal agencies dating back to 1972. The CRISP database can be searched to find information about the use of animals in federally funded research projects at universities, hospitals, and other research institutions. Information supplied about each project includes the name of the principal investigator, the name and address of the research institution, the starting and ending dates of the project, the federal agency providing funding, and a description of the project.

DRUG TESTING. According to the FDA, in "The Beginnings: Laboratory and Animal Studies" (January 30, 2006, http://www.fda.gov/fdac/special/testtubetopatient/studies.html), drug companies typically test new drugs on at least two different animal species to see if they are affected differently. Animal testing is performed to determine specific characteristics, such as:

- How much of the drug is absorbed into the bloodstream

- Any toxic side effects

- Appropriate dosage levels

- How the drug is metabolized (broken down) by the body

- How quickly the drug is excreted from the body

The results from animal tests tell researchers if and how new drugs should then be tested on humans.

Product Testing

Millions of research animals are used to test products intended for industrial and consumer markets in the United States. Product safety testing exposes animals to chemicals to determine factors such as eye and skin irritancy. Common product safety tests conducted with animals include:

- Acute toxicity tests determine the immediate effects of chemical exposure. The LD-50 test is an example. In this test animals are exposed to chemicals through ingestion, inhalation, or skin contact to determine the concentration necessary to kill 50% of the test group within a specific time period.

- Skin and eye irritancy tests determine the effects on skin and eyes of chemical exposure. One example is the Draize eye test. Rabbits are commonly used because they cannot blink and wash out the chemicals.

TABLE 5.5

Animals used at USDA-registered research facilities, fiscal year 2007

Species	All other covered species	Cats	Dogs	Guinea pigs	Hamsters	Nonhuman primates	Other farm animals	Pig	Rabbits	Sheep	Total by state
States											
AK	614	—	—	—	52	—	30	—	—	—	696
AL	2,730	211	1,904	503	214	1,463	610	1,174	1,807	28	10,644
AR	49	70	251	441	85	128	194	429	533	0	2,180
AZ	6,582	120	275	206	69	94	33	443	274	50	8,146
CA	16,380	2,195	3,498	27,774	6,175	4,470	7,241	4,970	49,396	2,056	124,155
CO	2,092	394	587	5,622	1,830	0	87	623	503	483	12,221
CT	763	36	592	622	2,408	339	10	584	525	51	5,930
DC	5,660	107	48	576	527	224	41	844	405	33	8,465
DE	932	266	377	5,158	1,481	0	507	41	16,176	570	25,508
FL	2,723	441	403	462	151	716	881	1,237	303	232	7,549
GA	7,024	1,037	1,940	1,214	10,226	3,334	166	1,269	5,043	76	31,329
HI	5	51	50	5	478	0	0	38	31	0	658
IA	1,337	2,180	2,229	5,646	43,809	23	919	974	5,163	512	62,792
ID	238	16	40	0	0	0	49	0	34	2	379
IL	4,513	975	3,074	2,788	3,046	652	761	1,792	5,051	300	22,952
IN	2,810	329	1,983	750	1,862	709	364	927	2,257	135	12,126
KS	1,350	565	1,533	670	813	220	112	138	667	0	6,068
KY	2,309	56	177	254	372	63	26	140	535	0	3,932
LA	1,029	237	380	4	240	2,561	359	83	1,032	7	5,932
MA	6,258	106	3,287	22,436	9,229	5,211	714	5,286	14,857	752	68,136
MD	8,462	87	810	19,849	5,061	6,304	1,725	1,656	7,465	377	51,796
ME	716	0	0	48	0	0	340	31	234	3	1,372
MI	6,493	463	6,784	15,291	913	3,361	286	2,912	4,482	563	41,548
MN	1,281	1,734	3,072	10,814	104	216	1,127	3,808	5,691	1,067	28,914
MO	1,440	1,874	2,413	3,978	8,126	108	450	1,813	3,373	66	23,641
MS	171	5	70	118	7	84	46	76	442	0	1,019
MT	26	9	0	28	532	5	125	0	313	84	1,122
NC	1,989	1,138	1,699	8,731	1,098	2,085	4,772	3,074	4,237	593	29,416
ND	36	149	21	3	2		81	24	952	443	1,711
NE	1,835	649	1,032	1,302	7,317	89	261	9,132	815	46	22,478
NH	394	23	9	1	265	16	0	256	7	31	1,002
NJ	3,692	135	6,427	13,668	2,193	4,461	42	1,284	8,260	0	40,162
NM	341	21	228	134	88	295	0	66	972	0	2,145
NV	1,947	0	121	163	0	0	9	0	188	380	2,808
NY	8,074	2,325	4,595	14,708	43,974	2,230	869	1,422	13,665	245	92,107
OH	4,159	1,113	6,052	13,438	3,884	2,151	192	4,304	13,827	137	49,257
OK	646	93	657	533	3	113	173	21	451	52	2,742
OR	576	46	37	1,022	101	2,369	645	708	416	299	6,219
PA	3,997	1,743	5,627	11,557	2,388	4,183	1,364	2,544	38,618	692	72,713
PR	971	0	0	0	287	3,066	0	36	14	0	4,374
RI	943	12	0	61	247	25	50	201	322	58	1,919
SC	635	238	199	248	55	471	44	289	617	0	2,796
SD	356	21	14	7	94	17	624	125	307	6	1,571
TN	2,179	120	466	161	990	171	239	1,440	732	11	6,509
TX	12,261	585	1,455	8,506	3,826	4,389	3,380	3,080	17,189	952	55,623
UT	1,418	107	291	423	4,190	16	14	214	791	198	7,662
VA	2,109	80	283	360	321	94	125	4,389	1,212	37	9,010
VT	213	18	17	450	0	0	12	89	137	1,280	2,216
WA	2,221	162	795	4,687	359	4,596	248	795	1,949	26	15,838
WI	955	300	6,192	1,820	2,972	8,859	722	834	3,914	203	26,771
WV	230	40	20	14	27	9	0	0	307	81	728
WY	345	5	23	3	7	0	37	0	20	23	463
Species total	**136,509**	**22,687**	**72,037**	**207,257**	**172,498**	**69,990**	**31,106**	**65,615**	**236,511**	**13,240**	
Report total											**1,027,450**

SOURCE: "Appendix 1. Animals Used in Research," in *Animal Care Annual Report of Activities: Fiscal Year 2007*, U.S. Department of Agriculture, Animal and Plant Health Inspection Service, September 2008, http://www.aphis.usda.gov/publications/animal_welfare/content/printable_version/2007_AC_Report.pdf (accessed January 13, 2009)

- Subchronic and chronic toxicity tests determine the effects of long-term chemical exposure.

- Genetic toxicity tests determine the effects of chemical exposure on reproductive organs.

- Birth defects tests determine the effects of chemical exposure on offspring.

- Cancer potential tests determine the potential of chemical exposures for causing cancer.

CONSUMER PRODUCTS. Some companies selling consumer products, such as cosmetics and household cleaners, advertise that they do not conduct animal testing on their products or that their products are "cruelty-free." In some

FIGURE 5.4

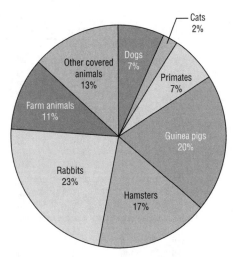

Animals used in research, by species, fiscal year 2007

Cats 2%
Dogs 7%
Primates 7%
Other covered animals 13%
Farm animals 11%
Guinea pigs 20%
Rabbits 23%
Hamsters 17%

SOURCE: Adapted from "Figure 1. Animals Used in Research, Experiments, Testing, and Teaching, FY 2007," in *Animal Care Annual Report of Activities: Fiscal Year 2007*, U.S. Department of Agriculture, Animal and Plant Health Inspection Service, September 2008, http://www.aphis.usda.gov/publications/animal_welfare/content/printable_version/2007_AC_Report.pdf (accessed January 13, 2009)

cases this statement may be somewhat misleading. For example, according to CAAT (September 14, 2007, http://altweb.jhsph.edu/faqs.htm#13), such claims can mean various things, including:

- Animal testing has not been performed on the products and/or their ingredients in the previous five years.

- Animal testing was performed on the products and/or ingredients by another company (e.g., a supplier).

- Nonanimal testing was performed on finished products made from ingredients already known to be safe because of previous animal testing.

CAAT points out that the vast majority of cosmetic ingredients used by the industry have been tested on animals at some point in time, or are known to be safe based on decades of use. It notes that smaller cosmetics companies tend to produce final products made from purchased ingredients, rather than from ingredients developed in-house. Larger companies that develop new ingredients for cosmetics must use animal testing or viable alternatives to prove that the ingredients are safe for consumer use.

In *Personal Care for People Who Care* (2007), the National Anti-Vivisection Society lists hundreds of companies that produce personal care (e.g., bath products, deodorants, and antiperspirants), household (e.g., bathroom and kitchen cleaners and furniture polishes), pet care, and cosmetic products and tells whether they do or do not test their products on animals.

In addition, the book identifies companies that do not use any animal-derived ingredients in their products. Other animal rights organizations, such as PETA, maintain similar types of lists. Some provide a seal that compliant companies can use to mark their products for easy identification by shoppers.

In February 2003 the Council of the European Union and the European Parliament approved the Seventh Amendment of Council Directive 76/768/EEC (the Cosmetics Directive). In "The Cosmetics Directive's Ban on Animals in Testing" (2009, http://www.colipa.eu/the-cosmetics-directives-ban-on-animals-in-testing.html), Colipa, a trade association for the European cosmetic, toiletry, and perfumery industries, indicates that a ban on the testing of cosmetic ingredients on animals in Europe went into effect in March 2009. In addition, a ban on the sale and import of new cosmetics tested on animals using specific tests also went into effect in March 2009. A final ban on the sale and import of cosmetics tested on animals using any test will go into effect in March 2013.

Dissection

Dead animals used for dissection in schools are believed to make up a small portion of all research animals. The HSUS states in the press release "Back to School Shouldn't Mean Back to Dissection Says the HSUS" (September 23, 2004, http://www.hsus.org/press_and_publications/press_releases/back_to_school_shouldnt_mean_back_to_dissection_says_the_hsus.html) that an estimated 6 million animals—mostly frogs, pig fetuses, and cats—are dissected by U.S. schoolchildren each year. Dissection has been considered a staple of biology classes since the 1960s, when the NSF urged schools to implement a more hands-on science curriculum.

The first legal challenge against school dissection lodged by a student occurred in California in 1987. A high school student sued her school for not allowing her to perform an alternative to dissection. California and Florida became the first states to allow students to opt out of dissection in the mid- to late 1980s. In "Dissection Laws" (February 4, 2009, http://www.hsus.org/animals_in_research/animals_in_education/dissection_laws.html), the HSUS notes that other states have since followed suit with choice-in-dissection laws or policies: Illinois, Louisiana, Maine, Maryland, Massachusetts, New Jersey, New Mexico, New York, Oregon, Pennsylvania, Rhode Island, Vermont, and Virginia.

By the early twenty-first century many students were expressing ethical and moral concerns about the practice of dissection in the classroom. Some school districts now offer students alternatives, such as computer models. The National Science Teachers Association defends dissection as a valuable learning tool for children, but urges teachers to be flexible in offering alternatives.

TABLE 5.6

Number of animals used in research, by species, fiscal years 1973–2007

Fiscal year	Dogs	Cats	Primates	Guinea pigs	Hamsters	Rabbits	Farm animals	Other covered animals	Totals
1973	195,157	66,165	42,298	408,970	454,986	447,570	—	38,169	1,653,345
1974	199,204	74,259	51,253	430,439	430,766	425,585	—	81,021	1,692,527
1975	154,489	51,439	36,202	436,446	456,031	448,530	—	42,523	1,625,660
1976	210,330	70,468	50,115	486,310	503,590	527,551	—	73,736	1,922,100
1977	176,430	62,311	53,116	348,741	393,533	439,003	—	46,535	1,519,669
1978	197,010	65,929	57,009	419,341	414,394	475,162	—	58,356	1,687,201
1979	211,104	69,103	59,359	457,134	419,504	539,594	—	76,247	1,832,045
1980	188,783	68,482	56,024	422,390	405,826	471,297	—	49,102	1,661,904
1981	188,649	58,090	57,515	432,632	397,522	473,922	—	50,111	1,658,441
1982	161,396	49,923	46,388	459,246	337,790	453,506	—	69,043	1,577,292
1983	174,542	53,344	54,926	485,048	337,023	466,810	—	108,549	1,680 242
1984	201,936	56,910	55,338	561,184	437,123	529,101	—	232,541	2,074,133
1985	194,905	59,211	57,271	598,903	414,460	544,621	—	284,416	2,153,787
1986	176141	54,125	48,540	462,699	370,655	521,773	—	144,470	1,778,403
1987	180,169	50,145	61,392	538,998	416,002	554,385	—	168,032	1,969,123
1988	140,471	42,271	51,641	431,457	331,945	459,254	—	178,249	1,635,288
1989	156,443	50,812	51,688	481,712	389,042	471,037	—	153,722	1,754,456
1990	109,992	33,700	47,177	352,627	311,068	399,264	66,702	257,569	1,578,099
1991	107,908	34,613	42,620	378,582	304,207	396,046	214,759	363,685	1,842,420
1992	124,161	38,592	55,105	375,063	396,585	431,432	210,936	529,308	2,134,182
1993	106,191	33,991	49,561	392,138	318,268	426,501	165,416	212,309	1,704,505
1994	101,090	32,610	55,113	360,184	298,934	393,751	180,667	202,300	1,624,649
1995	89,420	29,569	50,206	333,379	248,402	354,076	163,985	126,426	1,395,463
1996	82,420	26,035	52,327	299,011	246,415	338,574	154,344	146,579	1,345,739
1997	75,429	26,091	56,381	272,797	217,079	309,322	159,742	150,987	1,267,828
1998	76,071	24,712	57,377	261,305	206,243	287,523	157,620	142,963	1,213,814
1999	70,541	23,238	54,927	266,129	201,593	280,222	155,409	165,939	1,217,998
2000	69,516	25,560	57,518	266,873	174,146	258,754	159,711	166,429	1,286,412
2001	70,082	22,755	49,382	256,193	167,231	267,351	161,658	242,251	1,236,903
2002	68,253	24,222	52,279	245,576	180,000	243,838	143,061	180,351	1,137,580
2003	67,875	25,997	53,586	260,809	177,991	236,250	166,135	199,826	1,188,469
2004	64,932	23,640	54,998	244,104	175,721	261,573	105,678	171,312	1,101,958
2005	66,610	22,921	57,531	221,286	176,988	24 5,786	155,004	231,440	1,177,566
2006	66,314	21,637	62,315	204,809	167,571	239,720	105,780	144,567	1,012,713
2007	72,037	22,687	69,990	207,257	172,498	236,511	109,961	136,509	1,027,450

—Not reported

SOURCE: "Appendix 5. Number of Animals Used in Research from the First Reporting Year (FY 1973) to the Present," in *Animal Care Annual Report of Activities: Fiscal Year 2007*, U.S. Department of Agriculture, Animal and Plant Health Inspection Service, September 2008, http://www.aphis.usda.gov/publications/animal_welfare/content/printable_version/2007_AC_Report.pdf (accessed January 13, 2009)

Surgical/Medical Training and Behavior Research

It is estimated that the use of laboratory animals for surgical/medical training and behavior research makes up only a small part of the number of research animals used. However, this category is one that is particularly criticized by antivivisection groups. In the past, surgeons training to operate on humans and animals almost always practiced on live animals. Many of these surgeries are terminal surgeries, meaning that the animals are not allowed to regain consciousness. The animals are euthanized while they are under the effects of anesthesia.

The Physicians Committee for Responsible Medicine (PCRM) reports in "Alternatives to Animal Labs in Medical Schools" (January 30, 2007, http://www.pcrm.org/resch/anexp/alertliveanimallabs.html) that more than 90% of all U.S. medical schools have eliminated live animal labs to train medical students. Many veterinary schools are limiting the number of terminal surgeries required of their students. Some veterinary schools conduct dissection labs. According to the PCRM, many schools now use animal cadavers donated by people whose pets or livestock have died of natural causes or have been humanely euthanized because of illness or injury.

SOURCES OF RESEARCH ANIMALS

Research animals are obtained by laboratories from animal breeders and brokers licensed by the USDA. These licenses fall into two types:

- Class A—breeders who sell animals that they have bred and raised on their own premises and who buy animals only to replenish their breeding stock

- Class B—breeders, dealers, brokers, and operators of auction sales that purchase and/or resell live or dead animals, often obtained from city or county animal shelters

Breeders who sell fewer than 25 dogs and/or cats per year that were born and raised on their own premises, for research, teaching, or testing purposes, are exempt.

FIGURE 5.5

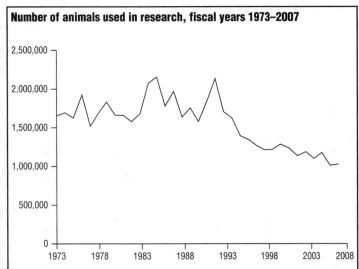

Number of animals used in research, fiscal years 1973–2007

SOURCE: Adapted from "Appendix 5. Number of Animals Used in Research from the First Reporting Year (FY 1973) to the Present," in *Animal Care Annual Report of Activities: Fiscal Year 2007*, U.S. Department of Agriculture, Animal and Plant Health Inspection Service, September 2008, http://www.aphis.usda.gov/publications/animal_welfare/content/printable_version/2007_AC_Report.pdf (accessed January 13, 2009)

APHIS reports in "Electronic Freedom of Information Act Reports" that in January 2009 there were 4,228 Class A breeders and 1,067 Class B breeders/dealers/brokers in the United States. Note that not all these licensees sell animals to research laboratories. Some sell animals to pet stores and other animal enterprises.

Lab animal suppliers advertise their animals in the *Lab Animal Buyer's Guide* (http://guide.labanimal.com/guide/index.html/). It lists more than 500 companies and over 800 products and services. Animals available include frogs, toads, salamanders, newts, cats, dogs, ferrets, chickens, ducks, cattle, goats, sheep, swine, rabbits, nonhuman primates (monkeys, chimpanzees, etc.), birds, fish, opossums, woodchucks, exotic animals, invertebrates, and a wide assortment of rodents.

Purpose-Bred Animals

The vast majority of laboratory research animals are purpose-bred, meaning that they are born and raised under controlled conditions and may be genetically manipulated. Purpose-breeding of laboratory animals is becoming more and more common as researchers demand animals with particular genetic makeups. For example, researchers investigating narcolepsy use dogs bred to be born with the condition. Charles River Laboratories in Wilmington, Massachusetts, is a leading breeder and supplier of purpose-bred animals.

Random-Source Animals

Live animals for research can also be purchased from random sources. For example, dogs and cats obtained from animal shelters are considered random-source animals. Researchers acquire these animals from dealers with USDA Class B licenses or directly from shelters. Class B dealers can acquire random-source dogs and cats for resale, but only from the following sources:

- Other USDA licensed dealers

- State-, county-, or city-owned and operated animal pounds or shelters

- Humane groups and contract pounds organized as legal entities under the laws of their state

- People who have bred and raised the animals on their own premises

Class B dealers are prohibited from obtaining dogs and cats from private individuals who did not breed and raise the animal on their own premises.

The rules that Class B dealers must follow when acquiring animals are primarily intended to prevent them from selling pets to research facilities. USDA regulations also require Class B dealers to hold live dogs and cats for specific time periods before reselling them, and the dealers have to keep records, including physical information about each animal (age, color, sex, species, and breed) and the names and addresses of the seller and buyer of each animal. (See Table 5.7.) This gives pet owners a chance to track down lost pets that were sold to Class B dealers by animal shelters. Random-source dealers are listed in the *Lab Animal Buyer's Guide*. Some animal protection groups also

TABLE 5.7

Holding periods required for dogs and cats held by USDA-licensed "B" dealers

IF the source is	AND the dog/cat's age is	THEN the holding period is
a private pound, contract pound or shelter	any age	10 full days, not including the day of acquisition and the time in transit
a state, city, or county operated pound or shelter	any age	5 full days, not including the day of acquisition and the time in transit
a private individual who bred and raised the dog/cat on his/her premises	< or = 120 days	24 hours, not including the time in transit
a private individual who bred and raised the dog/cat on his/her premises	>120 days	5 full days, not including the day of acquisition and the time in transit
another USDA licensed dealer or exhibitor who has already held the dog/cat for the required holding period	any age	24 hours, not including the time in transit
another USDA licensed dealer or exhibitor who has not held the dog/cat for the required holding period	any age	5 full days, not including the day of acquisition and the time in transit

SOURCE: "Licensed 'B' Dealer," in *Random Source Dog and Cat Dealer Inspection Guide*, U.S. Department of Agriculture, Animal and Plant Health Inspection Service, April 2000, http://www.aphis.usda.gov/animal_welfare/downloads/manuals/dealer/randomsource.pdf (accessed January 29, 2009)

maintain lists of Class B dealers they believe sell random-source dogs and cats to laboratories.

Random-source animals are used in research where genetic diversity is important. According to the MISMR, in "The Use of Pound Animals in Biomedical Research" (2009, http://www.mismr.org/educational/pound.html), random-source animals are primarily used in biomedical research on cardiovascular diseases, cancer, diabetes, arthritis, lung disorders, orthopedics, birth defects, hearing loss, and blindness. Dogs are the subject of choice for heart and kidney disease research. Cats are frequently used in research devoted to the central nervous system, strokes, and disorders of the brain, eyes, and ears. The MISMR (2009, http://www.mismr.org/about/) notes that use of these animals in research benefits not only human medicine but also veterinary medicine.

Random-source dogs and cats are far less expensive than those that are purpose-bred. The MISMR reports in "Use of Pound Animals in Biomedical Research" that in 2006 the cost of a shelter dog or cat was $60 to $200, compared to $422 to $580 for a purpose-bred one. It also claims that less than 2% of the 10 million animals that reside in shelters each year are used for medical research. The organization claims that these animals would be euthanized in the shelters anyway because of the pet overpopulation problem.

Animal welfare organizations disagree, however, noting that neither municipal animal shelters nor Class B dealers all follow the regulations. They may fail to keep animals for the assigned period or do not keep detailed records of the animals they sell. Despite regulations of the industry, lost family pets may become the subjects of experiments when they are not held for the entire waiting period. In addition, there has been much controversy over Class B dealers, some of whom have been known to steal pets from homes and yards. Welfarists and animal rights activists often criticize the NIH for funding research projects that use shelter dogs and cats. The NIH leaves source decisions to individual research institutions. Even though some people are pushing for legislation to outlaw the use of shelter animals in medical research, the MISMR argues that this would drive up the cost of research and the costs to local communities that must house and euthanize unwanted animals. Those involved in the animal welfare and rights movement respond with evidence that more and more animal shelters are adopting a "no-kill" policy—meaning they will euthanize only in cases of severe illness or temperament problems but not because of overpopulation—so shelter animals will not necessarily be euthanized and may instead be adopted.

CLASS B DEALER BUSTED BY THE USDA. In August 2003 federal authorities raided Martin Creek Kennels in Williford, Arkansas, and confiscated more than 100 dogs and one cat. The facility had a USDA Class B license to purchase and resell animals. The raid resulted from an undercover videotape obtained by the animal protection group Last Chance for Animals. The videotape documented many cases of abuse and neglect at the facility and several incidences of dogs being shot to death and thrown into mass graves. Brenda Shoss reports in "Pet Theft Thugs: They're Real. They're Nearby" (March 2005, http://www.animalsvoice.com/edits/editorial/features/compani/shoss_pet_thefts.html) that the kennel purchased stolen pets from bunchers (people who steal pets, pick up strays, and take in dogs and cats given away for free and sell them to Class B dealers). The kennel bought stolen pets for $5 to $30 per animal and sold them using falsified paperwork to research laboratories for $150 to $700 per dog and $50 to $200 per cat.

Shoss notes that the kennel had been in business for 16 years, and during that time it sold thousands of animals to research laboratories. In February 2005 C. C. Baird, the owner of the kennel, and his family were fined $262,700 by the USDA and had their Class B licenses revoked permanently. In 2006 HBO produced a documentary using footage from the Last Chance for Animals videotape called *Dealing Dogs.* The case also highlighted legislation proposed by the U.S. senator Daniel Akaka (1924–; D-HI), beginning in 1999, called the Pet Safety and Protection Act that would amend the Animal Welfare Act to make it illegal for research facilities to purchase dogs and cats from Class B dealers. The bill (also known as "Buck's Bill" for one of the dogs rescued from the Martin Creek Kennels who later died due to conditions at the kennel) was supported in the U.S. House of Representatives by Representatives Michael Doyle (1953–; D-PA), and Steve Israel (1958–; D-NY) and approved in the House and Senate Farm Bills in 2007, but it was later removed from the 2008 version of the Farm Bill. It is expected that the bill will be reintroduced to the 111th Congress in 2009.

Because of cases such as this, those in the animal rights and welfare community, as well as veterinarians, frequently warn against placing "free to good home" advertisements, fearing that the animals offered will end up in the hands of bunchers or Class B dealers.

REDUCTION, REFINEMENT, AND REPLACEMENT

In 1959 William Russell (1925–2006) and Rex Burch (1926–1996) published *Principles of Humane Experimental Technique,* which advocated three principles for the animal research industry: reduction, refinement, and replacement. Russell and Burch called these principles "the three R's for the removal of inhumanity" in the scientific community.

The book was largely ignored until the 1980s, when public protest against the use of animals in laboratory testing became more widespread. Scientists and animal welfare organizations then embraced the three Rs as scientifically reasonable and humane goals for the industry. The three Rs, however, are guiding principles, not legal requirements.

The three Rs are defined as follows:

- Reduction is a goal to reduce the number of animals used in research overall by reducing the number required for individual experiments or areas of study without sacrificing the statistical validity of the results. In other words, researchers are urged to use statistics to determine the minimum number of animals that can be used in an experiment and still provide valid data. Another goal is to reduce the number of procedures that require whole animals. For example, tissues from an animal used in one experiment could be used in other experiments in place of live whole animals.

- Refinement is a goal to refine experimental and care practices to reduce animal suffering and distress and encourage well-being. Such practices include the use of painkillers during and after experiments, the use of humane euthanasia techniques, and improvements in animals' living environments.

- Replacement is a goal to replace live laboratory animals with suitable alternatives (e.g., computer simulations) and to replace higher animal species with lower species.

Search for Alternatives to Animal Tests

In 1993 the National Institutes of Health Revitalization Act was passed, requiring the formation of an agency to oversee validation of alternatives to toxicological animal testing. The result was the Interagency Coordinating Committee for the Validation of Alternative Methods (ICCVAM) and the National Toxicology Program Interagency Center for the Evaluation of Alternative Toxicological Methods (NICEATM).

The ICCVAM is responsible for establishing validation criteria and for encouraging government agencies that regulate toxicity testing to accept validated methods. The NICEATM facilitates information sharing among all the parties involved.

Table 5.8 lists the alternative test methods that have been submitted to the ICCVAM for review and evaluation as of November 2008. Three of the tests are considered particularly promising: the local lymph node assay (LLNA), Corrositex, and in vitro pyrogenicity. The LLNA is a mouse-based test for determining if new chemicals cause allergic contact dermatitis (skin reactions). The traditional test for this condition used guinea pigs. The LLNA is reported to use fewer animals and cause much less pain and distress than the traditional test. It is also much faster. According to the ICCVAM, in 1999 the LLNA was accepted by regulatory agencies as an alternative to guinea pig testing for contact dermatitis. The use of LLNA for other testing applications is under review.

Corrositex is an in vitro (outside a living organism) test in which synthetic skin is used to test chemical irritancy. In vitro tests are commonly conducted in test tubes. The traditional test for skin irritancy relied on rabbits and could take

TABLE 5.8

Summary of alternative test methods evaluated by ICCVAM as of November 2008

Toxicity area	No.	Test method (no.)
Acute systemic toxicity	3	Up-and-down procedure (UDP)
		In vitro basal cytotoxicity methods [2]
Biologics testing	23*	In vivo alternatives
		Ex vivo alternatives
		In vitro cell-based methods
		In vitro enzymatic alternatives
Developmental toxicity	1	Frog embryo
		Teratogenesis assay: Xenopus (FETAX)
Endocrine disruptors	138	In vitro androgen receptor (AR) binding [11]
		In vitro AR transcriptional activation (TA) [18]
		In vitro estrogen receptor (ER) binding [14]
		In vitro ER TA [95]
Eye corrosion/irritation	7	In vitro test methods for detecting ocular corrosives and severe irritants [4]
		In vitro test methods for assessment of the eye irritation potential of antimicrobial cleaning products [3]
Pyrogenicity	5	In vitro pyrogenicity
Skin corrosion	4	Corrositex®
		EpiDerm™
		EPISKIN™
		Rat trancutaneous Electrical resistance (TER) assay
Skin sensitization	7	Murine local lymph node assay (LLNA)
		• Limit dose approach
		• Use for potency determination
		• Applicability domain
		• Performance standards
		LLNA non-radiolabelled methods [3]
Total	**188**	

No.= Number of methods reviewed in each toxicity area, OECD = Organisation for Economic Co-operation and Development.
*These methods were reviewed and discussed at an ICCVAM-NICEATM/ECVAM (Interagency Coordinating Committee on the Validation of Alternative Methods/NTP (National Toxicology Program) Interagency Center for the Evaluation of Alternative Toxicological Methods/European Centre for the Validation of Alternative Methods) sponsored workshop to review the state-of-the-science and current knowledge of alternatives that may reduce, replace, and refine (less pain and distress) the use of mice for botulinum toxin testing.

SOURCE: Adapted from "Test Methods Reviewed or under Consideration by ICCVAM," in *NICEATM and ICCVAM Test Method Evaluations*, National Institutes of Health, National Institute of Environmental Health Sciences, Interagency Coordinating Committee on the Validation of Alternative Methods, November 20, 2008, http://iccvam.niehs.nih.gov/docs/about_docs/MethodsSum.pdf (accessed January 29, 2009)

several weeks. The new one takes just a few minutes or hours. Corrositex was accepted by U.S. agencies in 2000. Other in vitro skin corrosion tests could be used to satisfy other types of corrosivity testing required by various agencies. The new tests would replace the current testing protocol in which corrosive substances are placed on the skin of living animals (usually rabbits) for specific lengths of time. The extent of tissue damage in the animals is assessed after the exposure time to determine the corrosivity of the chemicals.

Pyrogenicity is the ability to cause fever or inflammation. Drugs intended for human use are tested for pyrogenicity, typically in rabbits. In vitro pyrogenicity tests are conducted on human cells in test tubes. In "*In Vitro* Pyrogen Test Methods" (April 21, 2009, http://iccvam.niehs.nih.gov/methods/pyrogen/pyrogen.htm), the ICCVAM recommends the new test methods as an alternative to rabbit testing for certain types of drugs.

FIGURE 5.6

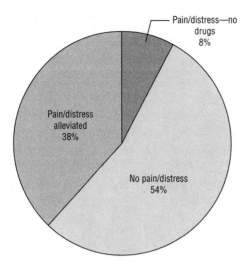

Pain and/or distress circumstances for animals used in research, fiscal year 2007

Pain/distress—no drugs 8%

Pain/distress alleviated 38%

No pain/distress 54%

SOURCE: Adapted from "Figure 2. Animals Experiencing Pain/Distress, Pain/Distress Relief, of No Pain/Distress during Experiments, FY 2007," in *Animal Care Annual Report of Activities: Fiscal Year 2007*, U.S. Department of Agriculture, Animal and Plant Health Inspection Service, September 2008, http://www.aphis.usda.gov/publications/animal_welfare/content/printable_version/2007_AC_Report.pdf (accessed January 13, 2009)

Pain and Distress

One of the goals of refinement is to relieve animal pain and distress. APHIS tracks the occurrence of pain and distress in regulated animals based on reports by research institutions. In FY 2007, 54% of the regulated animals experienced no pain or distress, 38% experienced pain or distress but were administered drugs for relief, and 8% suffered pain and distress but were not given drugs for relief. (See Figure 5.6.) Hamsters and guinea pigs were the species most involved in experiments in which pain and distress were not relieved. (See Table 5.9.) Nearly 62,000 of them fell into this category during FY 2007. In addition, just over 3,500 dogs, cats, and primates also suffered pain and distress that was not relieved.

Animal welfare groups express doubts about the validity of APHIS pain and distress numbers, saying that these numbers are greatly underreported by research institutions. In 1998 the HSUS launched a Pain and Distress Initiative to focus attention on issues involved in assessing and relieving pain in laboratory animals. The HSUS publishes the quarterly newsletter *Pain and Distress Report* to publicize these issues. The goal of the initiative is to eliminate pain and distress in research animals by 2020.

The HSUS (June 2008, http://www.hsus.org/animals_in_research/pain_distress/pain_distress_campaign/) acknowledges that animal rights advocates want to eliminate animal testing, not reform it. It states, "The HSUS would like to see the day when animals are no longer used in harmful research; however, we believe the most urgent public priority is eliminating pain and distress among laboratory animals."

GENETIC ENGINEERING

Genetic engineering is the scientific manipulation of genetic material. Animals have been the subject of genetic engineering research and experiments for several decades. Transgenic animals are animals that carry a foreign gene that has been deliberately inserted through genetic engineering. They are widely used in biomedical research and pharmaceutical development. Most of these animals are farm animals. Raising these transgenic animals for the cultivation of pharmaceutical products is known as pharming. For example, scientists have pharmed transgenic sheep and goats that produce foreign proteins in their milk. Production of these proteins could have enormous medical and industrial benefits for humans. As of April 2009, pharmed substances were still in the development stage and had not yet been commercialized.

Another growing area of genetic engineering is xenotransplantation. The term *xeno* comes from the Greek word *xenos*, meaning "foreign" or "strange." In xenotransplantation organs from animals are transplanted into humans. Research continues on the genetic engineering of pigs so that they can grow organs that will not be rejected by human bodies. Scientists believe that harvesting organs from transgenic pigs could one day solve the human organ shortage that at present exists, saving millions of human lives. The technology is almost to the point of making this possible. Some people consider this to be medical progress, whereas others see it as another injustice perpetrated against animals for the sake of humans, noting that there would not be an organ shortage if more people were willing to become organ donors.

Cloning is a form of genetic manipulation in which a later-born genetic twin can be produced. In July 1996 the first mammal cloned from adult cells was born, a product of research at the Roslin Institute in Edinburgh, Scotland. Dolly was cloned from an udder cell taken from a six-year-old sheep. She was a fairly healthy clone and produced six lambs of her own. Before she was euthanized by lethal injection on February 14, 2003, Dolly had been suffering from lung cancer and arthritis. An autopsy (postmortem examination) of Dolly revealed that, other than her cancer and arthritis, she was anatomically like other sheep. (See Figure 5.7.) Between 1996 and 2009 other animals were cloned, including sheep, mice, cows, a gaur (an endangered Asian ox), goats, pigs, rabbits, dogs, and cats. Not all the animals have survived, and some have been born with compromised immunity and genetic disorders. Cloning is still new technology, and the success rate is low.

TABLE 5.9

Animals that suffered pain and were not administered drugs at USDA-registered research facilities, fiscal year 2007

Species	All other covered species	Cats	Dogs	Guinea pigs	Hamsters	Nonhuman primates	Other farm animals	Pig	Rabbits	Sheep	Total by state
States											
AK	—	—	—	—	0	—	—	—	—	—	0
AL	0	0	0	36	0	0	70	0	0	0	106
AR	0	0	0	0	0	0	0	0	0	0	0
AZ	0	0	0	0	0	0	0	22	0	0	22
CA	351	6	61	2,175	25	39	0	78	233	28	2,996
CO	232	0	0	1,975	686	0	0	15	30	36	2,974
CT	6	0	33	220	1,215	42	0	0	0	0	1,516
DC	53	0	0	172	3	15	0	2	0	17	262
DE	10	0	88	1,010	483	0	0	0	764	0	2,355
FL	88	0	0	0	48	2	0	0	52	0	190
GA	139	9	0	0	1,572	19	24	0	1,982	8	3,753
HI	0	0	0	0	0	0	0	0	0	0	0
IA	11	253	131	627	15,524	0	0	0	0	0	16,546
ID	0	0	0	0	0	0	0	0	4	0	4
IL	57	0	0	526	89	33	0	135	104	0	944
IN	95	0	47	0	0	2	0	0	2	0	146
KS	0	0	0	0	585	0	0	0	8	0	593
KY	0	0	0	0	0	0	0	0	0	0	0
LA	145	0	0	0	0	0	3	0	40	0	188
MA	306	0	130	776	379	18	10	205	834	0	2,658
MD	89	0	3	4,858	351	335	0	66	638	0	6,340
ME	41	0	0	0	0	0	0	0	0	0	41
MI	0	0	10	7,248	0	61	0	0	3	24	7,346
MN	199	0	24	87	0	3	0	0	6	0	319
MO	0	0	0	0	1,861	0	0	0	30	0	1,891
MS	0	0	0	0	0	0	0	0	0	0	0
MT	0	0	0	0	0	0	0	0	0	0	0
NC	0	0	0	550	0	34	0	1	54	0	639
NE	63	23	4	51	1,186	0	0	0	0	0	1,327
NH	0	0	0	0	0	0	0	0	0	0	0
NJ	547	0	361	462	136	224	0	0	245	0	1,975
NM	17	0	0	130	0	142	0	0	329	0	618
NV	0	0	0	0	0	0	0	0	0	49	49
NY	424	360	440	1,455	7,396	55	0	0	187	0	10,317
OH	125	0	13	1,077	157	180	0	0	383	0	1,935
OK	0	0	0	0	0	0	0	0	0	0	0
OR	0	0	0	42	0	0	0	0	6	0	48
PA	37	19	137	956	25	86	0	704	407	0	2,371
PR	0	0	0	0	0	0	0	0	0	0	0
RI	0	0	0	0	0	0	0	0	0	0	0
SC	0	0	0	0	0	0	0	0	0	0	0
SD	0	0	0	0	0	0	0	112	0	0	112
TN	355	0	2	0	0	0	0	34	42	0	433
TX	220	0	2	1,206	742	28	149	0	492	3	2,842
UT	0	0	0	245	2,991	0	0	0	0	0	3,236
VA	0	0	9	0	231	21	0	0	0	0	261
VT	0	0	0	88	0	0	0	0	0	0	88
WA	0	0	0	191	0	4	0	0	1	0	196
WI	18	0	0	0	0	0	0	0	0	0	18
WV	0	0	0	0	0	0	0	0	111	0	111
WY	0	0	0	0	0	0	0	0	0	0	0
Species total	3,628	670	1,495	26,163	35,685	1,343	256	1,374	6,987	165	
Report total											77,766

SOURCE: "Appendix 3. Animals Used in Research," in *Animal Care Annual Report of Activities: Fiscal Year 2007*, U.S. Department of Agriculture, Animal and Plant Health Inspection Service, September 2008, http://www.aphis.usda.gov/publications/animal_welfare/content/printable_version/2007_AC_Report.pdf (accessed January 13, 2009)

A Gallup poll conducted in May 2008 found that 33% of those asked believed that cloning of animals was morally acceptable. (See Table 5.10.) Another 61% felt that animal cloning was morally wrong. These values have changed little since the question was first included in a Gallup poll in 2001. The Gallup Organization reports in *Cloning* (2007, http://www.gallup.com/poll/6028/Cloning.aspx) that in 2002, 38% of respondents favored the cloning of endangered species to keep them from becoming extinct. Only 15% favored the cloning of pets. Therefore, public support does not seem to be fully behind animal cloning, even though the practice proceeds in the laboratory.

FIGURE 5.7

Dolly, the first cloned mammal. *AP Images.*

TABLE 5.10

Public opinion on the morality of cloning animals, 2001–08

NEXT, I'M GOING TO READ YOU A LIST OF ISSUES. REGARDLESS OF WHETHER OR NOT YOU THINK IT SHOULD BE LEGAL, FOR EACH ONE, PLEASE TELL ME WHETHER YOU PERSONALLY BELIEVE THAT IN GENERAL IT IS MORALLY ACCEPTABLE OR MORALLY WRONG. HOW ABOUT . . . [RANDOM ORDER]?

CLONING ANIMALS

	Morally acceptable %	Morally wrong %	Depends on situation (vol.) %	Not a moral issue (vol.) %	No opinion %
2008 May 8–11	33	61	2	1	3
2007 May 10–13	36	59	2	1	3
2006 May 8–11	29	65	2	1	3
2005 May 2–5	35	61	1	*	3
2004 May 2–4	32	64	1	1	2
2003 May 5–7	29	68	1	*	2
2002 May 6–9	29	66	3	1	1
2001 May 10–14	31	63	2	1	3

*Less than 0.5%.
(vol.) = Volunteered response.

SOURCE: "Next, I'm Going to Read You a List of Issues. Regardless of Whether or Not You Think It Should Be Legal, for Each One, Please Tell Me Whether You Personally Believe That in General It Is Morally Acceptable or Morally Wrong. How about Cloning Animals?" in *Moral Issues*, The Gallup Organization, 2008, http://www.gallup.com/poll/1681/Moral-Issues.aspx (accessed January 13, 2009). Copyright © 2008 by The Gallup Organization. Reproduced by permission of The Gallup Organization.

CHAPTER 6

ANIMALS IN SPORTS

Merriam-Webster's Collegiate Dictionary (2003) defines a sport as recreation that includes physical activity. Most people would think of a sport as an athletic competition that demonstrates skills such as physical strength, stamina, agility, and speed. Humans recognized centuries ago that many animals possess such skills naturally and could be used in sporting events.

In the United States the major sports in which animals are involved are horse racing, greyhound racing, sled dog racing, rodeos, and organized animal fighting. Except for animal fighting, all these are considered legitimate sports.

The legitimate sports probably began as friendly competitions between people wanting to show off their animals, but the most popular evolved into businesses in which large amounts of money are involved. Horse racing and greyhound racing are intertwined with the legalized gambling industry. Rodeos and sled dog races largely depend on sponsors. Sponsors are companies that provide financial backing in exchange for being allowed to advertise during an event—for example, by placing advertisements around an arena, in programs, or on uniforms or vehicles. Even animal fighting has become a business of sorts, with profits driven almost entirely by illegal gambling.

In all these sports, skilled animals can be quite profitable for the people who own, train, and manage them. Some animals involved in the sports industry are well cared for during their athletic "careers"; others are horribly abused. Sports animals that are less skilled, injured, past their prime, or unwilling or unable to compete anymore have different prospects. Some retire and live comfortably, whereas others are sold to the slaughterhouse or are killed.

The fate and well-being of animals in sports lie in the hands of humans. To some animal rights activists, this is the root of the problem. They believe that animals should not be used by people for any purpose at all, including sports. Animal welfarists focus their attention on uncovering, publicizing, and outlawing practices in animal sports that they consider harmful to the animals. Animal participation is defended by insiders and fans who feel their right to enjoy a recreational activity is being threatened by overzealous activists who do not understand the nature of these sports. In May 2008 the Gallup Organization conducted its annual poll on animal-related issues. More than one-third (38%) of the people asked supported banning sports involving competition between animals (including horse racing and dog racing). (See Figure 6.1.) Fifty-nine percent of the respondents were opposed to such a ban.

MAJOR ANIMAL SPORTS CONTROVERSIES

Animal sports enthusiasts argue that the animals are doing what they do naturally. Horses and greyhounds love to run, cocks naturally fight with each other in the barnyard, wild dogs fight over who will lead the pack, and unbroken livestock naturally try to buck off a rider. People involved in legitimate animal sports argue that the animals are well cared for because their welfare is crucial to the success of the sport and the people involved. In other words, they say it makes no sense for the owner or manager of a sports animal to mistreat that animal and perhaps lose money as a result. They also insist that safeguards are in place to ensure that animals are not mistreated during a sporting event and receive proper medical care if they are injured.

Critics counter by explaining that animal sports are not sports at all, but performances forced out of animals that have no choice in the matter. They believe sports animals are not behaving naturally but are doing things that they are either trained to do or have been bred over many generations to do. Because so much money is involved in animal sports, animal welfare and rights advocates indicate that greed and financial advancement are the main motivators behind animal sports. General problems with animal sports revolve around four main issues:

- Overbreeding of the animals
- Mistreatment during training, performances, and the off-season
- Lack of veterinary care
- The ways in which unwanted sports animals are destroyed

FIGURE 6.1

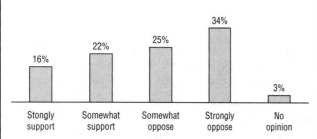

Public opinion on banning sports that involve competition between animals, May 2008

HERE ARE SOME SPECIFIC PROPOSALS CONCERNING THE TREATMENT OF ANIMALS. FOR EACH ONE, PLEASE SAY WHETHER YOU STRONGLY SUPPORT THIS PROPOSAL, SOMEWHAT SUPPORT IT, SOMEWHAT OPPOSE IT, OR STRONGLY OPPOSE THIS PROPOSAL. HOW ABOUT...?

BANNING SPORTS THAT INVOLVE COMPETITION BETWEEN ANIMALS, SUCH AS HORSE RACING OR DOG RACING

16%	22%	25%	34%	3%
Strongly support	Somewhat support	Somewhat oppose	Strongly oppose	No opinion

SOURCE: Frank Newport, "Here Are Some Specific Proposals Concerning the Treatment of Animals. For Each One, Please Say Whether You Strongly Support This Proposal, Somewhat Support It, Somewhat Oppose It, or Strongly Oppose This Proposal. How about Banning Sports That Involve Competition between Animals, Such As Horse Racing or Dog Racing?" in *Post-Derby Tragedy, 38% Support Banning Animal Racing*, The Gallup Organization, May 15, 2008, http://www.gallup.com/poll/107293/PostDerby-Tragedy-38-Support-Banning-Animal-Racing.aspx (accessed January 13, 2009). Copyright © 2008 by The Gallup Organization. Reproduced by permission of The Gallup Organization.

HORSE SPORTS

Horses are the most versatile sporting animal. Besides racing and rodeos, horses participate on a large scale in many other types of sports, shows, and competitions. (See Table 6.1.) However, none of these events are performed by horses alone. All of them include humans, who ride the horses, run alongside them, or are pulled behind in carts.

Thoroughbred Racing

Thoroughbred horse racing is the king of animal sports in the United States. It is a multibillion-dollar industry involving people who breed, manage, train, own, and ride the horses, and the people who own and manage racetracks. Indirectly, the industry provides income to feed and equipment suppliers, veterinarians, and other support personnel. The industry is also a source of income for those state governments that allow gambling at racetracks and/or off-track betting locations.

THE RACES. The Jockey Club reports in "Thoroughbred Racing and Breeding Worldwide" (2009, http://www.jockey club.com/factbook.asp?section=17) that in 2007 there were 51,304 Thoroughbred horse races in the United States and 5,057 in Canada. The number of Thoroughbred races held each year has generally declined since 1997. Purses increased through the late 1990s as gambling increased in popularity around the country before somewhat leveling off after 2002. In 2007 the total North American purse, or amount won by the

TABLE 6.1

Horse sports other than racing and rodeos

Category	Description	Organizations
Cattle events	Cutting or herd work: Rider on horseback selects a single calf from a herd in the arena, guides it into the center of the arena, and then using fast starts and turns, prevents it from escaping back to the herd. Reining: Rider maneuvers horse through various moves, including figure-eight patterns, 360 degree spins, and sliding stops. Cow work: Rider maneuvers horse to control the movements of a running steer, including herding it back and forth along a fence and circling around an arena. Team penning or sorting: Team of 2 or 3 riders on horseback must cut specifically marked cattle from a herd and herd them to designated areas.	National Reined Cow Horse Association, National Reining Horse Association, National Cutting Horse Association, United States Team Penning Association
Dressage	Rider moves horse through a series of carefully choreographed movements and patterns.	United States Dressage Federation
Endurance	Long-distance trail riding conducted over natural terrain.	American Endurance Ride Conference
Eventing or combined training	A three-in-one competition including dressage, cross-country jumping, and show jumping.	Fédération Equestre Internationale
Foxhunting	A sport in which riders and dogs hunt foxes in the countryside.	American Masters of Foxhound Association
Hunter-jumper	Equestrian event in which horses and riders jump over obstacles.	National Hunter and Jumper Association
Polo	Two teams of players riding thoroughbred horses play a game similar to hockey using a small ball and mallets.	United States Polo Association
Polocrosse	Combination of polo and lacrosse in which riders use racquets instead of mallets.	American Polocrosse Association
Ride and tie	Long-distance race in which two people and one horse form a racing team. During a race the people alternate riding the horse and running.	Ride and Tie Association
Steeple chase	Equestrian event in which horses and riders jump over fences.	National Steeplechase Association
Vaulting	Sport in which a rider uses gymnastic moves to vault onto and dismount from moving horse.	American Vaulting Association

SOURCE: Created by Kim Masters Evans for Gale, 2009

owners of the winning horses, was $1.3 billion—$1.2 billion for the United States and $127.6 million for Canada.

According to Trackinfo.com (December 20, 2007, http://www.trackinfo.com/index2.html), as of 2007 there were about 160 Thoroughbred racetracks in the United States. Some racetracks are only open seasonally, whereas those in warm climates are open year round. Racetracks vary in size and in ownership; some are government owned, and some are owned by private and public companies.

The three most prestigious Thoroughbred races in the United States are the Kentucky Derby at the Churchill Downs track in Kentucky, the Preakness Stakes at Pimlico in Maryland, and the Belmont Stakes at Belmont Park in New York. The races are held over a five-week period between May and June of each year. A horse that wins all three races in one year is said to have won the "Triple Crown." Only 11 horses have captured the Triple Crown—most recently, a horse named Affirmed in 1978.

WELFARE OF RACING HORSES. The racehorse industry prides itself on the enormous investments it has made in horse health issues. Millions of dollars have been spent on veterinarian research concerning the injuries and illnesses that affect racehorses. The Grayson-Jockey Club Research Foundation is the leading private source of funding for research into horse health issues. The foundation, which dates back to 1940, is operated by the Jockey Club, though it accepts donations from private individuals, Thoroughbred clubs, racetracks, and other organizations. The foundation notes in *2007 Annual Report* (2009, http://www.grayson-jockeyclub.org/resources/2007%20Annual%20Report.pdf) that in 2007 it allocated more than $1.1 million to universities conducting equine research projects. In the press release "Grayson-Jockey Club Research Foundation to Fund Record $1.2 Million in Equine Research in 2008" (February 15, 2008, http://www.grayson-jockeyclub.org/aboutDisplay.asp?section=12&story=320), the foundation notes that it had contributed over $15.5 million between 1983 and 2008. It receives financial support from donations and from special racing events staged by horse racetracks. In 2007 the foundation funded research in a variety of illnesses and injuries common to horses.

Most animal welfare groups are opposed to horse racing and contend that racehorses are treated as investments rather than as living beings. Specifically, they offer the following reasons for opposing the sport:

- Thoroughbred racehorses have been inbred to the point that their bodies are too heavy for their slender, fragile legs.
- Broodmares are forced to come into season too often and at unnatural times to lengthen the potential training season for their offspring.

- Racehorses are drugged when they have injuries or illnesses (such as hairline fractures) so that they can still compete.
- Track surfaces are too hard.
- The racing season is too long.
- Horses are run too young, risking damage to bones that are not fully mature.
- The industry is regulated by state governments that have a vested interest in making the industry profitable, not in safeguarding animal welfare.
- Racehorses suffer injuries and deaths during training and races.

Between 2006 and 2008 there was a series of on-track "breakdowns" by championship thoroughbreds. Barbaro won the Kentucky Derby in early May 2006 and then shattered a right leg while running the Preakness Stakes two weeks later. After suffering a series of complications from the injury, the horse was euthanized eight months later. Pine Island dislocated an ankle while competing in the November 2006 Breeders' Cup Distaff and was euthanized. Fleet Indian suffered a serious leg injury during the same race, and was retired from racing. In May 2008 Eight Belles had to be euthanized on the racetrack after breaking both front ankles during the Kentucky Derby.

Deaths among racehorses are not uncommon. According to the article "Study Shows 5,000 Racehorse Deaths since '03" (Associated Press, June 14, 2008), approximately 5,000 thoroughbred racehorse died between 2003 and 2008. Most of the horses were euthanized after suffering serious injuries on the racetrack. The article notes that "countless other deaths went unreported because of lax record keeping." The article "Racehorse Deaths by State in 2007" (Associated Press, June 14, 2008) provides a breakdown by state of the more than 1,000 known thoroughbred racehorse deaths that occurred during 2007. No data are provided for Arkansas, Michigan, and Nebraska, because those states reportedly do not compile such information.

As shown in Figure 6.2, there were 306 racehorse fatalities in California alone between 2007 and 2008. The vast majority (81%) of the fatalities were due to musculoskeletal injuries. (See Figure 6.3.) Thoroughbred racehorses sustained the most fatal injuries during training and racing. (See Figure 6.4.)

The slaughter of racehorses is a particularly controversial topic. Ray Paulick reports in "Death of a Derby Winner: Slaughterhouse Likely Fate for Ferdinand" (*Blood-Horse Magazine*, July 25, 2003) that Ferdinand, the winner of the 1986 Kentucky Derby, was possibly slaughtered for meat in Japan. Demand for horse meat has skyrocketed in parts of Asia and Europe because of the scare concerning mad cow disease. Horses intended for human consumption cannot be injected with drugs,

FIGURE 6.2

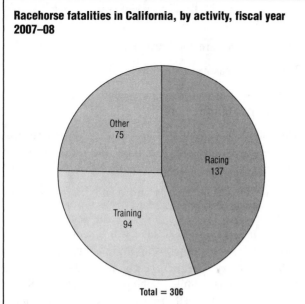

Racehorse fatalities in California, by activity, fiscal year 2007–08

Total = 306

SOURCE: "Figure 1. All Fatalities by Activity," in *Thirty-Eighth Annual Report of the California Horse Racing Board: A Summary of Fiscal Year 2007–08 Revenue and Calendar Year 2008 Racing in California*, California Horse Racing Board, 2009, http://www.chrb.ca.gov/annual_reports/2008_annual_report.pdf (accessed February 2, 2009)

FIGURE 6.3

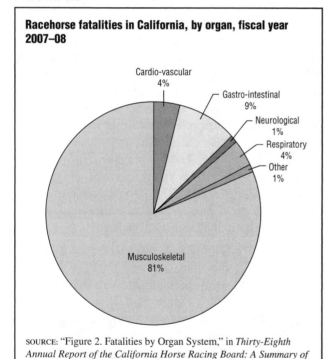

Racehorse fatalities in California, by organ, fiscal year 2007–08

SOURCE: "Figure 2. Fatalities by Organ System," in *Thirty-Eighth Annual Report of the California Horse Racing Board: A Summary of Fiscal Year 2007–08 Revenue and Calendar Year 2008 Racing in California*, California Horse Racing Board, 2009, http://www.chrb.ca.gov/annual_reports/2008_annual_report.pdf (accessed February 2, 2009)

FIGURE 6.4

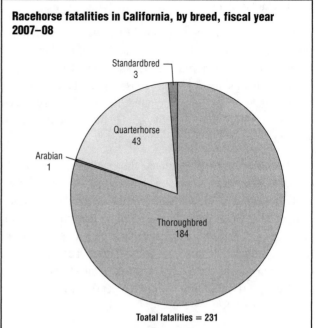

Racehorse fatalities in California, by breed, fiscal year 2007–08

Toatal fatalities = 231

SOURCE: "Figure 3. Racing and Training Fatalities by Breed," in *Thirty-Eighth Annual Report of the California Horse Racing Board: A Summary of Fiscal Year 2007–08 Revenue and Calendar Year 2008 Racing in California*, California Horse Racing Board, 2009, http://www.chrb.ca.gov/annual_reports/2008_annual_report.pdf (accessed February 2, 2009)

house, they are knocked unconscious, then have their throats cut (in the same way that cattle are slaughtered). By contrast, horses sold to rendering plants can be given drugs for pain in transit and can be euthanized by lethal injection.

Animal welfare groups allege that many injured racehorses are not humanely euthanized but are shipped off to slaughter without being given painkillers. Even though there were no horse meat slaughterhouses operating in the United States as of April 2009, there were several in Mexico and Canada. Welfarists complain that racehorses going to slaughterhouses travel for many hours in cramped carriers with no food or water.

RETIRED RACING HORSE ADOPTION. There are several organizations around the country that rescue retired racehorses and either adopt them out or provide lifetime sanctuary and care for them. The two largest are the Thoroughbred Retirement Fund (http://www.trfinc.org/) and the New Vocations Racehorse Adoption Program (http://www.horse adoption.com/). Both organizations report that many of its rescued racehorses come from miserable conditions and suffer because of serious neglect and untreated medical conditions.

Rodeos

The word *rodeo* comes from the Spanish word *rodear*, meaning "to surround." Originally, a rodeo was a roundup of cattle that happened once or twice per year. Open-range grazing was common in western North America during the

either as painkillers or as a humane method of euthanization. As such, horses sold for horse meat are given no painkillers in transit, and when they reach the slaughter-

1800s, and cowboys were hired to round up the cattle and herd them to market. Following these cattle drives, as they were called, the cowboys would often congregate and hold informal contests to show off their skills at riding and roping.

THE RODEO BUSINESS. Rodeos now take place all over North America, even in big cities. They are seen by their fans as wholesome family entertainment that glorifies the rugged and hardworking cowboys of the Old West.

Animal welfare groups estimate that several thousand rodeos take place each year. Professional rodeo stars travel from event to event and compete for millions of dollars in prize money. Most big-money rodeos in the United States are sponsored by the Professional Rodeo and Cowboy Association (PRCA). Besides professional rodeos, the organization also sponsors amateur rodeo events for children and youth.

The animals used in rodeos include horses, bulls, steers (male cattle that have been castrated before reaching sexual maturity), and calves. Typical rodeo events include bareback bull riding, saddle bronc riding (in which a bucking horse, or bronco, is ridden), bareback horse riding, steer wrestling, calf and steer roping, and barrel racing (in which riders guide their horses around barrels positioned around an arena).

WELFARE OF RODEO ANIMALS. The PRCA defends the treatment of animals used in rodeos it sponsors, claiming that it has an extensive animal welfare program that governs the care and handling of rodeo animals and requires that a veterinarian be on-site during a rodeo. Animal welfare organizations are opposed to rodeos. They argue that rodeos are not representative of Old West ranching ways but are businesses that use animals as pieces of athletic equipment. They say that most injured rodeo animals are not humanely euthanized but are sent to slaughterhouses without receiving veterinary attention or painkillers. They also point out that the rodeo animals of the twenty-first century are not naturally wild and unbroken as they might have been when rodeos first started in the 1800s but are relatively tame animals that must be physically provoked into displaying wild behavior. This is particularly true for the bucking animals.

Rodeo opponents say that bucking is unnatural behavior provoked in rodeo animals by tormenting them with painful straps and spurs. They also claim that bucking animals are sometimes poked with cattle prods or sharp sticks or rubbed with caustic ointments right before they are released from their chutes to incite more frenzied bucking action during the ride.

The PRCA notes that bucking horses do wear flank straps that encourage them to kick their legs high in the air. However, the PRCA requires that the flank strap be lined with fleece or neoprene and placed loosely around the horses. The animal rights group People for the Ethical Treatment of Animals (PETA) states in "Buck the Rodeo" (July 16, 2006, http://bucktherodeo.com/) that the straps are cinched tightly around the animals' sensitive abdomen and groin areas, causing the animals to buck to try to throw off the painful devices. The PRCA denies that the straps are pulled tight, arguing that a tight strap would actually restrict a horse's movement and not permit it to jump into the air.

Riders in several rodeo events wear and use spurs. The PRCA requires that the spur points be dull and that the wheel-like rowels on the spurs be able to roll along the animal's hide, rather than be locked. The organization contends that this prevents any injury to the animal from spurring. Riders who violate these rules or injure an animal are subject to disqualification. PETA argues that even dull spurs are painful because they are kicked into the animals' sides.

Gait Competitions

Some horses are bred and trained to walk with an exaggerated gait in which they lift their front legs high in the air. Walking horses, particularly Tennessee Walking Horses, are breeds associated with this gait. These horses compete in shows in which they demonstrate their high-stepping skills to earn prizes for their owners and trainers. Animal protection groups complain that many of the training methods used to elicit high stepping are abusive, for example, repeated use of heavy chains or other weights around the legs trains horses to use a lot of force to lift their legs to walk. Once the weights are removed, the same amount of force lifts the legs high in the air. Some unscrupulous owners and trainers use a process called soring on their horses to achieve an exaggerated gait. Soring is achieved by applying a caustic or irritating chemical substance to a horse's legs or hoofs, by putting objects between a horse's hoof and shoe, or by cutting a horse's hoof too short to expose sensitive underlying tissue. Sored horses lift their legs high because of the pain. Continued use of soring techniques can lead to permanent scarring.

The Horse Protection Act (HPA) prohibits sored horses from competing in horse shows. The U.S. Department of Agriculture (USDA) reports in "The Horse Protection Act" (*Animal Welfare Information Center Newsletter*, vol. 8, no. 2, Summer 1997) that the act was originally passed in 1970 after soring became a widespread practice during the 1960s. Under the HPA specially trained individuals called Designated Qualified Persons (DQPs) act on behalf of the USDA to inspect horses before shows, sales, and auctions. Sored horses are disqualified from competing, being sold, or being auctioned off. Owners and trainers accused of soring can face criminal or civil charges and can be disqualified from participating in future shows, sales, and auctions. Table 6.2 shows the federal funds appropriated to HPA enforcement for fiscal years (FY) 2002 to 2007. Table 6.3 lists the horse industry

TABLE 6.2

Federal appropriations for enforcement of the Horse Protection Act (HPA), fiscal years 2002–07

Fiscal year	Annual appropriations for HPA enforcement
2007	$497,000
2006	$492,000
2005	$493,000
2004	$487,000
2003	$490,000
2002	$415,000

SOURCE: "Table 12. Appropriations for Horse Protection, FY 2002–2007," in *Animal Care Annual Report of Activities: Fiscal Year 2007*, U.S. Department of Agriculture, Animal and Plant Health Inspection Service, September 2008, http://www.aphis.usda.gov/publications/animal_welfare/content/printable_version/2007_AC_Report.pdf (accessed January 13, 2009)

TABLE 6.3

Horse industry organizations with programs certified under the Horse Protection Act, 2007

Friends of Sound Horses
Heart of America Walking Horse Association
Horse Protection Commission
International Walking Horse Association
Kentucky Walking Horse Association
Missouri Fox Trotting Horse Breeding Association
National Horse Show Commission
National Walking Horse Association
Oklahoma Horse Association
Sound, Honest, Objective, Winning (SHOW)
Spotted Saddle Horse Breeders and Exhibitors Association
Tennessee Walking Horse Breeders and Exhibitors Association
United Mountain Horse, Inc.
Western International Walking Horse Association

SOURCE: "Table 13. Horse Industry Organizations," in *Animal Care Annual Report of Activities: Fiscal Year 2007*, U.S. Department of Agriculture, Animal and Plant Health Inspection Service, September 2008, http://www.aphis.usda.gov/publications/animal_welfare/content/printable_version/2007_AC_Report.pdf (accessed January 13, 2009)

organizations that had DQP programs certified by the USDA in FY 2007.

According to the Animal and Plant Health Inspection Service, in *Animal Care Annual Report of Activities: Fiscal Year 2007* (September 2008, http://www.aphis.usda.gov/publications/animal_welfare/content/printable_version/2007_AC_Report.pdf), DQPs examined horses at 506 horse shows in 2007 and reported 629 violations of horse protection regulations.

Dog Sports

Dogs participate on a large scale in three sports: greyhound racing, sled dog racing, and organized fighting. These sports differ widely in their legitimacy. Sled dog racing evolved as a sport to show off the skills of hardy dogs that have been pulling sleds in snowbound regions for centuries. By contrast, greyhound racing began as a competition between fast and graceful dogs but evolved into a gambling

pastime. Organized dogfighting is illegal in every state. Despite its illegitimacy, or maybe because of it, dogfighting continues to be popular. Its roots lie in the blood sports enjoyed by the ancient Romans at the Coliseum.

There are also a variety of new amateur sporting events that are emerging for dogs. Agility-based competitions, such as catching Frisbees and traversing obstacles, are growing in popularity. One of the newest dog sports is called fly ball. This is a relay event in which teams of dogs compete against each other to jump over hurdles and race to retrieve a ball. In 2000 the International Federation of Cynological Sports (IFCS) was formed in Europe to unite organizations holding dog sports in various countries around the world. (Cynology is the scientific study of canines.) The IFCS is working to bring dog sports, such as those involving agility, to the Olympic Games.

Greyhound Racing

As of February 2009, there were 34 greyhound racetracks operating around the country. (See Table 6.4.) Greyhound racing is most prevalent in Florida, where there were 13 tracks, the most of any state. The Florida Department of Business and Professional Regulation, Division of Pari-mutuel Wagering reports in *Division of Pari-mutuel Wagering 76th Annual Report Fiscal Year 2006–2007* (January 2008, http://www.myflorida.com/dbpr/pmw/documents/AnnualReport2006-2007.pdf) that $465.3 million was wagered at the state's greyhound tracks between FYs 2006 and 2007.

In "Greyhound Racing: Running for Their Lives" (February 8, 2008, http://www.hsus.org/pets/issues_affecting_our_pets/running_for_their_lives_the_realities_of_greyhound_racing/), the HSUS reports that revenue from greyhound racing declined by 45% in the 1990s, leading to the closure or cessation of live racing at many tracks around the country. In addition, seven states specifically banned live greyhound racing during the 1990s: Idaho, Maine, North Carolina, Nevada, Vermont, Virginia, and Washington. Pennsylvania and Massachusetts enacted bans in 2004 and 2008, respectively. The Massachusetts ban will go into effect in 2010.

Three major organizations manage greyhound racing in the United States: the National Greyhound Association (NGA), the American Greyhound Track Operators Association (AGTOA), and the American Greyhound Council (AGC; a joint effort of the NGA and AGTOA). The NGA represents greyhound owners and is the official registry for racing greyhounds. All greyhounds that race on U.S. tracks must first be registered with the NGA. The AGTOA represents greyhound track operators. The AGC manages the industry's animal welfare programs, including farm inspections and adoptions.

The AGC (2009, http://www.agcouncil.com/node/34) estimates that the greyhound racing industry pays $86

TABLE 6.4

North American Greyhound racetracks as of September 2007

State/track	City/town	Opened	Operation
Alabama			
Birmingham RC	Birmingham	1992	Year-round
Mobile GP	Theodore	1973	Year-round
VictoryLand	Shorter	1984	Year-round
Arizona			
Phoenix GP	Phoenix	1954	Year-round
Tucson GP	Tucson	1944	Year-round
Arkansas			
Southland Park	West Memphis	1956	Year-round[a]
Colorado			
Mile High	Commerce City	1949	Seasonal
Florida			
Ebro GT	Washington Co.	1995	Year-round
Daytona Beach KC	Daytona Beach	1948	Year-round
Flagler GT	Miami	1932	Year-round
Jefferson County	Monticello	1959	Year-round
Mardi Gras RT	Hollywood	1934	Year-round[a]
Melbourne GP	Melbourne	1991	Seasonal
Naples-Ft. Myers	Bonita Springs	1957	Year-round
Orange Park KC	Orange Park	1946	Seasonal
Palm Beach KC	W. Palm Beach	1932	Year-round
Pensacola GT	Pensacola	1946	Year-round
St. Petersburg KC	St. Petersburg	1925	Year-round
Sanford-Orlando	Longwood	1935	Year-round
Sarasota KC	Sarasota	1944	Year-round
Iowa			
Bluffs Run	Council Bluffs	1986	Year-round[a]
Dubuque GP	Dubuque	1985	Seasonal[a]
Kansas			
Woodlands	Kansas City	1989	Year-round
Massachusetts			
Raynham/Taunton	Raynham	1940	Year-round
Wonderland	Revere (Boston)	1935	Seasonal
New Hampshire			
Hinsdale GP	Hinsdale	1973	Seasonal
Seabrook GP	Seabrook	1973	Seasonal
The Lodge	Belmont	1975	Seasonal[b]
Rhode Island			
Twin River	Lincoln	1977	Year-round[a, c]
Texas			
Gulf GP	La Marque	1992	Year-round
Valley Race Park	Harlingen	2000	Seasonal
West Virginia			
Tri-State	Cross Lanes	1985	Year-round[a]
Wheeling Downs	Wheeling	1976	Year-round[a]
Wisconsin			
Dairyland GP	Kenosha	1990	Year-round
Mexico			
Agua Caliente	Tijuana	1940s	Year-round

[a]Offers casino-style gaming; referred to as a racino.
[b]Formerly known as Lakes Region Greyhound Park.
[c]Formerly known as Lincoln Park.
Notes: RC = Race Course. GP = Greyhound Park. KC = Kennel Club.
GT = Greyhound Track. RT = Racetrack.

SOURCE: Adapted from *Greyhound Racetracks Operating in North America as of September 2007*, Greyhound Network News, September 2007, http://www.greyhoundnetworknews.org (accessed February 2, 2009)

WELFARE OF RACING GREYHOUNDS. The HSUS and other animal welfare organizations are strongly opposed to greyhound racing for the following reasons:

- It is not governed by the Animal Welfare Act (AWA) under the USDA as are other commercial animal enterprises, such as zoos and circuses.

- The industry severely overbreeds greyhounds in the hopes of producing winners, leading to the destruction of thousands of puppies each year.

- A racing greyhound's career is typically over at the age of four, well below its average life span of 12 years, meaning that thousands of adult dogs are also destroyed each year when they are no longer useful.

The AGC states that it has adopted standard guidelines for the care of greyhounds and the maintenance of kennel facilities based on the veterinary textbook *The Care of the Racing and Retired Greyhound* (2007) by Linda L. Blythe et al. All the nation's greyhound breeding farms and kennels are subject to unannounced inspections to verify that they are complying with the industry's animal welfare guidelines. Violators can be expelled from the sport.

In "Adoption Programs" (2009, http://www.agcouncil.com/node/5), the AGC claims that greyhound tracks contribute approximately $2 million each year to local greyhound adoption programs and that more than 90% of all registered greyhounds are retired to farms for breeding purposes or adopted out as pets. Animal welfare groups claim that thousands of adult greyhounds are destroyed each year by the racing industry. The Greyhound Protection League (2002, http://www.greyhounds.org/gpl/contents/common.html) estimates that more than 1 million unwanted racing greyhounds have been culled (killed) by the industry since the 1930s.

MASS KILLING. David M. Halbfinger reports in "Dismal End for Race Dogs, Alabama Authorities Say" (*New York Times*, May 23, 2002) that in May 2002 Robert L. Rhodes was arrested and charged with felony animal cruelty after the remains of more than 2,000 greyhounds were found on his property in Baldwin County, Alabama. The man, who worked as a security guard at the Pensacola Greyhound Track in Florida, claimed that the track paid him $10 apiece to shoot the dogs and dispose of their carcasses on his 18-acre farm. He admitted to performing the service for 40 years at the request of race dog owners. Authorities report that autopsies indicate some of the dogs were not killed instantly and therefore suffered before they died. It is a felony in Alabama to torture an animal. Racetrack officials denied involvement in the case and fired Rhodes along with several other security guards and a kennel operator.

Alabama authorities eventually charged four greyhound owners and trainers under the state's animal cruelty law based on statements from Rhodes and Clarence Ray

million in federal, state, and local taxes and pumps approximately $356 million every year into the economy through the purchasing of goods and services.

Patterson, a kennel owner at the Pensacola Greyhound Track. At an April 2004 hearing, the Baldwin County sheriff testified that Rhodes, who died in 2003, had admitted killing between 2,000 and 3,000 greyhounds that were too sick or old to race. Florida investigators testified that Florida kennel owners and trainers paid Rhodes to shoot unwanted greyhounds because it was cheaper than having the animals humanely euthanized by a veterinarian. However, in 2005 the defendants' lawyers succeeded in having the case dropped after arguing that insufficient evidence existed and that the deceased Rhodes could not be cross-examined.

Sled Dog Racing

The sport of sled dog racing is small but extremely popular throughout Alaska, Canada, and parts of northern Europe. In North America the sport traces its origins to Native Americans, who for centuries have used hardy dogs bred for cold weather to pull their sleds. Typical draft animals, such as horses and oxen, were unsuitable for this purpose because of their weight and food requirements.

IDITAROD. The most famous sled dog race is the Iditarod Trail Sled Dog Race (commonly called the Iditarod). It is held in Alaska in early March of each year and includes dozens of teams competing for thousands of dollars in prize money. In general, the race covers roughly 1,150 miles (1,850 km; from Anchorage to Nome, Alaska) and is completed in anywhere from 8 to 16 days. The speed record (set in 2002) is eight days, 22 hours, and 46 minutes. Nearly $898,000 in prize money was awarded to winning racers for the 2009 Iditarod (2009, http://www.iditarod.com/archives/year/yearsummary_111.html).

Mushers (human sled drivers) are allowed to start the Iditarod with up to 16 dogs. A typical team includes 15 dogs, one of which is the leader. The others are arranged in pairs behind the lead dog. The pair closest to the sled carries the heaviest load among the dogs. No dog substitutions are allowed during the race. If one or more dogs drop out for any reason, they cannot be replaced. The remainder carry the load. The dogs wear booties on their paws to help protect against cuts and abrasions.

The Iditarod includes about 24 checkpoints along the way. Each team is required to take three breaks during the race: one 24-hour break and two eight-hour breaks. Mushers leave dogs that are sick, tired, or injured at one of the checkpoints for transport back to the starting point. According to race officials, each checkpoint has a veterinarian available.

Hazards of the race include weather conditions, wildlife, and unpredictable terrain. Temperatures can drop to as low as -40° F (-40° C) during the race. However, unusually warm temperatures (up to 50° F [10° C]) are also a problem as they can contribute to heat stress in the dogs and cause spoilage of dog food stored along the route.

The Iditarod received little media attention outside of Alaska until 1985, when Libby Riddles (1956–) became the first woman to win the race. Another woman, Susan Butcher (1954–2006), won the Iditarod four times between 1986 and 1990. The resulting publicity not only boosted the profile of the race but also brought more scrutiny and criticism from animal welfare organizations.

WELFARE OF SLED DOGS. The animal welfare group Sled Dog Action Coalition (SDAC; 2009, http://www.helpsleddogs.org/) opposes the Iditarod, citing the following problems:

- The race experiences dog deaths and injuries almost every year.

- At least 142 sled dogs are known to have died during the race since its inception in 1973. Dogs have died from heart and other organ failures due to overexertion, pneumonia, and injuries, including being strangled in towlines (the ropes that stretch from the dogs' harnesses to the sled) and rammed by sleds.

- At least three mushers have been disqualified from races for beating or kicking dogs or forcing dogs to run through dangerously deep slush. Two of the dogs in these cases died.

- Race dogs have suffered heat stress, dehydration, diarrhea, pulled tendons, and cut paws because of their participation in the Iditarod.

- Sled dog breeders kill puppies that are unable or unwilling to become good racers.

The SDAC also notes that most sled dogs are confined to short tethers in large dog yards when they are not racing. Tethering as a means of primary confinement is not permitted by the USDA for its licensed dog breeders and is opposed by the HSUS.

Iditarod mushers and supporters acknowledge that the race is grueling and can be dangerous, but they believe that sufficient rules and safeguards are in place to protect the dogs from injury and abuse. Many people involved in the sport believe that the dangers and wildness of the race enhance its allure. The SDAC calls for specific reforms to be made in race procedures to ensure the safety of the sled dogs.

COCKFIGHTING

A cock is the adult male of the domestic fowl (Gallus gallus), also known as a rooster. Cocks participate in only one organized sport: cockfighting. Cockfighting is illegal in most states and is considered a blood sport because the roosters that participate are frequently killed or mutilated during the fight. Cockfighting is performed by cocks outfitted with sharp spikes called gaffs on their legs. Two cocks are thrown into a pit together, where they

TABLE 6.5

Summary of cock fighting laws, by state, 2008

State	Cockfighting	Possession of birds for fighting	Spectator at a cockfight	Possession of implements	Rank
4 Felony					
Florida	Felony Max 5 years Max $5,000	Felony Max 5 years Max $5,000	Felony Max 5 years Max $5,000	Felony Max 5 years Max $5,000	1

Michigan	Felony
	Max 4 years
	$5,000–$50,000
	500–100 hours
	   community service
		Felony
		Max 4 years
		$5,000–$50,000
		500–100 hours
		   community service
			Felony
			Max 4 years
			$1,000–$5,000
			250–500 hours
			   community service
				Felony
				Max 4 years
				$1,000–$5,000
				250–500 hours
				   community service
					2

Colorado	Class 5 felony 1–3 years Max $1,000	Class 5 felony 1–3 years Max $1,000	Class 5 felony 1–3 years Max $1,000	Class 5 felony 1–3 years Max $1,000	3
Virginia	Class 6 felony Max 5 years Max $2,500	Class 6 felony Max 5 years Max $2,500	Class 6 felony Max 5 years Max $2,500	Class 6 Felony Max 5 years Max $2,500	4
3 Felony					
Iowa	Class D felony Max 5 years $750–$7,500	Class D felony Max 5 years $750–$7,500	Aggravated misdemeanor Max 2 years $500–$5,000	Class D felony Max 5 years $750–$7,500	5
Maryland	Felony Max 3 years Max $5,000	Felony Max 3 years Max $5,000	Misdemeanor Max 1 year Max $2,500	Felony Max 3 years Max $5,000	6
3 felony, 1 legal					
New Jersey	Crime of the 3rd degree 3–5 years $3,000–$5,000	Crime of the 3rd degree 3–5 years $3,000–$5,000	Crime of the 3rd degree 3–5 years $3,000–$5,000	Legal	7
Pennsylvania	3rd degree felony Max 7 years Max $15,000	3rd degree felony Max 7 years Max $15,000	3rd degree felony Max 7 years Max $15,000	Legal	8
New Hampshire	Class B felony Max 7 years Max $4,000	Class B felony Max 7 years Max $4,000	Class B felony Max 7 years Max $4,000	Legal	9
Nebraska	Class IV felony Max 5 years Max $10,000	Class IV felony Max 5 years Max $10,000	Class IV felony Max 5 years Max $10,000	Legal	10
Washington	Class C felony 5 years $10,000	Class C felony 5 years $10,000	Class C felony 5 years $10,000	Legal	11
Connecticut	Felony Max 5 years Max $5,000	Felony Max 5 years Max $5,000	Felony Max 5 years Max $5,000	Legal	12
Vermont	Felony Max 5 year Max $5,000	Felony Max 5 year Max $5,000	Felony Max 5 year Max $5,000	Legal	13

Massachusetts	Felony equivalent
	Max 5 years (state
	   prison) or
	Max 1 year (house of
	   correction)
	Max $1,000
		Felony equivalent
		Max 5 years (state
		   prison) or
		Max 1 year (house of
		   correction)
		Max $1,000
			Felony equivalent
			Max 5 years
			   (state prison) or
			Max 2.5 year (house
			   of correction)
			Max $1,000
				Legal	14

Delaware	Class F felony Max 3 years Discretionary fine	Class F felony Max 3 years Discretionary fine	Class G felony Max 2 years Discretionary fine	Legal	15
Rhode Island	Felony Max 2 years Max $1,000	Felony Max 2 years Max $1,000	Felony Max 2 years Max $1,000	Legal	16

fight to the death. Cockfighting was banned by most states during the 1800s. As of 2008, it was illegal in all states. (See Table 6.5.) It was a felony in 33 states and a misdemeanor offense in 17 others. States differ in their treatment of cockfight spectators and those caught in possession of birds for fighting.

Pet-abuse.com tracks and logs media reports about acts of animal abuse, including the use of animals in fighting. It notes that in 2008 there were 81 reports involving cockfighting (http://www.pet-abuse.com/pages/cruelty _database/). Authorities reportedly seized more than 8,000 birds while investigating these cases.

TABLE 6.5

Summary of cock fighting laws, by state, 2008 [CONTINUED]

State	Cockfighting	Possession of birds for fighting	Spectator at a cockfight	Possession of implements	Rank
2 Felony					
Illinois	Class 4 felony 1–3 years Max $25,000	Class 4 felony 1–3 years Max $25,000	Class A misdemeanor Max 1 year Max $2,500	Class C misdemeanor Max 30 days Max $1,500	17
Indiana	Class D felony 6 months–3 years Max $10,000	Class D felony 6 months–3 years Max $10,000	Class A misdemeanor Max 1 year Max $5,000	Class B misdemeanor Max 180 days Max $1,000	18
Oregon	Class C felony Max 5 years Max $125,000	Class C felony Max 5 years Max $125,000	Class A misdemeanor Max 1 year Max $6,250	Class C felony* Max 5 years Max $125,000	19
2 felony, 1 legal					
Minnesota	Felony Min 1 year 1 day	Felony Min 1 year 1 day	Misdemeanor Max 90 days Max $1,000	Legal	20
Arizona	Felony 9 months–2 years Max $150,000	Felony 9 months–2 years Max $150,000	Misdemeanor Max $25,000	Legal	21
Oklahoma	Felony Max 10 years Max $25,000	Felony 1–10 years $2,000–$25,000	Misdemeanor Max 1 year Max $5,000	Legal	22
Alaska	Class C felony Max 5 years Max $50,000	Class C felony Max 5 years Max $50,000	Violation No jail time Max $500	Legal	23
District of Columbia	Felony Max 5 years Max $25,000	Felony Max 5 years Max $25,000	Misdemeanor Max 180 days Max $1,000	Legal	24

Maine	Class C crime
	Court must impose a fine
	  of $500 max, in addition to:
	Max 5 years
	Max $5,000
		Class C crime
		Court must impose a fine
		  of $500 max, in addition to:
		Max 5 years
		Max $5,000
			Class D crime
			Max 1 year
			Max $2,000
				Legal	25

North Dakota	Class C felony Max 5 years Max $5,000	Class C felony Max 5 years Max $5,000	Class A misdemeanor Max 1 year Max $2,000	Legal	26
Wyoming	Felony Max 2 years Max $5,000	Felony Max 2 years Max $5,000	Misdemeanor Max 6 months Max $750	Legal	27
New York	Felony Max 4 years Max $25,000	Felony Max 4 years Max $25,000	Misdemeanor Max 1 year Max $15,000	Legal	28
Wisconsin	Class I felony Max 3 years, 6 months Max $10,000	Class I felony Max 3 years, 6 months Max $10,000	Class A misdemeanor Max 9 months Max $10,000	Legal	29
2 felony, 2 legal					
Montana	Felony 1–5 years Max $5,000	Felony 1–5 years Max $5,000	Legal	Legal	30
1 felony, 1 legal					
Missouri	Class D felony Max 10 years	Legal	Class A misdemeanor Min 6 months	Class A misdemeanor Min 6 months	31
1 felony, 3 legal					
Georgia	Felony 1–5 years Max $15,000	Legal	Legal	Legal	32

Because cockfighting is legal in Mexico and in many Asian countries, there is a commercial breeding industry in the United States. However, the AWA prohibits the exporting of fighting gamecocks to foreign countries.

Dogfighting

Dogfighting is widely considered to be a horrific form of animal abuse. In the United States dogfighting is an illegal, multimillion-dollar gambling industry, often associated with gangs, auto theft, arms smuggling, money laundering, and drug trafficking. Dogs most often used in dogfighting are pit bulls, which are not considered a specific breed but are rather a mix of breeds, the most predominant being the American Staffordshire terrier. Pit bulls are not necessarily aggressive by nature, but because they are extremely loyal to their owners and have powerful, muscu-

TABLE 6.5

Summary of cock fighting laws, by state, 2008 [CONTINUED]

State	Cockfighting	Possession of birds for fighting	Spectator at a cockfight	Possession of implements	Rank
Texas	Felony 180 days–2 years Max $10,000	Legal	Legal	Legal	33
North Carolina	Felony 3–8 months to 4–10 months	Legal	Legal	Legal	34
Misdemeanor					
California	Misdemeanor Max of 1 year Max of $5,000	Misdemeanor Max 6 months Max $1,000	Misdemeanor Max of 1 year Max of $5,000	Misdemeanor Max 6 months Max $1,000	35
Misdemeanor, 1 Legal					
Tennessee	Class A misdemeanor Max 11 months and 29 days Max $2,500	Class A misdemeanor Max 11 months and 29 days Max $2,500	Class C misdemeanor Max 30 days Max $50	Legal	36
West Virginia	Misdemeanor Max 1 year $100–$1,000	Misdemeanor Max 6 months $300–$2,000	Misdemeanor Max 1 year $100–$1,000	Legal	37
New Mexico	Petty misdemeanor Max 6 months Max $500	Petty misdemeanor Max $500 and max 6 months	Petty misdemeanor Max $500 and max 6 months	Legal	38
Ohio	4th degree misdemeanor Max 30 days Max $250	4th degree misdemeanor Max 30 days Max $250	4th degree misdemeanor Max 30 days Max $250	Legal	39
Misdemeanor, 2 Legal					
Nevada	Gross misdemeanor 1–4 years Max $5,000	Legal	Misdemeanor Max $1,000	Legal	40
South Carolina	Misdemeanor Max 1 year Max $1,000	Legal	Misdemeanor Max 1 year Max $1,000	Legal	41
Utah	Class B Misdemeanor Max 6 months Max $1,000	Legal	Class B misdemeanor Max 6 months Max $1,000	Legal	42
South Dakota	Class 1 Misdemeanor Max 1 year Max $2,000	Legal	Class 1 misdemeanor Max 1 year Max $2,000	Legal	43
Kansas	Misdemeanor Max 1 year Max $1,000	Legal	Misdemeanor Max 1 year Max $1,000	Legal	44
Louisiana	Misdemeanor Max 6 months Max $1,000	Legal	Misdemeanor Max 6 months Max $1,000	Legal	45
Misdemeanor, 3 Legal					
Hawaii	Misdemeanor Max 1 year Max $2,000	Legal	Legal	Legal	46
Arkansas	Misdemeanor Max 1 year Max $1,000	Legal	Legal	Legal	47
Kentucky	Class A misdemeanor Max 12 months Max $500	Legal	Legal	Legal	48
Idaho	Misdemeanor Max 6 months $100–$5,000	Legal	Legal	Legal	49
Mississippi	Misdemeanor 10–100 days $10–$100	Legal	Legal	Legal	50
Alabama	Misdemeanor $20.00–$50.00 fine	Legal	Legal	Legal	51

*Possession of gaffs and slashers is a class C felony; possession of all other cockfighting implements is a class A misdemeanor.

SOURCE: *Ranking of State Cockfighting Laws*, Humane Society of the United States, December 3, 2008, http://files.hsus.org/web-files/PDF/cockfighting_statelaws.pdf (accessed February 2, 2009)

lar bodies and strong jaws, they can be bred and trained to exhibit aggressive behavior toward other dogs. Fights typically go on for hours, sometimes to the death. Generally, a fight goes on until a dog gives up or an owner concedes defeat. Dogs that survive the fights frequently die hours or days later from shock, blood loss, or infections.

Fighting dogs are judged on their gameness, which is determined by a dog's willingness and eagerness to fight and its reluctance to yield or back down during the fight. Selective breeding and grueling, cruel training methods are used to enhance gameness. Fighting dogs are usually drugged with steroids and other stimulants to enhance their aggression.

Fighting dogs are often trained on treadmills or devices called catmills. A catmill holds an animal, such as a cat, rabbit, or small dog, just out of reach of the training dog while it runs. Police report that these bait animals are often pets stolen from local neighborhoods and are usually killed during the training. Mild-tempered pit bulls that show no fighting inclinations are also used as bait dogs.

Dogfighting is a felony in all 50 states. (See Table 6.6.) Possession of a dog for fighting and even being a spectator at a dogfight are felonies in some states. As noted earlier, Pet-abuse.com tracks media reports about animal abuse incidents. This includes incidents involving dogfighting. It notes that in 2008 there were 123 reports involving dogfighting (http://www.pet-abuse.com/pages/cruelty_database/).

Animal welfare groups want to strengthen state laws dealing with dogfighting. They also ask major newspapers not to accept advertisements selling dogs that use descriptive words such as *game dog* or *game bred*, as these terms imply that the dog is intended for fighting. The HSUS asks people to notify it whenever such ads appear in their local newspapers. HSUS activists monitor Web sites and magazines devoted to game dogs and alert police when they believe a dogfight is going to take place.

In 2007 dogfighting became national news after the Atlanta Falcons quarterback Michael Vick (1980–) was arrested for running a dogfighting operation on property he owned in Virginia. Investigators alleged that Vick and his coconspirators killed poorly performing fighting dogs by electrocuting, hanging, drowning, or beating them to death. In December 2007 Vick was sentenced to 23 months in prison for his role in the operation and for lying to authorities about his involvement. Vick lost his multimillion-dollar contract with the Atlanta Falcons and millions of dollars more in endorsement deals. He was released from prison in March 2009.

In "What Happened to Michael Vick's Dogs" (*Sports Illustrated*, December 23, 2008), Jim Gorant gives a detailed account on the fate of the surviving dogs rescued from Vick's dogfighting compound. Gorant reports that 51 dogs were originally rescued. Four died or were euthanized in shelters after being seized. Initially, some animal welfare groups—including the HSUS and PETA—called for all the dogs to be euthanized. Their reasoning was that the money and time required to rehabilitate the fighting dogs would be better spent on much more adoptable dogs already languishing in shelters. However, there was widespread public interest in the welfare of the surviving dogs. As a result, they were handed over to well-respected rescue groups and individuals experienced in rehabilitating former fighting dogs. Twenty-two of the dogs went to the Best Friends Animal Sanctuary in Nevada. Another 10 went to the group Bay Area Doglovers Responsible about Pitbulls in California. The remaining 15 dogs went to permanent homes or foster homes around the country. One of those dogs—Leo—became a certified therapy dog and visits cancer patients at a California hospital. According to Gorant, rescuers believe most of the dogs still in rehabilitation will eventually be adoptable.

Federal Legislation against Animal Fighting

One of the outcomes of the Vick case was intense public notice and concern about dogfighting. In May 2007 President George W. Bush (1946–) signed the Animal Fighting Prohibition Enforcement Act, which made it a felony to violate the animal fighting provisions of the AWA or to possess dogfighting or cockfighting implements. The new law also provides additional resources for federal investigation and enforcement related to animal fighting. The AWA prohibits the selling, purchasing, or transporting across state lines or in international commerce of an animal intended for fighting.

TABLE 6.6

Summary of dog fighting laws, by state, 2009

State	Dogfighting	Spectator at a dogfight	Possession of dogs for fighting	Rank
First tier: Three felony provisions				
NJ	Crime of the 3rd degree 3–5 years Max $15,000	Crime of the 3rd degree 3–5 years Max $15,000	Crime of the 3rd degree 3–5 years Max $15,000	1
LA	Felony 1–10 years $1,000–$25,000	Felony 1–10 years $1,000–$25,000	Felony 1–10 years $1,000–$25,000	2
AL	Class C felony 1–10 years Max of $5,000	Class C felony 1–10 years Max of $5,000	Class C felony 1–10 years Max of $5,000	3
CO	Class 5 felony 1–3 years $1,000–$100,000	Class 5 felony 1–3 years $1,000–$100,000	Class 5 felony 1–3 years $1,000–$100,000	4
MS	Felony 1–3 years $1,000–$5,000	Felony Max 1 year $500–$5,000	Felony 1–3 years $1,000–$5,000	5
AZ	Class 5 felony 9 months–2 years Max $150,000	Class 6 felony 6 months–1½ years Max $150,000	Class 5 felony 9 months–2 years Max $150,000	6
OH	4th degree felony 6–18 months $5,000	4th degree felony 6–18 months $5,000	4th degree felony 6–18 months $5,000	7
NC	Class H felony 4–8 months to 5–10 months	Class H felony 4–8 months to 5–10 months	Class H felony 4–8 months to 5–10 months	8
PA	3rd degree felony Max 7 years Max $15,000	3rd degree felony Max 7 years Max $15,000	3rd degree felony Max 7 years Max $15,000	9
NH	Class B felony Max 7 years Max $4,000	Class B felony Max 7 years Max $4,000	Class B felony Max 7 years Max $4,000	10
OR	Class C felony Max 5 years Max $125,000	Class C felony Max 5 years Max $125,000	Class C felony Max 5 years Max $125,000	11
NE	Class IV felony Max 5 years Max $10,000	Class IV felony Max 5 years Max $10,000	Class IV felony Max 5 years Max $10,000	12
WA	Class C felony Max 5 years Max $10,000	Class C felony Max 5 years Max $10,000	Class C felony Max 5 years Max $10,000	13
CT	Felony Max 5 years Max $5,000	Felony Max 5 years Max $5,000	Felony Max 5 years Max $5,000	14
FL	3rd degree felony Max 5 years Max $5,000	3rd degree felony Max 5 years Max $5,000	3rd degree felony Max 5 years Max $5,000	15
VT	Felony Max 5 year Max $5,000	Felony Max 5 year Max $5,000	Felony Max 5 year Max $5,000	16
VA	Class 6 felony Max 5 years Max $2,500	Class 6 felony Max 5 years Max $2,500	Class 6 felony Max 5 years Max $2,500	17
MA	Felony equivalent Max 5 years (state prison) or Max 1 year (house of correction) Max $1,000	Felony equivalent Max 5 years (state prison) or Max 2.5 years (house of correction) Max $1,000	Felony equivalent Max 5 years (state prison) or Max 1 year (house of correction) Max $1,000	18
MI	Felony Max 4 years $5,000–$50,000 500–100 hours community service	Felony Max 4 years $1,000–$5,000 250–500 hours community service	Felony Max 4 years $5,000–$50,000 500–100 hours community service	19

TABLE 6.6

Summary of dog fighting laws, by state, 2009 [CONTINUED]

State	Dogfighting	Spectator at a dogfight	Possession of dogs for fighting	Rank
First tier: Three felony provisions				
DE	Class F felony Max 3 years Discretionary Fine	Class G felony Max 2 years Discretionary fine	Class F felony Max 3 years Discretionary Fine	20
RI	Felony Max 2 years Max $1,000	Felony Max 2 years Max $1,500	Felony Max 2 years Max $1,000	21
NM	4th degree felony 18 months Max $5,000	4th degree felony 18 months Max $5,000	4th degree felony 18 months Max $5,000	22
GA	Felony 1–5 years Min $5,000	Misdemeanor Max 1 year Max $1,000	Felony 1–5 years Min $5,000	23
IL	Class 4 felony 1–3 years Max $25,000	Class A misdemeanor Max 1 year Max $2,500	Class 4 felony 1–3 years Max $25,000	24
MN	Felony Min 1 year 1 day	Misdemeanor Max 90 days Max $1,000	Felony Min 1 year 1 day	25
OK	Felony 1–10 years $2,000–$25,000	Misdemeanor Max 1 year Max $500	Felony 1–10 years $2,000–$25,000	26
TN	Class E felony 1–6 years Max $3,000	Class C misdemeanor Max of 30 days Max $50	Class E felony 1–6 years Max $3,000	27
KS	Level 10 nonperson felony 1–5 years Max $100,000	Class B nonperson misdemeanor Max 6 months Max $1,000	Level 10 nonperson felony 1–5 years Max $100,000	28
KY	Class D felony 1–5 years $1,000–$10,000	Class A misdemeanor Max 12 months Max $500	Class D felony 1–5 years $1,000–$10,000	29
IN	Class D felony 6 months–3 years Max $10,000	Class A misdemeanor Max 1 year Max $5,000	Class D felony 6 months–3 years Max $10,000	30
MO	Class D felony Max 10 years	Class A misdemeanor Min 6 months	Class D felony Max 10 years	31
AR	Class D felony Max 6 years Max $10,000	Class A misdemeanor Max 1 year Max $1,000	Class D felony Max 6 years Max $10,000	32
AK	Class C felony Max 5 years Max $50,000	Violation No jail time Max $500	Class C felony Max 5 years Max $50,000	33
DC	Felony Max 5 years Max $25,000	Misdemeanor Max 180 days Max $1,000	Felony Max 5 years Max $25,000	34
UT	3rd degree felony Max 5 years Max $25,000	Class B misdemeanor 6 months Max $1,000	3rd degree felony Max 5 years Max $25,000	35
IA	Class D felony Max 5 years $750–$7,500	Aggravated misdemeanor Max 2 years $500–$5,000	Class D felony Max 5 years $750–$7,500	36
ND	Class C felony Max 5 years Max $5,000	Class A misdemeanor Max 1 year Max $2,000	Class C felony Max 5 years Max $5,000	37
SC	Felony Must be 5 years or $5,000 or both	Misdemeanor Must be 6 months or $500 or both	Felony Must be 5 years or $5,000 or both	38

TABLE 6.6

Summary of dog fighting laws, by state, 2009 [CONTINUED]

State	Dogfighting	Spectator at a dogfight	Possession of dogs for fighting	Rank
ME	Class C crime Court must impose a fine of $500 max, in addition to: Max 5 years Max $5,000	Class D crime Max 1 year Max $2,000	Class C crime Court must impose a fine of $500 max: in addition to: Max 5 years Max $5,000	39
ID	Felony Max 5 years Max $50,000	Misdemeanor Max 6 months $100–$5,000	Felony Max 5 years Max $50,000	40
WI	Class I felony Max 3 years, 6 months Max $10,000	Class A misdemeanor Max 9 months Max $10,000	Class I felony Max 3 years, 6 months Max $10,000	41
MD	Felony Max 3 years Max $5,000	Misdemeanor Max 1 year Max $2,500	Felony Max 3 years Max $5,000	42
CA	Felony 16 months or 2 or 3 years Max $50,000	Misdemeanor Max 6 months Max $1,000	Felony 16 months or 2 or 3 years Max $50,000	43
WY	Felony Max 2 years Max $5,000	Misdemeanor Max 6 months Max $750	Felony Max 2 years Max $5,000	44
SD	Class 6 felony Max 2 years Max $4,000	Class 1 misdemeanor Max 1 year Max $2,000	Class 6 felony Max 2 years Max $4,000	45
Third tier: One felony provision				
WV	Felony 1–5 years $1,000–$5,000	Misdemeanor Max 1 year $100–$1,000	Misdemeanor Max 6 months $300–$2,000	46
NY	Felony Max 4 years Max $25,000	Misdemeanor Max 1 year Max $1,000	Misdemeanor Max 1 year Max $15,000	47
TX	State jail felony 180 days–2 years	Class A misdemeanor Max 1 year Max $4,000	Class A misdemeanor Max 1 year Max $4,000	48
Fourth tier: Allows possession or spectators				
MT	Felony 1–5 years Max $5,000	Legal	Felony 1–5 years Max $5,000	49
HI	Class C felony Max 5 years Max $10,000	Legal	Class C felony Max 5 years Max $10,000	50
NV	Category D felony 1–4 years Max $5,000	Misdemeanor Max 6 months Max $1,000	Legal	51

SOURCE: Ranking of State Dogfighting Laws, Humane Society of the United States, February 13, 2009, http://www.hsus.org/acf/fighting/dogfight/ranking_ state_dogfighting_laws.html (accessed February 20, 2009)

CHAPTER 7
ENTERTAINMENT ANIMALS

Entertainment animals are those that perform or are displayed publicly to amuse people. These animals appear in circuses, carnivals, animal shows and exhibits, amusement and wildlife theme parks, aquariums, zoos, museums, fairs, and motion pictures and television programs. Even though these venues are diverse, they all have one thing in common: They use animals for human purposes. Many of these purposes are purely recreational. Others combine recreation with educational goals, such as teaching the public about the conservation and preservation of endangered species. In either case, the animals are a source of income for their owners.

Entertainment animals include both wild and domesticated types. Wild exotic animals such as elephants, lions, and tigers are the most popular. They are objects of curiosity because people do not encounter them in their daily life. The word *exotic* means "foreign" or "not native" but also suggests an air of mystery and danger that is alluring to people, who will often pay to see exotic animals living in cages. By contrast, domestic animals must do something to make money, because most people will not pay to see ordinary dogs and cats lying around. They might, however, pay to see them jump through fiery hoops or walk on their hind legs pushing baby carriages. They will pay even more to see wild animals do such things.

This unnatural basis of the exotic animal business is what makes it unacceptable to animal rights groups. They believe wild animals should live in the wild, unaffected by human interference, and not be forced to do things that do not come naturally to them. Animal welfarists fear that exotic animals are not housed, trained, and cared for in a humane manner, particularly at circuses, carnivals, and roadside zoos and parks. The animals at these venues may be treated poorly, living in deplorable conditions without access to veterinary care. Performing animals must be trained to be entertainers, and trainers may use cruel and abusive methods.

Animal rights advocates feel that even nonperforming captive wild animals live unnatural existences. They are either removed from their natural habitats or born into captivity. Some people argue that this is beneficial to the animals and the perpetuation of their species. Animals in the wild face many dangers, including natural predators, starvation, hunters, and poachers. Their natural habitats in many parts of the world are shrinking as human development takes up more and more space.

Some exotic animals live longer in captivity than they would in the wild, and some species might die out completely if humans do not capture specimens of them to preserve. Large zoos often do this kind of work, and they may also take in exotic animals that have been surrendered by or rescued from smaller, less capable zoos and parks. However, even these large zoos are in the entertainment business, earning money by displaying captive animals to the public. Does the end justify the means? This is one of the fundamental questions in the debate over animals in entertainment.

HISTORY

The movie and television industry became a major media outlet for animal entertainment during the latter part of the twentieth century. Circuses and other traditional shows featuring live wild animal acts faded in popularity as they competed with new venues, such as theme parks and aquariums with exotic animals. In 1964 the first Sea-World marine park opened in San Diego, California. The San Diego Zoo's Wild Animal Park was established in 1969. Busch Gardens of Florida began in the late 1950s as a beer-tasting factory open to the public. Over the following two decades the company added elaborate bird and animal acts and amusement park rides to create a theme park. During the late 1990s SeaWorld and Walt Disney World both added massive animal theme parks to their existing attractions.

Exotic animal acts evolved during the twentieth century. These shows are often marketed as a chance for people to get closer to nature and to help protect endangered species. For example, tourists pay to swim with captive dolphins at beach resorts. SeaWorld in Orlando, Florida, advertises "amazing animal encounters" for its guests with orcas, dolphins, sea lions, and stingrays.

U.S. LEGISLATION AND REGULATION

Performing animals in the United States had little legal protection until 1970, when the Animal Welfare Act (AWA) was amended to include animals exhibited to the public. Regulation and enforcement of the act is handled by the U.S. Department of Agriculture's (USDA) Animal and Plant Health Inspection Service (APHIS). Animal exhibitors that show animals for compensation and either obtain or dispose of animals in commercial transactions must be licensed. Exhibitors that do not receive compensation and do not buy, sell, or transport animals only need to register.

Licensing is required for:

- Zoos (except those operated by the federal government)

- Exhibits, shows, and acts that feature captive marine mammals (dolphins, porpoises, whales, polar bears, sea otters, seals, walruses, and other mammals with fins or flippers)

- Tourist attractions exhibiting animals, such as roadside zoos

- Carnivals and circuses with animals

- Promotional exhibits in which regulated animals are used to promote or advertise goods and services

- Owners who exhibit animals doing tricks or otherwise performing for a live audience or on tape

Exemptions from the license requirement are granted for pet and horse shows, rodeos, hunting events, exhibits of farm animals at agricultural events, private collectors who do not publicly show or sell animals, enterprises that keep animals in a wild state (such as game and hunting preserves), and exhibits that feature animals not covered by the AWA—mainly birds, reptiles, and fish.

In "Zoo, Circus, and Marine Animals" (April 22, 2009, http://awic.nal.usda.gov/nal_display/index.php?tax_level=1&info_center=3&tax_subject=180), APHIS explains that under the AWA licensed exhibitors must provide "adequate care and treatment in the areas of housing, handling, sanitation, nutrition, water, veterinary care, and protection from extreme weather and temperatures." The exhibitors are required to keep records detailing the veterinary care that the animals receive. According to APHIS, in 2009 there were 2,712 licensed exhibitors (http://www.aphis.usda.gov/animal_welfare/efoia/downloads/reports/C_cert_holders.pdf) and

15 registered exhibitors (http://www.aphis.usda.gov/animal_welfare/efoia/downloads/reports/E_cert_holders.pdf) operating in 2009. California has the most licensed animal acts (270), followed by Florida (257), Texas (217), New York (126), and Illinois (122). Together, these five states accounted for more than one-third of all licensed exhibits. The number of regulated exhibitors has generally increased every year since fiscal year 2002.

Regulations are also designed to ensure public safety. Dangerous animals can be publicly exhibited only under the direct control of an experienced trainer. There are time limits for exhibits, and the animals have to be fed and watered and handled in a humane manner that prevents unnecessary stress or discomfort. Physical abuse and withholding food are not permissible training methods. Traveling exhibits have to submit their performance schedules to APHIS before each tour. Exhibitors that violate standards are subject to warnings and civil actions such as license suspensions or fines.

Criticisms of the AWA and APHIS

The AWA regulations are criticized by animal welfarists as being minimal standards that provide little protection and are poorly enforced. Penalties for violating the AWA are civil, not criminal. APHIS reports in *Animal Care Annual Report of Activities: Fiscal Year 2007* (September 2008, http://www.aphis.usda.gov/publications/animal_welfare/content/printable_version/2007_AC_Report.pdf) that it conducted 3,626 compliance inspections of animal exhibits in fiscal year 2007.

Entertainment animals are often protected by state and local anticruelty laws, but the Humane Society of the United States (HSUS) claims that some states exempt USDA-licensed animal acts (particularly circuses) from meeting anticruelty standards. Animal rights groups also indicate that the USDA refuses to allow its inspectors to testify in criminal cruelty cases. Some local governments forbid or tightly regulate animal acts.

The HSUS advocates one of two legislative approaches at the local level:

- A ban on any mental and physical harassment of wild animals for the purpose of entertainment and a ban on their use in unnatural behaviors (such as jumping through hoops, wrestling with people, etc.)

- A ban on the use of all wild animals for entertainment unless regulations are in place to ensure their safety and that of the public

CIRCUSES

Circuses have used performing animals, mostly horses, elephants, lions, tigers, bears, and monkeys, for centuries. Animal rights and welfare groups are critical of circuses that feature animals. They say the animals are treated poorly and spend long hours in small cages or chained to the ground. In "Circus Myths" (2009, http://www.hsus.org/wildlife/issues_facing_wildlife/circuses/circus_myths.html), the HSUS makes the following claims against circuses:

- Many circus animals are not owned by the circuses but are leased from exotic animal dealers under seasonal contracts.

- Circuses do not provide proper veterinary care for the animals they own or lease.

- Circus animals spend too much time in transport in trucks and railcars that are not air conditioned or heated.

- Traveling circus animals are often deprived of food and water for long periods.

- Circus training methods include beatings and food deprivation.

Major animal welfare and rights groups, such as the HSUS, People for the Ethical Treatment of Animals (PETA), and Born Free USA advocate animal-free circuses. Born Free USA lists in *Incidents from Circuses that Use Animals* (2009, http://www.bornfreeusa.org/popups/a1a_exhibited_circus_incidents.php) several animal incidents (escapes, attacks, and alleged abuse cases) associated with circuses.

ZOOS

In 1874 the first American zoo opened to the public in Philadelphia, Pennsylvania. It featured animals from around the world, as well as elaborate gardens, architecture, and art. Early zoos kept wild animals in cages, but during the mid-1800s the German exhibitor Carl Hagenbeck (1844–1913) advocated the use of natural settings for zoo animals. In 1907 he opened a zoo in which the animals were exhibited on artificial islands that resembled their natural habitats. He felt this approach was better for both the animals and the spectators. Even though few other zookeepers adopted his ideas at the time, they were one of the hallmarks of a top zoo by the end of the twentieth century.

Accredited Zoos

Originally founded in 1924 as the American Association of Zoological Parks and Aquariums, the Association of Zoos and Aquariums (AZA) is a nonprofit organization that works to advance conservation, education, science, and recreation at zoos and aquariums. According to the AZA (2008, http://www.aza.org/AboutAZA/), it is "dedicated to the advancement of accredited zoos and aquariums in the areas of animal care, wildlife conservation, education and science." Zoos and aquariums that meet AZA's professional standards can be accredited by the organization. In "Numbers, Numbers, Numbers" (2008, http://www.aza.org/Newsroom/Current Statistics/index.html), the AZA notes that in 2008 there

were 218 AZA-accredited zoos and aquariums, located mostly in North America, housing 735,173 animals. In 2007 these zoos attracted 175 million visitors. The AZA also works to ensure the long-term breeding and conservation of a variety of species.

The zoos accredited by the AZA in the United States are generally well respected by the public and even by many animal welfarists. For example, the HSUS acknowledges that large zoos educate the public about wildlife and help conserve, preserve, and restore endangered species. However, this does not spare accredited zoos from some criticisms.

Unwanted Animals

In "Cruel and Usual: How Some of America's Best Zoos Get Rid of Their Old, Infirm, and Unwanted Animals" (*U.S. News and World Report*, July 28, 2002), Michael Satchell examines the animal disposal practices of some major U.S. zoos. Satchell tracked down a dozen primates, birds, and other exotic animals that had left the prestigious Rosamond Gifford Zoo in Syracuse, New York, for a menagerie in Texas. He found the animals living in filthy cages alongside an interstate highway amid trash and weeds. The menagerie had gone out of business.

The AZA explains in "AZA Acquisition/Disposition Policy" (2008, http://www.aza.org/AboutAZA/ADPolicy/) that it requires accredited institutions to acquire animals from and dispose of animals to other AZA institutions or to non-AZA members with "the expertise, records management practices, financial stability, facilities, and resources required to properly care for and maintain the animals and their offspring." Satchell claims this procedure is often violated by AZA zoos that "loan" or "donate" unwanted animals to unaccredited roadside zoos and animal parks. These facilities are frequently substandard and provide poor care. Satchell quotes Richard Farinato of the HSUS as saying that the practice "is the big, respectable zoos' dirty little secret."

Satchell bases his accusations on a review of database records from the International Species Information System (http://www.isis.org/CMSHOME/), which is used by major zoos to track animal transfers, and from interviews with government, zoo, and animal rights personnel. Satchell concludes that large zoos in New York, California, Hawaii, Tennessee, Georgia, Colorado, Arizona, Alabama, Missouri, and the District of Columbia have transferred unwanted animals to substandard facilities and to dealers with alleged links to the exotic animal trade.

Captivity Effects on Carnivores

Carnivores are flesh-eating mammals. Ros Clubb and Georgia Mason of Oxford University studied the effects of zoo captivity on 35 carnivore species and published their findings in "Animal Welfare: Captivity Effects on

Wide-Ranging Carnivores" (*Nature*, vol. 425, no. 6957, October 2, 2003). They find that some carnivores, such as snow leopards and ring-tailed lemurs, adjust well and even thrive in captivity. However, carnivores that normally roam over large territories in the wild, such as Asian elephants, polar bears, and lions, experience health, behavior, and reproductive problems in captivity. Clubb and Mason believe these species are traumatized by a lack of roaming space in their zoo enclosures. They conclude that "the keeping of naturally wide-ranging carnivores should be either fundamentally improved or phased out."

Unaccredited Zoos

According to the AZA (2008, http://www.aza.org/Accreditation/AccreditationIntro/), it accredits less than 10% of U.S. zoos. As such, there are thousands of unaccredited small "roadside zoos," petting zoos, animal parks, and similar exhibits that display animals to the public. The HSUS says that these small zoos often barely meet minimal federal standards for animal care. Most of these facilities include exotic animals, such as lions and tigers. Many are run by entrepreneurs with little experience in the proper care of exotic animals and with limited financial resources. Some call themselves animal preserves and achieve tax-exempt status so that they can solicit donations for their "conservation" work.

All licensed animal exhibits are subject to USDA inspection, but animal welfare groups claim that poorly run facilities often receive bad inspection reports for years and are still not closed down. A case in point is ZooCats, Inc. (also known as Zoo Dynamics) in Kaufman, Texas. In 2008 APHIS (September 24, 2008, http://www.da.usda.gov/oaljdecisions/080924_AWA_03-0035DO.pdf) initiated an administrative proceeding against ZooCats and its owners for several AWA violations that occurred between 2002 and 2007. According to court records, ZooCats was registered with the USDA as a nonprofit corporation but had exhibited wild and exotic animals for profit at the Six Flags over Texas amusement park and other venues around the country, including shopping malls and fairs. These exhibits often included baby tigers that children were allowed to pet and feed without proper supervision. APHIS cited many deficiencies over several years found by APHIS inspectors with the handling, housing, feeding, and veterinary care provided for the tigers and other exotic animals, including prairie dogs, lions, and a bear, that were exhibited by ZooCats. Some of the tigers were malnourished and had untreated injuries and illnesses. In September 2008 an administrative law judge ruled that the ZooCats's USDA license should be revoked. He complained, "In addition to the astonishing lack of precaution taken by Respondents to protect the public and the animals from harm, Respondents also often failed to feed their animals properly or provide them with veterinary and other requisite kinds of care." Brett Shipp reports in "Big Cat Exhibitor Continues Operation after

License Revoked" (KVUE.com, January 14, 2009) that ZooCats had filed an appeal in the case in January 2009 and continued to operate its exhibits.

THE FIGHT OVER CIRCUS AND ZOO ELEPHANTS

The keeping of elephants in captivity by circuses and zoos is a highly controversial issue for animal welfare and rights groups. Elephants are difficult to keep in confinement because of their immense size. Welfarists claim that many circus elephants are mistreated, malnourished, and sick with tuberculosis. A common tool for training elephants is called an ankus or bullhook, which is a long rod with a sharp hook on the end. Critics charge that elephant trainers beat the animals with the rod and poke the hook into tender areas of the elephant's hide, such as behind its ears. In 2002 the animal rights group In Defense of Animals (IDA) sponsored speaking engagements around the country for a former circus animal trainer, who described beatings administered to elephants with bullhooks. He claimed that brutal training methods are routinely used at the Clyde Beatty–Cole Brothers Circus and the Ringling Brothers and Barnum and Bailey Circus. The IDA also obtained video footage of what it says are abusive training methods being practiced on circus elephants.

Zoos and circuses insist that keeping elephants in captivity is a conservation measure that will help ensure the survival of the species for the future. For example, the Ringling Brothers and Barnum and Bailey Circus defends its elephant training and breeding programs. The circus, which is owned by Feld Entertainment, operates an animal retirement facility and the Center of Elephant Conservation (CEC) in Florida. The CEC explains in "Ringling Bros. Center for Elephant Conservation Facts & Figures" (2009, http://www.elephantcenter.com/default.aspx?id=3630) that it was founded in 1995 to conserve, study, and breed Asian elephants. The CEC is a $5-million, 200-acre (81-ha) facility dedicated to preserving the species, of which only 35,000 are left in the wild. The center is not open to the public but admits researchers, conservationists, and academicians by arrangement. As of 2009, the CED had 22 births.

Animal rights groups contend that breeding elephants to work in the circus or display at zoos is not really conservation. They believe that wild animals should live undisturbed in their natural environments and that resources should be focused on protecting and expanding natural habitats. They oppose the use of captivity as a conservation tool.

The Hawthorn Elephants

PETA (February 2005, http://www.circuses.com/save lota.asp) describes the life of a circus elephant named Lota. She lived at the Milwaukee Zoo from 1954 until 1990, when she was acquired by the Hawthorn Corporation, a company that trains exotic animals and leases them to circuses. PETA claims that Hawthorn handlers beat Lota and that she suffered from malnutrition and tuberculosis. For years the company has been criticized by animal welfare groups for mistreating and being neglectful of the animals under its care.

Richard Farinato reports in "USDA Seizes the Moment, Orders Hawthorn to Give up 16 Elephants" (March 25, 2004, http://www.hsus.org/wildlife/wildlife_news/usda _seizes_the_moment_orders_hawthorn_to_give_up_16 _elephants.html) that in April 2003 the Hawthorn Corporation was charged by the USDA for AWA violations. Later that year the USDA confiscated an elephant named Delhi from the company and sent it to the Elephant Sanctuary in Hohenwald, Tennessee. In March 2004 the Hawthorn owner John F. Cuneo Jr. admitted to committing at least 19 violations of the AWA and agreed to relinquish ownership of all 16 of his elephants by August 2004 to settle the USDA lawsuit. He was assessed a $200,000 civil penalty. In July 2004 Cuneo filed court motions seeking to vacate the consent order against him. A long series of legal maneuvers began that extended well beyond the original August 2004 deadline for relinquishing the elephants.

In *Hawthorn Elephant Update* (February 14, 2006, http://www.aphis.usda.gov/animal_welfare/downloads/ stakeholder/stakeholder4.pdf), Chester A. Gipson of APHIS notes that two of the elephants (Tess and Sue) subsequently died in Hawthorn facilities. In late 2004 two more elephants (Lota and Misty) went to live at the Elephant Sanctuary. Lota died there in February 2005 after a long battle with tuberculosis. Two other elephants were placed with other facilities approved by the USDA. In January 2006 eight more Hawthorn elephants were sent to the Elephant Sanctuary. More than a year later, the Performing Animal Welfare Society (PAWS) sanctuary in San Andreas, California, took the remaining two Hawthorn elephants named Nicholas and Gypsy.

The Case against Ringling Brothers

The Ringling Brothers and Barnum and Bailey Circus (commonly called the Ringling Brothers) is owned by Feld Entertainment. The company has long been criticized by animal welfare groups for its handling and use of Asian elephants. In 2000 Ringling Brothers and Feld Entertainment were sued by a group of plaintiffs including PAWS, the American Society for the Prevention of Cruelty to Animals (ASPCA), the Animal Welfare Institute, the Fund for Animals, and Tom Rider, a former Ringling Brothers elephant handler.

The suit claims that Ringling Brothers has violated the "taking" provision under the Endangered Species Act. The act's definition of taking includes harming, harassing, and/or wounding. Specifically, the circus is accused of physically abusing its elephants with bullhooks, chaining the elephants for up to 20 hours at a time, and forcibly separating elephant mothers from their babies at an early age. In 2001 PAWS dropped out of the lawsuit due to separate litigation brought against it by Feld Entertainment. Between February and March 2009, after many years of delays, *ASPCA et al. v. Feld Entertainment, Inc.* was finally heard in federal court. As of April 2009, a decision had not been made public.

Feld Entertainment has staunchly denied the allegations in the lawsuit. In the pretrial press release "Feld Entertainment, Inc. Trial Update: Trial Set for Feb. 4, 2009 in Case Filed by Animal Special Interest Groups" (February 3, 2009, http://www.ringlingbrostrialinfo.com/ uploadedFiles/Media%20Stmt%20V.F..pdf), the company states, "Feld Entertainment will show during the trial that its elephants are healthy, alert, and thriving, and it intends to debunk the misinformation that has been spread by those who do not own or know how to care for an elephant." The company accuses the animal groups of waging "a long-running crusade to eliminate animals from circuses, zoos and wildlife parks."

Elephant Welfare under the AWA

In 2006 the IDA petitioned APHIS to issue regulations dealing specifically with the space and living conditions for captive elephants, because they did not have specific standards under the AWA, but fell under the general standards for warm-blooded animals. APHIS published a request for comments on the petition in the *Federal Register* (August 9, 2006, vol. 71, no. 153). Specifically, the agency asked for public input on the causes of arthritis in elephants, proper foot care practices and substrates (standing surfaces) for captive elephants, and exercise and other welfare standards for the animals.

In *Animal Care Annual Report of Activities*, APHIS states that it received 2,100 comments in response to the public notice and was still reviewing all the input. The agency promised that when the comment review process was completed, "a determination will be made as to constructive actions that can be taken appropriately under the AWA to address elephant welfare in specific terms."

Zoo Conditions for Elephants

In January 2008 the IDA published its annual "Ten Worst Zoos for Elephants in 2007" (http://www.idausa.org/ news/currentnews/nr_080109.html). The IDA states that seven elephants died at AZA-accredited zoos in 2007, most from disorders the IDA claims are "caused by lack of space and inadequate, unnatural zoo exhibits." The group is also critical of the keeping by some zoos of only one elephant and of frequent transfers of elephants between zoos. The IDA complains that "elephants do not naturally live in isolation and require social interaction with other elephants." Transfers between zoos and poor living conditions are blamed for aiding the spread of the elephant herpes virus, a deadly infectious disease.

According to the article "Phila. Zoo Elephant Dies" (*Philadelphia Business Journal*, June 9, 2008), the Philadelphia Zoo decided to close its elephant exhibit in 2006 because it could not afford renovations to provide more space for its three elephants—Petal, Kallie, and Bette. In June 2008 Petal was found dead in her stall of unknown causes. The other two elephants were scheduled to move to the Pittsburgh Zoo's International Conservation Center. As of April 2009, they had not yet been transferred. The IDA notes that in 2007 the Philadelphia Zoo transferred a fourth elephant—Dulary—to the Elephant Sanctuary in Tennessee. The Alaska Zoo in Anchorage, Alaska, transferred its lone elephant—Maggie—to the PAWS sanctuary in California in 2007. Both zoos had endured years of criticism from animal welfare groups about their lack of space for elephants, and, in the Alaska's zoo case, for keeping a solitary elephant. Also in 2007 the Los Angeles Zoo transferred an elephant named Ruby to the PAWS sanctuary. The zoo began a $40 million renovation to build a 3.5-acre (1.4-ha) habitat for its remaining elephant Billy. Corina Knoll notes in "Bob Barker Donates $1.5 Million for L.A. Zoo Elephant" (*Los Angeles Times*, January 26, 2009) that the former television personality Bob Barker (1923–) had offered to donate $1.5 million to move Billy to the PAWS sanctuary. He and other animal welfare proponents believe the proposed zoo habitat will be too small for the elephant. Barker donated $300,000 the previous year to move Ruby to PAWS. Nevertheless, the Los Angeles City Council voted on January 28, 2009, to continue construction of the elephant habitat for Billy.

The IDA has publicly criticized the Buffalo Zoo for its elephant confinement area. According to Tricia Cruz, in "Animal Rights Group Comes down on Zoo" (January 7, 2009, http://www.wivb.com/dpp/news/animal_rights _group_comes_down_on_zoo_090106), the zoo spent $1 million renovating its elephant quarters. An IDA spokesperson complained that "they now cram three elephants into an 1800 square foot area that's about the size of a small suburban home." Cruz notes that the zoo had been ranked by the IDA as one of the ten worst zoos for elephants. Donna Fernandes, the zoo president, is quoted as responding, "I think that the list is unfortunate, it does harm to a community that's working hard to support an important cultural asset."

MOVIES AND TELEVISION

Animals have been performing in movies and television shows ever since those media were invented. Rin Tin Tin was a famous war dog that starred in silent movies during the 1920s. The story of another dog, Lassie, appeared in book form in 1940, in a movie in 1943, and on television in 1954. The original television show ran for 17 years. Another dog gained fame in the title role of the movie *Benji* in 1974. Popular animal movies of the 1980s included *White Fang* and *Turner and Hooch*.

The orca Keiko became famous because of the 1993 movie *Free Willy*. In the movie Keiko portrayed a whale liberated from captivity with the help of a boy. In "Won't Somebody Please Save This Whale?" (*Life*, November 1993), JoBeth McDaniel described the irony of the poor conditions in which Keiko lived in a Mexican amusement park. In response, the Free Willy Foundation raised millions of dollars to have Keiko moved in 1996 to an aquarium in Oregon. (See Figure 7.1.) There he gained weight and recuperated from various health ailments. In 1998 he was flown to Iceland to live in a bay pen in his native waters. Keiko's handlers tried to teach him skills he would need in the wild, such as catching live fish on his own. Keiko was released in 2002. However, he did not join an ocean pod of whales as was hoped. Instead, he took refuge in a calm bay in Norway and remained semidependent on humans for food until his death in 2003 from pneumonia.

During the 1990s animal stories in the media became so popular that an entire cable television network was devoted to them. Animal Planet was launched in 1996 as a project of Discovery Communications. It broadcasts popular shows such as *Animal Cops*, *Animal Precinct*, *The Jeff Corwin Experience*, and *The Planet's Funniest Animals*.

Animal Precinct is a reality show that goes on patrol with New York City's Humane Law Enforcement (HLE) agents. These agents are empowered to respond to cruelty complaints, perform investigations, and arrest people for crimes against animals. They were granted this power in 1866 when the ASPCA established its original charter with the state of New York. *Animal Cops* is a similar series based on the work of the Detroit-based Michigan Humane Society. Due to the popularity of such shows, additional programs were created in Houston, Texas, Miami, Florida, and San Francisco, California. Since their inception, these shows have gained an enormous fan base, and the featured agents and officers have earned celebrity status because of their work.

The American Humane Association Monitors Animal Welfare

During the filming of the 1939 movie *Jesse James*, a horse was killed when it was forced to jump off a cliff for a scene. Public complaints led to the formation of the film-monitoring unit of the American Humane Association (AHA). The AHA opened an office in Los Angeles in 1940.

In 1980 the AHA was awarded a contract with the Screen Actors Guild (SAG) to monitor the safety and welfare of animals appearing in movies and television shows featuring SAG performers filmed in the United States. The Producer-Screen Actors Guild Codified Basic Agreement of 1998 includes a provision that producers must notify the AHA before using animals on a set and

FIGURE 7.1

Keiko, a killer whale, at the Oregon Coast Aquarium, Newport, Oregon, 1998. *AP Images.*

provide AHA representatives with access to the set while animals are being filmed. This applies to movies, television shows, commercials, and music videos that include SAG performers.

The AHA reviews scripts and works with animal trainers and production staff to ensure that animals are not harmed during filming. The AHA monitors hundreds of productions each year in the United States. The AHA's contractual authority does not extend beyond the United States. However, producers sometimes invite the AHA to oversee animal filming at foreign locations. The AHA has no oversight authority on non-SAG productions, such as reality shows and documentaries.

The AHA guidelines are laid out in *American Humane Association Guidelines for the Safe Use of Animals in Filmed Media* (October 2005, http://www.americanhumane.org/assets/docs/protecting-animals/PA-FILM-guidelines.pdf). The guidelines cover what filmmakers and crew should do before and during production to ensure animal safety. In "Movie Search" (http://www.ahafilm.info/movies/search.phtml), the AHA lists its ratings for hundreds of movies based on their adherence to these guidelines. The AHA also details how particular animal scenes were filmed in dozens of movies by use of deceptive camera

angles, body doubles, fake blood, computer graphics, and other tricks.

ANIMAL THEME PARKS

Animal theme parks are large tourist attractions that combine elements of zoos (or aquariums) and amusement parks to entertain the public. The first oceanarium (a large saltwater aquarium) in the United States is thought to be Marine Studios of Florida, later named Marineland. In 1963 came the release of the popular movie *Flipper*, about a dolphin who befriends a young boy. It became a hit television show a year later. (See Figure 7.2.) Public demand for performing dolphins and other sea creatures skyrocketed. In 1964 George Millay (1929–2006) developed a marine life park called SeaWorld in San Diego, California, and in 1965 SeaWorld acquired Shamu, a female orca captured from the wild.

Shamu was one of many orcas captured during the early 1960s for use in the entertainment industry. According to *Frontline*, in *A Whale of a Business* (November 1997, http://www.pbs.org/wgbh/pages/frontline/shows/whales/), the first captive orca had been collected for Marineland of the Pacific in 1961. The animal lived for only one day. She repeatedly smashed herself against the walls of her tank

FIGURE 7.2

The cast members Tommy Norden, Brian Kelly, and Luke Halpin with the dolphin star Bebe, who played Flipper on the 1960s television show of the same name. *AP/Wide World Photos/NBC. Reproduced by permission.*

until she died. *Frontline* lists 133 known orcas captured between 1961 and 1997, along with their life spans in captivity. Many lived only for a few months, whereas the average life span for an orca in the wild is 40 to 60 years. *Frontline* estimates that 102 of the 133 captive orcas had died.

The original Shamu survived for six years. In the intervening years SeaWorld has continued to acquire orcas and call at least one of them by the stage name Shamu for performance purposes. Eventually, the company trademarked the name.

During the 1970s and 1980s SeaWorld marine parks opened in Ohio, Florida, and Texas. In 1989 they were purchased by Anheuser-Busch, which already operated Busch Gardens, a popular park in Florida featuring bird acts, animal shows, and amusement park rides. In 2000

the company opened another theme park, also in Florida, named Discovery Cove, where visitors can experience wildlife up close and swim with dolphins and stingrays. The stingers are cut off of the stingrays to make them harmless to people. An aviary includes hundreds of exotic birds that people can hand feed. According to company officials (April 2, 2009, http://www.orlandowelcomecenter.com/discovery-cove-environment.htm), the SeaWorld marine parks, Busch Gardens, and Discovery Cove are home to approximately 60,000 animals. The officials note that "these animals serve as ambassadors for their species by helping to entertain, educate and inspire millions of people."

Many animal welfare and rights groups are critical of the Anheuser-Busch theme parks and Disney's Animal Kingdom, an attraction that opened at Walt Disney World in Florida in 1998. PETA notes in "Deadly Destinations" (2009, http://www.helpinganimals.com/travel_feat_deadlydest.asp) that hundreds of animals have died at these facilities because of improper care. PETA argues that living conditions are not healthy for the animals in captivity and disputes claims by the owner companies of animal parks that they further conservation efforts.

The HSUS focuses its efforts on eliminating dolphin petting pools at animal theme parks. These are areas of shallow water around which visitors can gather and touch and feed dolphins. In *Biting the Hand That Feeds: The Case against Dolphin Petting Pools* (Spring 2003, http://www.hsus.org/web-files/PDF/Biting_The_Hand_That_Feeds.pdf), the HSUS indicates that animal theme parks are increasingly offering such opportunities for the public to experience physical contact with wild animals and marine life via feeding, petting, and swimming programs. The HSUS provides a number of arguments against holding cetaceans (dolphins, whales, porpoises, etc.) in captivity to entertain humans and particularly against using them in petting pools. HSUS field investigations conducted between 1996 and 2003 reveal that visitors to petting pools are not properly supervised by theme park staff and expose themselves and the animals to various health and safety hazards. The HSUS also notes that many of the dolphins in petting pools appear obese and show signs of injury from aggressive competition over food. Allowing the public to feed captive dolphins also sets a dangerous precedent, the HSUS believes, given that the government actively discourages people from feeding wild dolphins under the Marine Mammal Protection Act. Finally, the HSUS disputes the claim by the theme park industry that petting pools are educational, noting that "hand-feeding dead fish to obese dolphins in a cramped, overcrowded and featureless tank of chemically treated water provides visitors with scant insight into normal dolphin behavior in the natural environment."

CHAPTER 8
SERVICE ANIMALS

Service animals are those that work for humans doing particular tasks. These tasks may be as mundane as pulling plows or as sophisticated as finding underwater mines. Throughout history animals have helped humans hunt wildlife, herd livestock, guard people and property, and wage warfare. Animals are also trained for more humanitarian causes, such as rescuing the lost and providing aid and comfort to people with certain physical and psychological needs.

Whatever the task may be, the common factor is that service animals help humans with their needs and desires. Some people see this as a clever use of resources. Many believe it is a mutually beneficial bond, but others see it as a form of slavery. Some animal rights activists believe that animals should not be used for any purpose by humans. Even though they rarely speak out against uses that the public views as benevolent, they are extremely critical of military uses of animals because the animals are exposed to great danger. This is also true for animals doing some police and rescue jobs.

Welfarists are also concerned that working animals should be trained and treated with care. Animal groups recommend that only positive reinforcement be used when service animals are trained. They also point out that service animals should be carefully screened to ensure that they are a good match with their potential human partners. Finally, they remind people that the needs of service and assistance animals must be considered along with the needs of the people being served. In general, however, welfarists tend to support programs that train service and therapeutic animals because so many of these programs rescue homeless animals from shelters.

HISTORY

The role of service animals in hunting, agriculture, transportation, and warfare changed little over thousands of years. In the United States service animals continued in their traditional roles until the late 1800s. Then the urbanization and innovations of the Industrial Revolution slowly eliminated the need for many of them. Motorized vehicles took over nearly all the work formerly done by horses and beasts of burden in transportation, warfare, and agriculture. Over the next century many people turned to electronics instead of dogs to guard their property and to chemicals instead of cats to kill rodents. Some vital tasks previously performed by working animals have become activities of recreation—for example, hunting and herding with dogs and using horses to pull carriages.

The use of animals (particularly dogs) in military and public service, however, continues to grow. In addition, animals serve as aides and provide companionship and therapy to people with specific physical and mental needs.

HUNTING
Falconry

Falconry is a form of hunting conducted with the use of trained birds of prey, such as falcons, hawks, owls, or eagles. (See Figure 8.1.) These birds are also called raptors. According to the California Hawking Club (January 14, 2009, http://www.calhawkingclub.org/app_info.htm), in 2009 there were approximately 7,000 falconers in the United States. Falconry has strict licensing requirements because it uses wild birds that are protected species. Animals commonly hunted using falconry are rabbits, squirrels, pigeons, quail, and waterfowl.

Dogs

Dogs have historically been used in hunting. In the United States dogs are used to hunt upland game birds and waterfowl, such as pheasant, quail, partridge, ducks, and pigeons. Dogs are also used to hunt squirrels, bears, raccoons, mountain lions, foxes, and other prey. The primary dog breeds used in hunting are beagles, spaniels, griffons,

FIGURE 8.1

A peregrine falcon. *Image copyright Jeff Banke, 2009. Used under license from Shutterstock.com.*

retrievers, setters, pointers, and hounds. Dogs that hunt mostly by scent are called scent hounds, and dogs that hunt mostly by sight are called sight hounds. Hunting dogs perform a variety of tasks, including tracking prey, pointing prey out to the hunter, and retrieving downed prey after it is shot.

CONTROVERSIES OVER USING HUNTING DOGS. Hunting with dogs has become a controversial issue in some areas where it is common. In "Hunters Howling" (*Atlanta Journal-Constitution*, April 13, 2003), Stacy Shelton reports on increasing conflicts in southern Georgia between hunters using dogs and landowners. Dog running, as it is called, is a long-standing tradition in rural areas of the state. Landowners accused hunters of letting their dogs trespass onto private property during deer hunting season (mid-October to mid-January). Hunters said that property owners were being unreasonable and had killed at least one hunting dog. The landowners claimed that hunters had threatened them and told them that they should fence their property if they did not want hunting dogs on it.

In July 2003 the Georgia legislature passed a bill that severely restricts the hunting of deer with dogs in the state. It can only be conducted on large pieces of property of at least 1,000 acres (405 ha). The owners or lessees of the property must obtain a permit from the state before allowing a hunt. All hunters have to label their dogs and vehicles with the permit number. In this way, trespassers can be easily identified and reported to authorities. Some companies that own huge tracts of land in southern Georgia, such as the International Paper Company, have decided not to allow hunting with dogs on their property anymore.

One particularly controversial form of hunting conducted with the help of dogs and horses is foxhunting. Hunters on horseback pursue foxes across the countryside using packs of hounds. Though foxhunting has been practiced in the United Kingdom for hundreds of years, animal welfare groups have been trying to get it outlawed since the 1940s because they consider it cruel to the foxes. In February 2002 Scotland passed a bill outlawing mounted hunting with dogs. After much political maneuvering, a similar bill was passed in England and Wales that went into effect in February 2005. The debate over the bill in the United Kingdom was generally divided between social classes, with upper-class landowners opposing it. Foxhunting has traditionally been a sport of the wealthy in the United Kingdom, including members of the royal family.

According to the Masters of Foxhounds Association of North America, in "American Foxhunting" (February 17, 2009, http://www.mfha.com/abfo.htm), there are 171 recognized foxhunting clubs in North America. This number has reportedly grown over the last decade as foxhunting becomes more popular in the United States.

GUARD DUTY

Guard duty encompasses several tasks performed by animals. One is to alert humans to danger. Another is to provide physical protection from danger. Many animals can provide alerts but not protection. For example, canaries were once used in mines to warn miners that dangerous gases were present. Because canaries are sensitive to small dosages of these gases, their deaths gave the miners time to leave dangerous areas before they, too, were overcome. This was not a trained or voluntary response by the canaries. By contrast, dogs can alert people to an approaching predator and defend them against it.

Dogs are still the most popular type of guarding animals. Besides their traditional guard duties, dogs are increasingly used to warn humans about impending natural phenomena, such as earthquakes. For years, researchers have been studying claims that dogs can somehow sense when an earthquake is about to happen. The speculation is that dogs may hear rumbling noises or sense vibrations occurring deep within the earth that precede actual ground movement.

Guarding Territory and People

Dogs are the most popular animal used for guarding territory and people. This job requires large breeds that are strong, protective, and territorial. The breeds most often used for this work are Doberman pinschers, rottweilers, komondors, German shepherds, and chows.

Guard dogs are not the same as watchdogs. Watchdogs bark when a stranger approaches them or their territory. Even small dogs, such as Chihuahuas, make good watchdogs. Guard dogs are intended to scare away and even attack intruders. Many guard dogs are employed by security companies. They work with handlers and human guards to patrol sites or protect individuals. Other guard dogs work without human accompaniment. They are placed on commercial and industrial properties, such as junkyards, at night.

Animal welfarists are highly critical of the use of unaccompanied guard dogs at commercial and industrial sites. They claim these working dogs are given a minimum amount of food, water, and veterinary care; are kept in isolation in dangerous environments; and are treated cruelly to instill aggressive behavior.

Megan Metzelaar describes in "Guard Dog Update" (*ActionLine*, winter 2002–03) the hardships endured by some New Jersey guard dogs. According to Metzelaar, many guard dogs are leased from security companies. They are rotated around to different properties so that the dogs will not become accustomed to and possibly friendly with people in that area. The constant uncertainty makes the dogs feel vulnerable and insecure, which makes them even more aggressive. Critics say that the constant movement also makes it difficult for concerned people to monitor the condition of the dogs and report abuse and neglect to authorities.

MANUAL LABOR

Manual labor is work that requires physical skill and energy. In the United States mechanized equipment has replaced most of the work done by beasts of burden. Draft horses and mules are still used by a few farmers, particularly those in communities that use traditional farming techniques, such as the Amish. In addition, nearly all developing countries rely heavily on draft animals for agricultural work. (See Figure 8.2.)

In the United States some tasks historically performed by animals have become activities of leisure. For example, entrepreneurs in many large cities offer carriage rides to tourists. Animal welfarists are critical of these ventures, saying that carriage horses are forced to work under hazardous conditions on city streets crowded with traffic and often do not receive proper housing and care.

Since 2006 the animal protection group Coalition for New York City Animals has waged a campaign to ban horse-drawn carriages in that city. In "Let Carriage Horses Run Free: It's Time to Ban the Practice in New York City" (*New York Daily News*, January 12, 2009), Elizabeth Forel, a spokesperson for the organization, notes that there are approximately 200 carriage horses operating in New York City. She argues that the carriages interfere with traffic and are a danger to humans and horses. She complains, "Horses are shy, prey animals—meaning, they are programmed to flee from a frightening noise or situation. It is abhorrent for them to work in noisy traffic, breathing in car exhaust. In these conditions, they have no opportunity to graze in pasture or even to scratch an itch, instead they are being worked between the shafts of their carriage for nine hours straight." Forel claims that the Coalition for New York City Animals had acquired 35,000 signatures in a petition drive to ban the carriage industry in New York City. She notes that Councilman Tony Avella had introduced a bill imposing such a ban. As of April 2009, the ban was still under consideration by the New York City Council.

In April 2009 People for the Ethical Treatment of Animals (PETA) urged the city of Charleston, South Carolina, to ban horse-drawn carriages after a horse spooked by construction noise bolted out of control down a city street, causing the carriage to overturn. Only the driver was onboard at the time and was not injured. According to Greg Hambrick, in "Updated: Mayor Responds to PETA Carriage Request" (*Charleston City Paper*, April 7, 2009), the incident was the sixth such incident in the city since January 2008. Charleston's mayor responded that the city's carriage horse industry was "very safe" and showed "care and respect" for the horses involved.

LAW ENFORCEMENT

Law enforcement agencies around the world use animals (mostly dogs and horses) to help them perform security work. Dogs are, by far, the most common animals used.

Dogs

Many dogs are used by U.S. law enforcement agencies at the local and national levels to perform important tasks. These agencies include police and sheriff departments, arson investigators, the Federal Bureau of Investigation, the Federal Bureau of Prisons, the U.S. Customs and Border Protection, the U.S. Department of Agriculture (USDA), and the U.S. Drug Enforcement Administration.

The dogs are specially trained to work with officers during searches and arrests and to sniff out illegal substances. Dogs have incredibly sensitive noses. Their sense of smell is several thousand times better than that of humans. Dogs can smell tiny quantities of substances and can distinguish

FIGURE 8.2

Plowing oxen. *Image copyright Vera Bogaerts, 2009. Used under license from Shutterstock.com.*

particular scents with amazing accuracy. This natural ability has proven to be an extremely useful tool in law enforcement applications.

Many fire departments use dogs as part of their arson investigation teams. Arson dogs are specially trained to sniff for the presence of accelerants, such as gasoline, at sites where arson is suspected. Because of their incredible sense of smell, arson dogs can detect tiny amounts of accelerants lingering on surfaces inside buildings and vehicles or on people's clothes. The dogs indicate a find by either sitting or attempting to gain eye contact with their handlers. Because arsonists often hang around the scene of the crime, arson dogs are discreetly led through crowds gathered to watch fires to sniff for the presence of accelerants on people's clothing or belongings. Any suspicious finds are subjected to detailed laboratory testing.

Federal agencies that guard U.S. borders have used dogs since the 1970s. In 1970 the U.S. Customs Service began using dogs to sniff out narcotics being smuggled into the country at major border crossings. The U.S. Immigration and Naturalization Service also used dogs to help intercept illegal aliens and prevent smuggling.

In 2003 these agencies were grouped together into the U.S. Department of Homeland Security. The canine resources of the individual agencies were combined into a new agency called U.S. Customs and Border Protection. Drug-sniffing dogs are also sometimes used in schools. In "Drug-Detecting Police Dog Dies of Nose Cancer from Sniffing out Cocaine" (*New York Daily News*, January 27, 2009), Lauren Johnston reports that in January 2009 a retired drug-sniffing dog in England died from a rare type of nose cancer. Max was a nine-year-old Springer spaniel. The dog's veterinarian believes that sniffing drugs, particularly cocaine, during his years of service to the police department was a factor in the development of cancer.

Horses

Horses have been used in law enforcement work for centuries. They were the fastest and surest form of transportation for officers for many years. Even after cars became common, many law enforcement agencies continued to use mounted patrols. According to MountedPolice.com (April 26, 2009), there are hundreds of jurisdictions around the United States that use horse-mounted officers.

Mounted units are popular in both rural and metropolitan areas. The United Mounted Peace Officers of Texas (November 11, 2008, http://www.tumpot.org/about.htm) indicate that in 2008 Texas authorities used 102 mounted units for patrols around the state. They are particularly useful in backcountry areas on dirt roads and rugged terrain. Several large U.S. police departments use mounted patrols for crowd control and to provide greater visibility of officers on the streets.

Mounted units are not without controversy. There have been injuries to horses, police, and members of the public. Because mounted units often perform crowd control during protests and demonstrations, the horses and the riders are exposed to people who may be angry and confrontational. There are reports of police horses being pelted with marbles and even garbage. Protesters claim that police often charge their horses into crowds, knocking over and injuring people.

Walking for many hours on city streets under stressful conditions is not easy on the horses. A few instances are reported each year of police horses throwing off or kicking their riders.

SEARCH, RESCUE, AND RECOVERY

Search and rescue (SAR) and body recovery work are performed by a variety of public service agencies in conjunction with private organizations. Some SAR units use dogs to help find missing humans, rescue people in danger, and recover bodies after disasters strike. Animals that assist in SAR work are generally considered valuable and noble by modern societies.

In "SAR Dog Fact Sheet" (2009, http://www.nasar.org/nasar/sar_dog_fact_sheet.php), the National Association for Search and Rescue notes that there were over 150 SAR dog units across the country in 2009. The breeds most often used for this work are German shepherds, Dobermans, rottweilers, golden retrievers, giant schnauzers, and Labrador retrievers.

One of the most remarkable displays of SAR dogs in action occurred after the September 11, 2001 (9/11), terrorist attacks on the United States. More than 350 dogs scoured the rubble of the World Trade Center in New York City, along with their human trainers, looking for survivors and corpses. These dogs were from all over the United States and from foreign countries. The work was difficult. SAR dogs suffered from paw cuts and burns, dehydration, burning eyes, and psychological stress. Some handlers reported that their dogs became depressed after not finding any live victims and could not eat or sleep normally. Campaigns were begun to collect donated booties and other items needed by the SAR dogs who participated in helping during the 9/11 aftermath, and donations poured in from around the world.

HUMANITARIAN MINE DETECTION

Since World War II (1939–1945) trained dogs have been used in military applications to detect land mines on the battlefield. In 1988 the United Nations called on the international community to devote resources to humanitarian demining—detecting and removing mines left over from many civil and regional conflicts around the world. A collaboration of governments, nongovernmental organizations (NGOs), and commercial enterprises has resulted to tackle the problem. The organization Adopt-a-Minefield (April 24, 2009, http://www.landmines.org/Page.aspx?pid=789) estimates that 70 million to 80 million land mines remain in the ground in dozens of countries.

According to the Marshall Legacy Institute (2009, http://www.marshall-legacy.org/!our_dogs/dog-overview.html), approximately 700 dogs are used in humanitarian demining operations around the world. The dogs' excellent sense of smell is particularly effective for detecting mines made up of nonmetal components. These mines are not detectable using metal detecting equipment.

In the early 1990s Bart Weetjens seized on the idea of training rats to detect underground mines. He began the NGO Anti-Persoonsmijnen Ontmijnende Product Ontwikkeling (APOPO; Anti-personnel Mines Demining Product Development). The APOPO collects Gambian giant pouched rats from Africa and trains them to detect mines while wearing harnesses controlled by human handlers.

MEDICAL SERVICE

Animals that provide for the physical and mental well-being of humans are perhaps the most admired of all working animals. They guide, aid, assist, and comfort people with all kinds of physical and mental disabilities, impairments, and problems.

Aiding the Physically Impaired

Many people troubled with physical impairments rely on trained dogs to improve their quality of life. According to Assistance Dogs International Inc. (2009, http://www.adionline.org/), a coalition of nonprofit organizations that

FIGURE 8.3

A trained seeing eye dog. *Image copyright Boris Djuranovic, 2009. Used under license from Shutterstock.com.*

train and place assistance dogs, assistance dogs fall into three broad categories:

- Guide dogs for the blind and visually impaired
- Hearing dogs for the deaf and hearing impaired
- Service dogs for those with other physical disabilities

HELP FOR THE BLIND OR VISUALLY IMPAIRED. Guide dogs have been trained to assist blind people for nearly two centuries. Figure 8.3 shows a guide dog at work. According to the Seeing Eye (2009, http://www.seeingeye.org/about Us/default.aspx?M_ID=165), guide dogs for the blind typically work for seven to eight years and are then adopted as pets by their owners or others.

Guide Dog Users Inc. (GDUI) is an affiliate of the American Council of the Blind. The organization reports increasing problems with attacks on guide dogs by aggressive dogs while walking on city streets. It wants state laws enacted that will protect blind people and their guide dogs from any harassment or obstruction. The GDUI estimates that it costs up to $60,000 to properly train a guide dog team.

HELP FOR THE DEAF OR HEARING IMPAIRED. Hearing dogs are specially trained to alert their deaf or hard-of-

hearing owners to particular noises, such as a doorbell, knock at the door, oven timer, crying baby, alarm clock, or smoke alarm. When the dogs hear these noises, they make physical contact with their owners and lead them to the source of the noise.

HELP FOR OTHER PHYSICAL CONDITIONS. Service dogs do a variety of tasks for people with debilitating conditions, such as paralysis, lameness, epilepsy, or Parkinson's disease. The dogs are trained to pick up dropped items, fetch objects (such as a phone), pull wheelchairs, open and close doors, turn light switches on and off, and perform other tasks as needed. They can even assist people who are unsteady on their feet by providing a means of support and balance. Some service dogs are trained to summon help if their partner needs it.

"Seizure alert dogs" are trained to identify signs—generally undetectable to humans—that their human companion is going to have a seizure. Some dogs have demonstrated an ability to predict when a person is going to have a seizure up to an hour before it happens. No one knows exactly how these dogs know when a person is going to have a seizure, but some scientists speculate that the dogs may be aware of certain physical or behavioral changes such as dilated pupils or slight changes in skin color or facial expressions that occur. The dog may be trained to remain with the person throughout the seizure, sometimes lying on top of the person to steady him or her and prevent injury, and helping him or her up afterward.

NOT ALL CASES ARE SUCCESSFUL. Even though the vast majority of service dogs are greatly appreciated for their work, there have been cases of abuse. In February 2002 a blind man in Pennsylvania was charged with brutally killing his guide dog, Inky. The man allegedly went into a rage while intoxicated and kicked the dog to death. He was sentenced to 23 months in prison and ordered to pay $1,000 to a guide dog association. Animal welfarists use the case to point out that service animals and their human partners must be carefully screened and monitored to ensure that a good match is made and that the animals will be cared for properly.

One controversial issue associated with guide dogs is the use of breeding programs to produce them. Many organizations and training schools rescue dogs from pounds and animal shelters. This provides good homes for dogs that might otherwise be euthanized. Animal welfarists are critical of schools that breed their own dogs because there are already so many unwanted dogs in the country.

Mental and Physical Therapy

Another medical service that animals provide is therapeutic rather than utilitarian. Therapy animals provide emotional support or assist in rehabilitation activities. For example, therapy animals can comfort people undergoing psychological counseling. Many organizations working with abused children use therapy dogs in their programs. Petting and hugging the dogs relaxes the children and allows them to open up to counselors. Similar programs are used to calm children suffering from autism.

Therapy dogs also visit hospitals, orphanages, and nursing homes to cheer people who may be lonely or depressed. Only gentle and social dogs with good dispositions are used in this work. They must go through rigorous training and receive Canine Good Citizenship certification. The human participants are screened beforehand to ensure that they like animals and find them comforting.

Dogs are even used in medical detection, thanks to their extremely keen sense of smell. Dermatologists have reported stories about patients whose dogs sniffed at moles on their owners' bodies. The moles turned out to be cancerous and were removed. Doctors speculate that dogs may be able to smell some unique scent emitted by cancerous skin cells. Dogs have also been tested for their ability to detect by smell the presence of cancerous cells in the urine or breath of cancer patients. Michael McCulloch et al. report in "Diagnostic Accuracy of Canine Scent Detection in Early- and Late-Stage Lung and Breast Cancers" (*Integrative Cancer Therapies*, vol. 5, no. 1, March 2006) that specially trained dogs correctly detected 99% of the sam-

ples from lung cancer patients and 88% from breast cancer patients. The dogs made incorrect detections in 1% of lung cancer patients and in 2% of breast cancer patients. It is believed that the dogs are able to detect trace amounts of chemicals not ordinarily present in the breath of healthy people.

MILITARY SERVICE

Of all the service and assistance animals in use, animals used by the military are the most controversial. To animal welfarists and animal rights activists, the use of animals by the military can be extremely disturbing. These animals are often put into tremendous danger, and many of them die during their service. On the contrary, members of the military say that service animals have saved many human lives in battle. They argue that animal deaths in war are regrettable but permissible if human lives are saved. Animal rights activists and welfarists argue that animals involved in warfare do not know what they are fighting for or against and have poor chances of surviving.

Even though some animal work is classified, it is known that the U.S. military has used horses, pigeons, dogs, chickens, dolphins, beluga whales, sea lions, and other marine mammals during combat. Besides horses, many of these animals are still used in modern warfare.

History

According to *Wild Horses: An American Romance* (January 15, 2008, http://netnebraska.org/extras/wildhorses/wh_man/wh_war.html), most of the 6 million horses that served the U.S. military in World War I (1914–1918) were killed. The deaths of millions of other horses in military service to other countries severely depleted the world's horse population. World War I was the last war in which horses played a major role in combat. By 1942 all U.S. cavalry units were disbanded or mechanized.

Coincidentally, this was the same year that dogs were first officially inducted into the U.S. Army. A group called Dogs for Defense asked Americans to donate dogs to the army. Dogs were trained for guard and police duty, to pull sleds, to carry packs and messages, to help reconnaissance patrols find hidden enemy soldiers, and to help the medical corps find and rescue wounded soldiers.

Following World War II the surviving dogs were returned to their owners. This was not the case in later wars. Military officials were afraid of a trained military dog attacking someone in civilian life. It became common practice to euthanize unusable and retired war dogs or leave them behind on the battlefield. Animal welfarists and soldiers were strongly against this policy, particularly after the Vietnam War (1954–1975).

Military historians estimate that war dogs saved thousands of U.S. soldiers from death or injury during the Vietnam War. Approximately 4,000 service dogs guarded troops, alerted them to booby traps, and pulled the wounded to safety. The U.S. War Dog Association (April 12, 2008, http://www.uswardogs.org/id31.html) lists the names of nearly 300 dogs that were killed in action during the war. Most service dogs that survived the war were left behind in Vietnam when U.S. troops pulled out. The fate of these dogs is unknown. Many veterans, including the Vietnam Dog Handlers Association, are lobbying for a national memorial to be built in the District of Columbia to honor the service of war dogs.

In November 2000 President Bill Clinton (1946–) signed a new law into effect that allows retired military dogs to be adopted rather than euthanized. New owners have to agree not to hold the government responsible for any injuries or damages caused by former military dogs. Because of their extensive training, the dogs are expected to be useful in law enforcement and rescue work. In December 2005 President George W. Bush (1946–) signed legislation allowing the military to adopt out active-duty military dogs to their handlers under certain circumstances.

Current Uses

According to Donna Miles, in "Military Working Dogs Protect Forces, Bases during Terror War" (September 3, 2004, http://www.defenselink.mil/news/Sep2004/n09032004_2004090306.html), as of September 2004 about 2,300 dogs were working as sentries, detecting land mines and bombs, and performing SAR tasks for the U.S. military. Many were stationed in Afghanistan or Iraq to deal with ongoing military conflicts in those countries. Military dogs are trained at the Military Working Dog Center at Lackland Air Force Base in San Antonio, Texas. The most common breeds used are German shepherds, Dutch shepherds, and Belgian Malinois (a variety of Belgian shepherd). The military conducts its own breeding program and purchases suitable dogs from other breeders. Most dogs have a military career of around 10 years and are then retired from the service.

Hundreds of animals were used by the U.S. military during the 2003 invasion of Iraq, including dogs, dolphins, pigeons, and chickens. The use of animals was criticized by animal rights and welfare groups, including PETA, the Humane Society of the United States (HSUS), and the United Poultry Concerns. Other activists have accused the military of wasting animals needlessly when sophisticated equipment could be used instead.

U.S. forces used two bottle-nosed Atlantic dolphins named Makai and Tacoma to seek out underwater mines along the Iraqi coast. The dolphins were trained to find the mines without detonating them and then alert handlers to their presence.

Frontline reports on the U.S. Navy's historical use of dolphins and other marine mammals in *A Whale of a Business* (November 1997, http://www.pbs.org/wgbh/pages/frontline/shows/whales/). The navy began its Marine Mammal Program in 1960. Marine mammals were trained to perform tasks such as filming objects underwater, retrieving and delivering equipment, and guarding vessels against enemy divers. They were used during the Vietnam War and later in the Persian Gulf during the 1980s.

Dolphins are trained to detect enemy divers and attach restraining devices to them so they can be apprehended by human handlers. These devices include a line with a buoy that floats to the surface. Sea lions are trained to actually pursue any fleeing divers who go ashore. Mine-hunting dolphins identify and mark mines so that they can be decommissioned or later exploded safely. In 2007 the U.S. Navy announced plans to use dolphins and sea lions to patrol the waters off a naval base near Seattle, Washington. The marine animals are trained to detect and catch potential terrorists attacking from the water.

Stray Animals Offer Comfort during War

Besides the dogs in official U.S. military service, soldiers stationed around the world often befriend stray dogs and cats in other countries. Soldiers report that these dogs and cats provide them with much-needed comfort and companionship during military conflicts. Some military personnel serving in Iraq found that they wanted to adopt the strays they had grown to love. Because only military animals are allowed to fly on U.S. Department of Defense planes, the soldiers must find alternative means of transporting their adopted friends back to the United States. Flying an animal across international borders and dealing with bureaucratic issues can be very expensive, so international animal welfare groups and military support organizations have joined together to raise money and enlist volunteers to transport these animals to their new homes.

Adopting a pet while on a tour of duty is, however, strictly against U.S. military rules. Under General Order 1A, soldiers may receive a reduction in rank or a court-martial if they are caught with a pet while in active service overseas. According to the armed forces, this is due largely to the threat of disease from strays in foreign countries. Dru Sefton notes in "Despite Military Rules, War Zone Pets Make It to States" (Newhouse News Service, February 23, 2005) that the U.S. Air Force reported in early 2005 that 53 people were treated for rabies after coming into contact with an infected stray at Bagram Air Base in Afghanistan.

However, media stories about soldiers rescuing and trying to adopt dogs in war zones have brought public attention to the issue. In 2007 the Society for the Prevention of Cruelty to Animals launched Operation Baghdad Pups (http://www.baghdadpups.com/) to assist soldiers stationed in the Middle East with transporting rescued dogs and cats to their home countries. One of these dogs, Ratchet, had been rescued as a puppy from a burning trash heap by U.S. Army Specialist Gwen Beberg. Ratchet made headlines in October 2008, when Beberg's commanding officer seized the dog and refused to let it travel to the Baghdad International Airport to fly to Beberg's home in Minnesota. Widespread publicity about Beberg's plight prompted calls from the public and politicians for Ratchet's release. The U.S. Army relented and allowed Operation Baghdad Pups to transport the dog to the United States. In January 2009 Beberg was reunited with her dog after her tour of duty ended in Iraq.

CHAPTER 9

PETS

Pets are animals that humans keep for pleasure rather than utility. Their value to humans is mostly emotional. They help to fulfill human desires for companionship, affection, entertainment, and ownership. Historians are not sure when humans first started keeping animals as pets. Keeping an animal for pleasure rather than for food or work was possible only for people who were well off and had the resources to feed extra mouths. For centuries pet ownership was mostly limited to the upper classes of society—royalty, aristocrats, and landowners. The modern age of pet keeping began in the mid-1800s, when a thriving middle class emerged in society. This was the first time that many people had the time and money to keep animals solely for companionship and pleasure. Owning pets eventually became more and more popular.

The American Pet Products Association (APPA, formerly the American Pet Products Manufacturers Association) was founded in 1958 and is the nation's leading pet industry trade group. More than 900 companies were members of the association in 2009. Every two years the APPA releases data on pet ownership. In *2007–2008 National Pet Owners Survey* (2008, http://www.americanpetproducts.org/press_industrytrends.asp), the APPA indicates that in 2008, 382.2 million animals were kept as pets in the United States. Freshwater fish, cats, and dogs were the most popular. Other common pets included birds, horses, reptiles, saltwater fish, and various small animals. Sixty-three percent of U.S. households had a pet in 2006, up from 56% in 1988. The APPA estimates that U.S. pet owners spent $43.2 billion in 2008 on pet supplies, equipment, and services. This is more than double the $17 billion spent in 1994.

The Gallup Organization conducted a poll in April 2007 to learn more about Americans and their pets. Gallup found that 59% of the people polled owned a dog and/or cat. (See Figure 9.1.) A breakdown by owner demographics is included in Table 9.1. White people, people between the ages of 18 and 49, and people with incomes of $75,000 or more per year were found to be the most likely pet owners. Gallup asked dog and cat owners to name the main reason they owned a pet. The results are shown in Table 9.2 for dogs and in Table 9.3 for cats. Companionship/friendship was cited as the reason by 42% of the dog owners. Liking or loving animals was named by 27% of the cat owners.

Pets have a unique status. Legally, they are considered personal property. This offers them some protection under the law, because damaging someone else's property is a crime. From a psychological standpoint some pets enjoy a higher value and are considered members of the family, almost like children. The federal government acknowledged this bond with passage of the Pets Evacuation and Transportation Standards Act of 2006. The act requires that federal, state, and local emergency preparedness officials include pets and service animals (such as seeing-eye dogs) in their plans for evacuating and sheltering people during disasters. The law was spurred by events following Hurricane Katrina along the Gulf Coast during 2005. Many distressed pet owners were forced to leave their animals behind when they were evacuated. Others refused to leave without their pets, putting themselves in great danger.

It surprises many pet owners to learn that some animal rights groups are opposed to the idea of keeping pets. Pet ownership is a thorny issue in the animal rights debate. Some activists believe that any use of any animal for any human purpose is wrong. However, when it comes to pets, many consider this stance too radical. A great number of those who work to improve animal welfare are pet owners. Most animal rights groups and animal welfarists focus their attention on particular pet problems, such as neglect, abuse, and overpopulation. They are particularly critical of breeders and pet stores that sell pets to the public. The keeping of wild animals as pets is condemned by all major organizations working for animal rights and welfare.

FIGURE 9.1

Cat and dog ownership, April 2007

"THINKING OF YOUR OWN SITUATION, DO YOU PERSONALLY OWN A CAT, A DOG, BOTH, OR NEITHER?"

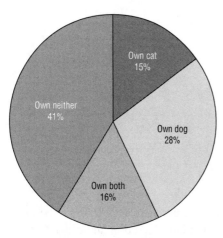

Own cat 15%
Own neither 41%
Own dog 28%
Own both 16%

SOURCE: Adapted from Jeffrey M. Jones, "Thinking of Your Own Situation, Do You Personally Own a Cat, a Dog, Both, or Neither?" in *Companionship and Love of Animals Drive Pet Ownership*, The Gallup Organization, November 30, 2007, http://www.gallup.com/poll/102952/Companionship-Love-Animals-Drive-Pet-Ownership.aspx (accessed January 13, 2009). Copyright © 2007 by The Gallup Organization .Reproduced by permission of The Gallup Organization.

TABLE 9.1

Dog and cat ownership, by demographics, April 2007

	Own a dog %	Own a cat %
Age		
18 to 49 years	51	37
50+ years	36	23
Race		
White	47	35
Nonwhite	32	17
Income		
Under $30,000	32	24
$30,000 to $74,999	45	35
$75,000 or more	54	34
Marital status		
Married	52	36
Not married	34	25
Children under 18		
Yes	49	36
No	41	28

SOURCE: Jeffrey M. Jones, "Dog and Cat Ownership, by Demographic Subgroup," in *Companionship and Love of Animals Drive Pet Ownership*, The Gallup Organization, November 30, 2007, http://www.gallup.com/poll/102952/Companionship-Love-Animals-Drive-Pet-Ownership.aspx (accessed January 13, 2009). Copyright © 2007 by The Gallup Organization. Reproduced by permission of The Gallup Organization.

Some groups state that people keep pets for the wrong reasons. They argue that some people get pets to compensate for their inability to engage in healthy social contact with other people. Pets may be a crutch or a time-filler to these

TABLE 9.2

Main reasons for owning a dog, April 2007

WHAT IS THE MAIN REASON WHY YOU OWN A DOG? [OPEN-ENDED]

[Based on 455 dog owners]

	%
For companionship/friendship	42
Like/love animals	24
Family wanted one	17
For protection/security	10
Dogs are fun/entertaining	5
For recreational purposes (hunting/exercise)	5
Rescued dog	3
Have always had a dog	3
Dog was given to respondent	2
Other	2
No reason in particular	1
No opinion	*

*Less than 0.5%.
Percentages add to more than 100% due to multiple responses.

SOURCE: Jeffrey M. Jones, "What Is the Main Reason Why You Own a Dog?" in *Companionship and Love of Animals Drive Pet Ownership*, The Gallup Organization, November 30, 2007, http://www.gallup.com/poll/102952/Companionship-Love-Animals-Drive-Pet-Ownership.aspx (accessed January 13, 2009). Copyright © 2007 by The Gallup Organization. Reproduced by permission of The Gallup Organization.

TABLE 9.3

Main reasons for owning a cat, April 2007

WHAT IS THE MAIN REASON WHY YOU OWN A CAT? [OPEN-ENDED]

[Based on 344 cat owners]

	%
Like/love animals	27
For companionship/friendship	25
Family members wanted cat	17
Rescued the cat	14
Cats are independent/easier to care for/lower maintenance	8
Keep mice/critters away	6
Entertaining/fun	4
Cat was given to respondent	2
Other	4
No reason in particular	2
No opinion	1

Percentages add to more than 100% due to multiple responses.

SOURCE: Jeffrey M. Jones, "What Is the Main Reason Why You Own a Cat?" in *Companionship and Love of Animals Drive Pet Ownership*, The Gallup Organization, November 30, 2007, http://www.gallup.com/poll/102952/Companionship-Love-Animals-Drive-Pet-Ownership.aspx (accessed January 13, 2009). Copyright © 2007 by The Gallup Organization. Reproduced by permission of The Gallup Organization.

people. Others rely on pets to build their egos or to make them feel good about themselves in some way. The ability to control another living being can be a powerful motivator. Some people see pets as disposable items to be kept as long as they are useful or fun, and discarded when they are not. Many people think that taking care of a pet is educational for children because it teaches them responsibility and respect for other living creatures. Some people believe keeping a pet has a spiritual basis and that it brings them closer to nature.

The common thread in all these reasons is that they focus on the needs and wants of the pet owner rather than the pet. Some people feel this is only fair, as it is the pet owner who provides food, shelter, and care. Should people be allowed to keep animals as pets as long they take care of them? There is a movement by some humane organizations to refer to pets as companion animals and to owners as guardians. These terms demonstrate the desire of these groups to elevate pets from property status to wards or dependents.

SHELTERS, POUNDS, AND EUTHANASIA

Despite the popularity of pets, every year millions of them wind up in public and private shelters. The vast majority are cats and dogs. They are either turned in by owners who no longer want them or are picked up as strays. Some are lost pets that can be reunited with their owners, but many are homeless animals with no place to go. In "HSUS Pet Overpopulation Estimates" (July 7, 2008, http://www.hsus.org/pets/issues_affecting_our_pets/pet_overpopulation_and_ownership_statistics/hsus_pet_overpopulation_estimates.html?print=t), the HSUS estimates that U.S. shelters receive 6 million to 8 million cats and dogs each year. Approximately half of these animals are euthanized (killed). The remainder are adopted or reclaimed by owners.

Euthanasia

The word *euthanasia* comes from a Greek term meaning "good death." During the 1800s it was first used to describe mercy killing conducted with the approval of the law. In the twentieth century euthanasia of shelter animals was conducted on a massive scale. However, euthanasia rates have been generally declining since the late twentieth century. The HSUS reports in *The State of the Animals: 2001* (June 2001, http://www.hsus.org/press_and_publications/humane_bookshelf/the_state_of_the_animals_2001.html) that the number of euthanized cats and dogs dropped considerably in the United States, from about 13.5 million deaths in 1973 to 4 million to 6 million deaths in 2000, whereas over the same period the total number of cats and dogs nearly doubled.

Animal People is an animal organization that issues the monthly publication *Animal People News*. Each year in its July–August edition the newspaper compiles data collected over the three previous years on the number of animals killed in shelters in selected representative cities and states around the country. These data are used to estimate national shelter killing rates. *Animal People News* (http://www.animalpeoplenews.org/08/7/JulyAugust08.pdf) estimates that 4.2 million shelter animals were euthanized in the United States in 2007. Table 9.4 compares this estimate with estimates from previous years dating back to 1950. The number of shelter animals euthanized per 1,000 Americans was 13.8 in 2007, down from a high of 115 in 1970. Table 9.5 provides a breakdown of shelter animal euthanasia numbers by region and species (i.e., dogs and cats). The South

TABLE 9.4

Estimated number of dogs and cats killed in shelters, selected years, 1950–2007

Year	Millions of dogs and cats killed	Killed per 1,000 Americans
1950	2.0	13.5
1970	23.4	115.0
1985	17.8	74.8
1997	4.9	21.1
1998	4.9	19.4
1999	4.5	16.6
2000	4.5	16.8
2001	4.4	15.7
2002	4.2	15.3
2003	4.5	14.8
2004	4.9	17.4
2005	4.4	14.8
2006	4.0	13.6
2007	4.2	13.8

SOURCE: "U.S. Progress v. Shelter Killing," in *Animal People News*, vol. 18, no. 6, July/August 2008, http://www.animalpeoplenews.org/08/7/JulyAugust08.pdf (accessed February 2, 2009)

TABLE 9.5

Estimated number of dogs and cats killed in shelters, by region, 2007

Region	Cats	Dogs	Ratio
Northeast	36,282	18,690	66/34
Mid-Atlantic	137,050	80,490	63/37
So. Atlantic	497,777	459,485	52/48
Appalachia	220,557	187,882	54/46
Gulf Coast	444,203	378,395	54/46
West	156,911	184,200	46/54
Midwest	491,442	418,636	54/46
Pacific	308,271	145,069	68/32
U.S. total	**2,292,493**	**1,872,847**	**55/45**

SOURCE: "Cat/Dog Shelter Killing by Region," in *Animal People News*, vol. 18, no. 6, July/August 2008, http://www.animalpeoplenews.org/08/7/JulyAugust08.pdf (accessed February 2, 2009)

Atlantic states were estimated to have the highest number of euthanized animals in 2007, followed by the Midwest and the Gulf Coast states. The ratio of euthanized dogs to cats was highest in the Pacific states (68/32) and nearly evenly in the South Atlantic states (52/48).

According to Animal People, there are regional differences in shelter killing rates. In general, shelters located in the Northeast have the lowest euthanasia rates, whereas shelters in the Southeast have the highest rates. This is attributed to several factors, including the weather, the availability of low-cost spay-neuter programs, and animal control policies. The cold winters in the Northeast lower the fertility rates of cats and dogs and claim the lives of stray animals so that fewer end up in shelters. Animal welfare organizations are much more predominant in the Northeast and provide low-cost spay-neuter programs that help control populations of unwanted animals. Many northeastern municipalities charge pet owners licensing fees with higher amounts for unfixed animals. This is far less common in the South.

Euthanasia Methods

Even though the public assumes that animals euthanized at shelters are killed by lethal injection, this is not always true. The American Veterinary Medical Association (AVMA) maintains a list of approved euthanasia methods for various types of animals. In *Guidelines for Humane Euthanasia of Animals* (June 2007, http://www.avma.org/issues/animal_welfare/euthanasia.pdf), the AVMA states, "Euthanasia techniques should result in rapid loss of consciousness followed by cardiac or respiratory arrest and the ultimate loss of brain function. In addition, the technique should minimize distress and anxiety experienced by the animal prior to loss of consciousness." However, the AVMA admits that "the absence of pain and distress cannot always be achieved."

Acceptable euthanasia methods for cats and dogs include intravenous injection of barbiturates (such as sodium pentobarbital or secobarbital) or potassium chloride/anesthetic, or gassing the animals with inhalant anesthetics (such as ether), carbon dioxide, or carbon monoxide gas. In addition, gassing with nitrogen or argon is considered acceptable with some reservations on cats and dogs, as are the use of electrocution and penetrating captive bolts (bolts shot at point-blank range from a gun into the animal's skull, which if shot at the proper location destroy enough brain tissue to kill the animal instantly) on dogs only.

The AVMA notes that intravenous injection of barbiturates is the preferred method of euthanasia for horses, dogs, cats, and other small animals. Advantages include rapid and smooth action, minimal physical distress to the animal if the procedure is performed correctly, and relatively low cost compared to other options. The main disadvantages are that each animal must be personally restrained for the procedure, and personnel must be properly trained in giving injections. Also, barbiturates are federally controlled substances that can be purchased only using a U.S. Drug Enforcement Administration registration and order form. Their use is controlled by state law, and there are specific record-keeping requirements that must be met.

Lethal injection is a hands-on procedure in which animals and personnel come into close physical contact. When shelters began practicing humane euthanasia, it was thought that a hands-off approach would be easier for the workers performing euthanasia. Gas chambers were common because the euthanizer could perform the procedure from outside the chamber by opening a valve or flipping a switch.

Many shelters still use gassing to euthanize unwanted animals. Even though the use of poisonous gases is considered acceptable by the AVMA, the organization notes that "any gas that is inhaled must reach a certain concentration in the alveoli before it can be effective; there-fore, euthanasia with any of these agents takes some time." Animal welfarists roundly condemn gassing as a means of euthanasia and have worked to convince state legislators to ban the practice. Andrew Seaman reports in "Six States Seek Ban on Gas Euthanasia of Shelter Animals" (*USA Today*, April 2, 2009) that as of April 2009, 12 states had already enacted a ban: Arizona, Arkansas, California, Delaware, Florida, Maine, Maryland, New Jersey, Oregon, Rhode Island, Tennessee, and Virginia. In addition, the legislatures of six other states were considering a ban: Georgia, Illinois, Michigan, North Carolina, New York, West Virginia, and Pennsylvania.

Animal shelter workers have an incredibly stressful and emotionally demanding job. Many get into the line of work because they care about animals but become frustrated by the public's seeming lack of concern for the tragic fate of many millions of unwanted pets. Most humane organizations believe the solution to the euthanization problem lies in aggressive sterilization campaigns, better education of pet owners, and successful adoption programs.

Spaying and Neutering

The overpopulation of cats and dogs is a tremendous problem. It is aggravated by the fact that these animals reproduce at high rates. Experts generally agree that massive and sustained birth control methods must be implemented on cat and dog populations to bring the problem under control. Surgical sterilization of female animals is called spaying, or removal of the ovaries, fallopian tubes, and uterus. Male animals are neutered or castrated by having their testicles removed. Pet owners commonly refer to these sterilization procedures as fixing or altering an animal. Increasingly, animal groups use the term *neuter* to refer to sterilization of either males or females.

Veterinarians have been promoting spaying and neutering of pets for several decades. According to the animal organization SPAY USA, in "Benefits of Spay/Neuter for Cats and Dogs" (2009, http://www.spayusa.org/main_directory/02-facts_and_education/benefits_sn.asp), sterilization has many medical, behavioral, and social benefits, including:

- Female pets do not go into heat (have fertile cycles) during which scents are emitted that attract male animals. Sterilization eliminates the problems associated with male animals that gather and often fight over females in heat.

- Sterilization usually stops male cats (toms) from marking their territory by spraying strong-smelling urine.

- Sterilization makes pets more likely to stay at home than wander.

- Sterilized females cannot develop ovarian or uterine infections and are less likely to develop mammary cancer.

- Sterilized males usually become less aggressive.

- Sterilization helps reduce the number of stray and unwanted animals in the community. This is advantageous for public health and safety reasons and reduces the enormous cost to taxpayers and private agencies of capturing, impounding, and destroying millions of unwanted animals each year.

Some pet owners are resistant to spaying and neutering their pets. Their reasons can include one or more of the following common myths:

- Surgery costs too much or is too painful for the pet.

- Having a litter can be good for the pet and educational for children.

- Fixed animals get fat and lazy.

- Backyard breeding is a fun hobby that brings in extra money.

- Male animals do not need to be fixed because they do not have litters.

- Neutering male dogs robs them of their masculinity and makes them less protective as guard dogs.

- Sterilization is unnatural.

Many states and municipalities actively encourage spaying and neutering of pets as a means to reduce overpopulation. Those with licensing programs usually charge pet owners a lower registration fee if their pets are sterilized. A number of states also sell special license plates that benefit spay-neuter programs.

Increasingly, animal shelters spay and neuter cats and dogs before adoption or require new owners to do so within a certain time period after adoption. In 1998 California passed a law that requires preadoption sterilization of cats and dogs. The San Francisco Society for the Prevention of Cruelty to Animals (SPCA) was one of the first humane groups in the United States to offer low-cost and early spay-neuter surgery.

Low-cost clinics are often run by humane organizations. They operate under a nonprofit status, which allows them to save on overhead and tax costs. They offer discounted rates either to the general public or to those people who have adopted an animal from their shelter. The rates can be substantially lower than those charged by veterinarians in private practice. Such clinics are not without controversy. Some veterinarians complain that the clinics have an unfair advantage because of their nonprofit status. A few states have passed laws that prohibit veterinarians associated with nonprofit groups from operating low-cost spay-neuter clinics. Advocates of the clinics insist that they provide a much-needed service and help reduce animal overpopulation.

No-Kill Shelters

Some animal welfarists and members of the public criticize shelters for using euthanasia at all. They believe every animal that enters a shelter deserves the opportunity to be adopted no matter how long it takes. Critics say this viewpoint is unrealistic. They point out that some animals are too aggressive, injured, or sick to be adopted. There is no practical alternative but to euthanize them. Also, some pet owners rely on shelters rather than private veterinarians to euthanize their sick and elderly pets.

During the 1990s the concept of no-kill shelters became popular. The name implies that no animals are ever euthanized in these shelters—an idea that appeals to many people. In reality, most no-kill shelters still euthanize animals that are unadoptable because of illness or temperament. Some traditional shelters (or open-admission shelters, as they are called) do not like the use of the term *no-kill*. They feel it can be misleading and accuse some organizations of using the term just to gain financial support and political favor. Welfare organizations argue among themselves about the exact definition of no-kill and which animals are adoptable.

The truth is that all shelters (public and private) operate with limited space, personnel, and financial budgets. The people who run them must make life-and-death decisions about the animals that enter the facilities. These decisions are based on moral, political, social, and financial considerations. In "Hayden Law Update" (2004, http://www.maddies fund.org/Resource_Library/Hayden_Law_Update.html), Taimie Bryant argues that traditional shelters are reluctant to give up the use of euthanasia, seeing it as a necessary evil and an issue that pits themselves, performers of a public service, against a public that refuses to spay and neuter its pets. By contrast, shelters feel euthanasia is the most compassionate option, though not at all a desirable one.

Even though many people and organizations wish that euthanasia was not necessary, they also recognize some of the practical drawbacks of the no-kill idea. In "What Would It Take?" (*Animal Sheltering*, January–February 2002), Nancy Lawson and Carrie Allen describe how the no-kill idea became an advertising and fund-raising slogan for some animal organizations that use it to set themselves apart from traditional shelters.

The popularization of the no-kill idea is generally credited to Richard Avanzino, the president of the San Francisco SPCA from 1976 to 1999. During this period the city achieved the lowest euthanasia rate of any urban city in the nation. The San Francisco SPCA started adoption, spay-neuter, and animal management programs that became models for every other welfare organization. In 1992 Avanzino spoke at an HSUS workshop in Las Vegas on the no-kill movement. He advocated no-kill as a concept and a mission for welfarists, not as a weapon to use against traditional shelters in fund-raising campaigns.

Lawson and Allen also address the difficulties that some organizations encounter when they try to become no-kill shelters. In 1995 the Humane Society of Gallatin Valley in Bozeman, Montana, decided to institute a no-euthanasia policy. However, as the only shelter in the city it also decided to continue accepting any animal that was relinquished. The shelter soon became overwhelmed, and animal welfare suffered. Ganay Johnson, the shelter director, reported that "animals who came in 'adoptable' quickly became unadoptable in a crowded environment that wore on their temperaments and made them sick."

The same problem led some organizations to limit their shelter admissions. Critics state that such shelters do not really serve their communities by accepting only the "cute and cuddly" and turning away difficult-to-adopt animals. This practice is seen as self-serving. It allows these shelters to practice a true no-kill policy but burdens neighboring shelters with the animals they turn away. Yet, the opposite policy can be just as troublesome. Lawson and Allen cite well-meaning shelter groups that refuse to euthanize any animals, even typically unadoptable animals such as aggressive dogs. These animals take up cage space and resources that can be devoted to animals with a reasonable chance of being adopted. Deciding which course of action is better is difficult to make.

The no-kill label is a powerful public relations tool. Many people prefer to donate money to an organization or shelter that advertises itself as no-kill, but no-kill does not necessarily mean no-euthanasia. It also does not guarantee that the animals are being properly cared for and kept in clean, uncrowded, disease-free conditions. Critics state that some people who want to warehouse or hoard animals adopt the label to raise funds. Others may begin with the best of intentions and quickly become overwhelmed by the number of animals with severe physical and emotional problems requiring extensive surgery and/or rehabilitation.

Several major cities are already operating or working toward no-kill status. In 1994 the San Francisco SPCA formed an adoption pact with city animal control officials to become the first U.S. city with a no-kill policy. Shelters in other cities have followed suit.

Some organizations and shelters that follow the no-kill philosophy downplay use of the label to describe themselves. For example, the Best Friends Animal Sanctuary (2009, http://www.bestfriends.org/aboutus/) was founded in 1984 and is the largest animal sanctuary in the United States. Funded by private donations and located on 33,000 acres (13,355 ha) near Kanab, Utah, the sanctuary housed approximately 2,000 animals in 2009. Most were cats and dogs. The remainder included horses, burros, birds, rabbits, goats, livestock, and other animals. Best Friends takes in animals from all over the country and occasionally from other countries. Some come from shelters where the animals were considered unadoptable and were going to be euthanized. They may be old, crippled, or sick with chronic illnesses, or may have been traumatized by abuse or neglect. In exchange for taking these animals, the sanctuary asks many of the shelters to take back adoptable animals from Best Friends.

According to Best Friends (2009, http://www.best friends.org/aboutus/faq.cfm), many of the animals that come into the sanctuary are readily adoptable or become so following rehabilitation. Others are kept permanently at the sanctuary. The sanctuary defines no-kill to mean that "animals are not destroyed except in cases of terminal and painful illness, when compassion demands euthanasia because there is no reasonable alternative." As of 2009, Best Friends did not display a no-kill label on its Web site. Instead, it used the slogan "No More Homeless Pets."

Another major organization that supports the no-kill idea is Maddie's Fund. It was founded in 1999 by the billionaire Dave Duffield (1941–) and his wife, Cheryl, and named after their beloved miniature schnauzer Maddie, who died of cancer in 1997. Maddie's Fund is a pet rescue foundation that advocates a community approach in which animal control agencies, shelters, humane organizations, and private-practice veterinarians work together to achieve no-kill status. Maddie's Fund provides grants to community coalitions, veterinary medical associations, and colleges of veterinary medicine for programs that advance the no-kill goal.

In 2003 officials in New York City announced plans to convert all the city's shelters to no-kill, and in 2005 Maddie's Fund pledged $15.5 million to help New York City achieve this status. The effort is being spearheaded by the Mayor's Alliance for NYC's Animals, Inc.—a coalition of dozens of animal welfare groups. Experts believe the program has an excellent chance of success because the Mayor's Alliance is a neutral party rather than a particular animal group with its own agenda. The program will increase public awareness about adoptions and spay-neuter programs at the shelters. A new agreement was reached on how the city's animal control operations will coordinate with rescue groups and shelters to reach the no-kill goal. The Mayor's Alliance (April 23, 2009, http://www.animalalliancenyc.org/aboutus/index.htm) notes that the euthanasia rate for animals entering the city's Animal Care and Control has been reduced from 74% in 2002 to 39% in 2008.

Oddly enough, some major animal rights and welfare groups support (or excuse) the use of euthanasia on unwanted pets. Jeneen Interlandi reports in "PETA and Euthanasia" (*Newsweek*, April 28, 2008) that PETA shelters have euthanized more than 17,000 animals since 1998. That amounts to almost 85% of the animals the organization has taken in. Interlandi quotes a PETA spokesperson as saying, "We would rather offer these animals a painless death than have them tortured, starved or sold for research." PETA supports spay and neuter programs to prevent unwanted animals and ultimately reduce animal suffering. According to Interlandi, the HSUS president Wayne Pacelle has publicly stated his belief that the no-kill idea is "almost unachievable." This pessimism is harshly criticized by other animal advocates. The no-kill proponent Nathan Winograd complains that "with the resources at their disposal, PETA and the Humane Society of the U.S. could become no-kill in no time.... Instead they have become leading killers of cats and dogs, and the animal-loving public unwittingly foots the bill."

Owner Turn-ins

The National Council on Pet Population Study and Policy (NCPPSP) is a coalition founded in 1993 of animal organizations devoted to discovering the causes and possible solutions to pet overpopulation. The NCPPSP collects statistical data from animal shelters around the country on the number of animals relinquished by the public and the reasons for relinquishment. As of April 2009, the most recently available compilation of these data are for 1994 to 1997. The NCPPSP (http://www.petpopulation.org/research.html) lists published analyses of the data.

One of these studies is Mo D. Salman et al.'s "Human and Animal Factors Related to Relinquishment of Dogs and Cats in 12 Selected Animal Shelters in the United States" (*Journal of Applied Animal Welfare Science*, vol. 1, no. 3, July 1998), in which 12 shelters around the country were surveyed to find out why cat and dog owners are relinquishing their pets. In general, the researchers find that the owners had unrealistic expectations for their pets and lacked the knowledge or will to work out problems that arose. Moving was the number-one reason given by owners relinquishing their dogs to the shelters. However, the researchers find on interviewing these owners that there were deeper issues involved, mainly behavior problems. In other words, owners who were moving decided to give up their dogs rather than take them along, because the dogs were unruly. Salman et al. indicate that if the dogs were better behaved, they might have been kept and taken along to the new residence. Similar findings have been reported by humane organizations investigating dog turn-ins at other shelters.

Many organizations believe shelters need to place greater emphasis on behavior problems. Some shelters now offer training classes to new dog owners or have volunteers work with shelter dogs on basic obedience lessons. It is hoped that this will reduce the number of shelter-adopted dogs that are later relinquished. Breeders and veterinarians are being urged to encourage new dog owners to enroll in obedience classes or seek help from professional trainers. All people involved in reducing pet overpopulation agree that pet owners need to be better educated about the responsibilities and issues involved in raising pets.

Pound Seizure

Following World War II (1939–1945), the use of animals in laboratory testing and experimentation increased greatly. Researchers turned to pounds and shelters for a quick and cheap supply of unwanted animals. Many states passed laws that required publicly operated shelters to turn over animals to institutions that requested them, a practice called pound seizure. Animal welfarists were disturbed by this development and blamed the National Society for Medical Research (now the National Association for Biomedical Research) for pushing pound seizure legislation. Many welfare organizations contracted with their local municipalities to privatize shelter operations so that their shelters would not be subject to the laws.

In 1990 the Animal Welfare Act (AWA) was amended to set a minimum holding period of five days for shelter animals before release to research institutions. This holding period is designed to provide a window of opportunity for owners to find their missing pets or for the animals to be adopted by new owners. The AWA also includes record-keeping requirements for dealers who sell shelter animals to research institutions.

Animal rights activists and welfarists universally condemn pound seizure. In "Ban Pound Seizure" (April 16, 2009, http://www.aavs.org/campaign02.html), the American Anti-Vivisection Society (AAVS) notes that three states—Minnesota, Oklahoma, and Utah—still require publicly funded shelters to provide cats and dogs for research purposes. Most states legally allow pound seizure or do not address the issue. In some states the decision is left up to local government authorities. A few states require owners giving up animals to indicate whether or not they give permission for release to research institutions. The AAVS (2009, http://www.banpoundseizure.org/yourstate.shtml) provides a state-by-state listing of laws regarding pound seizure.

Those who support pound seizure argue that animals that are going to be euthanized by shelters anyway should be used in research. They feel the benefits to humans outweigh animal welfare concerns. Welfarists fear that pets turned over to laboratories will suffer from poor care and die slow, painful deaths as the subjects of medical experiments. They believe that euthanasia at the shelter is preferable to this alternative.

PUREBRED DOG INDUSTRY

Many animal welfare groups blame dog overpopulation in part on the purebred dog industry. Purebred dogs are those that have been bred from members of a recognized breed over many generations. This ensures that certain appearance and behavior traits are maintained

TABLE 9.6

Terminology used in purebred industry

Breed standard	Set of detailed guidelines established to define the particular characteristics of a breed
Conformation points	Specific criteria within the breed standard (e.g., fur color, shape of paws, size, etc.)
Consanguineous	Descended from the same ancestor
Dam	Mother dog
Fault	A characteristic of a purebred dog that doesn't meet a conformation point
Inbreeding	Breeding of immediate relatives (e.g., brother with sister, father with daughter, etc.)
Linebreeding	Breeding of close relatives (e.g., aunt with nephew, grandfather with granddaughter, cousin with cousin, etc.) or of animals with many common ancestors
Outcrossing	Breeding two dogs from different lines
Pedigree	A listing of ancestors; the family tree
Sire	Father dog
True to type	Showing desired breed characteristics. Also desired characteristics are so ingrained that offspring can be certain to have them also.
Type	Overall appearance including characteristics important to the breed standard
Typey	An adjective used to describe a dog that seems to capture the essence of the breed or closely meets the breed standard
Whelped	Born

SOURCE: Created by Kim Masters Evans for Gale, 2005

within a breed. Breeding of this type has been practiced for centuries. It was popularized during the Middle Ages by European monks who earned money by breeding dogs with particular traits for aristocrats and members of royalty. It resulted in breeds that were notable for a specific task, such as hunting wildfowl, or had desirable features in their size, shape, fur, ears, and so forth.

Maintaining desirable qualities in a bloodline requires a careful choice of mating partners. For example, an excellent hunting dog mated with a poor hunting dog will likely produce offspring that are not good hunters, and so the desirable qualities will be lost. Mating together two excellent hunting dogs will greatly increase the likelihood that the offspring will also be great hunters. This makes them much more valuable. Purebred enthusiasts are passionate about protecting certain qualities within a breed, and reputable breeders work to ensure that breed characteristics are maintained and that purebred puppies are placed in good homes. Purebred puppies and dogs can sell for hundreds or even thousands of dollars. Demand for purebred puppies and dogs has resulted in a multibillion-dollar industry based on breeding, showing, selling, and registering these dogs. Some common terms used in the purebred dog industry are defined in Table 9.6.

Registration, Pedigree, and Papers

The American Kennel Club (AKC) was formed in 1884. It is the largest nonprofit organization in the United States that registers purebred dogs. The second-largest registry is maintained by the United Kennel Club (UKC), which was founded in 1898. These are the two most respected purebred

registries in the United States. For a fee they provide registration certificates or "papers" showing that dogs are recognized as belonging to a particular breed. These papers provide a written record of a particular dog's ancestry. Each organization is supported by hundreds of local and regional kennel and breed clubs around the country.

The registration papers for purebred dogs are based on information supplied by breeders who are members of their respective clubs. Breeders can register litters born to registered purebred dogs. The registration papers are then turned over to the puppies' new owners. Each owner chooses a unique name for a registered dog that cannot be repeated. Owners can also request a copy of a pedigree (a family tree) for their registered dogs that goes back several generations.

Purebreds and Genetic Problems

Dogs as a species are prone to genetic diseases. Jonathan Amos states in "Pedigree Dog Health to be Probed" (BBC News, January 22, 2004) that "dogs are plagued by the greatest number of documented, naturally occurring genetic disorders of any non-human species." There are approximately 400 inherited disorders associated with dogs. As long as the breeding population remains large, the chances of passing along a genetic disorder are small. This is because the dog blueprint is based on around 30,000 genes.

Individual genes determine characteristics of a particular dog, such as hair color. Some genes can also carry the triggers for serious diseases and disorders. Two dogs can carry genes with these dangerous triggers but not suffer from the diseases themselves because the genes are recessive rather than dominant in their genetic makeup. However, if these two dogs mate with each other, there is a good chance that some of their puppies will inherit the problem genes from both parents and develop the disorder. At the very least, most of the puppies will inherit the recessive problem gene and later pass it along to their offspring.

In purebred dogs this inheritance problem is extremely aggravated because closely related dogs are bred with one another. This significantly raises the chances that problem genes will be passed on from parents to offspring.

Amos notes that common genetic diseases within specific breeds include heart disease in boxers, bleeding problems in Dobermans, lymphomas in pointers, hip dysplasia in Labrador retrievers, and eye problems in Irish setters.

In 1966 a group of veterinarians teamed with representatives from the Golden Retriever Club of America and the German Shepherd Club of America to found the Orthopedic Foundation for Animals (OFA). The OFA maintains a database of specific genetic disorders in individual purebred dogs. This information allows conscientious breeders to make informed decisions about which dogs should be mated. The OFA encourages breeders to submit health information for many generations so that trends in inheritance can be deduced. The OFA also issues health ratings for dogs in its database to provide potential consumers with important information. For example, the OFA can certify the condition of hips and elbows in particular dogs. This information can be included with the registration papers issued by the AKC. Another certifying organization is the Canine Eye Registration Foundation (CERF). CERF maintains a database on eye health and can certify that a particular purebred dog's eyes are free of genetic disorders.

Papers Do Not Guarantee Quality or Health

Neither the AKC nor the UKC guarantees the quality or health of a purebred dog. The AKC (2009, http://www.akc.org/reg/about.cfm) makes the following warning: "There is a widely held belief that 'AKC' or 'AKC papers' guarantee the quality of a dog. This is not the case. AKC is a registry body. A registration certificate identifies the dog as the offspring of a known sire [father] and dam [mother], born on a known date. It in no way indicates the quality or state of health of the dog."

The AKC and UKC simply track ancestry records based on the information they are given by breeders. It is an honor system. Unscrupulous breeders can provide false information and register dogs that are not really purebreds, but mixes (or mutts). Such breeders can also purposely breed dogs with known genetic disorders just to achieve a look that is popular with purebred buyers.

Purebred Dog Competitions

The AKC and UKC hold thousands of competitions each year in which registered dogs can compete. Some of these events are called dog shows or conformation shows and are designed to show off dogs that exemplify breed standards. These are basically beauty contests in which the focus is on distinctive features that characterize particular breeds. Other competitions highlight skills in hunting, agility, or obedience.

Purebred Registries Compete

The AKC and UKC are recognized as reputable purebred registries in the United States. In addition, some breed clubs maintain well-respected registries—for example, the Australian Shepherd Club of America. However, a number of other registries exist that may operate for dubious purposes. Dog enthusiasts state that unscrupulous registries make money by issuing papers indiscriminately to dogs that are not even purebreds or for dogs that are not from recognized breeds. This allows breeders to sell the dogs for high prices to unsuspecting consumers. Many of these unscrupulous registries are believed to have been started by breeders who have been kicked out of the AKC or UKC for rules violations.

Alternative registries often allow crossbreeds to be registered. These are puppies resulting from mating two desirable breeds together. Usually, the parents are AKC or UKC registered. However, the puppies cannot be registered by these agencies. Crossbreeds are popular with some consumers because they are novel. Examples include:

- Schoodle—mix of schnauzer and poodle
- Labradoodle—mix of Labrador retriever and poodle
- Cockapoo or Spoodle—mix of cocker spaniel and poodle
- Yorkiepoo—mix of Yorkshire terrier and poodle
- Goldendoodle—mix of golden retriever and poodle
- Bug—mix of beagle and pug

USDA Licenses

All dog breeders meeting certain criteria must be licensed by the Animal and Plant Health Inspection Service (APHIS) of the U.S. Department of Agriculture (USDA). These licenses fall into two types:

- Class A—breeders who sell animals that they have bred and raised on their own premises. People with three or fewer breeding females who sell offspring for pets or exhibition are exempt. People who sell animals directly to owners are exempt.
- Class B—people who purchase and resell animals, including dealers, brokers, and auction house operators. Retail pet stores selling nondangerous "pet-type" animals are exempt. Class B licensees may also breed the animals they sell. However, according to APHIS, in *Animal Care Annual Report of Activities: Fiscal Year 2007* (September 2008, http://www.aphis.usda.gov/publications/animal_welfare/content/printable_version/2007_AC_Report.pdf), these dealers "typically buy and resell animals from other sources."

Table 9.7 and Table 9.8 show the number of Class A and B licenses, respectively, by state as of January 2009. The states with the most Class A licenses were Missouri (1,370), Oklahoma (498), Iowa (393), Kansas (362), and Arkansas (308). Together, these five states accounted for 69% of all Class A licenses. As shown in Table 9.8, Missouri had the highest number of Class B license holders (159). Table 9.9 shows the number of licensed dealers for fiscal years 2002 to 2007. The vast majority of licensed breeders raise puppies for the purebred market. Breeders and brokers sell purebred puppies to pet stores, who in turn sell them to the public. Annual APHIS license fees for Class A and B licenses are listed in Table 9.10. A $10 application fee is required for first-time applicants.

Puppy Mills

Puppy mills are facilities that breed puppies in inferior conditions and sell them in commercial markets. The HSUS states in "Stop Puppy Mills: The Truth about Commercial Dog Breeding" (2009, http://www.hsus.org/) that

TABLE 9.7

Number of licenses granted to Class A breeders, by state, January 2009

State	Number	Percentage of total
Alabama	12	0.30
Alaska	None	—
Arizona	3	0.10
Arkansas	308	7.00
California	21	0.50
Colorado	13	0.30
Connecticut	3	0.07
D.C.	None	—
Delaware	None	—
Florida	37	0.90
Georgia	25	0.60
Guam	None	—
Hawaii	None	—
Idaho	1	0.02
Illinois	44	1.00
Indiana	93	2.20
Iowa	393	9.00
Kansas	362	9.00
Kentucky	12	0.30
Louisiana	11	0.30
Maine	1	0.02
Maryland	4	0.10
Massachusetts	13	0.30
Michigan	15	0.40
Minnesota	64	1.50
Mississippi	6	0.10
Missouri	1370	32.00
Montana	7	0.20
Nebraska	142	3.40
Nevada	2	0.00
New Hampshire	4	0.09
New Jersey	5	0.10
New Mexico	3	0.07
New York	43	1.00
North Carolina	7	0.20
North Dakota	13	0.30
Ohio	161	3.80
Oklahoma	498	11.80
Oregon	20	0.50
Pennsylvania	202	4.80
Puerto Rico	None	—
Rhode Island	None	—
South Carolina	2	0.00
South Dakota	102	2.00
Tennessee	10	0.20
Texas	91	2.00
Utah	1	0.02
Vermont	None	—
Virginia	23	0.50
Washington	9	0.20
West Virginia	1	0.00
Wisconsin	67	2.00
Wyoming	4	0.10
Total	**4,228**	

— Not applicable

SOURCE: Adapted from *Breeders*, U.S. Department of Agriculture, Animal and Plant Health Inspection Service, January 9, 2009, http://www.aphis.usda.gov/animal_welfare/efoia/downloads/reports/A_cert_holders.pdf (accessed February 6, 2009)

TABLE 9.8

Number of licenses granted to Class B breeders/dealers, by state, January 2009

State	Number	Percentage of total
Alabama	6	1.0
Alaska	None	—
Arizona	2	0.2
Arkansas	24	2.0
California	22	2.0
Colorado	16	1.0
Connecticut	3	0.0
D.C.	None	—
Delaware	3	0.3
Florida	71	7.0
Georgia	14	1.0
Guam	None	—
Hawaii	None	—
Idaho	1	0.1
Illinois	43	4.0
Indiana	27	3.0
Iowa	57	5.0
Kansas	54	5.0
Kentucky	8	0.7
Louisiana	9	1.0
Maine	2	0.2
Maryland	10	1.0
Massachusetts	10	1.0
Michigan	29	3.0
Minnesota	40	4.0
Mississippi	6	0.6
Missouri	159	15.0
Montana	2	0.2
Nebraska	12	1.0
Nevada	6	1.0
New Hampshire	None	—
New Jersey	12	1.0
New Mexico	6	0.6
New York	25	2.0
North Carolina	29	3.0
North Dakota	2	0.2
Ohio	34	3.0
Oklahoma	44	4.0
Oregon	16	1.0
Pennsylvania	50	5.0
Puerto Rico	None	—
Rhode Island	2	0.2
South Carolina	7	1.0
South Dakota	13	1.0
Tennessee	17	2.0
Texas	103	10.0
Utah	5	0.0
Vermont	1	0.1
Virginia	14	1.0
Washington	11	1.0
West Virginia	7	1.0
Wisconsin	32	3.0
Wyoming	1	0.1
Total	**1,067**	

— Not applicable

SOURCE: Adapted from *Dealers*, U.S. Department of Agriculture, Animal and Plant Health Inspection Service, January 9, 2009, http://www.aphis.usda.gov/animal_welfare/efoia/downloads/reports/B_cert_holders.pdf (accessed February 6, 2009)

puppy mills do not provide adequate veterinary care, food, shelter, and socialization for their puppies. According to the HSUS, thousands of puppy mills existed in the United States in 2009. Animal welfare groups maintain that puppy mills cause suffering of mother dogs and puppies. Female dogs are bred too often and destroyed when they quit producing puppies. The puppies are often transported over long distances in cramped cages and frequently suffer from debilitating conditions and diseases.

Breeding purebred puppies is big business in the Midwest. (See Table 9.7.) It was encouraged by the government following World War II as a way for rural people to make more income. Many traditional farmers switched from rais-

TABLE 9.9

Dealers licensed under the Animal Welfare Act, by class, fiscal years 2002–07

Fiscal year	Total dealers	Class A dealers	Class B dealers
2007	5,239	4,218	1,021
2006	5,197	4,202	995
2005	4,500	3,625	875
2004	4,571	NA	NA
2003	4,179	NA	NA
2002	3,893	NA	NA

Notes: NA = Not available

SOURCE: Adapted from "Table 5. Licensed Dealers, FY 2005–2007," in *Animal Care Annual Report of Activities: Fiscal Year 2007*, U.S. Department of Agriculture, Animal and Plant Health Inspection Service, September 2008, http://www.aphis.usda.gov/publications/animal_welfare/content/printable_version/2007_AC_Report.pdf (accessed January 13, 2009); *FY 2004 AWA Inspections*, U.S. Department of Agriculture, Animal and Plant Health Inspection Service, 2004, http://www.aphis.usda.gov/animal_welfare/downloads/awreports/awreport2004.pdf (accessed February 2, 2009); *FY 2003 AWA Inspections*, U.S. Department of Agriculture, Animal and Plant Health Inspection Service, 2003, http://www.aphis.usda.gov/animal_welfare/downloads/awreports/awreport2003.pdf (accessed February 2, 2009); and *FY 2002 AWA Inspections*, U.S. Department of Agriculture, Animal and Plant Health Inspection Service, 2002, http://www.aphis.usda.gov/animal_welfare/downloads/awreports/awreport2002.pdf (accessed February 2, 2009)

TABLE 9.10

USDA license fees for dealers, brokers, and operators of auction sales

Over	But not over	Initial license fee	Annual or changed class of license fee
$0	$500	$30	$40
500	2,000	60	70
2,000	10,000	120	130
10,000	25,000	225	235
25,000	50,000	350	360
50,000	100,000	475	485
100,000	—	750	760

SOURCE: "Table 1. Dealers, Brokers, and Operators of an Auction Sale—Class "A" and "B" License," in "Animal Welfare; Inspection, Licensing, and Procurement of Animals, Final Rule," *Federal Register*, vol. 69, no. 134, July 14, 2004, http://edocket.access.gpo.gov/2004/pdf/04-15878.pdf (accessed February 20, 2009)

ing pigs to raising puppies when market conditions were favorable. This was particularly true in Missouri.

MISSOURI: "THE PUPPY PIPELINE." Missouri leads the nation in APHIS Class A and B licenses. (See Table 9.7 and Table 9.8.) The state accounts for 32% of all Class A licenses and 15% of all Class B licenses. It is widely agreed that Missouri is the nation's top source for purebred puppies. In December 2003 the radio station KMOX of St. Louis, Missouri, aired the award-winning series *Missouri: The Puppy Pipeline* by Megan Lynch. According to Lynch, the state had an estimated 1,000 licensed puppy breeding facilities in 2003, far more than any other state. Experts estimated that as many as 1,000 additional unlicensed puppy farms were operating illegally. The state is home to the Hunte

Corporation, the world's largest distributor of puppies to pet stores. In 2003 puppy breeding was an estimated $2-billion-a-year business in Missouri. Lynch reviews the history of the puppy farming industry in the state and reports on many problems revealed by state auditors.

In 1992 the Missouri legislature passed the Animal Care Facilities Act to establish minimum standards for businesses, shelters, and pounds dealing with cats and dogs. The Missouri Department of Agriculture (MDA) oversees the program, which has regulations that are largely identical to USDA regulations for animal facilities. In *Audit of Animal Care Facilities Inspection Program* (February 15, 2001, http://www.auditor.mo.gov/press/2001-09.pdf), Claire McCaskill of the state auditor office was highly critical of the MDA's oversight of the state's puppy breeding industry. In *Follow-up Review of Animal Care Facilities Inspection Program* (December 16, 2004, http://www.auditor.mo.gov/press/2004-91.pdf), McCaskill notes that "most" of the problems cited in the 2001 audit had not been corrected.

McCaskill warns, "These problems have eroded the integrity of the inspection program which is designed to help ensure canines are safely and humanely treated." Auditors accompanying inspectors observed unsanitary and unsafe conditions at some puppy farms. A listing of the most serious problems is provided in Table 9.11. In addition, McCaskill mentions many problems with record-keeping, both by inspectors and facility operators.

NOTABLE PUPPY MILL CASES. According to the HSUS, in the press release "1,000 Freed from W. Va. Puppy Mill" (August 24, 2008, http://www.hsus.org/hsus_field/hsus_disaster_center/disasters_press_room/a_thousand_dogs_freed_from_wv_082408.html), in August 2008 authorities in West Virginia rescued 1,000 dogs and puppies from the Whispering Oaks Kennel in Parkersburg, which had been in operation since 1961. The property owner, Sharon Roberts, agreed to relinquish the dogs to authorities and cease operating her puppy breeding farm to avoid criminal charges. Most of the dogs were small breeds, such as Yorkies, poodles, and Jack Russell terriers. The dogs were kept in rabbit cages scattered around the property. Some reportedly had no access to water. The rescued dogs were turned over to animal welfare groups to be evaluated and adopted out.

The American Society for the Prevention of Cruelty to Animals (ASPCA) reports in "Lyles, Tennessee—June 2008" (June 2008, http://www.aspca.org/fight-animal-cruelty/puppy-mills/lyles-tennesseejune-2008.html) that in June 2008 over 700 dogs and puppies were removed from a puppy mill in Lyles, Tennessee—the largest rescue in the state's history. Patricia Adkisson, the owner of Pine Bluffs Kennels, had been previously charged in 1998 with 195 counts of animal neglect and cruelty after a similar raid. Those charges were dropped after a court ruled that her property had been improperly searched. The ASPCA and

TABLE 9.11

Violations observed by Missouri auditors at puppy breeding facilities, 2004

Inspection type	Violations observed by auditor at puppy breeding facilities	Response of inspector
Pre-licensing	Cages with inadequate flooring	Did not observe
	Accumulated fecal material	Did not observe
	Multiple shelters in poor condition	Did not observe
	Improper food storage	Did not observe
	Operator selling puppies prior to obtaining license	Observed, but did not report, told operator "you really shouldn't be doing that"
Annual	Pens with large amounts of fecal accumulation	Observed, but did not report
	Housing facility that did not protect dogs from weather	Observed, but did not report, decided to revisit facility before winter to ensure building was completed
Annual	A piece of unsecured metal covering a drain channel inside the outdoor runs	Did not observe
Pre-licensing	No veterinary care available	Gave applicant up to 30 days to correct, but did not reinspect for 138 days
	Fecal accumulation under and in pens	
	Dirty water or no water in bowls	
Re-inspection of above facility	Fecal accumulation under and in pens	Gave applicant time to correct
	Dirty water or no water	
	Pens with no shelter or shade	
	No food or moldy food in feed bowls	
	Dogs with skin problems	
	A puppy that had been dead for several days in pen	
	28 new violations	
Re-inspection of above facility	14 violations still existing from previous inspections, plus 7 new violations	Gave applicant time to correct
Re-inspection of above facility	15 violations still existing from previous inspections, plus 11 new violations	Gave applicant time to correct

SOURCE: Adapted from *Follow-Up Review of Animal Care Facilities Inspection Program*, Office of the Missouri State Auditor, December 16, 2004, http://www.auditor.mo.gov/press/2004-91.pdf (accessed February 20, 2009).

many other national and local animal organizations assisted law enforcement officials with the 2008 raid. They found 747 animals, including approximately 500 adult dogs and 200 puppies. An assortment of other animals were also removed. Melinda Merck, a crime scene investigator for the ASPCA, called it "one of the worst situations I have ever seen." She noted that "animals were in extreme states of neglect and illness. Some were dead. The overcrowding, the unsanitary conditions, the flea and parasite infestation, as well as the stress of competing for food and coping with untreated illnesses—all were severe." The kennel owner had advertised her puppies and dogs for sale on the Internet, where she described them running and playing on a "scenic and beautiful" farm. In August 2008 a grand jury indicted Adkisson on 24 felony counts of animal cruelty and more than a dozen misdemeanor counts. As of April 2009, the case had not gone to trial.

BUYER BEWARE. In response to negative publicity about puppy mills, several states have passed lemon laws to protect consumers who buy puppies at pet stores. Such laws typically enable consumers to be reimbursed by pet stores that sell them puppies that turn out to be in poor health. The HSUS hopes that such laws motivate pet stores to pressure breeders to improve the conditions in which puppies are raised. Table 9.12 shows HSUS tips on how consumers can identify a good dog breeder.

Consumers are urged to contact APHIS and ask for copies of federal inspection reports conducted on the breeder and broker of any puppy they purchase. Backyard breeders and hobby breeders do not have to register with APHIS. Dog enthusiasts encourage consumers to buy only from reputable local breeders and to ask to see the sire and dam of the puppy they are interested in purchasing. A personal visit ensures the consumer that the breeder is operating a clean and well-kept business with healthy, well-adjusted dogs.

ORGANIZATIONS RESPOND. All major animal welfare organizations are opposed to commercial puppy breeding because of the severe pet overpopulation problem. They do not believe that puppies should be commercially bred because millions of unwanted puppies and dogs are euthanized at shelters every year. The HSUS notes in "HSUS Pet Overpopulation Estimates" that approximately 25% of the dogs that wind up in shelters are purebred. Purebred dogs can generally be identified by their coloring, fur, and characteristic appearance.

The AKC does not support random large-scale breeding of dogs for commercial purposes. The organization conducts inspections of breeders who use the AKC registry and of breeders, retail pet shops, and brokers who conduct 25 or more registration transactions per year or breed seven or more litters of puppies per year.

FERAL CATS

Feral cats are cats that have reverted to a semiwild state because of lack of human contact and socialization. They avoid humans and often live in large groups called colonies.

TABLE 9.12

Tips from the Humane Society on picking a good dog breeder

A GOOD DOG BREEDER ...

Keeps her dogs in the home and as part of the family—not outside in kennel runs.

Has dogs who appear happy and healthy, are excited to meet new people, and don't shy away from visitors.

Shows you where the dogs spend most of their time—an area that is clean and well maintained.

Encourages you to spend time with the puppy's parents—at a minimum, the pup's mother—when you visit.

Breeds only one or two types of dogs, and is knowledgeable about what are called "breed standards" (the desired characteristics of the breed in areas such as size, proportion, coat, color, and temperament).

Has a strong relationship with a local veterinarian and shows you records of veterinary visits for the puppies. Explains the puppies' medical history and what vaccinations your new puppy will need.

Is well versed in the potential genetic problems inherent in the breed—there are specific genetic concerns for every breed—and explains to you what those concerns are. The breeder should have had the puppy's parents tested (and should have the results from the parents' parents) to ensure they are free of those defects, and she should be able to provide you with documentation for all testing she has done through organizations such as the Orthopedic Foundation for Animals (OFA).

Gives you guidance on caring and training for your puppy and is available for assistance after you take your puppy home.

Provides references of other families who have purchased puppies from her.

Feeds high quality "premium" brand food.

Doesn't always have puppies available but rather will keep a list of interested people for the next available litter.

Actively competes with her dogs in conformation trials (which judge how closely dogs match their "breed standard"), obedience trials (which judge how well dogs perform specific sets of tasks on command), or tracking and agility trials. Good breeders will also work with local, state, and national clubs that specialize in their specific breed.

Encourages multiple visits and wants your entire family to meet the puppy before you take your puppy home.

Provides you with a written contract and health guarantee and allows plenty of time for you to read it thoroughly. The breeder should *not* require that you use a specific veterinarian.

SOURCE: "How to Identify a Good Dog Breeder—Tips from the Humane Society of the United States," in *How to Find a Good Dog Breeder*, Humane Society of the United States, 2005, http://files.hsus.org/web-files/PDF/good_breeder_checklist.pdf (accessed February 20, 2009)

They may be born into this condition or adjust to it after being stray, lost, or abandoned for a long time. Feral cats are often confused with strays, but there is a difference. Stray cats generally appear scruffy and unclean because they do not groom themselves. They are accustomed to human care and suffer from stress and hunger without it. Feral cats are adjusted to a wild manner of living. If a natural food source is prevalent, they survive fairly well.

The problem is that they also reproduce well. Many animal welfare groups advocate a trap-neuter-return (TNR) management plan for feral colonies. In these programs feral cats are humanely trapped, vaccinated, sterilized, and returned to their colonies. In most cases volunteers feed the colonies and conduct TNR activities. Kittens and particularly tame adult cats go into adoption programs. In general, it is difficult to turn a truly feral cat into a pet. Where it is possible, it requires a great deal of time and effort. Most welfarists believe their time is better spent sterilizing the cats than trying to tame them.

Alley Cat Allies was founded in 1990 in the District of Columbia to advocate on behalf of feral and stray cats. Many animal control departments try to control feral cat colonies by capturing and euthanizing the cats. According to Alley Cat Allies (2009, http://www.alleycat.org/NetCommunity/Page.aspx?pid=434), the TNR approach is much more effective and less costly. It prevents the animals from producing kittens, and the adult population gradually decreases.

PET ABUSE AND NEGLECT

Tracking animal abuse cases is difficult because there is no government database of all cases. In 2001 Alison Gianotto of California began an online database of abuse cases—Pet-abuse.com—after her cat was stolen and set on fire. As of February 2009, the database listed information on nearly 13,000 cases in the United States. The largest number of cases involved neglect or abandonment (32.2%), followed by shooting (11.7%), hoarding (11.3%), fighting (8.9%), and beating (6.9%). Dogs (excluding pit bull breeds) and cats are the most common victims noted.

Data in the database can be searched by state, date, perpetrator name, type of animal, type of abuse, or sex of perpetrator. Photographs are included for some cases. Each case description includes media and/or law enforcement or court references so that information can be verified. Pet-abuse.com includes data on animal cruelty cases in which there is also documented neglect of a child or elderly person in the household.

Animal Hoarding

Animal hoarding is a form of animal abuse. Animal hoarders collect large numbers of pets and do not provide proper care for them. Most hoarders start out with good intentions, taking in a few strays to care for, but the situation can quickly grow out of control as the animals breed or the person takes in more and more animals. The animals are often kept inside the home and allowed to urinate and defecate there. Hoarders are oblivious to the negative effects of their actions on their pets and even on themselves. They see themselves as animal rescuers. Most will not admit that the severe overcrowding is unsanitary and unhealthy for the animals.

Pet-abuse.com lists 165 hoarding cases for 2008 involving thousands of animals. Three of the cases involve 800 small dogs and 82 parrots kept by an elderly couple in Avra

Valley, Arizona; more than 450 cats kept at the Tiger Ranch rescue facility near Tarentum, Pennsylvania; and 464 dogs, cats, birds, sheep, rabbits, and other animals living with a couple in Las Cruces, New Mexico. In all of these cases, investigators reported finding animals in very poor condition due to overcrowding and lack of proper care.

The Hoarding of Animals Research Consortium was founded in 1997 by Gary Patronek to study the hoarding problem and work to increase awareness among mental health and social service workers. The group believes that hoarding is a pathological problem. Some psychiatrists suspect that it is a psychological disorder similar to obsessive-compulsive behavior.

In 2001 Illinois became the first state to pass legislation dealing specifically with animal hoarding as a crime separate from animal cruelty or neglect. The Illinois law is considered by some animal activists to be model legislation for other states because it recognizes that hoarding may be a mental health problem and recommends psychiatric treatment for offenders.

EXOTIC PETS

The word *exotic* means "foreign" or "not native," but when the word is used to describe pets, it refers to wild animals that are not normally considered pets. These include lions, tigers, wolves, bears, primates, certain rodents and reptiles, and many other species. Exotic pets appeal to people because they are different and, in some cases, dangerous and threatening to others.

Many people feel they have the right to keep any animal as long as they provide proper care for it. Critics say that exotic animals belong in their natural habitats and not in cages, where they can suffer from abuse, neglect, and boredom. Welfarists believe that even well-treated exotic pets should not be kept in captivity because it violates their wild nature. Law enforcement and animal control officers point out that exotic pets pose a health hazard to people because their temperaments can be unpredictable.

Some people think it is wrong to keep wild animals in captivity, even those born in captivity. Exotic breeders argue that an animal born and raised in a cage does not miss the wild because the animal has never experienced it. Critics do not agree with this argument. They believe captive-born wild animals retain the natural urges and instincts of their species.

Exotic pets are offered for sale in pet stores, on the Internet, at auctions, and in trade publications, such as the *Animal Finder's Guide* (http://www.animalfindersguide .com/). The National Alternative Pet Association (NAPA) provides a list of breeders, dealers, and shops that specialize in exotic pets. The association also provides information and Internet links for a variety of clubs and organiza-

tions for exotic pet owners. NAPA complains that people with exotic pets suffer from discrimination and have difficulties finding food, supplies, veterinarians, shelters, and rescue groups for their animals. Zoos are often unwilling to provide needed information and will not take unwanted exotic pets.

Exotic pets are banned or regulated in many states. In "Summary of State Laws Relating to Private Possession of Exotic Animals" (2009, http://www.bornfreeusa .org/b4a2_exotic_animals_summary.php), Born Free USA lists states that completely or partially ban private ownership of big cats, wolves, bears, reptiles, and most nonhuman primates.

NAPA (2009, http://www.altpet.net/) indicates that "even though many exotic pet species have been bred in captivity for a long time now, the laws still treat them like second class pets in some areas." The organization believes that a few bad incidents involving exotic pets have been blown out of proportion and that exotic pet owners are unfairly blamed for declining populations of endangered species. NAPA insists that captive breeding is the only chance for some species. It claims that many public shelters and wildlife rescue groups give preference to zoos and will euthanize exotic animals instead of allowing private individuals to take them.

All major animal rights and welfare groups oppose the keeping of exotic pets, expressing concern about the degradation of natural populations and the care that captive animals receive. Wildlife collectors are blamed for harming sensitive habitats and killing nontarget animals. Animal rights activists and welfarists tend to be opposed to the removal of wild animals from their natural habitats for any purpose. Besides the obvious dangers to the animals, removal can have devastating consequences on the natural habitats of the animals left behind.

Exotic animals kept as pets can suffer from poor nutrition and care at the hands of inexperienced and uninformed owners. The animals may be subjected to painful procedures such as wing clipping, defanging, and declawing. Welfarists believe that only accredited zoos and sanctuaries should care for wild animals kept in captivity. This ensures the proper care for the animals and protects the public safety.

Tigers

In his testimony before the U.S. House of Representatives' Subcommittee on Fisheries Conservation, Wildlife, and Oceans, Eric Miller (June 12, 2003, http://www.aza .org/RC/Documents/TestimonyCaptiveWildlifeSafetyAct .pdf), the director of the St. Louis Zoological Park, stated that there are between 5,000 and 10,000 pet tigers in the United States and that this number exceeds the number of wild tigers living throughout Asia. Wild tigers are an endangered species, and private ownership of them is prohibited by the Endangered Species Act. However, ownership of a captive-born endangered animal is legal in many states.

Accredited zoos have been collecting wild tigers for decades. Many of these tigers were bred in captivity to produce popular zoo babies to bring in crowds. This resulted in an oversupply of adult tigers, many of which wound up in private hands. Pet owners, breeders, circuses, and roadside zoos have interbred different varieties of these animals, resulting in a large population of generic (not purebred) tigers.

Accredited zoos work to preserve endangered tiger species through selective breeding programs. Only pure-bred tigers with traceable ancestries are used. Generic tigers, or mutts, as they are called, have no value to these programs. Welfarists state that pet tigers are often kept chained or confined in small enclosures and may be beaten into submission.

Nonhuman Primates

The issue of nonhuman primates kept as pets captured national attention in February 2009, when a Connecticut woman was attacked and critically injured by her friend's pet chimpanzee. Stephanie Gallman reports in "Chimp Attack Victim Moved to Cleveland Clinic" (CNN, February 19, 2009) that Travis, a 200-pound (91-kg) male chimp, was 14 years old. His owner, a 70-year-old woman, reportedly bathed and slept in the same bed as the chimp, who had previously been featured in television commercials for various products. Travis was shot and killed by a police officer after the attack. The victim, a 50-year-old woman, suffered severe injuries to her face, including the loss of her eyelids, nose, lips, and sight, and had both hands nearly torn off at the wrists, eventually resulting in the loss of both hands.

The attack spurred calls for tougher laws against the ownership of nonhuman primates as pets. The HSUS and other animal welfare and wildlife and zoo organizations urged the federal government to pass the Captive Primate Safety Act, which would prohibit interstate commerce in primates for the pet trade. As of April 2009, the act had been passed by the U.S. House of Representatives, but had not yet been considered in the U.S. Senate.

HEALTH AND SAFETY ISSUES
Risks to People from Exotic Pets

The largest health risks to people from pets are zoonoses and animal bites. Zoonoses are diseases that can be passed from animals to humans. Scientists report that there are more than 250 distinct zoonoses that have been documented in medical literature. Zoonoses can occur in domesticated and wild animals. However, zoonoses in livestock, cats, and dogs are well known, heavily researched, and largely controlled through vaccination programs. Diseases

passed to humans from most other animals, particularly exotic pets, are a different matter. Little is known about them, and they are more difficult to control.

In May 2003 an outbreak of monkeypox in the Midwest captured widespread media attention. Monkeypox is a disease that is related to smallpox but not nearly as lethal. Scientists believe that several people caught monkeypox from pet prairie dogs, which in turn had caught the disease from infected Gambian rats. The import of all African rats was subsequently banned by the U.S. Department of Health and Human Services. Health experts fear that other zoonoses not previously seen in the United States will emerge unless the trade in wild and exotic pets is curtailed.

In "Hedgehog Zoonoses" (*Emerging Infectious Diseases*, vol. 11, no. 1, January 2005), Patricia Y. Riley and Bruno B. Chomel of the University of California, Davis, solidify these concerns by stating, "Overall, ownership of exotic pets should not be encouraged because exotic animals and wildlife do not usually make good pets and can transmit zoonotic agents."

SALMONELLOSIS. Salmonellosis, an infection caused by the bacteria *Salmonella*, can cause diarrhea, fever, and abdominal cramps in patients for several days. Even though it does not generally require hospitalization, it can be quite serious for patients with weak immune systems, children, and the elderly. The infection is caused by eating contaminated food or through direct or indirect contact with reptiles and amphibians, such as lizards, snakes, turtles, frogs, and newts. *Salmonella* occurs naturally in the gastrointestinal tracts of these animals. According to the CDC, in "Diseases from Reptiles" (2009, http://www.cdc.gov/healthypets/animals/reptiles.htm), approximately 70,000 people per year contract salmonellosis from contact with reptiles in the United States.

DOG BITES. Determining the number of dog bites and related injuries that occur in the United States is extremely difficult because there is no nationwide tracking system. In "Dog Bite Prevention" (October 28, 2008, http://www.cdc.gov/HomeandRecreationalSafety/DogBites/biteprevention.html), the CDC indicates that approximately 4.5 million people experience dog bites each year. Approximately 885,000 of the dog bite victims require medical attention. The most recent comprehensive and published data on dog bites as of mid-2009 were collected in 1994 and are summarized by the CDC in "Nonfatal Dog Bite-Related Injuries Treated in Hospital Emergency Departments—United States, 2001" (*Morbidity and Mortality Weekly Report*, vol. 52, no. 26, July 4, 2003). The CDC notes that in 1994 approximately 4.7 million Americans were bitten by dogs—more than half of the victims were children. Nearly 800,000 people sought medical attention for dog bites, with 333,700 going to hospital emergency rooms. Approximately 6,000 of these patients required hospitalization. The remainder were treated and released.

The CDC provides an analysis of dog bite injury data collected in 2001 from 66 emergency rooms around the country. Based on these limited data, the CDC estimates that approximately 368,000 people required treatment for dog bite injuries at U.S. emergency rooms during 2001. Children under the age of 14 accounted for an estimated 42% of the cases. The data collected in 2001 indicate that dog bites occurred mostly during the warm months, primarily during July. Nearly half of all injuries were to the arms and hands, and children were most likely to be bitten in the head or neck. Puncture and laceration wounds were the most common types of injuries.

Even though this report does not note the breeds of dogs associated with the bite injuries, breed information has been collected by the CDC for fatal injuries from dog bites. After examining the records for 304 fatalities due to dog bites from 1979 to 1996, the CDC concludes in "Dog-Bite-Related Fatalities—United States, 1995–1996" (*Morbidity and Mortality Weekly Report*, vol. 46, no. 21, May 30, 1997) that the dog breed (or primary cross breed) could

be identified in 199 of the cases. Pit bulls were blamed for 70 of the attacks; rottweilers accounted for 32 fatalities; German shepherds caused 30 deaths; huskies were associated with another 20 fatalities; and wolf hybrids were blamed for 14 deaths. Other breeds identified with fatal dog attacks included Alaskan malamutes, Doberman pinschers, chows, Great Danes, St. Bernards, and Akitas. The CDC notes that unaltered dogs (particularly males) were more likely to bite than spayed/neutered dogs.

Public fears about aggressive dogs have led some jurisdictions around the country to ban particular dog breeds. Some jurisdictions ban breeds outright, whereas others require owners to carry liability insurance or muzzle their dogs in public. Many animal protection organizations and industry groups, including the AKC and the ASPCA, are opposed to breed-specific legislation. They believe that irresponsible breeders and pet owners should be targeted instead, particularly those who train dogs to be aggressive or refuse to keep their dogs fenced or on leashes. Better enforcement of existing animal control legislation is seen as a more effective measure than breed-specific bans.

IMPORTANT NAMES
AND ADDRESSES

American Anti-Vivisection Society
801 Old York Rd., Ste. 204
Jenkintown, PA 19046
(215) 887-0816
1-800-729-2287
E-mail: aavs@aavs.org
URL: http://www.aavs.org/

American Greyhound Council
PO Box 543
Abilene, KS 67410-0543
(785) 263-4660
URL: http://www.agcouncil.com/

American Humane Association
63 Inverness Dr. East
Englewood, CO 80112
(303) 792-9900
1-800-227-4645
FAX: (303) 792-5333
E-mail: info@americanhumane.org
URL: http://www.americanhumane.org/

American Meat Institute
1150 Connecticut Ave. NW, 12th Floor
Washington, DC 20036
(202) 587-4200
FAX: (202) 587-4300
URL: http://www.meatami.com/

American Pet Products Association
255 Glenville Rd.
Greenwich, CT 06831
(203) 532-0000
1-800-452-1225
FAX: (203) 532-0551
URL: http://www.americanpetproducts.org/

**American Rescue Dog
Association**
PO Box 613
Bristow, VA 20136
1-888-775-8871
E-mail: information@ARDAinc.org
URL: http://www.ardainc.org/

**American Society for the Prevention of
Cruelty to Animals**
424 E. 92nd St.
New York, NY 10128-6804
(212) 876-7700
URL: http://www.aspca.org/

American Veterinary Medical Association
1931 N. Meacham Rd., Ste. 100
Schaumburg, IL 60173-4360
(847) 925-8070
FAX: (847) 925-1329
E-mail: avmainfo@avma.org
URL: http://www.avma.org/

Animal Legal Defense Fund
170 E. Cotati Ave.
Cotati, CA 94931
(707) 795-2533
FAX: (707) 795-7280
E-mail: info@aldf.org
URL: http://www.aldf.org/

Animal People
PO Box 960
Clinton, WA 98236
(360) 579-2505
FAX: (360) 579-2575
E-mail: anpeople@whidbey.com
URL: http://www.animalpeoplenews.org/

**Animal and Plant Health Inspection
Service**
U.S. Department of Agriculture
4700 River Rd.
Riverdale, MD 20737
URL: http://www.aphis.usda.gov/

Animal Protection Institute
1122 S St.
Sacramento, CA 95811
(916) 447-3085
FAX: (916) 447-3070
E-mail: info@bornfreeusa.org
URL: http://www.bornfreeusa.org/

Animal Welfare Institute
PO Box 3650
Washington, DC 20027
(202) 337-2332
FAX: 1-888-260-2271
E-mail: awi@awionline.org
URL: http://www.awionline.org/

Association of Zoos and Aquariums
8403 Colesville Rd., Ste. 710
Silver Spring, MD 20910-3314
(301) 562-0777
FAX: (301) 562-0888
URL: http://www.aza.org/

Best Friends Animal Society
5001 Angel Canyon Rd.
Kanab, UT 84741-5000
(435) 644-2001
E-mail: info@bestfriends.org
URL: http://www.bestfriends.org/

**Center for Alternatives to Animal
Testing**
615 N Wolfe Street, W7032
Baltimore, MD 21205
(410) 614-4990
FAX: (410) 614-2871
E-mail: caat@jhsph.edu
URL: http://caat.jhsph.edu/

**Centers for Disease Control and
Prevention**
1600 Clifton Rd.
Atlanta, GA 30333
1-800-232-4636
E-mail: cdcinfo@cdc.gov
URL: http://www.cdc.gov/

Compassion over Killing
PO Box 9773
Washington, DC 20016
(301) 891-2458
E-mail: info@cok.net
URL: http://www.cok.net/

Defenders of Wildlife
1130 17th St. NW
Washington, DC 20036
1-800-385-9712
E-mail: defenders@mail.defenders.org
URL: http://www.defenders.org/

Friends of Animals
777 Post Rd., Ste. 205
Darien, CT 06820
(203) 656-1522
FAX: (203) 656-0267
E-mail: info@friendsofanimals.org
URL: http://www.friendsofanimals.org/

Fund for Animals
200 W. 57th St.
New York, NY 10019
1-888-405-3863
E-mail: info@fundforanimals.org
URL: http://www.fundforanimals.org/

Greyhound Protection League
PO Box 669
Penn Valley, CA 95946
1-800-446-8637
URL: http://www.greyhounds.org/

Guide Dog Users Inc.
14311 Astrodome Dr.
Silver Spring, MD 20906
(301) 598-5771
1-866-799-8436
URL: http://www.gdui.org/

Humane Society of the United States
2100 L St. NW
Washington, DC 20037
(202) 452-1100
URL: http://www.hsus.org/

Humane Society Veterinary Medical Association
2100 L St. NW
Washington, DC 20037
(202) 452-1100
URL: http://www.hsvma.org/

In Defense of Animals
3010 Kerner Blvd.
San Rafael, CA 94901
(415) 488-0048
FAX: (415) 454-1031
E-mail: idainfo@idausa.org
URL: http://www.idausa.org/

International Institute for Animal Law
30 N. LaSalle St., Ste. 2900
Chicago, IL 60602
(312) 917-8850
FAX: (312) 263-5013
E-mail: IIAL@AnimalLawIntl.org
URL: http://www.animallawintl.org/

Jockey Club
40 E. 52nd St.
New York, NY 10022

(212) 371-5970
FAX: (212) 371-6123
URL: http://www.jockeyclub.com/

Maddie's Fund
2223 Santa Clara Ave., Ste. B
Alameda, CA 94501
(510) 337-8989
FAX: (510) 337-8988
E-mail: info@maddiesfund.org
URL: http://www.maddiesfund.org/

Michigan Society for Medical Research
PO Box 3237
Ann Arbor, MI 48106-3237
(734) 763-8029
FAX: (734) 930-1568
E-mail: mismr@umich.edu
URL: http://www.mismr.org/

National Agricultural Statistics Service U.S. Department of Agriculture
1400 Independence Ave. SW
Washington, DC 20250
1-800-727-9540
E-mail: nass@nass.usda.gov
URL: http://www.nass.usda.gov/

National Animal Interest Alliance
PO Box 66579
Portland, OR 97290-6579
(503) 761-1139
URL: http://www.naiaonline.org/

National Association for Biomedical Research
818 Connecticut Ave. NW, Ste. 900
Washington, DC 20006
(202) 857-0540
FAX: (202) 659-1902
E-mail: info@nabr.org
URL: http://www.nabr.org/

National Greyhound Association
PO Box 543
Abilene, KS 67410
(785) 263-4660
E-mail: nga@ngagreyhounds.com
URL: http://www.ngagreyhounds.com/

National Institute for Animal Agriculture
1910 Lyda Ave.
Bowling Green, KY 42104-5809
(270) 782-9798
FAX: (270) 782-0188
E-mail: NIAA@animalagriculture.org
URL: http://www.nih.gov/

National Institutes of Health
9000 Rockville Pike
Bethesda, MD 20892
(301) 496-4000
E-mail: NIHinfo@od.nih.gov
URL: http://www.nih.gov/

National Trappers Association
2815 Washington Ave.
Bedford, IN 47421

(812) 277-9670
FAX: (812) 277-9672
URL: http://www.nationaltrappers.com/

National Wildlife Federation
11100 Wildlife Center Dr.
Reston, VA 20190
1-800-822-9919
URL: http://www.nwf.org/

New England Anti-Vivisection Society
333 Washington St., Ste. 850
Boston, MA 02108
(617) 523-6020
FAX: (617) 523-7925
URL: http://www.neavs.org/

People for the Ethical Treatment of Animals
501 Front St.
Norfolk, VA 23510
(757) 622-7382
URL: http://www.peta.org/

Performing Animal Welfare Society
PO Box 849
Galt, CA 95632
(209) 745-2606
FAX: (209) 745-1809
E-mail: info@pawsweb.org
URL: http://www.pawsweb.org/

Pet-abuse.com
PO Box 5
Southfields, NY 10975
1-888-523-PETS
E-mail: info@pet-abuse.com
URL: http://www.pet-abuse.com/

Physicians Committee for Responsible Medicine
5100 Wisconsin Ave. NW, Ste. 400
Washington, DC 20016
(202) 686-2210
E-mail: pcrm@pcrm.org
URL: http://www.pcrm.org/

Professional Rodeo Cowboys Association
101 Pro Rodeo Dr.
Colorado Springs, CO 80919
(719) 593-8840
URL: http://www.prorodeo.com/

Sled Dog Action Coalition
PO Box 562061
Miami, FL 33256
E-mail: SledDogAC@aol.com
URL: http://www.helpsleddogs.org/

Society for Animal Protective Legislation
PO Box 3650
Washington, DC 20027
(202) 337-2332

FAX: 1-888-260-2271
E-mail: awi@awionline.org
URL: http://www.saplonline.org/

Society and Animals Forum
PO Box 1297
Washington Grove, MD 20880-1297
(301) 963-4751
E-mail:
kshapiro@societyandanimalsforum.org
URL: http://www.psyeta.org/

Spay/USA
2261 Broadridge Ave.
Stratford, CT 06614-3898
1-800-248-7729
URL: http://www.spayusa.org/

TRAFFIC North America
1250 24th St. NW
Washington, DC 20037

(202) 293-4800
FAX: (202) 775-8287
E-mail: tna@wwfus.org
URL: http://www.traffic.org/

United Gamefowl Breeders Association, Inc.
PO Box 457
Daleville, AL 36322
(334) 503-4336
E-mail: united069@centurytel.net
URL: http://www.ugba.info

United Poultry Concerns
PO Box 150
Machipongo, VA 23405
(757) 678-7875
E-mail: info@upc-online.org
URL: http://www.upc-online.org/

U.S. Bureau of Land Management
1849 C St. NW, Rm. 5665
Washington, DC 20240
(202) 208-3801
FAX: (202) 208-5242
URL: http://www.blm.gov/

U.S. Fish and Wildlife Service
U.S. Department of Interior
1849 C St. NW
Washington, DC 20240
1-800-344-WILD
URL: http://www.fws.gov/

U.S. Sportsmen's Alliance
801 Kingsmill Pkwy.
Columbus, OH 43229
(614) 888-4868
FAX: (614) 888-0326
E-mail: info@ussportsmen.org
URL: http://www.wlfa.org/

RESOURCES

Several resources useful to this book were published by agencies of the U.S. Department of Agriculture, including the Animal and Plant Health Inspection Service, the Economic Research Service, and the National Agricultural Statistics Service. Other federal agencies providing information were the Bureau of Land Management, the Centers for Disease Control and Prevention, the National Institutes of Health, the National Marine Fisheries Service, the National Park Service, the U.S. Customs and Border Protection, the U.S. Fish and Wildlife Service, the U.S. Food and Drug Administration, and the U.S. Forest Service.

The U.S. Government Accountability Office (GAO) is the investigative arm of Congress. The GAO publications used for this book were *Wildlife Services Program: Information on Activities to Manage Wildlife Damage* (November 2001) and *Effective Long-Term Options Needed to Manage Unadoptable Wild Horses* (October 2008).

Information on animal industries and businesses was obtained from associations including the American Greyhound Council, the American Kennel Club, the American Meat Institute, the American Pet Products Association, the American Veal Association, the Association of Zoos and Aquariums, the International Whaling Commission, the Jockey Club, the National Renderers Association, and the U.S. Fur Commission.

The Web sites of the Ringling Brothers and Barnum and Bailey Circus (http://www.ringling.com/) and the Hanneford Family Circus (http://www.hannefordcircus.com/) were informative. Temple Grandin's Web site (http://www.grandin.com/) was particularly useful as a resource on animal husbandry and slaughtering in the modern agriculture industry.

Organizations involved in animal issues that provided helpful statistics and information include the American Veterinary Medical Association, Assistance Dogs International, the Foundation for Biomedical Research, the Mich-igan Society for Medical Research, MountedPolice.com, the National Alternative Pet Association, the National Association for Search and Rescue, the Physicians Committee for Responsible Medicine, the U.S. Sportsmen's Alliance, and the U.S. War Dog Association. The following resources describe a variety of issues that also affect animals: *The Ecologist* magazine, Monterey Bay Aquarium, Sierra Club, *Society and Animals: Journal of Human-Animal Studies*, the Union of Concerned Scientists, the United Egg Producers, and *Vegetarian Journal*.

A wealth of information was obtained from groups devoted to the causes of animal protection, welfare, and rights. These include Alley Cat Allies, the American Humane Association, the Animal Legal Defense Fund, Animal People, the Animal Protection Institute, the Animal Welfare Institute, the Best Friends Animal Sanctuary, Defenders of Wildlife, Fund for Animals, the Greyhound Protection League, the Humane Society of the United States, In Defense of Animals, Last Chance for Animals, Maddie's Fund, the National Anti-Vivisection Society, the New England Anti-Vivisection Society, People for the Ethical Treatment of Animals, Pet-abuse .com, the Sled Dog Action Coalition, the Elephant Sanctuary, and United Poultry Concerns.

Animal rights activists and opponents have written some important books that were valuable resources for this work. They include *Beast and Man: The Roots of Human Nature* (1978) and *Animals and Why They Matter* (1983) by Mary Midgley; *Animal Liberation: A New Ethics for Our Treatment of Animals* (1975) by Peter Singer; *Animals, Property, and the Law* (1995) by Gary L. Francione; *Putting Humans First: Why We Are Nature's Favorite* (2004) by Tibor R. Machan; *The Animal Rights Debate* (2001) by Carl Cohen and Tom Regan; *The Case for Animal Rights* (1983) by Tom Regan; *Interests and Rights: The Case against Animals* (1980) and *Rights, Killing, and Suffering: Moral Vegetarianism and Applied Ethics* (1983) by Raymond G. Frey; *The*

Animals Issue: Moral Theory in Practice (1992) by Peter Carruthers; *Speciesism* (2004) by Joan Dunayer; *The Animal Rights Crusade: The Growth of a Moral Protest* (1992) by James M. Jasper and Dorothy Nelkin; *Animal Liberators: Research and Morality* (1988) by Susan Sperling; and *Making a Killing: The Political Economy of Animal Rights* (2007) by Bob Torres.

Various news organizations and outlets were useful for providing timely stories related to animals, particularly *Animal People News*, BBC News, *Los Angeles Times*, *National Geographic*, *Nature*, *New York Times*, *Scientific American*, and *Sports Illustrated*. The *Frontline* documentary *A Whale of a Business* (November 1997) was very helpful. The Gallup Organization supplied polling results on animal issues.

INDEX

H

Hagenbeck, Carl, 115
Halbfinger, David M., 103
Hambrick, Greg, 125
Hamsters
    number of regulated research animals, 85
    pain/distress of, 93
Harris, Eric, 9
Harrison, Ruth, 55
Harvard University
    patent for OncoMouse, 23
    vivisection laboratory at, 7, 79
Hawthorn Corporation, 116–117
Hawthorn Elephant Update (Gipson), 117
"Hayden Law Update" (Bryant), 137
Hazardous substance, 85
Health problems
    of dairy cows, 61–62
    of ducks/geese, 70
    of elephants in captivity, 116, 117
    of exotic pets, 146
    of purebred dogs, 140–141
    of racing horses, 99–100
    of veal calves, 62
Health Research Extension Act (HREA), 84
Health/safety
    health of farm animals and, 75
    issues of pets, 147–148
    risks of exotic pets, 146
    wildlife damage to, 35
    wildlife regulation for protection of, 34
Hearing dogs, 128
Heavenly bodies, 2, 3t
Hebrew tribes, 3
"Hedgehog Zoonoses" (Riley & Chomel), 147
Heifers, 59
"Henry Spira, 71, Animal Rights Crusader" (Feder), 22
Hens
    egg consumption per capita, 68(f4.13)
    egg production, 66, 68(f4.12)
    laying hens, 67–69
HFAC (Humane Farm Animal Care), 74–75
Hides, 48
Hill, Carla, 69
Hinduism, 2–3
Hirschfeld, Rachel, 26–27
History
    of animal rights debate, 22–24
    of animals used for military service, 129–130
    of beef cattle, 59
    of entertainment animals, 113–114
    of research animals, 78–82
    of service animals, 123
    of wildlife management, 32–33
    See also Human-animal interaction
History of Animals (Aristotle), 4

Hoarding, of animals, 145–146
Hoarding of Animals Research Consortium, 146
Hogarth, William, 6
Hogs and pigs
    definition of, 70
    hog farm reforms, 74
    hog-raising practices, 71–72
    modern hog industry, 70–71
    outlawing of small crate enclosures, 55
    percent operations and inventory, by herd size, 71f
    pig transport operation investigation, 54–55
    population of, 53
    pork consumption, 56
    routine farming practices, 57
    slaughter of, 72
Holding period
    for dogs/cats held by USDA-licensed "B" dealers, 90t
    for shelter animals, 139
Hormones
    BGH, 61–62
    for chickens, 66
    in duck/goose production, 70
    given to beef cattle, 60
    for hogs, 71
    organic farming is without, 74
Horse Protection Act (HPA)
    federal appropriations for enforcement of, 102(t6.2)
    horse industry organizations with programs certified under, 102(t6.3)
    soring prohibited by, 101–102
"The Horse Protection Act" (USDA), 101
Horse sports
    gait competitions, 101–102
    horse industry organizations with programs certified under HPA, 102(t6.3)
    horse racing, 97
    horse sports other than racing/rodeos, 98t
    HPA, federal appropriations for enforcement of, 102(t6.2)
    racehorse fatalities in California, by activity, 100(f6.2)
    racehorse fatalities in California, by breed, 100(f6.4)
    racehorse fatalities in California, by organ, 100(f6.3)
    rodeos, 100–101
    Thoroughbred racing, 98–100
"Horse Transport" (APHIS), 72
Horses
    Arabic cultures and, 4
    ban on slaughter of, 55
    cave painting of, 2f
    for foxhunting, 124
    horsemeat controversy, 72–73

    for law enforcement work, 127
    for manual labor, 125
    for military service, 129
    number of horses in U.S., 72
    in Roman Empire, 4
    wild horse and burro program statistics, 41(t3.4)
    Wild Horse Annie Act, 8
    wild horses/burros, management of, 35, 39
    wild horses/burros, removed/adopted, 42(f3.5)
    wild horses/burros managed by BLM, estimated population of, 42(f3.6)
"How Many Adults Are Vegetarian?" (Stahler), 74
"How the 'Mouse Man' Changed Medical Research" (Oosthoek), 77
HPA. *See* Horse Protection Act
HREA (Health Research Extension Act), 84
HSLF (Humane Society Legislative Fund), 10
HSUS. *See* Humane Society of the United States
"HSUS and Others Seek Injunction to Halt USDA in Its Attempt to Buck Congress on Horse Slaughter" (HSUS), 72–73
HSUS Animal Protection Litigation Section, 9
"HSUS Pet Overpopulation Estimates" (HSUS), 135, 144
"The HSUS's Campaign to Ban Battery Cages" (HSUS), 67, 69
"Human and Animal Factors Related to Relinquishment of Dogs and Cats in 12 Selected Animal Shelters in the United States" (Salman et al.), 139
Human interests
    endangered species vs., 43–44
    government wildlife regulation goals and, 34–35
Human rights, 21
Human-animal interaction
    ancient cultures/religions and, 2–4
    AWA and its amendments, 8t
    AWA enforcement cases, 12(t1.7)
    AWA funding, 11f, 11t
    AWA inspections, 12(t1.6)
    AWA inspections, by facility type, inspection category, 12(t1.5)
    blood sports, 5–6
    British law for, 6–7
    cave painting of horse, 2f
    Chinese zodiac, 3t
    domestication of animals, 1–2
    federal animal protection legislation passed or amended, 10t
    link between animal abuse and violence against people, 9
    in medieval period, 4–5
    in modern times, 7–9

J

Jaguars, 44
Jainism, 3
Japan, killing of whales, 52
Jasper, James M., 21
Jerusalem, 5
Jesse James (movie), 118
Jesus Christ, 4
Jews, 65
Jockey Club
  contact information, 150
  Grayson-Jockey Club Research
    Foundation, 99
  on races, 98
Johnson, Ganay, 138
Johnston, Lauren, 126–127
Judaism, 3

K

Kant, Immanuel, 6, 25
Keiko (orca), 118, *119f*
Kentucky Derby, 99
Killing
  of animals, in animal rights debate,
    21–22
  animals killed by hunting, 45, 46
  of big cats, 51
  of elephants, 51
  euthanasia, 135–136
  of fighting dogs, 108
  of nuisance wildlife, 35
  of racing greyhounds, 103–104
  shelters, estimated number of dogs/cats
    killed in, 135(*t*9.4)
  shelters, estimated number of dogs/cats
    killed in, by region, 135(*t*9.5)
  trapping, 46–47
  of wild horses, 35
  Wildlife Services, top twenty animals
    killed by, 41(*t*3.3)
  See also Euthanization; Slaughter
Klebold, Dylan, 9
Knoll, Corina, 118
Koran, 3–4
Kosher slaughter, 65–66
Krauss, Clifford, 49–50

L

Lab Animal Buyer's Guide, 90
Labeling
  Federal Hazardous Substances Labeling
    Act, 85
  of meat/poultry, 75
Labor, wild animals for, 31
Laboratory Animal Welfare Act
  passage of, 8
  requirements of, 80
Laboratory animals. *See* Research animals
Lacey Act of 1900, 33

"Ladder of nature," 4
Lameness, 61, 62
"Largest Recall of Ground Beef Is
  Ordered" (Martin), 65
Lash-Lure, 80
Lassie (dog), 118
Last Chance for Animals, 91
Law enforcement, service animals for,
  125–127
Laws
  on animal hoarding, 146
  animal-related legislation, recent record
    of, 9–10
  British animal rights law, 6–7
  cockfighting laws, by state, 105*t*–107*t*
  dogfighting laws, by state, 109*t*–111*t*
  federal animal protection legislation
    passed or amended, 10*t*
  federal laws impacting wildlife, 33*t*
  federal legislation against animal
    fighting, 108
  first modern law against animal
    cruelty, 6
  livestock protection laws, 54–55
  public support for strict laws concerning
    treatment of farm animals, 55*f*
  state animal anticruelty laws, 13*t*–19*t*
  U.S. law for animal rights, 7
  wildlife regulation laws of federal
    government, 33
  See also Legislation and international
    treaties
Lawson, Nancy, 137–138
Laying hens. *See* Hens
LD-50 test, 86
Legal system, 23–24
Legislation and international treaties
  Animal Care Facilities Act, 143
  Animal Enterprise Protection Act, 81, 82
  Animal Fighting Prohibition
    Enforcement Act, 108
  Animal Welfare Act, animal fighting
    and, 108
  Animal Welfare Act, elephant welfare
    under, 117
  Animal Welfare Act, entertainment
    animals and, 114
  Animal Welfare Act, exclusion of
    livestock, 55
  Animal Welfare Act, holding period for
    shelter animals, 139
  Animal Welfare Act and its
    amendments, 8*t*
  Animal Welfare Act enforcement cases,
    12(*t*1.7)
  Animal Welfare Act funding, 11*f*, 11*t*
  Animal Welfare Act inspections,
    12(*t*1.6)
  Animal Welfare Act inspections, by
    facility type, inspection category,
    12(*t*1.5)

Captive Primate Safety Act, 147
Conyers-Burton Prevention of Equine
  Cruelty Act of 2009, 73
Cosmetics Directive, 88
Cruelty to Animals Act, 79
Downed Animal Protection Act, 65
Endangered Species Act, 41, 44, 117
federal animal protection legislation
  passed or amended, 10*t*
Federal Hazardous Substances Labeling
  Act, 85
Federal Insecticide, Fungicide, and
  Rodenticide Act of 1947, 85
Federal Meat Inspection Act of 1906, 72
Food, Drug, and Cosmetic Act, 7, 80,
  84–85
Health Research Extension Act, 84
Horse Protection Act, 101–102,
  102(*t*6.2), 102(*t*6.3)
Humane Methods of Slaughter Act of
  1958, 7, 55, 65, 69, 72
Laboratory Animal Welfare Act, 8
Lacey Act of 1900, 33
Marine Mammal Protection Act, 121
Migratory Bird Hunting and
  Conservation Stamp Act of 1934, 33
National Institutes of Health
  Revitalization Act, 92
Omnibus Appropriations Bill, 35
Pet Safety and Protection Act, 91
Pets Evacuation and Transportation
  Standards Act of 2006, 133
Pure Food and Drug Act, 80
state animal anticruelty laws, 13*t*–19*t*
Toxic Substances Control Act of 1976,
  85
28-Hour Law of 1873, 7, 54–55
Wild Horse Annie Act, 8
Lemon laws, 144
Leonardo da Vinci, 23
Leopards, 51
"Let Carriage Horses Run Free: It's Time to
  Ban the Practice in New York City"
  (Forel), 125
Lethal injection, 136
Liberationists
  advocates of Singer's theory, 25
  practical implications of animal rights, 27
Licenses
  Class A breeders, number of licenses
    granted to, by state, 142(*t*9.7)
  Class B breeders/dealers, number of
    licenses granted to, by state, 142(*t*9.8)
  dealers licensed under AWA, by class,
    143(*t*9.9)
  for dog breeders/dealers, 141, 143
  for entertainment animal exhibitors, 114
  for falconry, 123
  for fishing, hunting, 44
  license fees, USDA, for dealers, brokers,
    operators of auction sales, 143(*t*9.10)

wildlife damages/threats reported by Wildlife Services, 40(*f*3.3)

from zoonotic diseases, 34

"The Three R's," 91–93

"Three Wrong Leads in a Search for an Environmental Ethic: Tom Regan on Animal Rights, Inherent Values, and 'Deep Ecology'" (Partridge), 23

Tigers

as exotic pets, 146–147

killing of for parts, 51

Timber wolf, 43*f*

Tischler, Joyce, 22

Toe clipping, 66, 67

Torres, Bob, 24

Toxic Substances Control Act of 1976, 85

Toxicity

product testing, 86, 87

testing for, 85

Trackinfo.com, 99

Trade

ban on ivory trade, 51

control of wildlife trade, 33

species trade restrictions, 44

TRAFFIC North America, 151

Training

circus training methods, 115

of elephants, 116

of fighting dogs, 108

of horses for gait competitions, 101

laboratory animals for, 89

of medical service dogs, 129

of military dogs, 130

of performance animals, 114

of racehorses, 99

of service animals, 123

Transgenic animals, 93

Transmissible spongiform encephalopathies (TSEs), 75

Transplants, 93

Transportation

of horses for slaughter, 72, 73

of livestock, law regarding, 54–55

Trap-neuter-return (TNR) plan, 145

Trapping, 46–47

Travis (chimpanzee), 147

"Triple Crown," 99

Trophy hunting

canned hunting, 47–48

states with Internet hunting bans, 49*f*

Trust, 27

TSEs (transmissible spongiform encephalopathies), 75

Tuna, 52

Turkeys, production of, 69–70, 70*f*

Turner, Ted, 74

Turner and Hooch (movie), 118

Twain, Mark (Samuel Clemens), 79

28-Hour Law of 1873, 7, 54–55

"2005 Poultry Welfare Audits: National Chicken Council Animal Welfare Audit for Poultry Has a Scoring System That Is Too Lax and Allows Slaughter Plants with Abusive Practices to Pass" (Grandin), 69

2006 National Survey of Fishing, Hunting, and Wildlife-Associated Recreation (USFWS), 47, 48

2007 Annual Report (Grayson-Jockey Club Research Foundation), 99

2007 Census of Agriculture (USDA)

on bison, 74

on factory farms, 58

farm animal statistics of, 53

on fish farming, 73

on horses, 72

on mink farms, 75

"2007 Restaurant Animal Welfare and Humane Slaughter Audits in Federally Inspected Beef and Pork Slaughter Plants in the U.S. and Canada" (Grandin), 64, 72

2007–2008 National Pet Owners Survey (APPA), 133

"2008 Restaurant Animal Welfare and Humane Slaughter Audits in Federally Inspected Beef and Pork Slaughter Plants in the U.S. and Canada" (Grandin), 64, 72

U

UKC (United Kennel Club), 140, 141

Unaccredited zoos, 116

"Understanding the Effect of Animal-Rights Activism on Biomedical Research" (Morrison), 26

United Egg Producers, 69

United Egg Producers Animal Husbandry Guidelines for U.S. Egg Laying Flocks (United Egg Producers), 69

United Gamefowl Breeders Association, 151

United Kennel Club (UKC), 140, 141

United Kingdom, foxhunting in, 124

United Mounted Peace Officers of Texas, 127

United Nations

Food and Agriculture Organization of, 52

Universal Declaration of Human Rights, 21

United Poultry Concerns (UPC)

on chicken slaughter, 69

contact information, 151

farm animal protection legislation, 55

on humane treatment of chickens, 67

United States

animal rights in modern times, 7–9

early animal rights laws, 7

endangered/threatened animal species, 43*t*

wildlife management history in, 32–33

Universal Declaration of Human Rights (United Nations), 21

Unwanted zoo animals, 115

UPC. *See* United Poultry Concerns

"Updated: Mayor Responds to PETA Carriage Request" (Hambrick), 125

U.S. Customs and Border Protection

use of dogs, 126

wildlife control by, 33

U.S. Customs Service, 126

U.S. Declaration of Independence, 21

U.S. Department of Agriculture (USDA)

animals used at USDA-registered research facilities, 87*t*

AWA enforcement by, 9

on bison, 74

cattle slaughtering and, 64, 65

dog breeder licenses, 141

elephants and, 117

entertainment animals regulation by, 114

on factory farms, 58

farm animal statistics, 53

on fish farming, 73

on hog-raising practices, 71

holding periods for dogs/cats held by USDA-licensed "B" dealers, 90*t*

horsemeat controversy, 72–73

on HPA, 101

on labeling, 75

laboratory animals, protection of, 80

license fees, for dealers, brokers, operators of auction sales, 143(*t*9.10)

on milk production, 61

on mink farms, 75

on organic farming, 74

pig transport operation investigation, 55

research facilities, registration with, 84

slaughterhouse investigation, 66

sources of research animals and, 90, 91

unaccredited zoos and, 116

on wildlife collisions, 34

wildlife control by, 33

U.S. Department of Health and Human Services, 147

U.S. Department of Homeland Security, 126

U.S. Department of Justice, 81

U.S. Environmental Protection Agency (EPA)

on animal feeding operations, 58

laws governing chemicals, 85

U.S. Fish and Wildlife Service (USFWS)

contact information, 151

on endangered/threatened species, 41, 43

federal wildlife regulation laws, 33

on hunting, 46, 47

mission of, 27

protection of endangered species, 44

wildlife management by, 33

wildlife-related recreation, survey on, 44

U.S. Food and Drug Administration (FDA)
approval of drugs, cosmetics, 85
cattle feed and, 57
on drug testing, 86
U.S. Forest Service (USFS), 43
U.S. Fur Commission, 75
U.S. General Accounting Office. *See* U.S. Government Accountability Office
U.S. Government Accountability Office (GAO)
on BLM's wild horse management, 39
on wildlife damage, 35
U.S. Immigration and Naturalization Service, 126
"U.S. Moves to Prohibit Beef from Sick or Injured Cows" (Martin), 65
U.S. Navy, 130
"US Production, Consumption, and Export of Rendered Products for 2002–2007" (National Renderers Association), 56
U.S. Sportsmen's Alliance (USSA), 47, 151
U.S. War Dog Association, 130
USDA. *See* U.S. Department of Agriculture
"USDA Seizes the Moment, Orders Hawthorn to Give up 16 Elephants" (Farinato), 117
"The USDA's Role in Equine Health Monitoring" (APHIS), 70–71, 72
"The Use of Pound Animals in Biomedical Research" (MISMR), 91
USFS (U.S. Forest Service), 43
USFWS. *See* U.S. Fish and Wildlife Service
Utah, pound seizure in, 139
Utilitarianism, 24–25
Utility, 24

V

Vaccination, 34
Value
farm animal commodities, percentage breakdown of value of production of, 54*f*
farm animal commodities, value of production of, 54(*t*4.1)
poultry/poultry products, value of production for, 66, 66*f*
production value of farm animals, 53
valuable wildlife categories, 31
Veal
controversy over, 62
outlawing of small crate enclosures, 55
veal consumption per capita, in pounds, 63*f*
Vegan, 74
Vegetarians
animal rights activists as, 26
moral, 23
reasons for being, 74
Vesalius, Andreas, 5

Veterinarian
care of entertainment animals, 114
genetic problems of purebred dogs and, 140
for research facility, under AWA, 83
for rodeo animals, 101
spaying/neutering of pets, 136–137
surgical/medical training, animals used for, 89
Vick, Michael, 108
Victoria, Queen of England, 7
Victorian Street Society, 79
Vietnam War, 129–130
Violence, 9
Vivisection
antivivisection groups, 80–81, 82
description of, 5
history of, 78–79
in U.S., 7
use of term, 77
Voltaire, 6

W

Walking horses, 101–102
Walt Disney World, Animal Kingdom, 113, 120–121
Warrick, Joby, 64–65
Watchdogs, 125
Weetjens, Bart, 127
Weier, John, 43
Welfare state, 24
Welfare-friendly farming, 74–75
Welfarism
animal rights movement and, 27
beliefs of, 24
welfare-friendly farming, 74–75
See also Animal welfarists
West Virginia, puppy mill in, 143
Westland/Hallmark Meat Company (Chino, CA), 65
A Whale of a Business (*Frontline*), 119–120, 130
Whales
of animal theme parks, 119–120
humpback whale, 32*f*
Keiko (orca), 118, 119*f*
Whaling, 51–52
"What Happened to Michael Vick's Dogs" (Gorant), 108
"What Is Pet Trust" (Hirschfeld), 26–27
"What Would It Take?" (Lawson & Allen), 137–138
Whispering Oaks Kennel (Parkersburg, WV), 143
White Fang (movie), 118
Wild animal commodities
animal organizations worldwide that support the Protect Seals Network, 51*t*
big cats, 51
elephants, 51

most common, 48–49
seals, 49–50
Wild animals
as entertainment animals, 113
ownership of, 27
Wild Horse Annie Act, 8
Wild Horses: An American Romance (netnebraska.org), 129
Wild horses and/or burros
managed by BLM, estimated population of, 42(*f*3.6)
management of, 35, 39
program statistics, 41(*t*3.4)
removed/adopted, 42(*f*3.5)
"Wild Horses Sold by U.S. Agency Sent to Slaughter" (Mott), 35
Wildlife
anglers, number of, 50(*f*3.17)
animal rights debate, 32
categories of valuable wildlife, 31
commercial fishing, 52
definition of, 31
federal laws impacting wildlife, 33*t*
fishing days, number of, 50(*f*3.18)
fishing expenditures, 50(*f*3.19)
government agencies that control, 33–34
government wildlife regulation, goals of, 34–35, 39, 41, 43–44
history of wildlife management, 32–33
humpback whale, 32*f*
hunters, number of, 45(*f*3.9)
hunters, number of, total and by animal, 46(*f*3.12)
hunting days, number of, 46(*f*3.10)
hunting expenditures, 46(*f*3.11)
Internet hunting bans, states with, 49*f*
Protect Seals Network, animal organizations worldwide that support, 51*t*
resources damaged by wildlife, by state/type of injurious wildlife, 36*t*–40*t*
Sport Fish and Wildlife Restoration Program excise taxes, distribution of, 45(*f*3.8)
Sport Fish Restoration Program excise tax, 50*t*
spotted owl recovery plan study areas, 44*t*
timber wolf, 43*f*
U.S. endangered/threatened animal species, list of, 43*t*
whaling, 51–52
wild animal commodities, 48–51
wild horse and burro program statistics, 41(*t*3.4)
wild horses/burros, removed/adopted, 42(*f*3.5)
wild horses/burros managed by BLM, estimated population of, 42(*f*3.6)
wildlife damages/threats reported by Wildlife Services, 40(*f*3.3)